DRABBLE

WALLY! YOU'RE BACK FROM THE VET! THAT WASN'T SO BAD, WAS IT?
© 2000 United Feature Syndicate, Inc.
3-16
IF YOU ASK ME, THAT VET WAS A LITTLE PUSHY!
www.comics.com

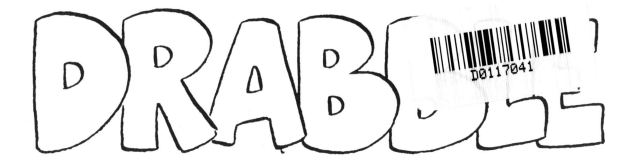

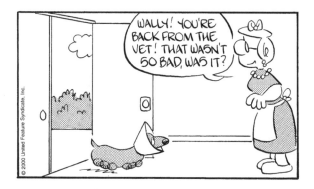

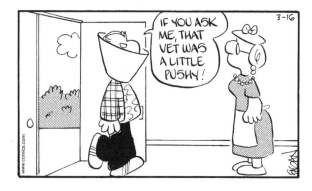

DRABBLE

WHO WANTS TO BE A FENDERHEAD

By KEVIN FAGAN

NANTIER · BEALL · MINOUSTCHINE
Publishing inc.
new york

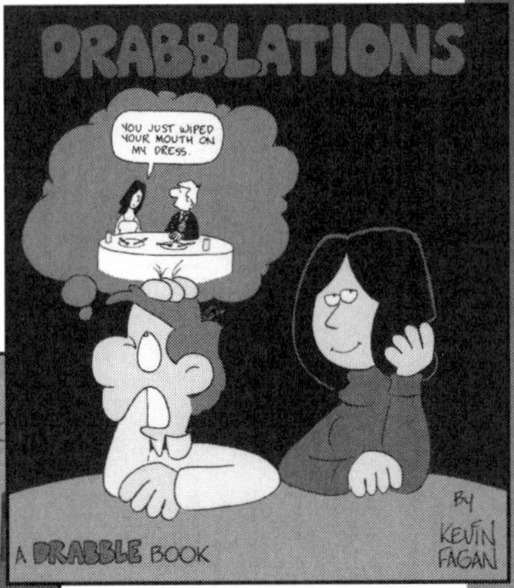
DRABBLATIONS
YOU JUST WIPED YOUR MOUTH ON MY DRESS.
A DRABBLE BOOK
BY KEVIN FAGAN

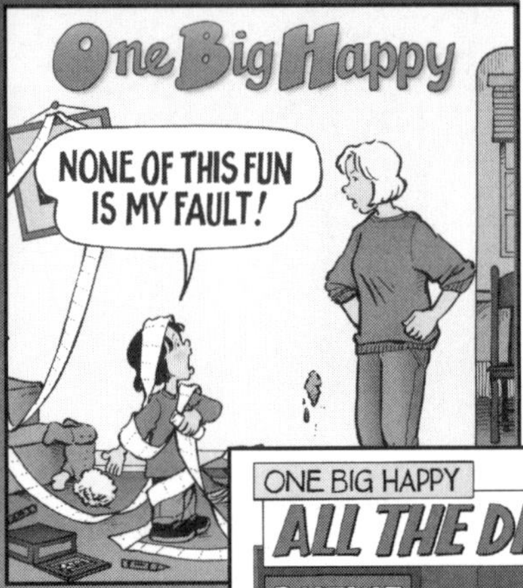
One Big Happy
NONE OF THIS FUN IS MY FAULT!

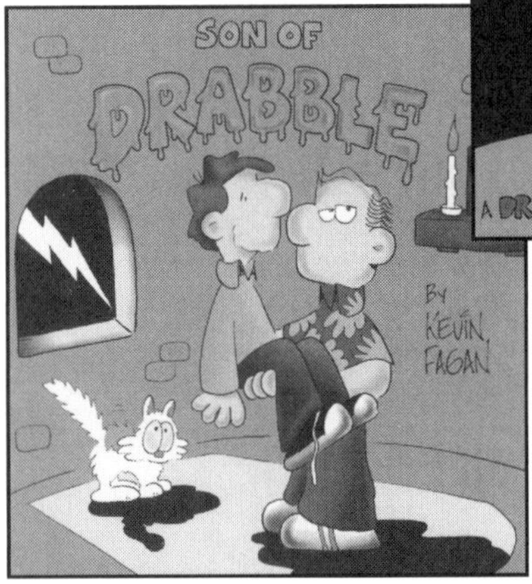
SON OF DRABBLE
BY KEVIN FAGAN

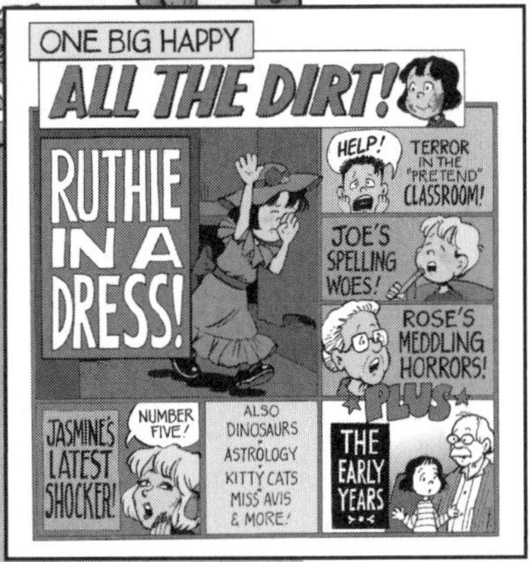
ONE BIG HAPPY
ALL THE DIRT!
RUTHIE IN A DRESS!
HELP!
TERROR IN THE "PRETEND" CLASSROOM!
JOE'S SPELLING WOES!
ROSE'S MEDDLING HORRORS!
PLUS
JASMINE'S LATEST SHOCKER!
NUMBER FIVE!
ALSO DINOSAURS ASTROLOGY KITTY CATS MISS AVIS & MORE!
THE EARLY YEARS

Also Available:
Drabble: “Son of Drabble”, $9.95
Drabble: “Mall Cops, Ducks and Fenderheads”, $9.95
Drabble: “Drabblations”, $9.95
One Big Happy: “Should I Spit On Him?”, $9.95
One Big Happy: “None Of This Fun Is My Fault!”, $9.95
One Big Happy: “Nice Costs Extra!”, $9.95
One Big Happy: “All The Dirt!”, $9.95
Beetle Bailey: “Still Lazy After All These Years”, $9.95
Beetle Bailey: “50 Years of Beetle Bailey”, $9.95
Funky Winkerbean: “Could Be a Book Deal Here”, $9.95
(plus $3 P&H 1st item, $1 each addt’l)

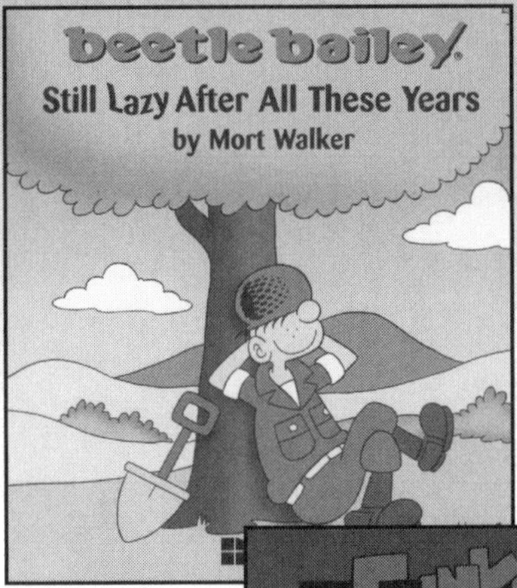
beetle bailey
Still Lazy After All These Years
by Mort Walker

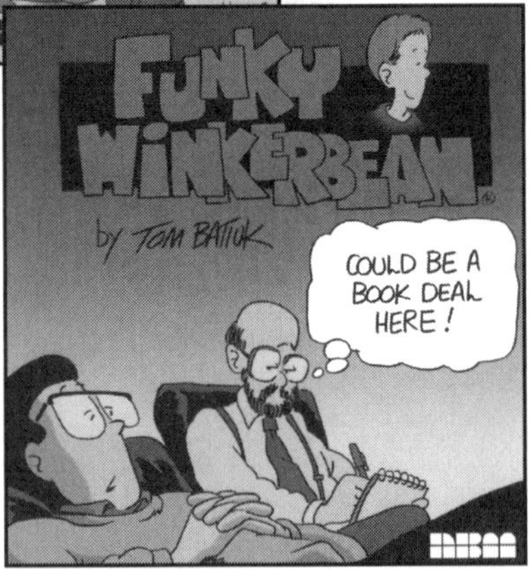
FUNKY WINKERBEAN
by TOM BATIUK
COULD BE A BOOK DEAL HERE!

NBM has over 150 graphic novels available
Please write for a free color catalog to:
NBM -Dept. S
555 8th Ave. Ste. 1202
New York, N.Y. 10018
www.nbmpublishing.com/comicstrips

See more Kevin Fagan
www.comics.com/comics/drabble

ISBN 1-56163-302-X

Printed in Canada

5 4 3 2 1

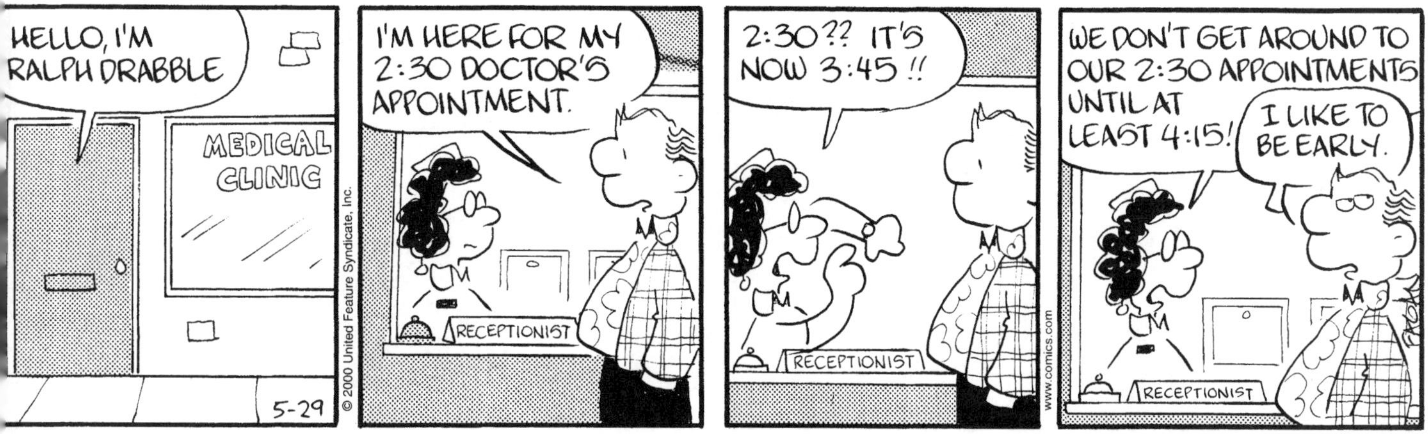
HELLO, I'M RALPH DRABBLE
MEDICAL CLINIC
5-29
© 2000 United Feature Syndicate, Inc.
I'M HERE FOR MY 2:30 DOCTOR'S APPOINTMENT.
RECEPTIONIST
2:30?? IT'S NOW 3:45!!
RECEPTIONIST
www.comics.com
WE DON'T GET AROUND TO OUR 2:30 APPOINTMENTS UNTIL AT LEAST 4:15!
I LIKE TO BE EARLY.
RECEPTIONIST

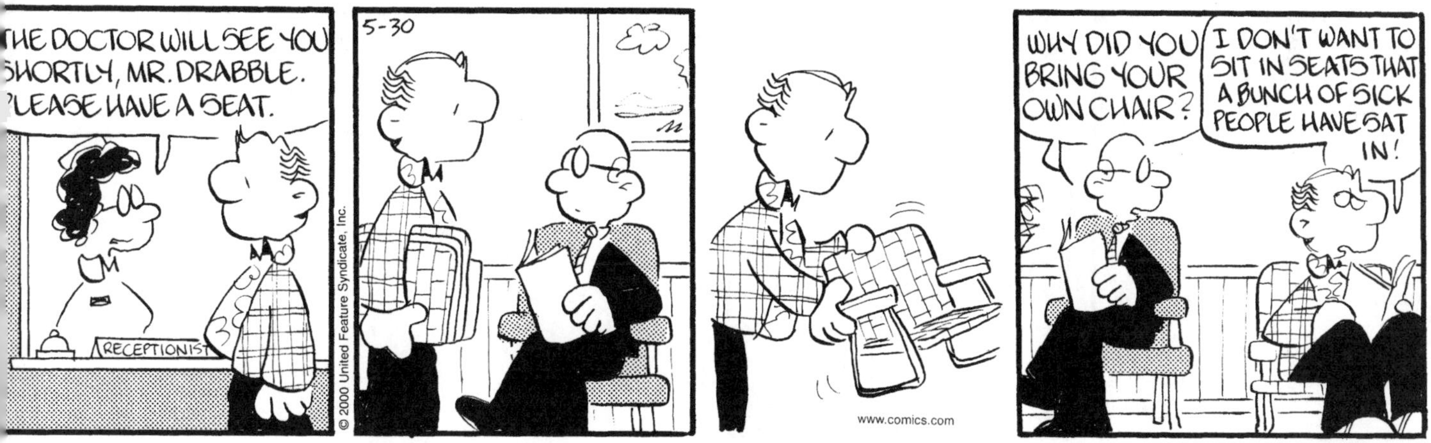
THE DOCTOR WILL SEE YOU SHORTLY, MR. DRABBLE. PLEASE HAVE A SEAT.
RECEPTIONIST
© 2000 United Feature Syndicate, Inc.
5-30
www.comics.com
WHY DID YOU BRING YOUR OWN CHAIR?
I DON'T WANT TO SIT IN SEATS THAT A BUNCH OF SICK PEOPLE HAVE SAT IN!

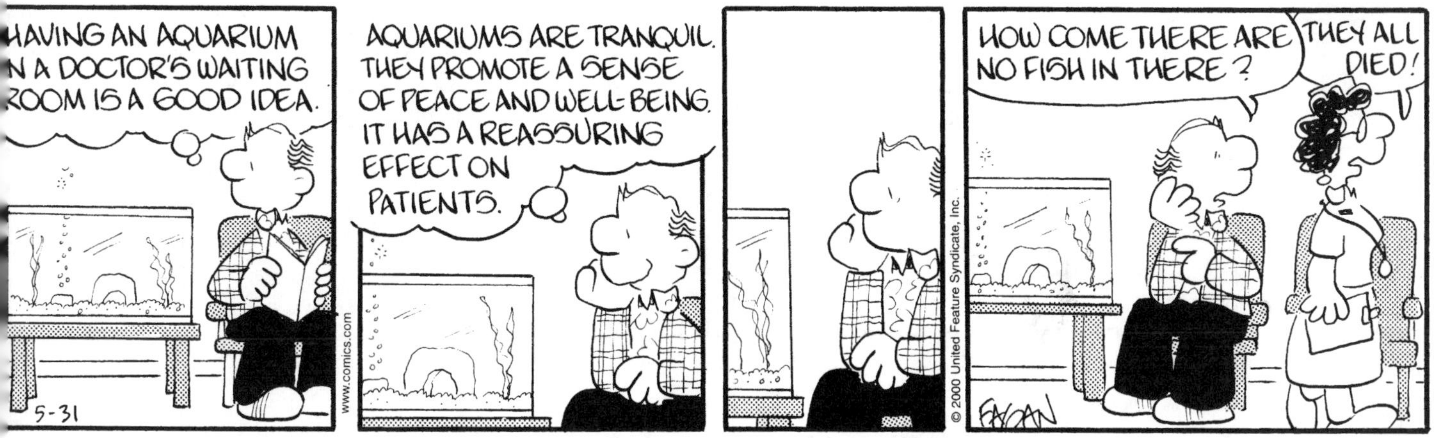
HAVING AN AQUARIUM IN A DOCTOR'S WAITING ROOM IS A GOOD IDEA.
5-31
www.comics.com
AQUARIUMS ARE TRANQUIL. THEY PROMOTE A SENSE OF PEACE AND WELL-BEING. IT HAS A REASSURING EFFECT ON PATIENTS.
© 2000 United Feature Syndicate, Inc.
HOW COME THERE ARE NO FISH IN THERE?
THEY ALL DIED!
FAGAN

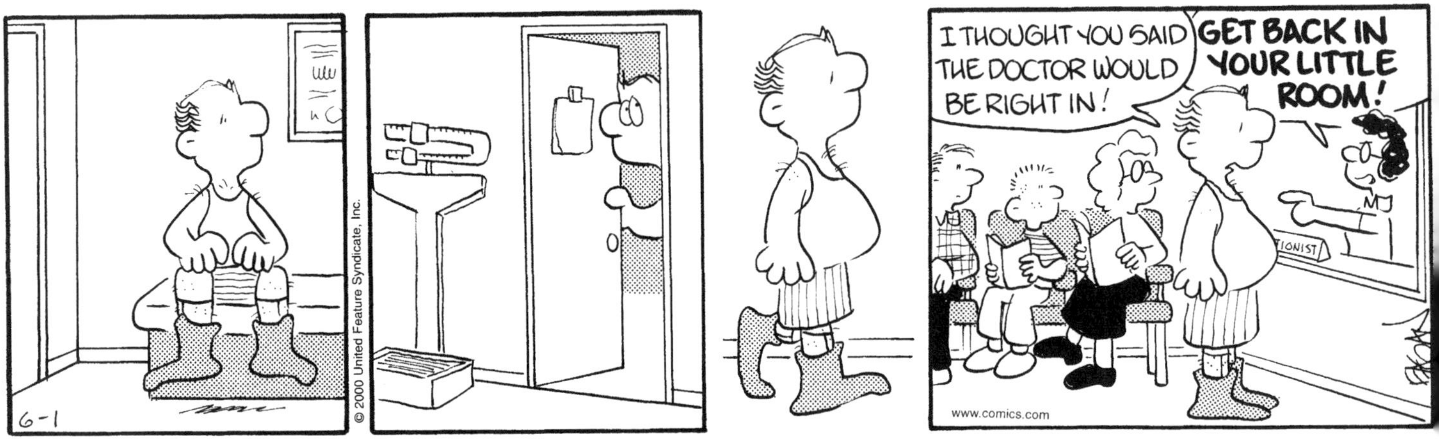
6-1
© 2000 United Feature Syndicate, Inc.
I THOUGHT YOU SAID THE DOCTOR WOULD BE RIGHT IN!
GET BACK IN YOUR LITTLE ROOM!
www.comics.com

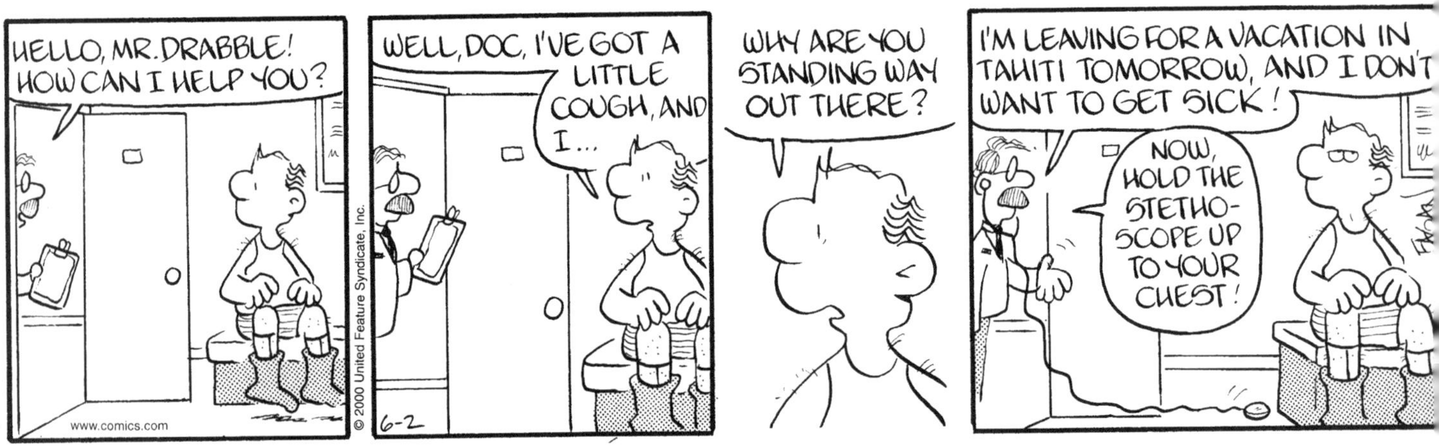
HELLO, MR. DRABBLE! HOW CAN I HELP YOU?
www.comics.com
© 2000 United Feature Syndicate, Inc.
WELL, DOC, I'VE GOT A LITTLE COUGH, AND I...
6-2
WHY ARE YOU STANDING WAY OUT THERE?
I'M LEAVING FOR A VACATION IN TAHITI TOMORROW, AND I DON'T WANT TO GET SICK!
NOW, HOLD THE STETHO-SCOPE UP TO YOUR CHEST!

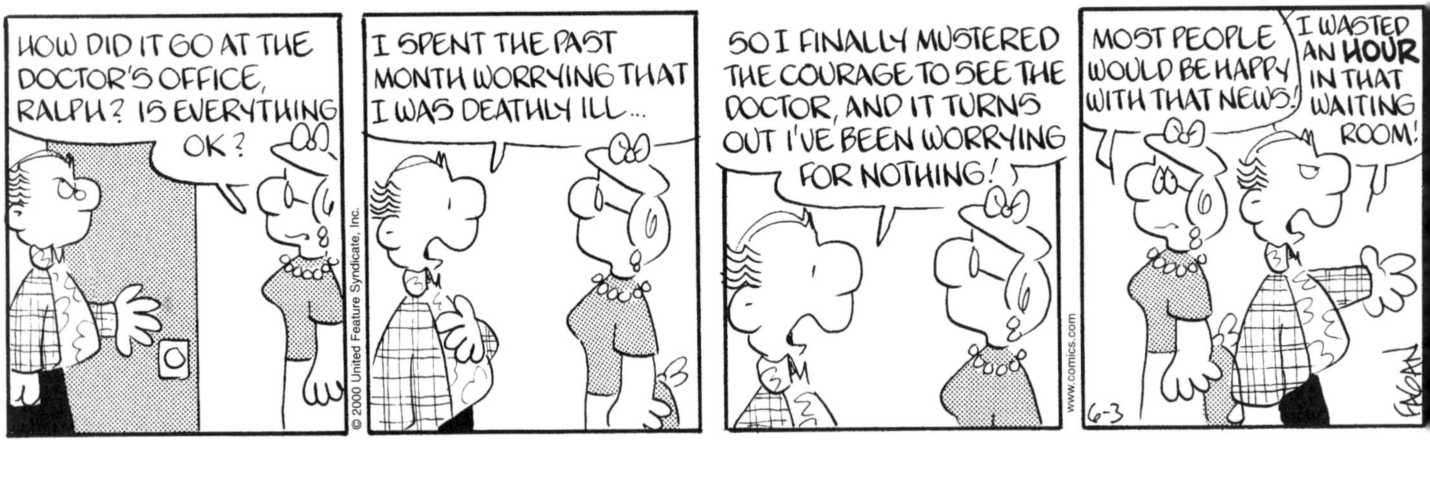
HOW DID IT GO AT THE DOCTOR'S OFFICE, RALPH? IS EVERYTHING OK?
© 2000 United Feature Syndicate, Inc.
I SPENT THE PAST MONTH WORRYING THAT I WAS DEATHLY ILL...
SO I FINALLY MUSTERED THE COURAGE TO SEE THE DOCTOR, AND IT TURNS OUT I'VE BEEN WORRYING FOR NOTHING!
www.comics.com
MOST PEOPLE WOULD BE HAPPY WITH THAT NEWS!
I WASTED AN **HOUR** IN THAT WAITING ROOM!
6-3

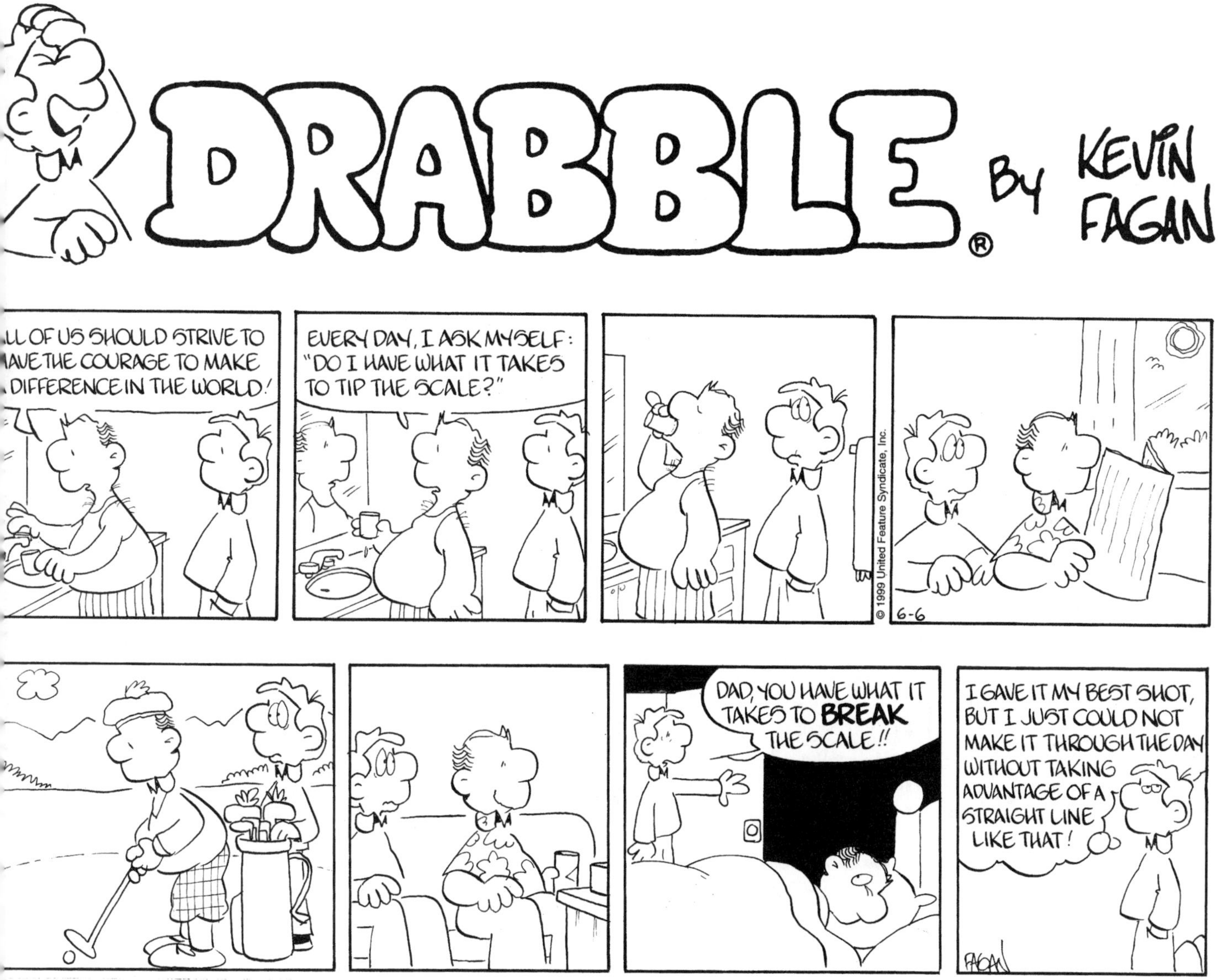
DRABBLE
By KEVIN FAGAN
LL OF US SHOULD STRIVE TO AVE THE COURAGE TO MAKE DIFFERENCE IN THE WORLD!
EVERY DAY, I ASK MYSELF: "DO I HAVE WHAT IT TAKES TO TIP THE SCALE?"
© 1999 United Feature Syndicate, Inc.
6-6
DAD, YOU HAVE WHAT IT TAKES TO BREAK THE SCALE!!
I GAVE IT MY BEST SHOT, BUT I JUST COULD NOT MAKE IT THROUGH THE DAY WITHOUT TAKING ADVANTAGE OF A STRAIGHT LINE LIKE THAT!
FAGAN

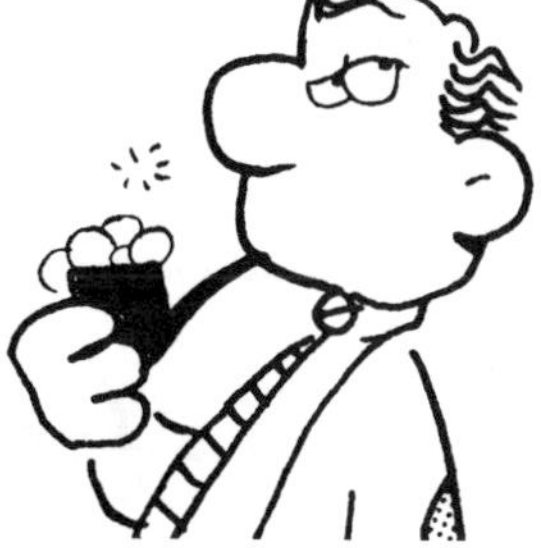

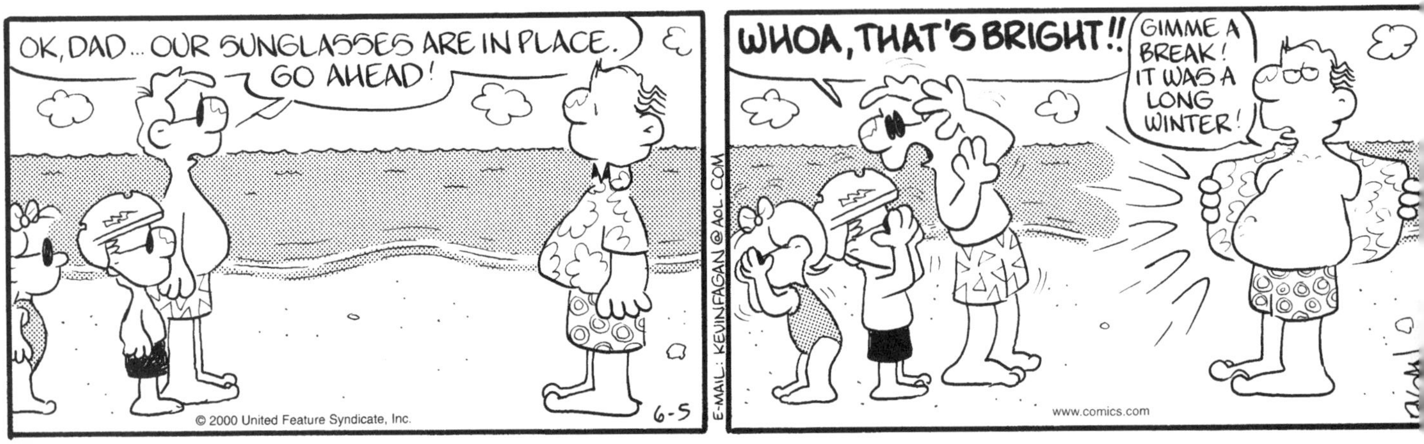
OK, DAD... OUR SUNGLASSES ARE IN PLACE. GO AHEAD!
© 2000 United Feature Syndicate, Inc.
6-5
E-MAIL: KEVINFAGAN@AOL.COM
WHOA, THAT'S BRIGHT!!
GIMME A BREAK! IT WAS A LONG WINTER!
www.comics.com

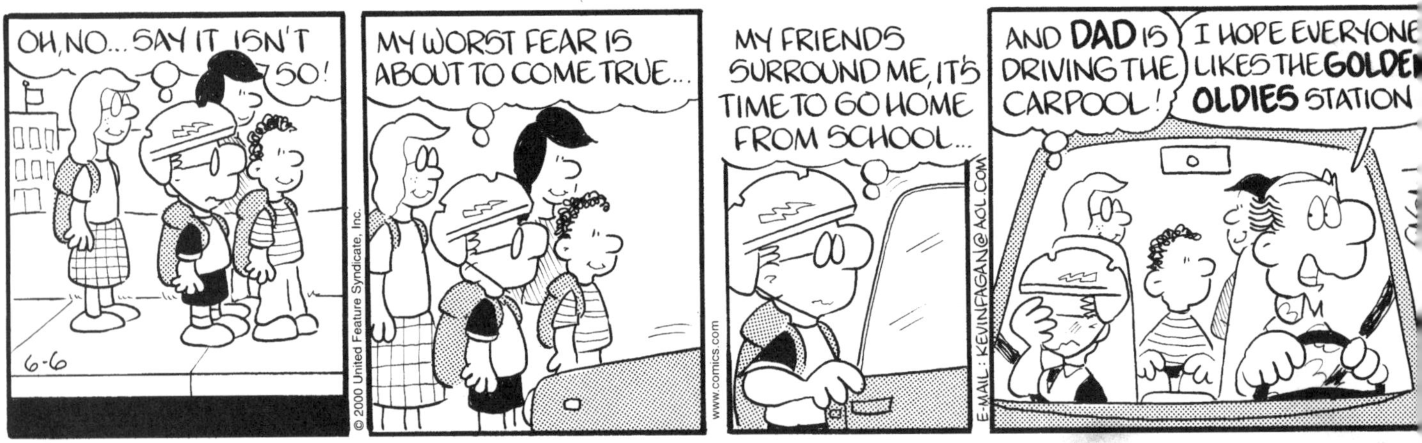
OH, NO... SAY IT ISN'T SO!
6-6
© 2000 United Feature Syndicate, Inc.
MY WORST FEAR IS ABOUT TO COME TRUE...
www.comics.com
MY FRIENDS SURROUND ME, IT'S TIME TO GO HOME FROM SCHOOL...
E-MAIL: KEVINFAGAN@AOL.COM
AND DAD IS DRIVING THE CARPOOL!
I HOPE EVERYONE LIKES THE GOLDE OLDIES STATION

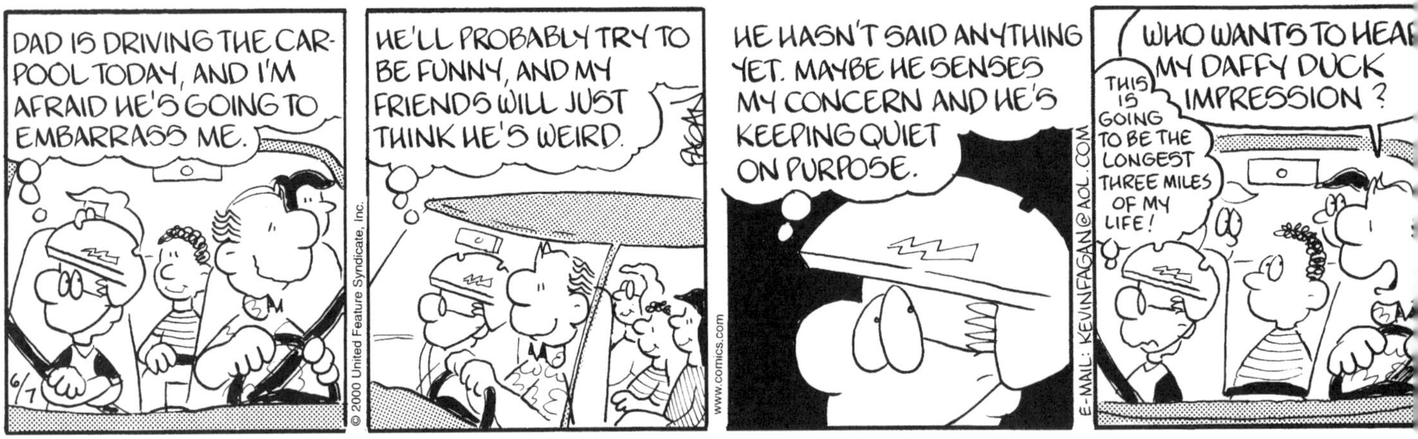
DAD IS DRIVING THE CAR-POOL TODAY, AND I'M AFRAID HE'S GOING TO EMBARRASS ME.
6/7
© 2000 United Feature Syndicate, Inc.
HE'LL PROBABLY TRY TO BE FUNNY, AND MY FRIENDS WILL JUST THINK HE'S WEIRD.
www.comics.com
HE HASN'T SAID ANYTHING YET. MAYBE HE SENSES MY CONCERN AND HE'S KEEPING QUIET ON PURPOSE.
E-MAIL: KEVINFAGAN@AOL.COM
WHO WANTS TO HEA MY DAFFY DUCK IMPRESSION?
THIS IS GOING TO BE THE LONGEST THREE MILES OF MY LIFE!

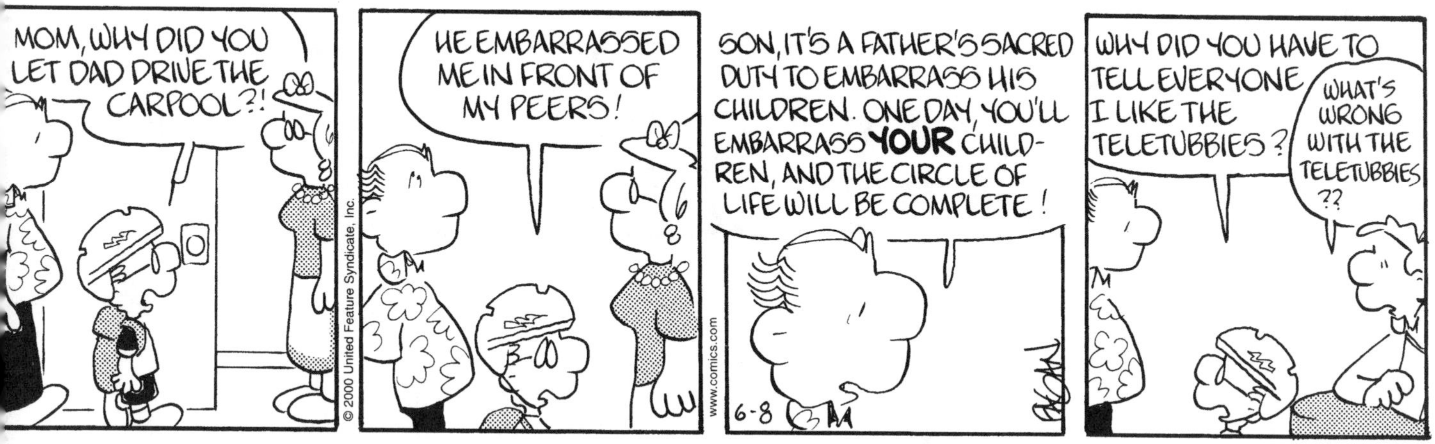
MOM, WHY DID YOU LET DAD DRIVE THE CARPOOL?!
HE EMBARRASSED ME IN FRONT OF MY PEERS!
© 2000 United Feature Syndicate, Inc.
SON, IT'S A FATHER'S SACRED DUTY TO EMBARRASS HIS CHILDREN. ONE DAY, YOU'LL EMBARRASS **YOUR** CHILDREN, AND THE CIRCLE OF LIFE WILL BE COMPLETE!
www.comics.com
6-8
FAGAN
WHY DID YOU HAVE TO TELL EVERYONE I LIKE THE TELETUBBIES?
WHAT'S WRONG WITH THE TELETUBBIES??

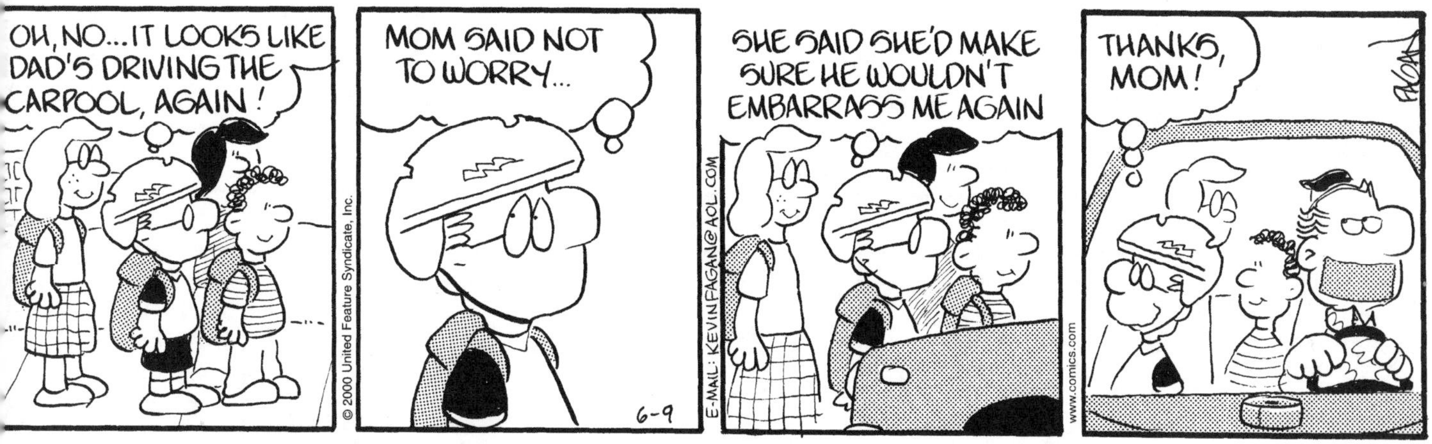
OH, NO...IT LOOKS LIKE DAD'S DRIVING THE CARPOOL, AGAIN!
© 2000 United Feature Syndicate, Inc.
MOM SAID NOT TO WORRY...
6-9
E-MAIL: KEVINFAGAN@AOL.COM
SHE SAID SHE'D MAKE SURE HE WOULDN'T EMBARRASS ME AGAIN
www.comics.com
THANKS, MOM!
FAGAN

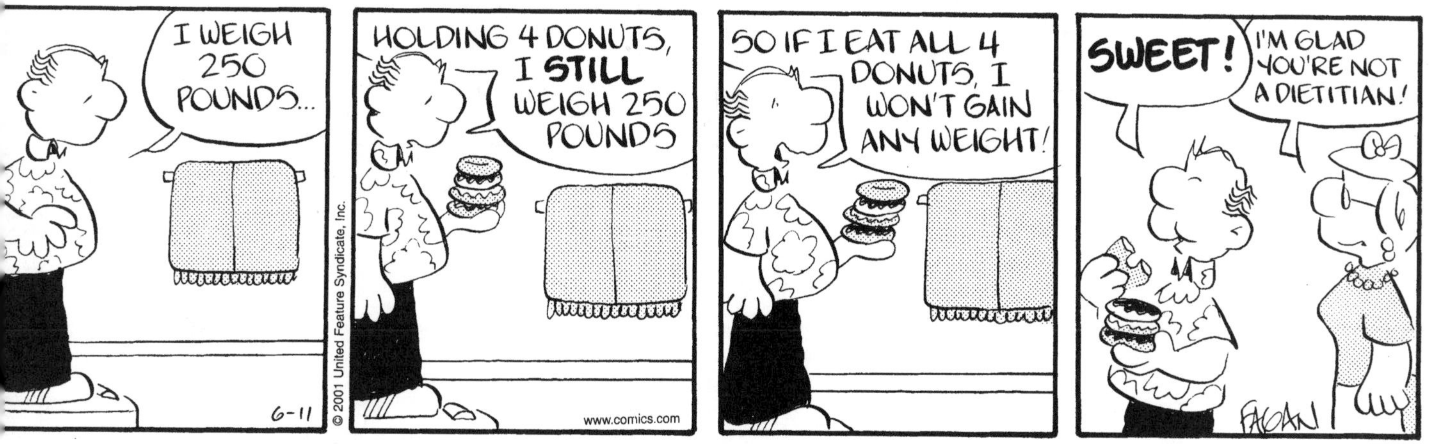
I WEIGH 250 POUNDS...
6-11
© 2001 United Feature Syndicate, Inc.
HOLDING 4 DONUTS, I **STILL** WEIGH 250 POUNDS
www.comics.com
SO IF I EAT ALL 4 DONUTS, I WON'T GAIN ANY WEIGHT!
SWEET!
I'M GLAD YOU'RE NOT A DIETITIAN!
FAGAN

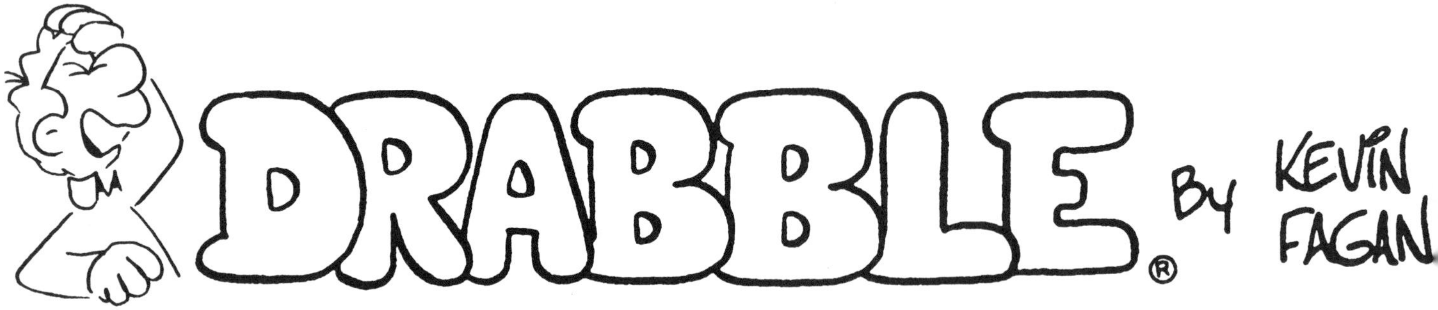
DRABBLE®
By KEVIN FAGAN

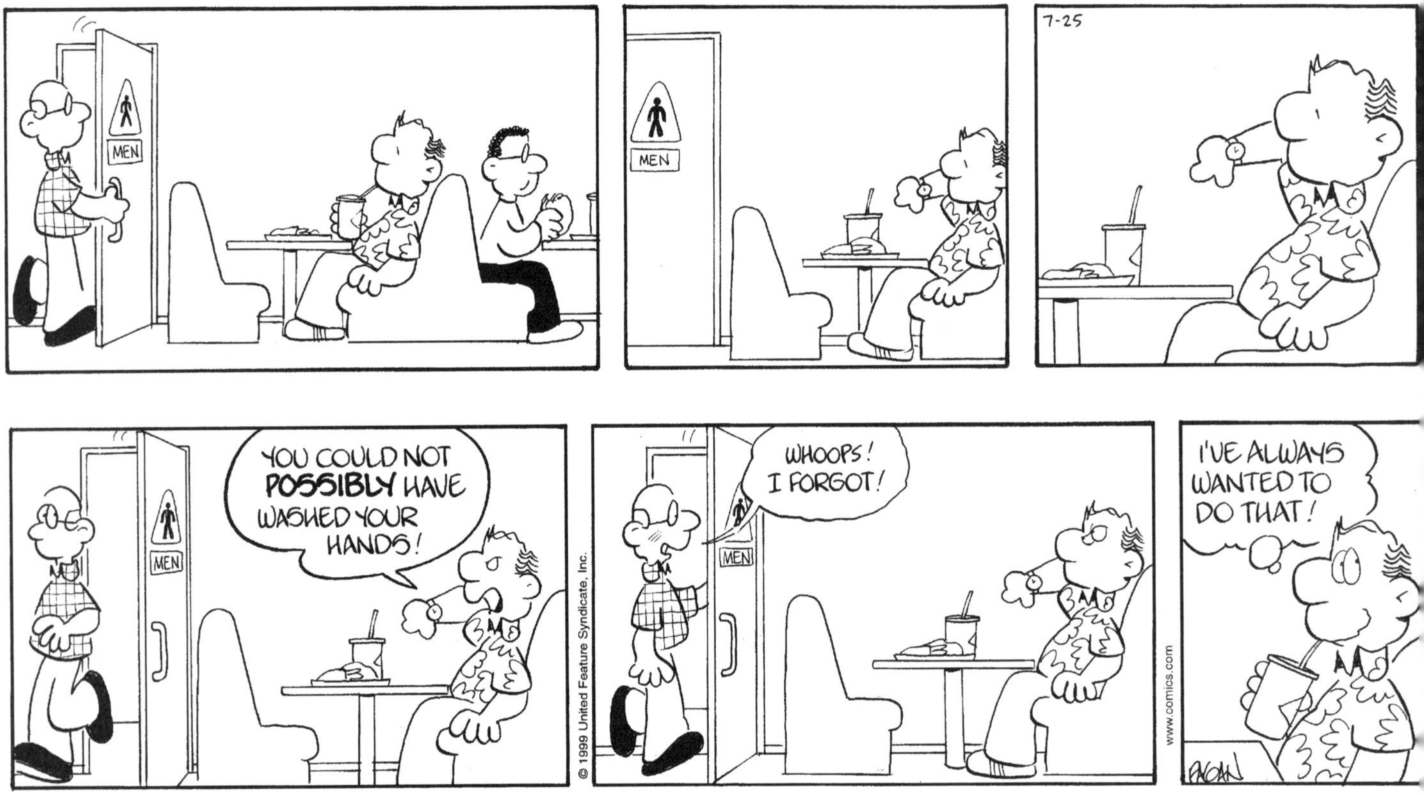
MEN
7-25
YOU COULD NOT POSSIBLY HAVE WASHED YOUR HANDS!
© 1999 United Feature Syndicate, Inc.
WHOOPS! I FORGOT!
www.comics.com
I'VE ALWAYS WANTED TO DO THAT!
FAGAN

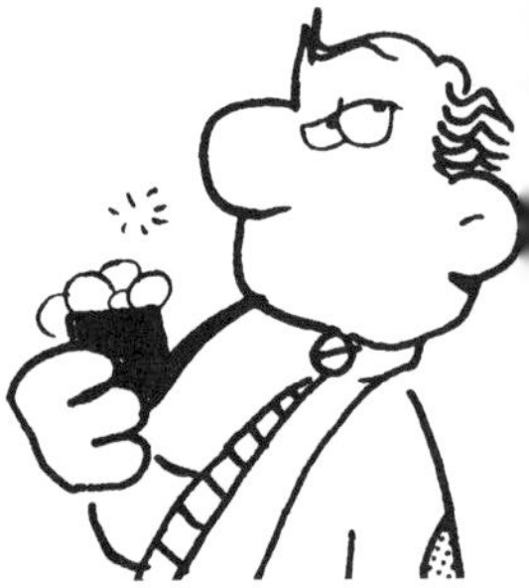

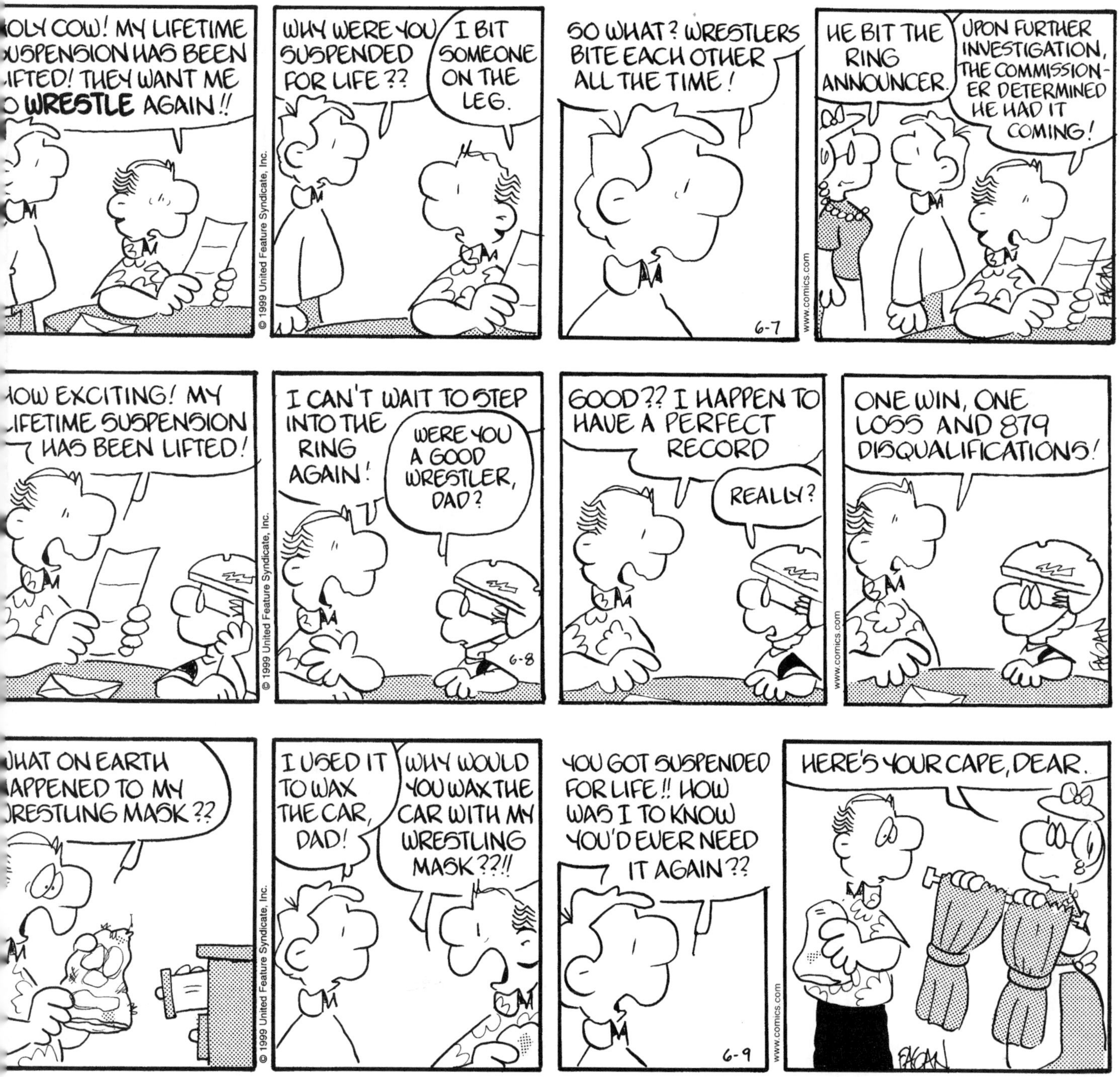
OLY COW! MY LIFETIME USPENSION HAS BEEN IFTED! THEY WANT ME O WRESTLE AGAIN!!
© 1999 United Feature Syndicate, Inc.
WHY WERE YOU SUSPENDED FOR LIFE??
I BIT SOMEONE ON THE LEG.
SO WHAT? WRESTLERS BITE EACH OTHER ALL THE TIME!
6-7
www.comics.com
HE BIT THE RING ANNOUNCER.
UPON FURTHER INVESTIGATION, THE COMMISSIONER DETERMINED HE HAD IT COMING!
OW EXCITING! MY IFETIME SUSPENSION HAS BEEN LIFTED!
© 1999 United Feature Syndicate, Inc.
I CAN'T WAIT TO STEP INTO THE RING AGAIN!
WERE YOU A GOOD WRESTLER, DAD?
6-8
GOOD?? I HAPPEN TO HAVE A PERFECT RECORD
REALLY?
www.comics.com
ONE WIN, ONE LOSS AND 879 DISQUALIFICATIONS!
HAT ON EARTH APPENED TO MY RESTLING MASK??
© 1999 United Feature Syndicate, Inc.
I USED IT TO WAX THE CAR, DAD!
WHY WOULD YOU WAX THE CAR WITH MY WRESTLING MASK??!!
YOU GOT SUSPENDED FOR LIFE!! HOW WAS I TO KNOW YOU'D EVER NEED IT AGAIN??
6-9
www.comics.com
HERE'S YOUR CAPE, DEAR.
FAGAN

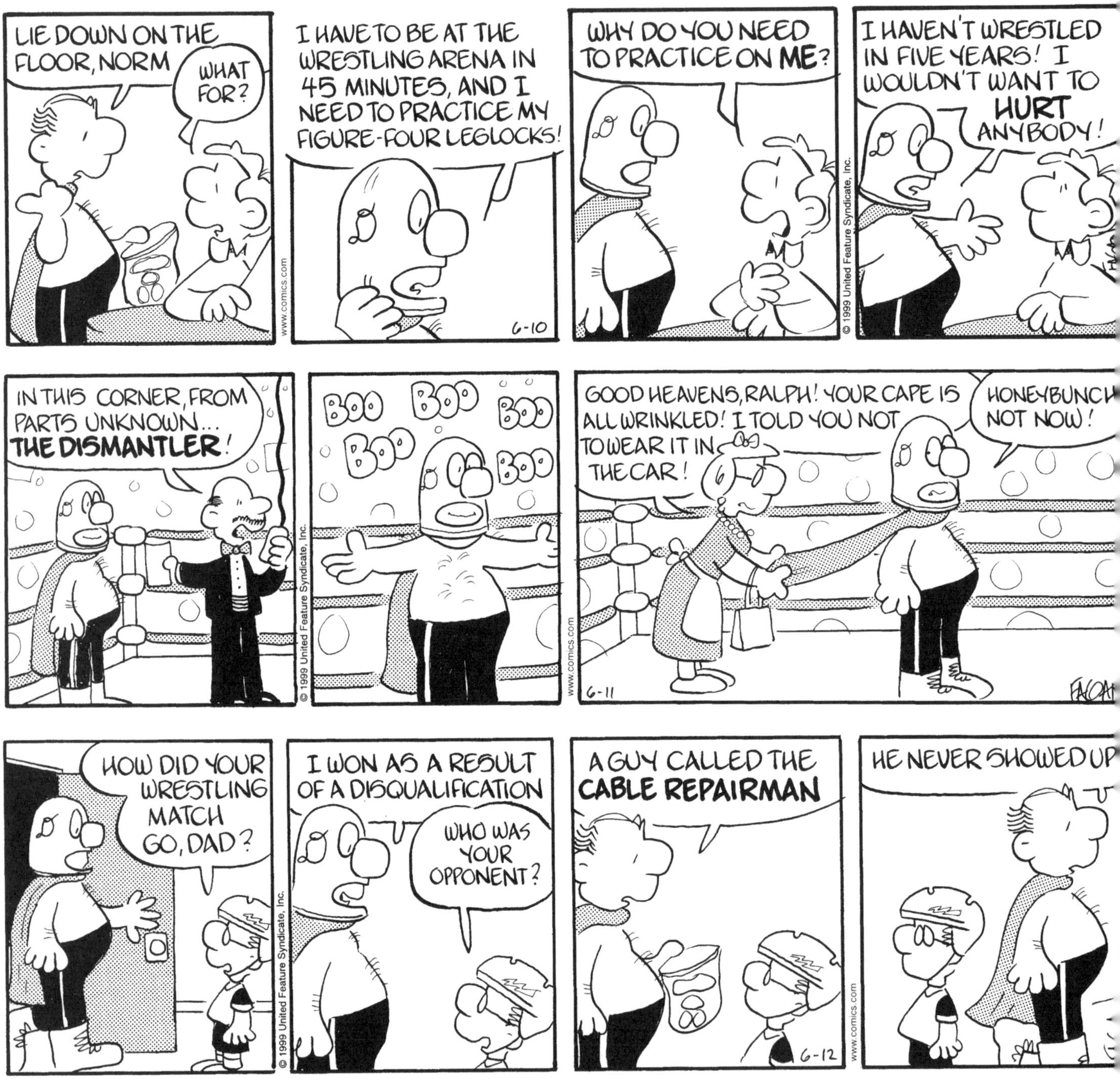
LIE DOWN ON THE FLOOR, NORM
WHAT FOR?
www.comics.com
I HAVE TO BE AT THE WRESTLING ARENA IN 45 MINUTES, AND I NEED TO PRACTICE MY FIGURE-FOUR LEGLOCKS!
6-10
WHY DO YOU NEED TO PRACTICE ON ME?
© 1999 United Feature Syndicate, Inc.
I HAVEN'T WRESTLED IN FIVE YEARS! I WOULDN'T WANT TO HURT ANYBODY!
IN THIS CORNER, FROM PARTS UNKNOWN... THE DISMANTLER!
© 1999 United Feature Syndicate, Inc.
BOO BOO BOO BOO BOO
www.comics.com
6-11
GOOD HEAVENS, RALPH! YOUR CAPE IS ALL WRINKLED! I TOLD YOU NOT TO WEAR IT IN THE CAR!
HONEYBUNCH NOT NOW!
HOW DID YOUR WRESTLING MATCH GO, DAD?
© 1999 United Feature Syndicate, Inc.
I WON AS A RESULT OF A DISQUALIFICATION
WHO WAS YOUR OPPONENT?
A GUY CALLED THE CABLE REPAIRMAN
6-12
www.comics.com
HE NEVER SHOWED UP

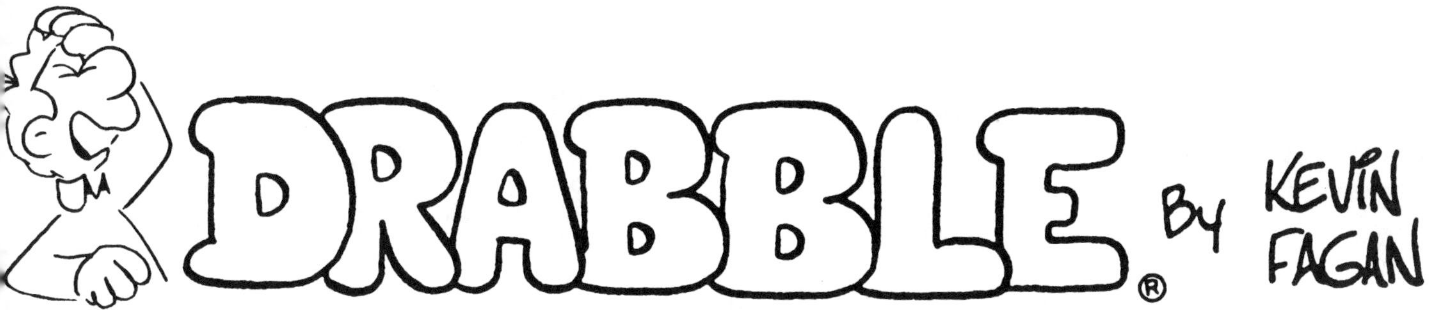

DRABBLE®
By KEVIN FAGAN

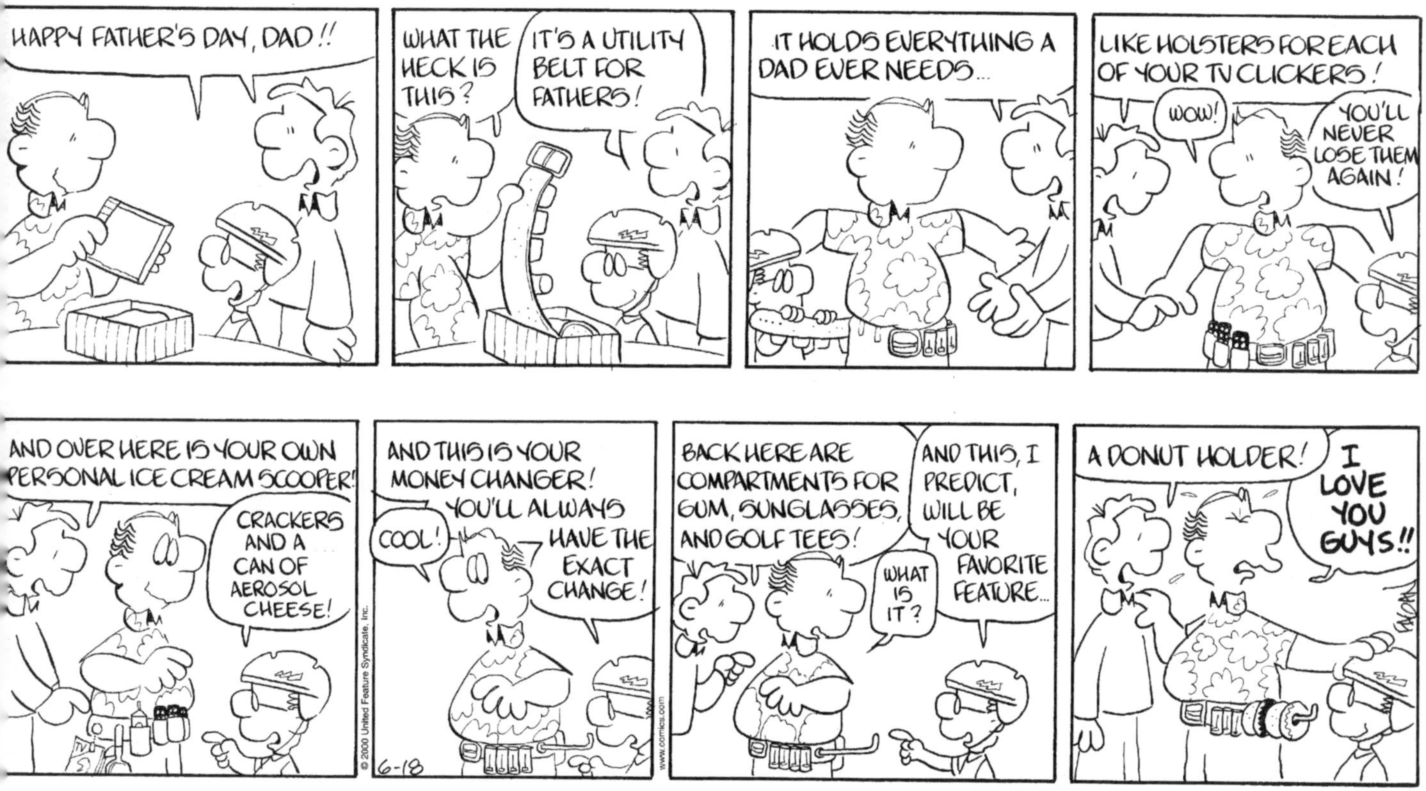

HAPPY FATHER'S DAY, DAD!!
WHAT THE HECK IS THIS?
IT'S A UTILITY BELT FOR FATHERS!
IT HOLDS EVERYTHING A DAD EVER NEEDS...
LIKE HOLSTERS FOR EACH OF YOUR TV CLICKERS!
WOW!
YOU'LL NEVER LOSE THEM AGAIN!
AND OVER HERE IS YOUR OWN PERSONAL ICE CREAM SCOOPER!
CRACKERS AND A CAN OF AEROSOL CHEESE!
© 2000 United Feature Syndicate, Inc.
AND THIS IS YOUR MONEY CHANGER!
YOU'LL ALWAYS HAVE THE EXACT CHANGE!
COOL!
6-18
www.comics.com
BACK HERE ARE COMPARTMENTS FOR GUM, SUNGLASSES, AND GOLF TEES!
AND THIS, I PREDICT, WILL BE YOUR FAVORITE FEATURE...
WHAT IS IT?
A DONUT HOLDER!
I LOVE YOU GUYS!!
FAGAN

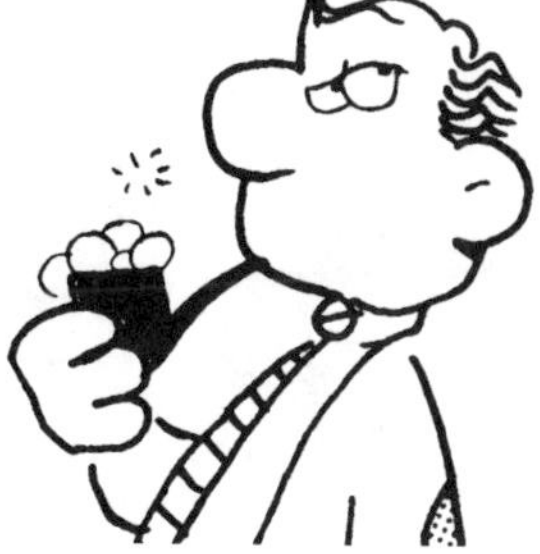

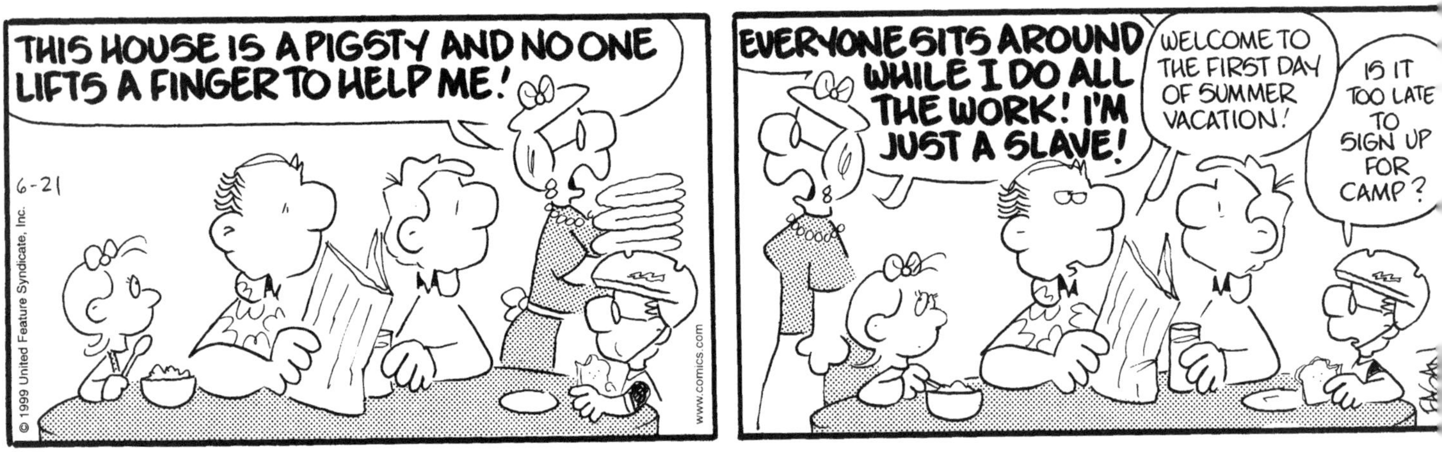
THIS HOUSE IS A PIGSTY AND NO ONE LIFTS A FINGER TO HELP ME!
6-21
© 1999 United Feature Syndicate, Inc.
www.comics.com
EVERYONE SITS AROUND WHILE I DO ALL THE WORK! I'M JUST A SLAVE!
WELCOME TO THE FIRST DAY OF SUMMER VACATION!
IS IT TOO LATE TO SIGN UP FOR CAMP?

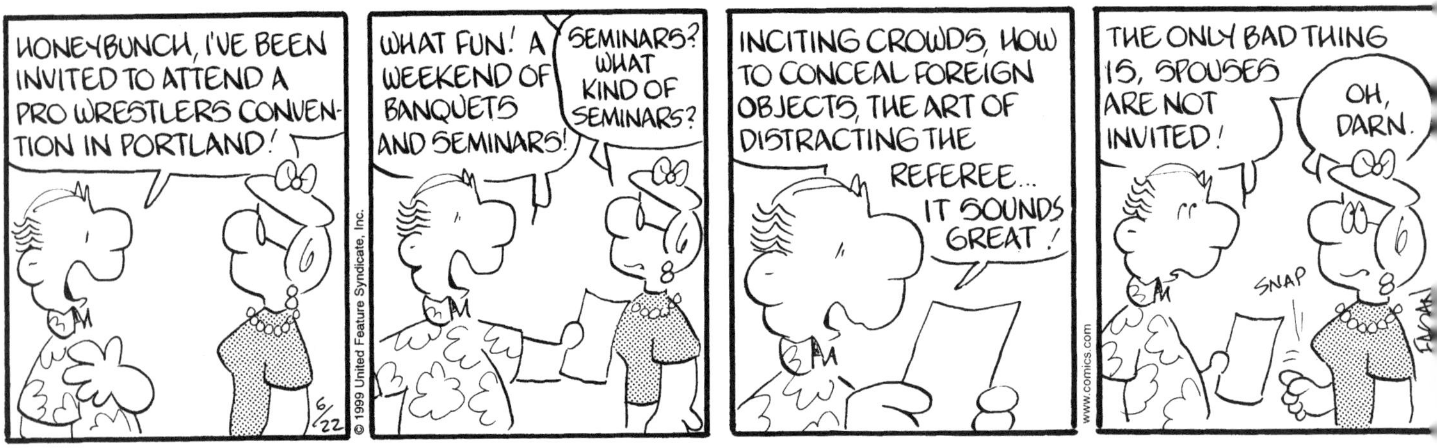
HONEYBUNCH, I'VE BEEN INVITED TO ATTEND A PRO WRESTLERS CONVENTION IN PORTLAND!
6/22
© 1999 United Feature Syndicate, Inc.
WHAT FUN! A WEEKEND OF BANQUETS AND SEMINARS!
SEMINARS? WHAT KIND OF SEMINARS?
INCITING CROWDS, HOW TO CONCEAL FOREIGN OBJECTS, THE ART OF DISTRACTING THE REFEREE...
IT SOUNDS GREAT!
www.comics.com
THE ONLY BAD THING IS, SPOUSES ARE NOT INVITED!
OH, DARN.
SNAP

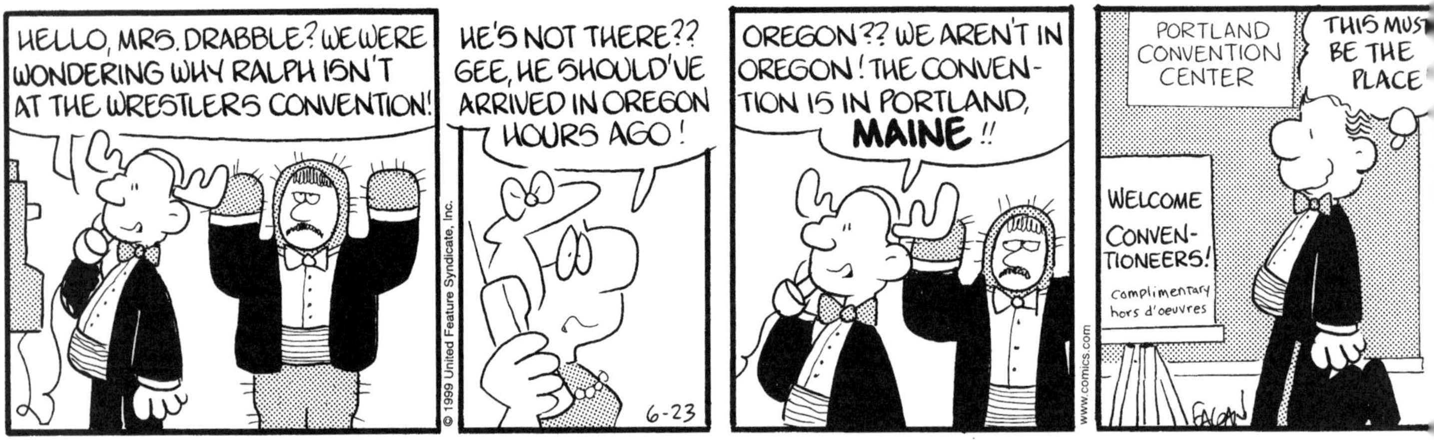
HELLO, MRS. DRABBLE? WE WERE WONDERING WHY RALPH ISN'T AT THE WRESTLERS CONVENTION!
© 1999 United Feature Syndicate, Inc.
HE'S NOT THERE?? GEE, HE SHOULD'VE ARRIVED IN OREGON HOURS AGO!
6-23
OREGON?? WE AREN'T IN OREGON! THE CONVENTION IS IN PORTLAND, MAINE!!
www.comics.com
PORTLAND CONVENTION CENTER
THIS MUST BE THE PLACE
WELCOME CONVENTIONEERS!
Complimentary hors d'oeuvres

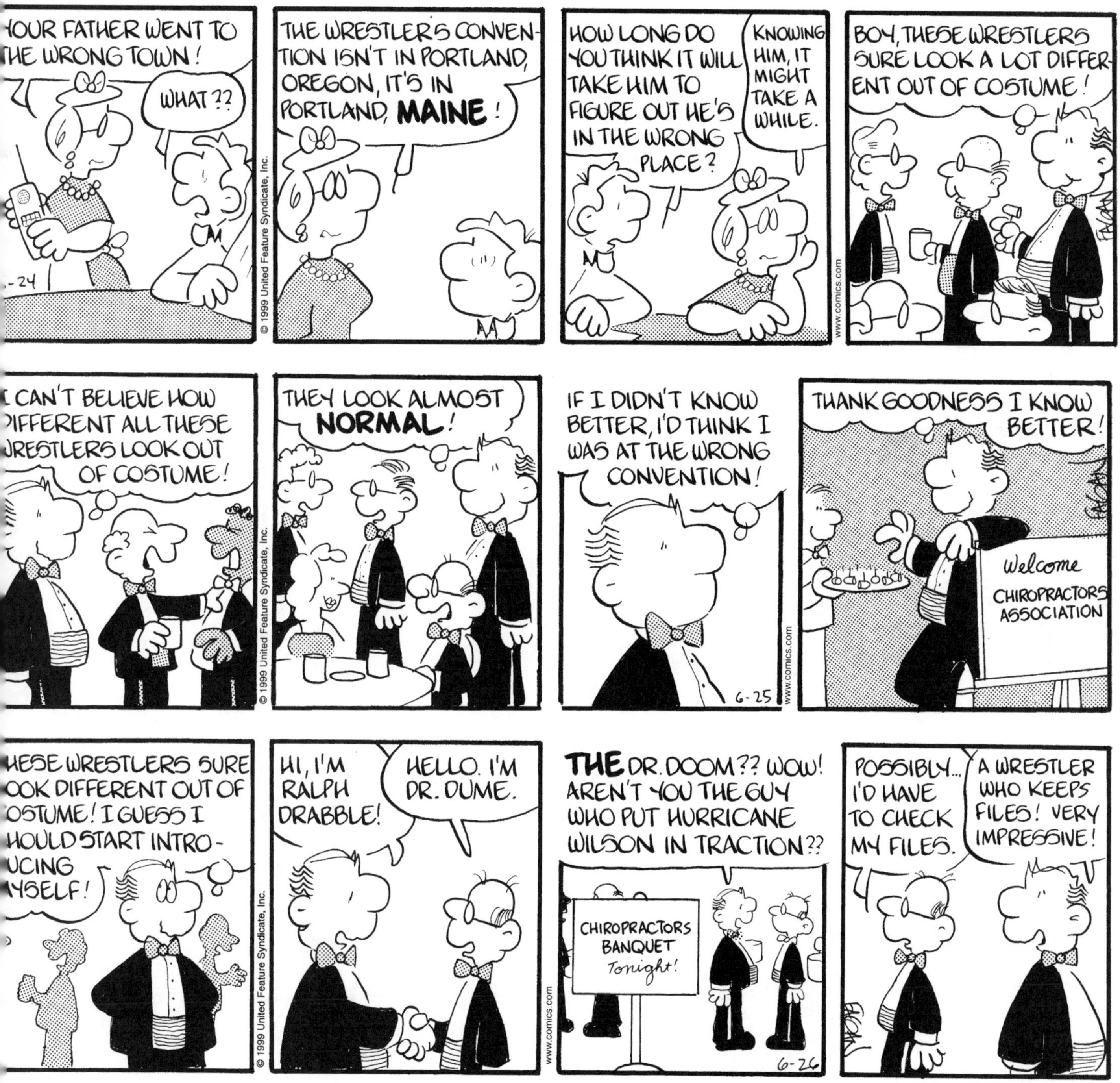
YOUR FATHER WENT TO THE WRONG TOWN!
WHAT??
6-24
© 1999 United Feature Syndicate, Inc.
THE WRESTLER'S CONVENTION ISN'T IN PORTLAND, OREGON, IT'S IN PORTLAND, MAINE!
HOW LONG DO YOU THINK IT WILL TAKE HIM TO FIGURE OUT HE'S IN THE WRONG PLACE?
KNOWING HIM, IT MIGHT TAKE A WHILE.
www.comics.com
BOY, THESE WRESTLERS SURE LOOK A LOT DIFFERENT OUT OF COSTUME!
I CAN'T BELIEVE HOW DIFFERENT ALL THESE WRESTLERS LOOK OUT OF COSTUME!
© 1999 United Feature Syndicate, Inc.
THEY LOOK ALMOST NORMAL!
IF I DIDN'T KNOW BETTER, I'D THINK I WAS AT THE WRONG CONVENTION!
6-25
www.comics.com
THANK GOODNESS I KNOW BETTER!
Welcome
CHIROPRACTORS ASSOCIATION
THESE WRESTLERS SURE LOOK DIFFERENT OUT OF COSTUME! I GUESS I SHOULD START INTRODUCING MYSELF!
© 1999 United Feature Syndicate, Inc.
HI, I'M RALPH DRABBLE!
HELLO. I'M DR. DUME.
www.comics.com
THE DR. DOOM?? WOW! AREN'T YOU THE GUY WHO PUT HURRICANE WILSON IN TRACTION??
CHIROPRACTORS BANQUET
Tonight!
6-26
POSSIBLY... I'D HAVE TO CHECK MY FILES.
A WRESTLER WHO KEEPS FILES! VERY IMPRESSIVE!

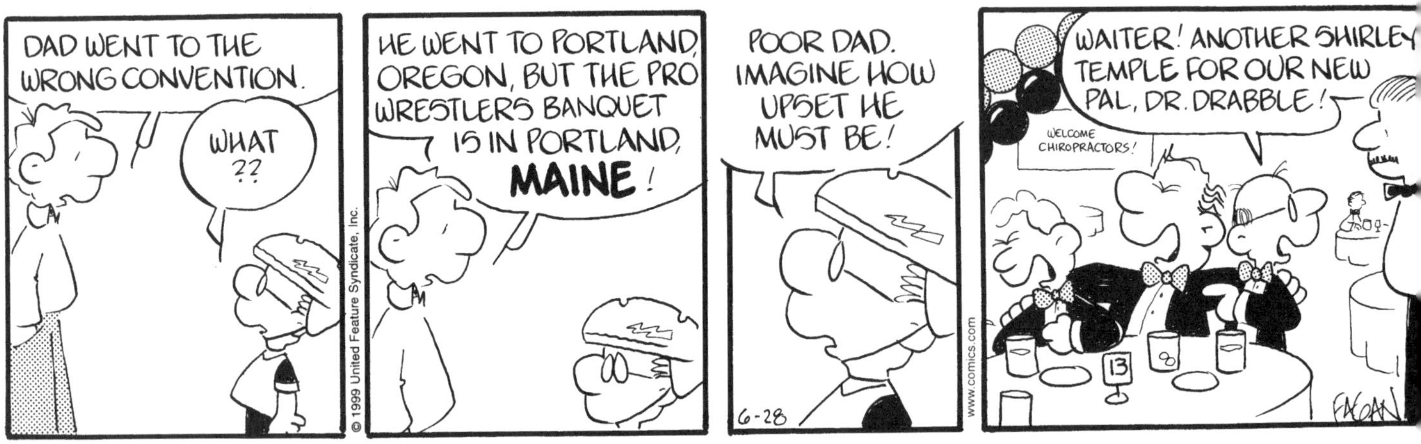
DAD WENT TO THE WRONG CONVENTION.
WHAT ??
HE WENT TO PORTLAND, OREGON, BUT THE PRO WRESTLERS BANQUET IS IN PORTLAND, **MAINE**!
© 1999 United Feature Syndicate, Inc.
POOR DAD. IMAGINE HOW UPSET HE MUST BE!
6-28
www.comics.com
WELCOME CHIROPRACTORS!
WAITER! ANOTHER SHIRLEY TEMPLE FOR OUR NEW PAL, DR. DRABBLE!
13
FAGAN

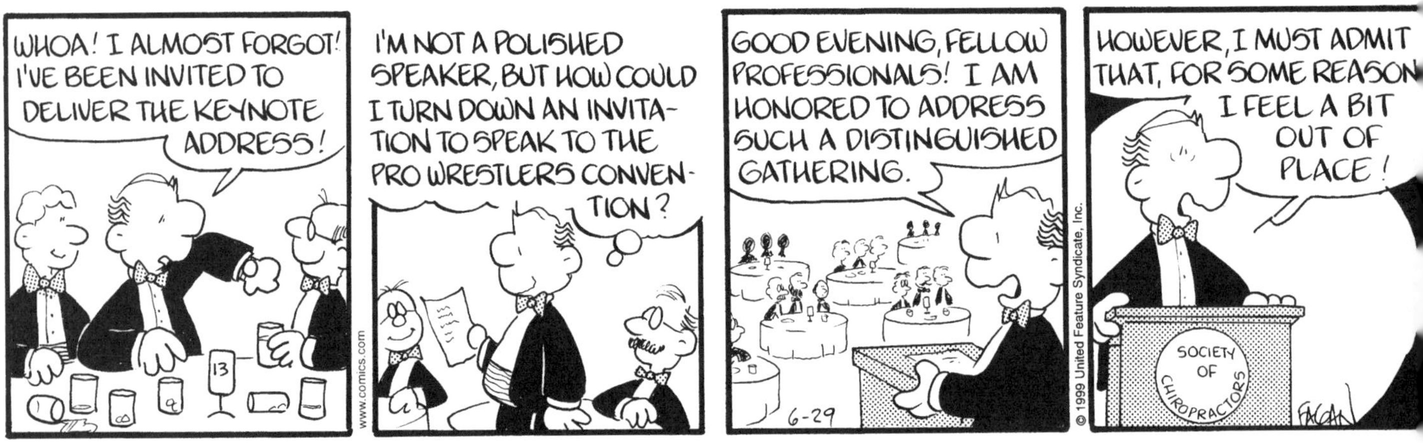
WHOA! I ALMOST FORGOT! I'VE BEEN INVITED TO DELIVER THE KEYNOTE ADDRESS!
13
www.comics.com
I'M NOT A POLISHED SPEAKER, BUT HOW COULD I TURN DOWN AN INVITATION TO SPEAK TO THE PRO WRESTLERS CONVENTION?
GOOD EVENING, FELLOW PROFESSIONALS! I AM HONORED TO ADDRESS SUCH A DISTINGUISHED GATHERING.
6-29
© 1999 United Feature Syndicate, Inc.
HOWEVER, I MUST ADMIT THAT, FOR SOME REASON I FEEL A BIT OUT OF PLACE!
SOCIETY OF CHIROPRACTORS
FAGAN

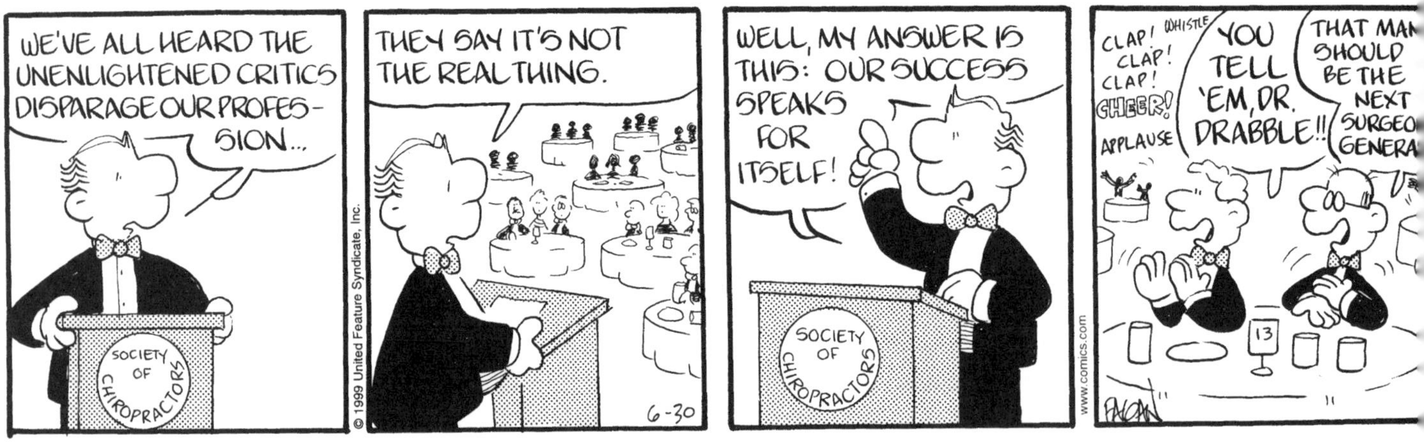
WE'VE ALL HEARD THE UNENLIGHTENED CRITICS DISPARAGE OUR PROFESSION...
SOCIETY OF CHIROPRACTORS
© 1999 United Feature Syndicate, Inc.
THEY SAY IT'S NOT THE REAL THING.
6-30
WELL, MY ANSWER IS THIS: OUR SUCCESS SPEAKS FOR ITSELF!
SOCIETY OF CHIROPRACTORS
www.comics.com
CLAP! CLAP! CLAP! WHISTLE CHEER! APPLAUSE
YOU TELL 'EM, DR. DRABBLE!!
THAT MA SHOULD BE THE NEXT SURGEO GENERA
13
FAGAN

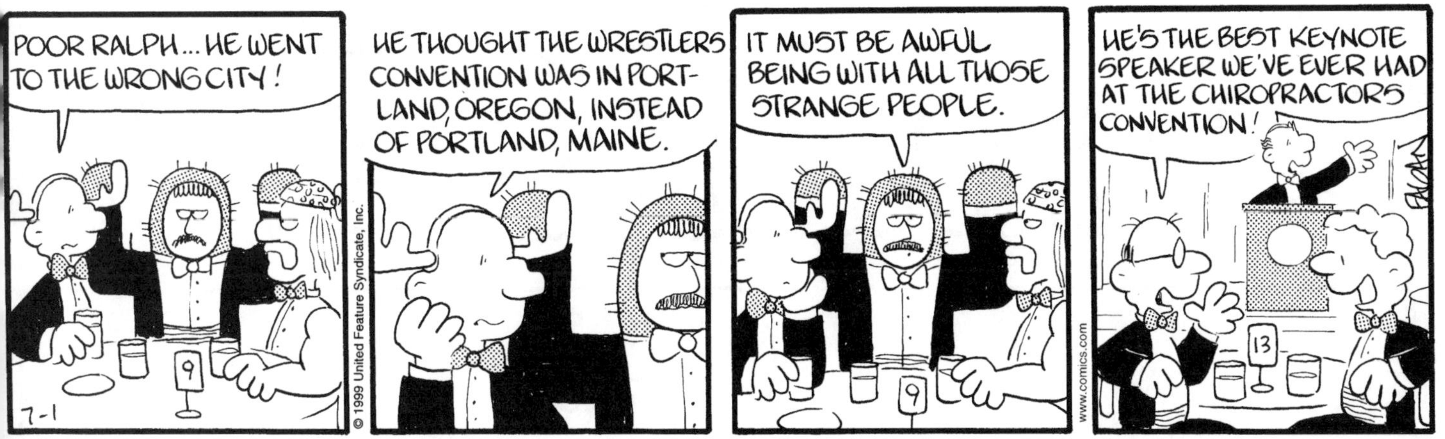
POOR RALPH... HE WENT TO THE WRONG CITY!
7-1
© 1999 United Feature Syndicate, Inc.
HE THOUGHT THE WRESTLERS CONVENTION WAS IN PORTLAND, OREGON, INSTEAD OF PORTLAND, MAINE.
IT MUST BE AWFUL BEING WITH ALL THOSE STRANGE PEOPLE.
www.comics.com
HE'S THE BEST KEYNOTE SPEAKER WE'VE EVER HAD AT THE CHIROPRACTORS CONVENTION!

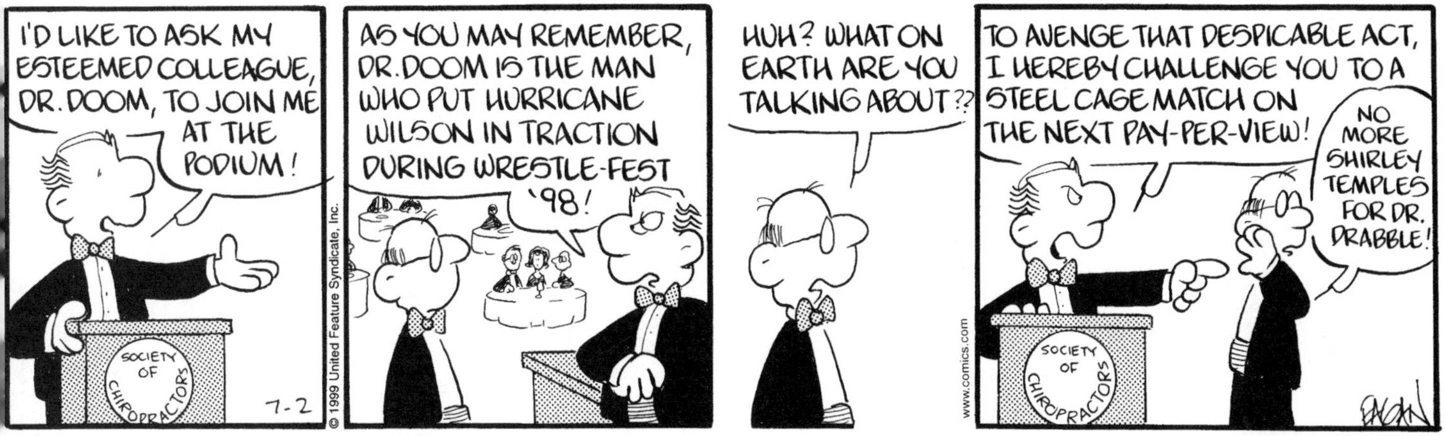
I'D LIKE TO ASK MY ESTEEMED COLLEAGUE, DR. DOOM, TO JOIN ME AT THE PODIUM!
SOCIETY OF CHIROPRACTORS
7-2
© 1999 United Feature Syndicate, Inc.
AS YOU MAY REMEMBER, DR. DOOM IS THE MAN WHO PUT HURRICANE WILSON IN TRACTION DURING WRESTLE-FEST '98!
HUH? WHAT ON EARTH ARE YOU TALKING ABOUT??
www.comics.com
TO AVENGE THAT DESPICABLE ACT, I HEREBY CHALLENGE YOU TO A STEEL CAGE MATCH ON THE NEXT PAY-PER-VIEW!
NO MORE SHIRLEY TEMPLES FOR DR. DRABBLE!
SOCIETY OF CHIROPRACTORS

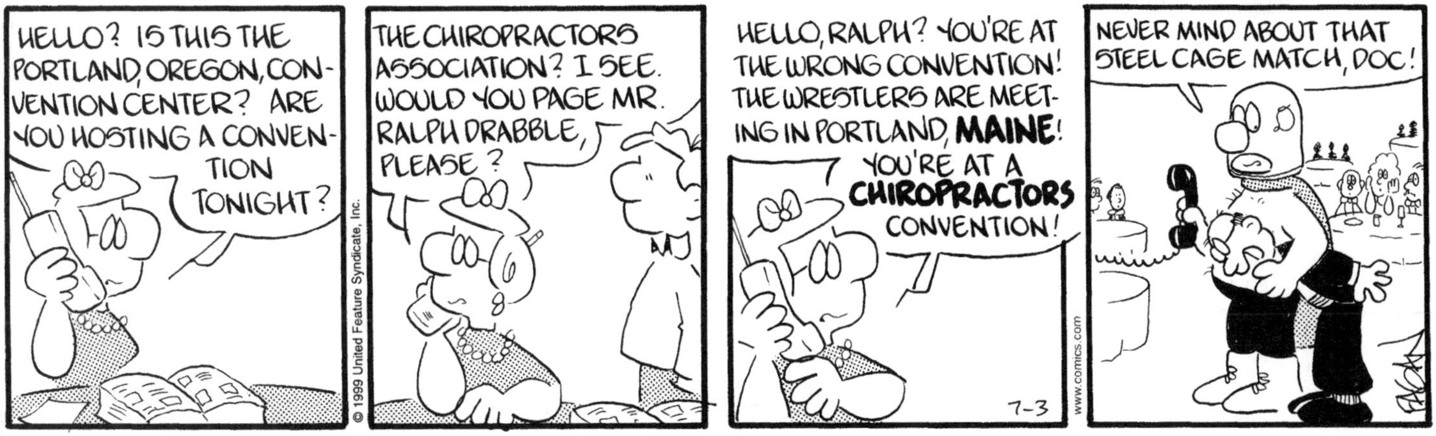
HELLO? IS THIS THE PORTLAND, OREGON, CONVENTION CENTER? ARE YOU HOSTING A CONVENTION TONIGHT?
© 1999 United Feature Syndicate, Inc.
THE CHIROPRACTORS ASSOCIATION? I SEE. WOULD YOU PAGE MR. RALPH DRABBLE, PLEASE?
HELLO, RALPH? YOU'RE AT THE WRONG CONVENTION! THE WRESTLERS ARE MEETING IN PORTLAND, MAINE!
YOU'RE AT A CHIROPRACTORS CONVENTION!
7-3
www.comics.com
NEVER MIND ABOUT THAT STEEL CAGE MATCH, DOC!

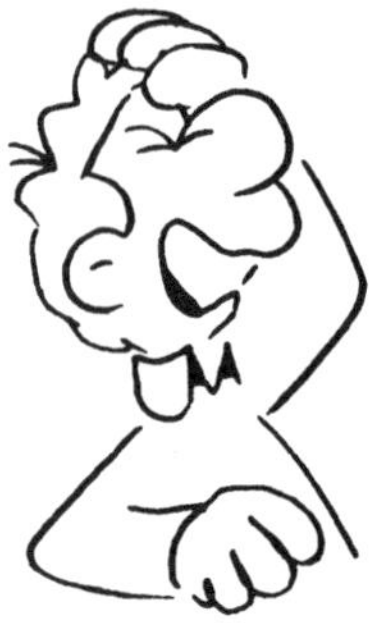

DRABBLE® By KEVIN FAGAN

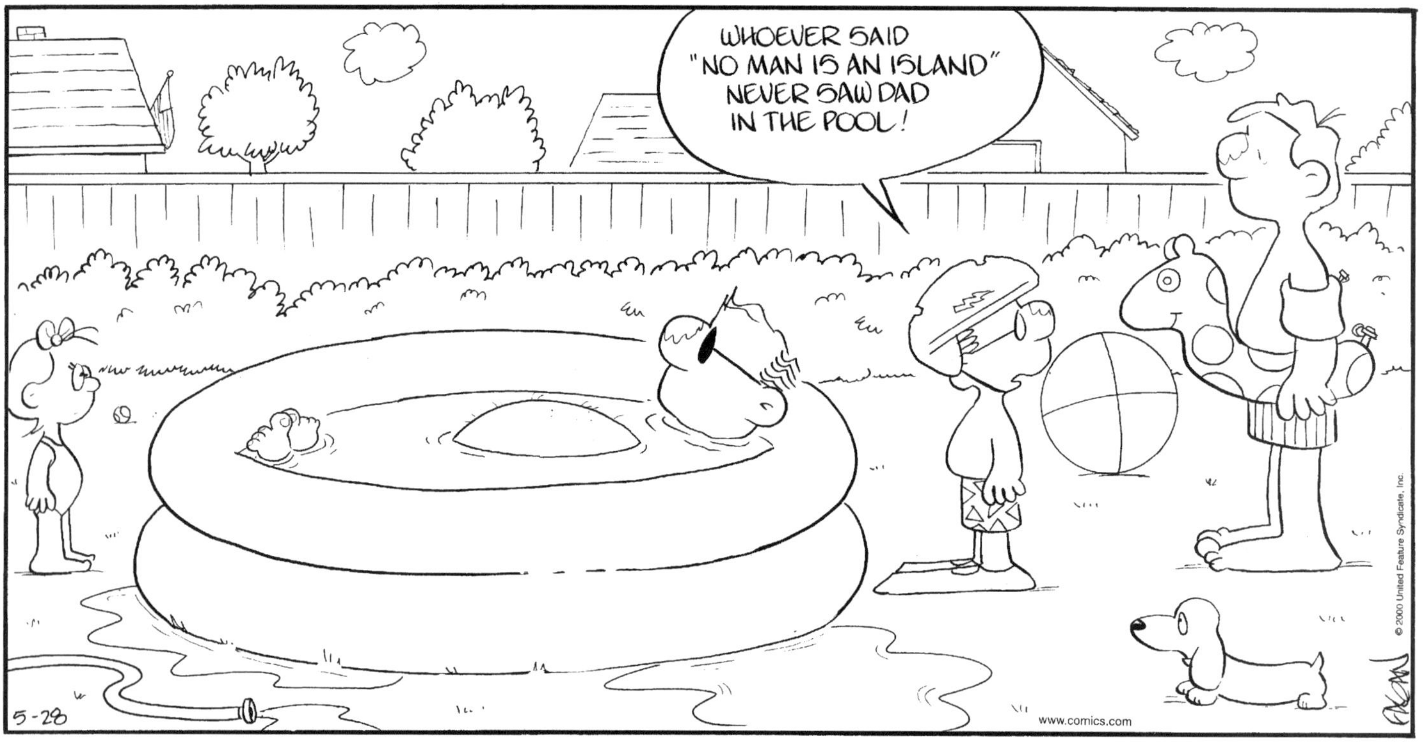
WHOEVER SAID "NO MAN IS AN ISLAND" NEVER SAW DAD IN THE POOL!
5-28
© 2000 United Feature Syndicate, Inc.
www.comics.com

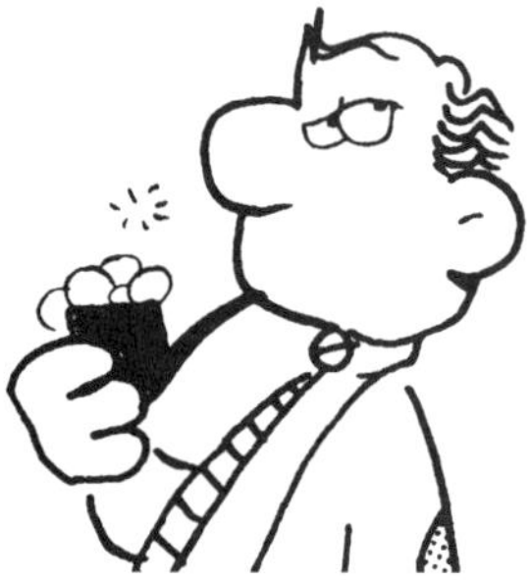

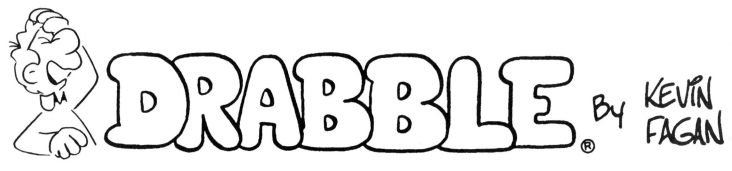

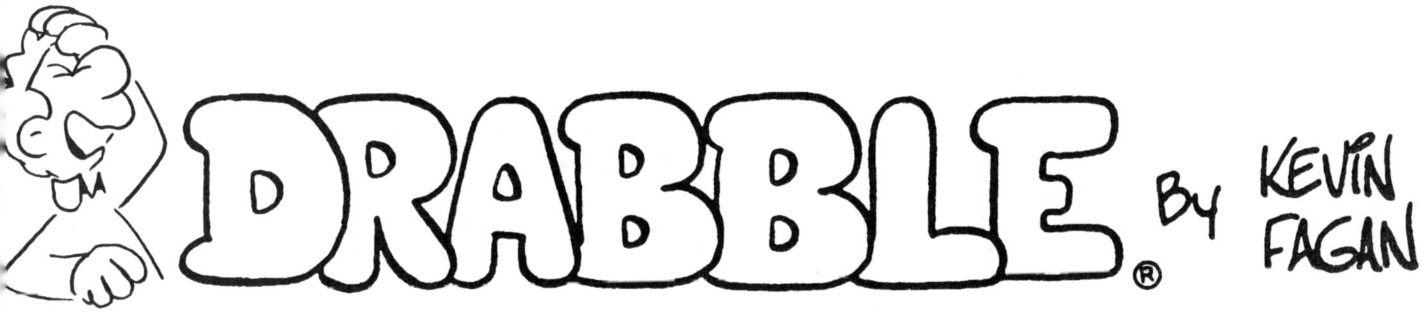
DRABBLE®
By KEVIN FAGAN

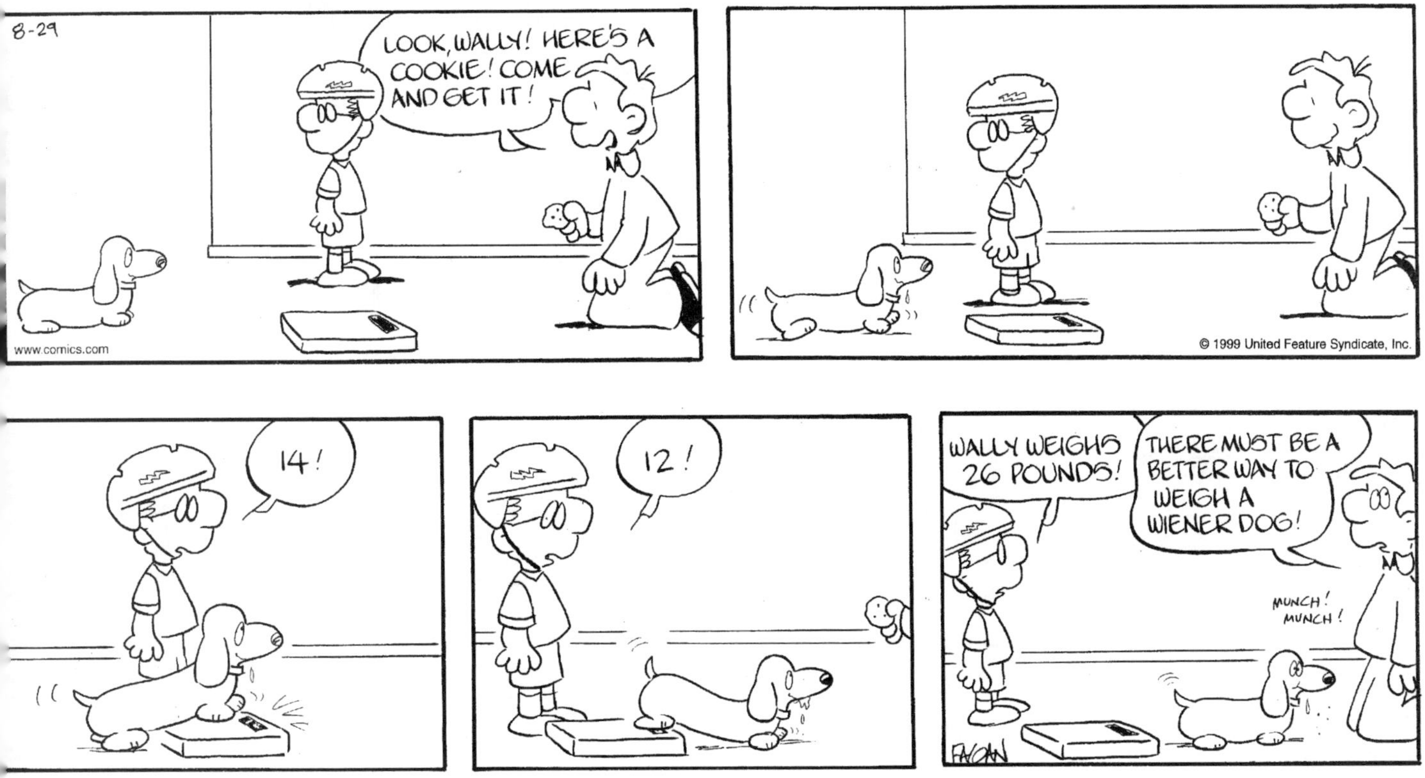
8-29
LOOK, WALLY! HERE'S A COOKIE! COME AND GET IT!
www.comics.com
© 1999 United Feature Syndicate, Inc.
14!
12!
WALLY WEIGHS 26 POUNDS!
THERE MUST BE A BETTER WAY TO WEIGH A WIENER DOG!
MUNCH! MUNCH!
FAGAN

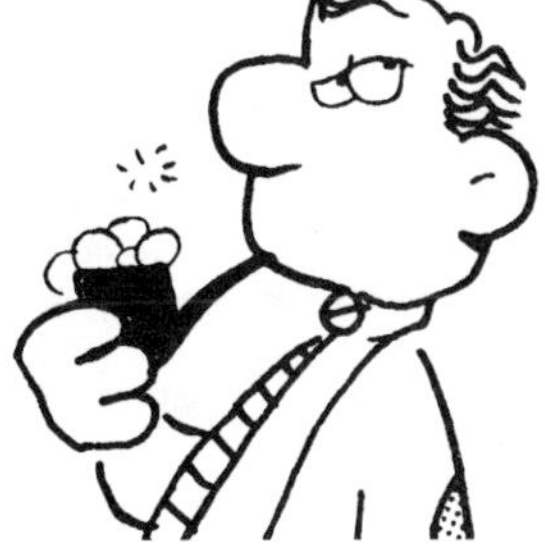

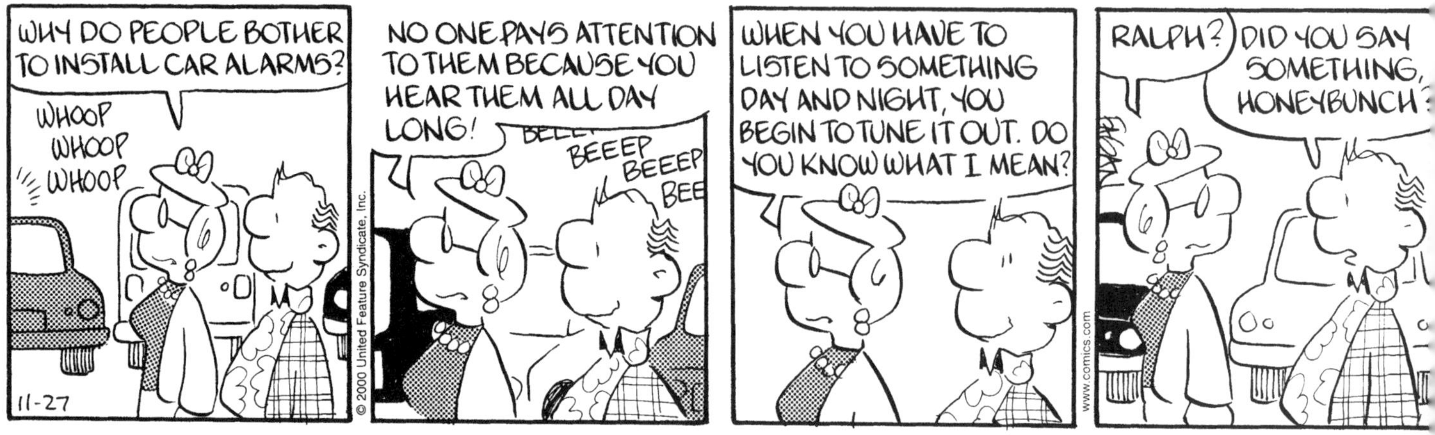
WHY DO PEOPLE BOTHER TO INSTALL CAR ALARMS?
WHOOP WHOOP WHOOP
11-27
NO ONE PAYS ATTENTION TO THEM BECAUSE YOU HEAR THEM ALL DAY LONG!
BEEEP BEEEP
© 2000 United Feature Syndicate, Inc.
WHEN YOU HAVE TO LISTEN TO SOMETHING DAY AND NIGHT, YOU BEGIN TO TUNE IT OUT. DO YOU KNOW WHAT I MEAN?
www.comics.com
RALPH?
DID YOU SAY SOMETHING, HONEYBUNCH?

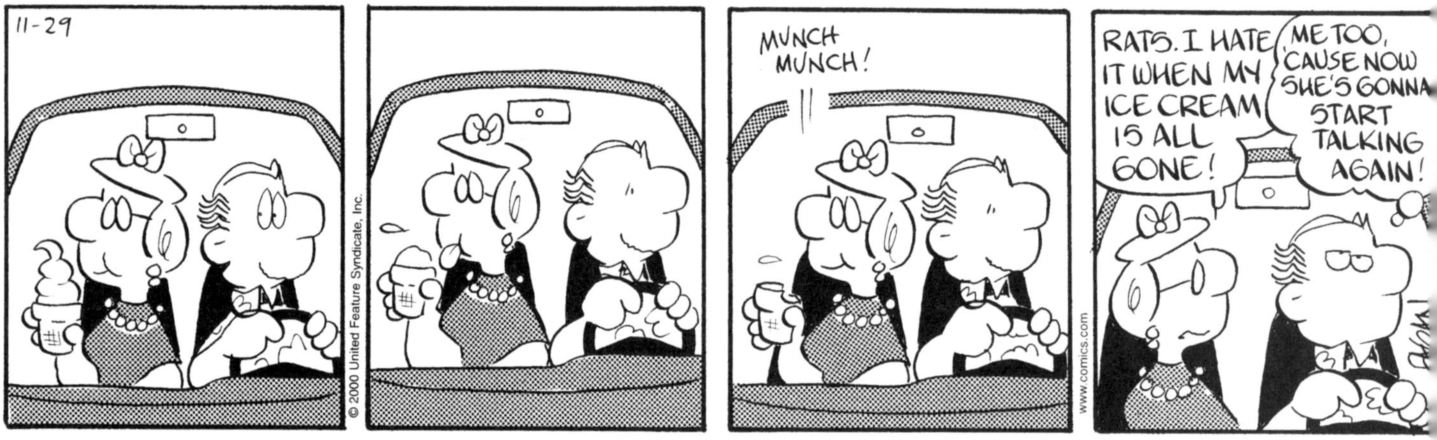
11-29
© 2000 United Feature Syndicate, Inc.
MUNCH MUNCH!
www.comics.com
RATS. I HATE IT WHEN MY ICE CREAM IS ALL GONE!
ME TOO, CAUSE NOW SHE'S GONNA START TALKING AGAIN!

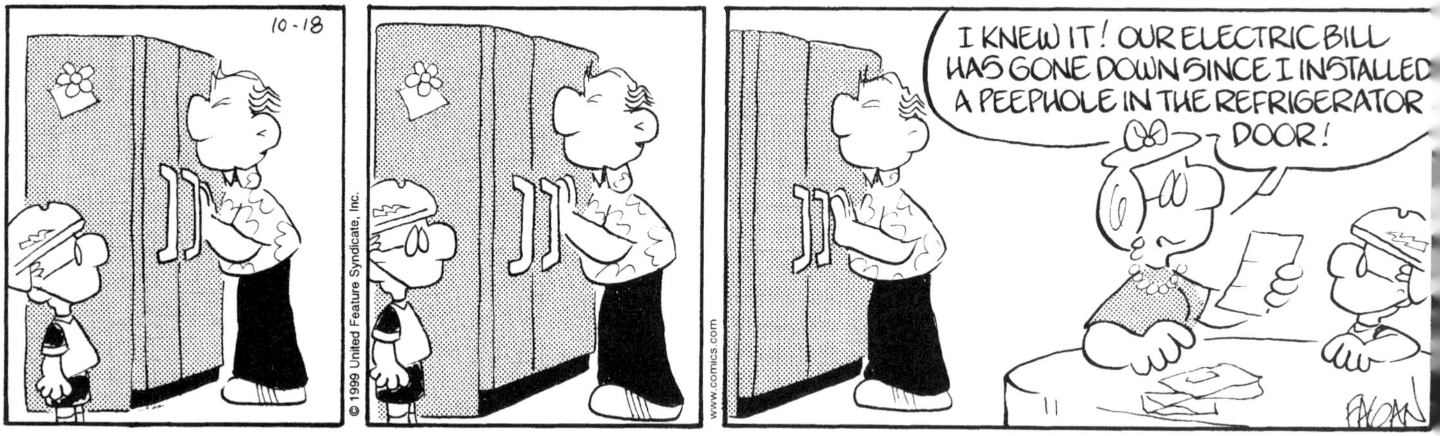
10-18
© 1999 United Feature Syndicate, Inc.
www.comics.com
I KNEW IT! OUR ELECTRIC BILL HAS GONE DOWN SINCE I INSTALLED A PEEPHOLE IN THE REFRIGERATOR DOOR!
FAGAN

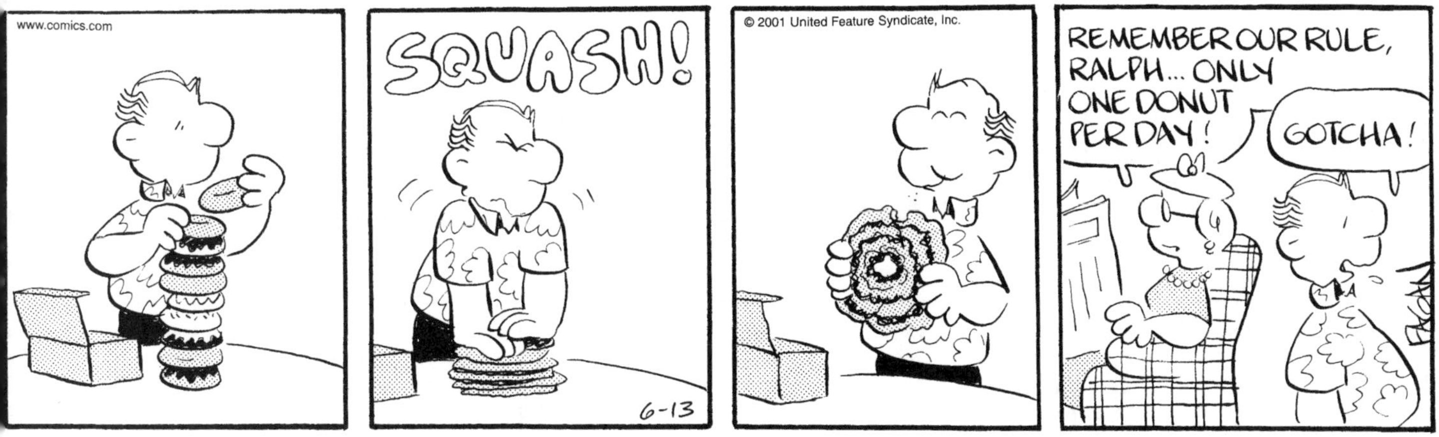
www.comics.com
SQUASH!
6-13
© 2001 United Feature Syndicate, Inc.
REMEMBER OUR RULE, RALPH... ONLY ONE DONUT PER DAY!
GOTCHA!

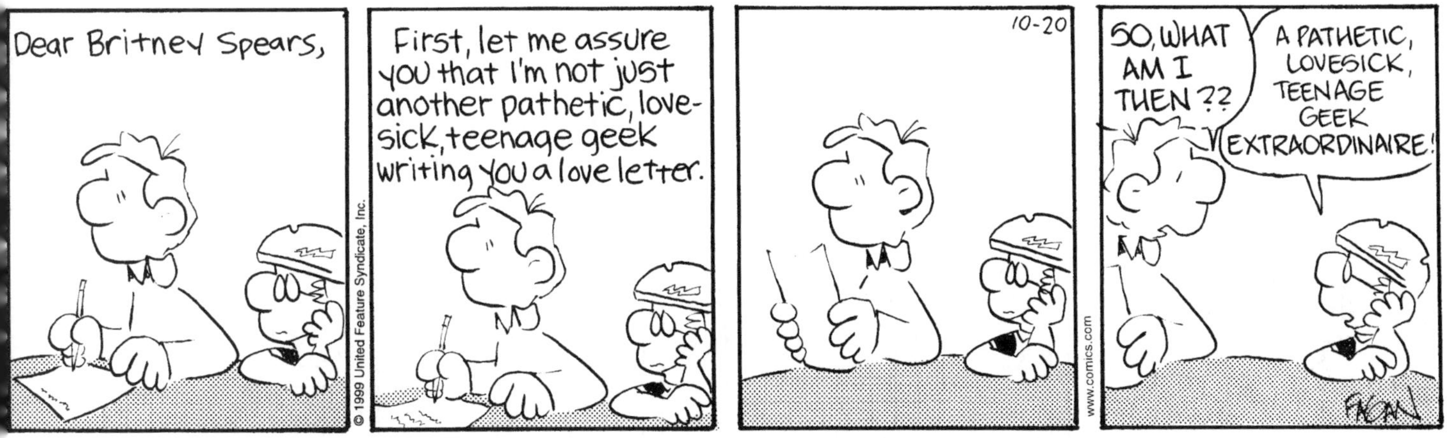
Dear Britney Spears,
© 1999 United Feature Syndicate, Inc.
First, let me assure you that I'm not just another pathetic, love-sick, teenage geek writing you a love letter.
10-20
www.comics.com
SO, WHAT AM I THEN??
A PATHETIC, LOVESICK, TEENAGE GEEK EXTRAORDINAIRE!

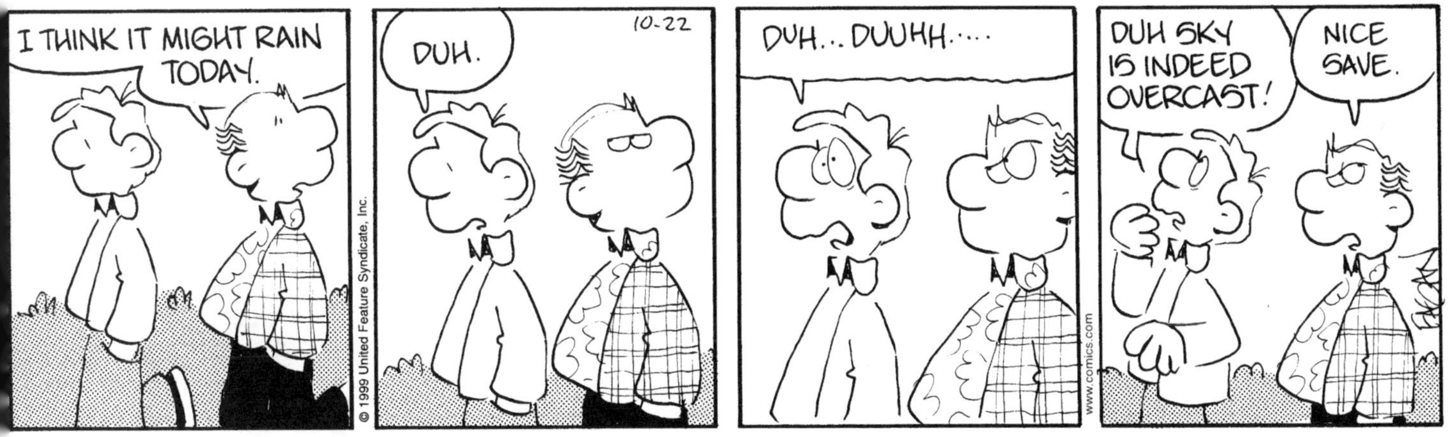
I THINK IT MIGHT RAIN TODAY.
© 1999 United Feature Syndicate, Inc.
DUH.
10-22
DUH... DUUHH....
www.comics.com
DUH SKY IS INDEED OVERCAST!
NICE SAVE.

DRABBLE. BY KEVIN FAGAN

Panel 1: YOUR USUAL, MR. DRABBLE?
NOT TODAY, ERNIE. I'M SORT OF ON A DIET, SO I'M TRYING TO CUT BACK ON MY DAILY DONUT INTAKE!

© 1999 United Feature Syndicate, Inc.

Panel 2: INSTEAD OF THREE CHOCOLATE DONUTS, JUST GIVE ME TWO!

Panel 3: WE'RE HAVING A TWO-FOR-ONE SALE TODAY, RALPH. FOR THE PRICE OF TWO DONUTS, YOU COULD HAVE FOUR!
REALLY? OK... GIMME FOUR!

Panel 4: IF YOU BUY FIVE, WE'LL THROW IN AN EXTRA ONE FREE!
WELL, OK! MAKE IT FIVE!

Panel 5: AND SINCE YOU NOW HAVE SIX, WE'LL GIVE YOU ANOTHER HALF DOZEN FOR ONLY A DOLLAR MORE!
GOSH, YA' CAN'T BEAT A DEAL LIKE THAT!
9-19

www.comics.com

Panel 6: NOW THAT YOU HAVE AN EVEN DOZEN, YOU'RE ENTITLED TO ANOTHER DOZEN AT 60% OFF!
REALLY??

Panel 7: WELL, I SEE YOUR NEW DIET IS OFF TO A FLYING START!
I MAY BE FAT, BUT I'M A SHREWD BUSINESSMAN!

FAGAN

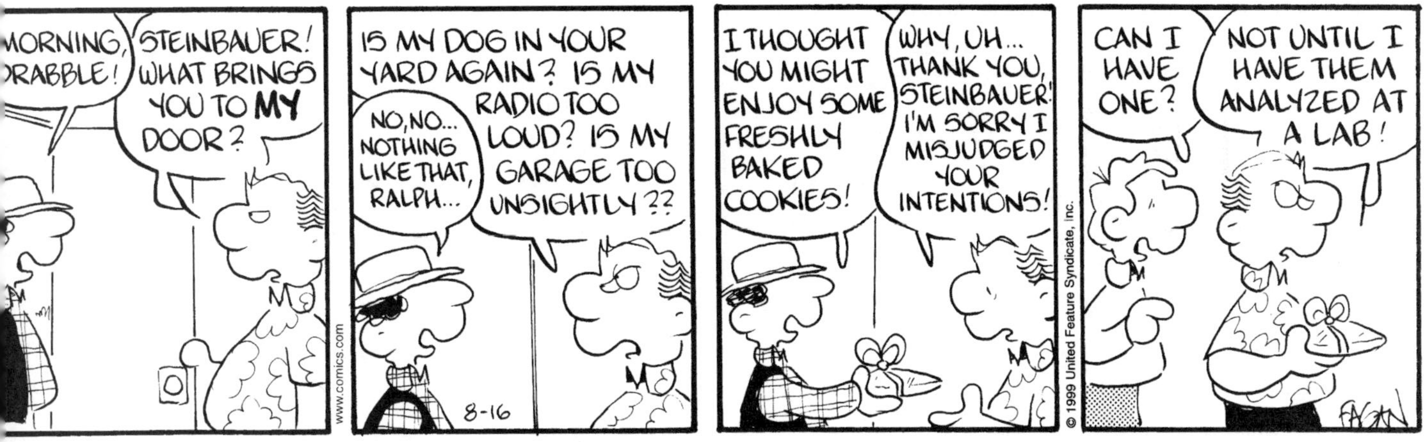
'MORNING, DRABBLE!
STEINBAUER! WHAT BRINGS YOU TO MY DOOR?
www.comics.com
IS MY DOG IN YOUR YARD AGAIN? IS MY RADIO TOO LOUD? IS MY GARAGE TOO UNSIGHTLY??
NO, NO... NOTHING LIKE THAT, RALPH...
8-16
I THOUGHT YOU MIGHT ENJOY SOME FRESHLY BAKED COOKIES!
WHY, UH... THANK YOU, STEINBAUER! I'M SORRY I MISJUDGED YOUR INTENTIONS!
© 1999 United Feature Syndicate, Inc.
CAN I HAVE ONE?
NOT UNTIL I HAVE THEM ANALYZED AT A LAB!
FAGAN

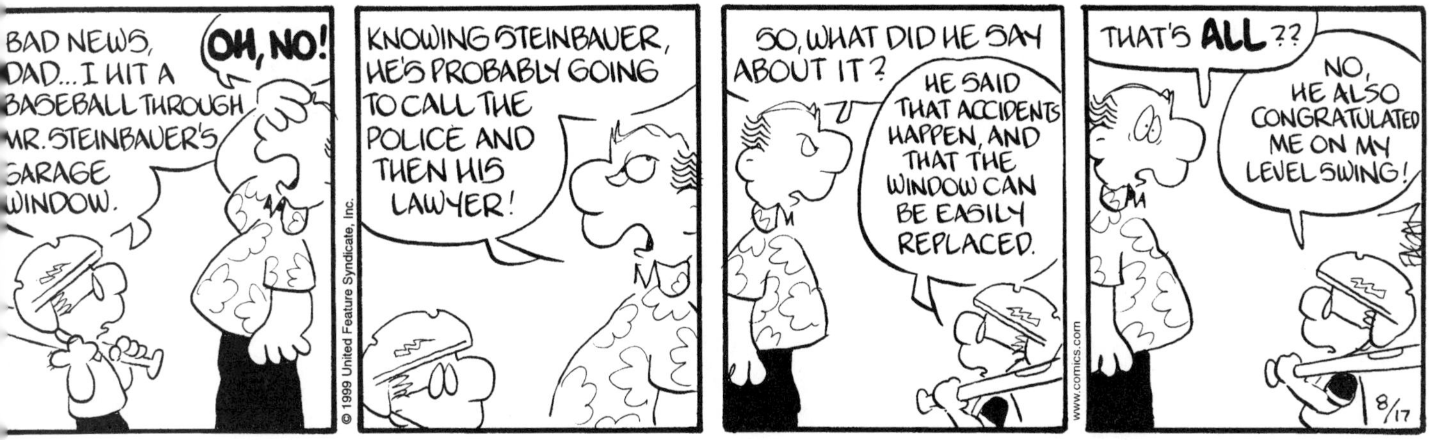
BAD NEWS, DAD... I HIT A BASEBALL THROUGH MR. STEINBAUER'S GARAGE WINDOW.
OH, NO!
© 1999 United Feature Syndicate, Inc.
KNOWING STEINBAUER, HE'S PROBABLY GOING TO CALL THE POLICE AND THEN HIS LAWYER!
SO, WHAT DID HE SAY ABOUT IT?
HE SAID THAT ACCIDENTS HAPPEN, AND THAT THE WINDOW CAN BE EASILY REPLACED.
www.comics.com
THAT'S ALL??
NO, HE ALSO CONGRATULATED ME ON MY LEVEL SWING!
8/17

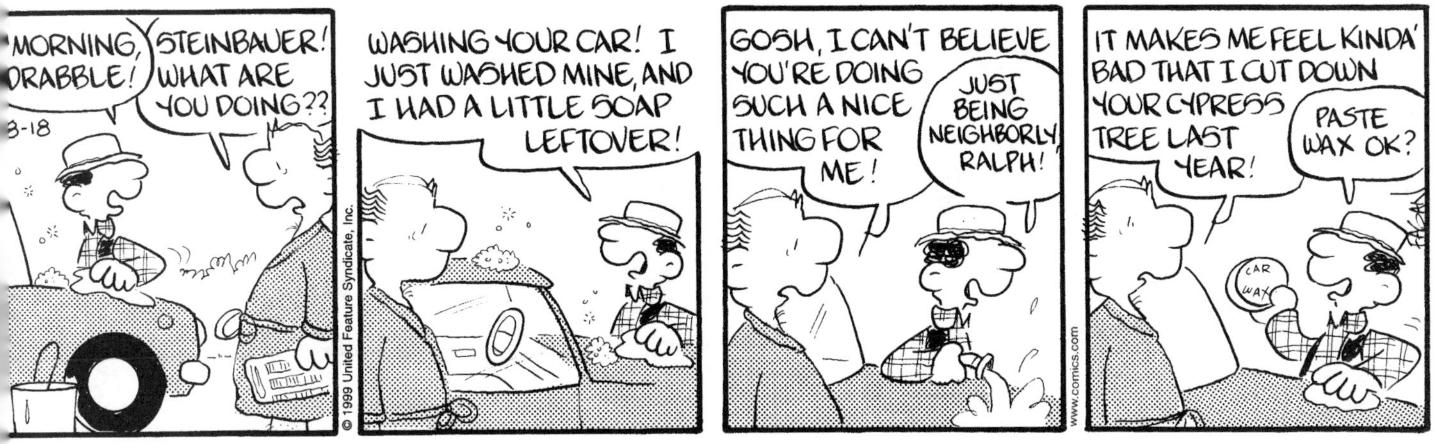
'MORNING, DRABBLE!
STEINBAUER! WHAT ARE YOU DOING??
8-18
© 1999 United Feature Syndicate, Inc.
WASHING YOUR CAR! I JUST WASHED MINE, AND I HAD A LITTLE SOAP LEFTOVER!
GOSH, I CAN'T BELIEVE YOU'RE DOING SUCH A NICE THING FOR ME!
JUST BEING NEIGHBORLY, RALPH!
www.comics.com
IT MAKES ME FEEL KINDA' BAD THAT I CUT DOWN YOUR CYPRESS TREE LAST YEAR!
PASTE WAX OK?
CAR WAX

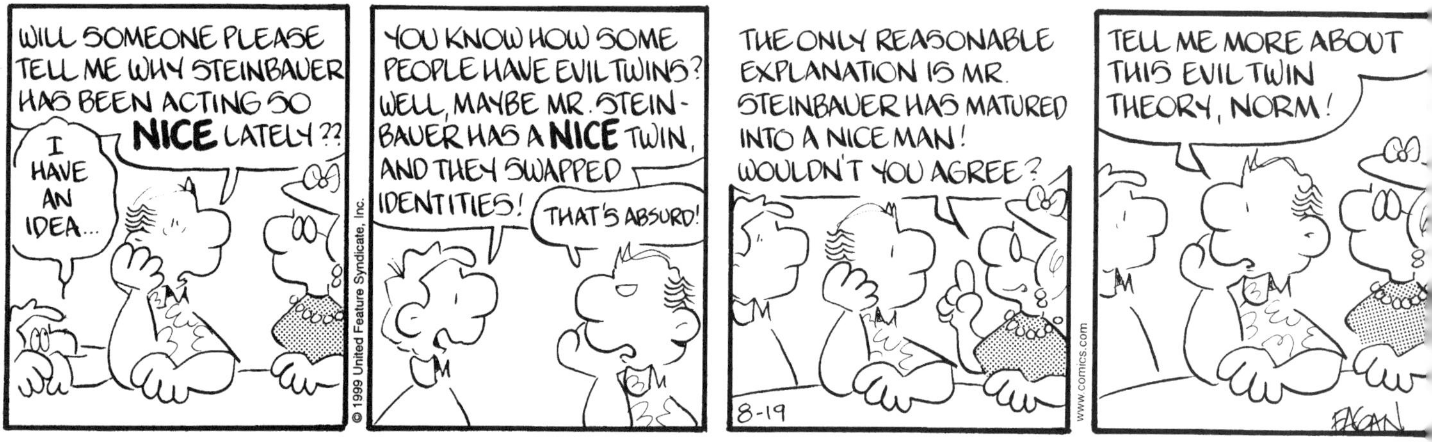
WILL SOMEONE PLEASE TELL ME WHY STEINBAUER HAS BEEN ACTING SO NICE LATELY??
I HAVE AN IDEA...
© 1999 United Feature Syndicate, Inc.
YOU KNOW HOW SOME PEOPLE HAVE EVIL TWINS? WELL, MAYBE MR. STEINBAUER HAS A NICE TWIN, AND THEY SWAPPED IDENTITIES!
THAT'S ABSURD!
THE ONLY REASONABLE EXPLANATION IS MR. STEINBAUER HAS MATURED INTO A NICE MAN! WOULDN'T YOU AGREE?
8-19
www.comics.com
TELL ME MORE ABOUT THIS EVIL TWIN THEORY, NORM!
FAGAN

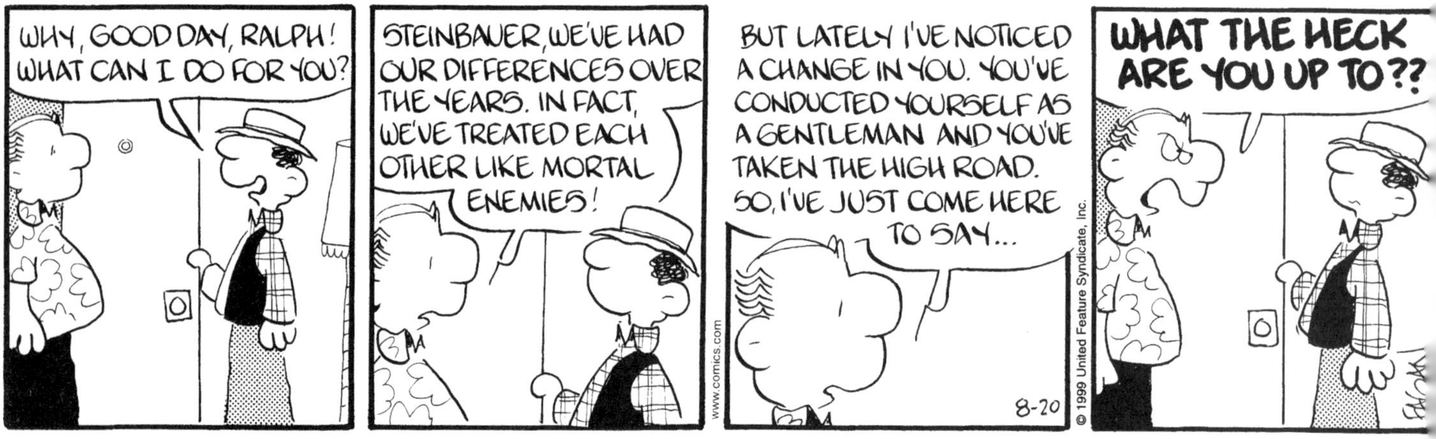
WHY, GOOD DAY, RALPH! WHAT CAN I DO FOR YOU?
STEINBAUER, WE'VE HAD OUR DIFFERENCES OVER THE YEARS. IN FACT, WE'VE TREATED EACH OTHER LIKE MORTAL ENEMIES!
www.comics.com
BUT LATELY I'VE NOTICED A CHANGE IN YOU. YOU'VE CONDUCTED YOURSELF AS A GENTLEMAN AND YOU'VE TAKEN THE HIGH ROAD. SO, I'VE JUST COME HERE TO SAY...
8-20
© 1999 United Feature Syndicate, Inc.
WHAT THE HECK ARE YOU UP TO??

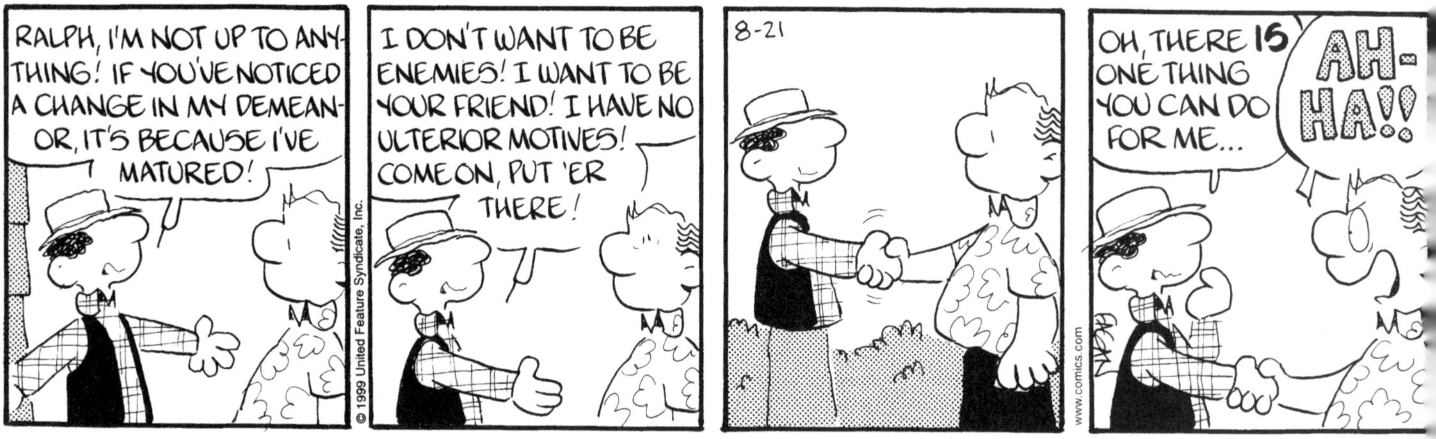
RALPH, I'M NOT UP TO ANYTHING! IF YOU'VE NOTICED A CHANGE IN MY DEMEANOR, IT'S BECAUSE I'VE MATURED!
© 1999 United Feature Syndicate, Inc.
I DON'T WANT TO BE ENEMIES! I WANT TO BE YOUR FRIEND! I HAVE NO ULTERIOR MOTIVES! COME ON, PUT 'ER THERE!
8-21
www.comics.com
OH, THERE IS ONE THING YOU CAN DO FOR ME...
AH-HA!!

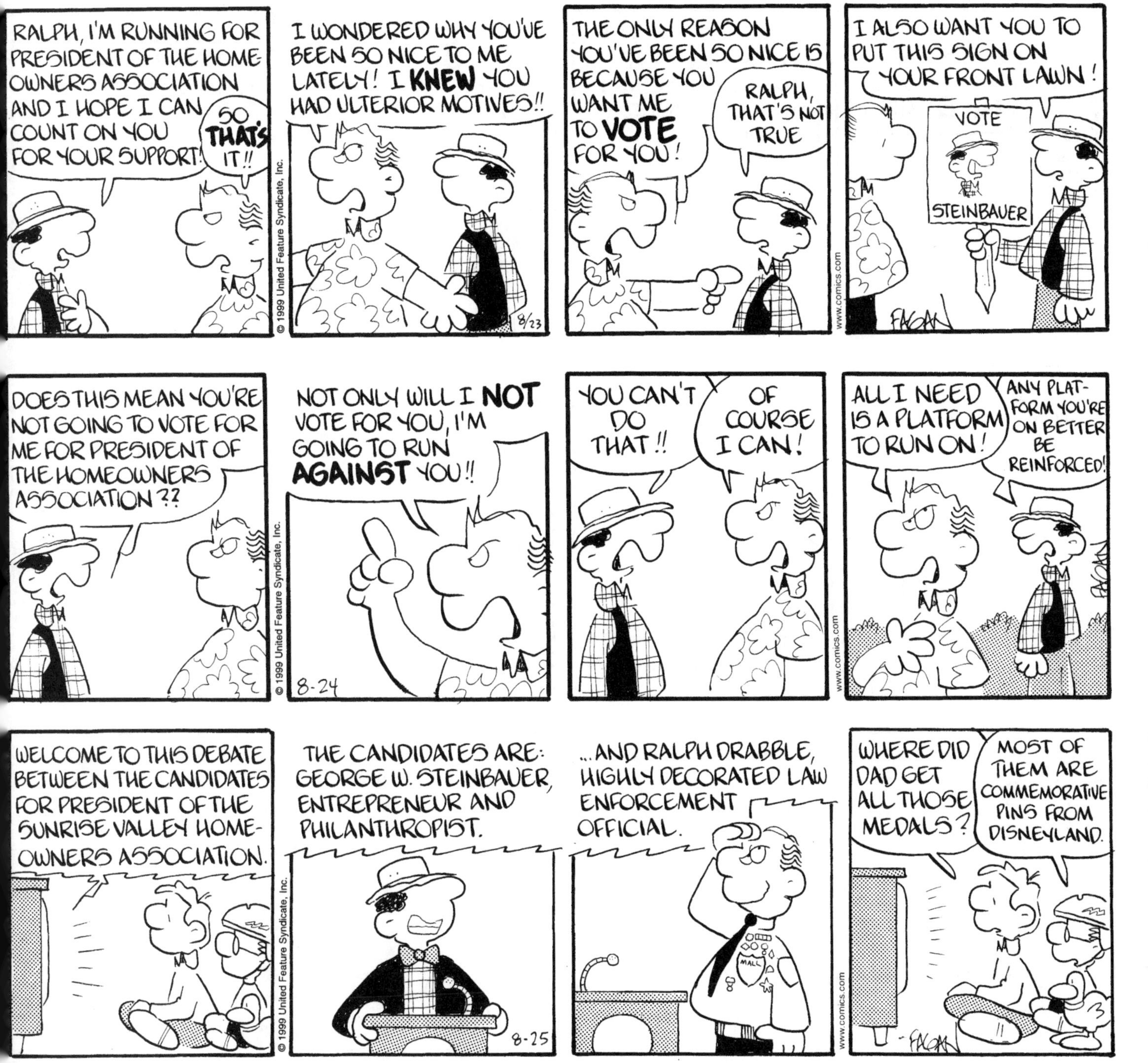
RALPH, I'M RUNNING FOR PRESIDENT OF THE HOME-OWNERS ASSOCIATION AND I HOPE I CAN COUNT ON YOU FOR YOUR SUPPORT!
SO THAT'S IT!!
© 1999 United Feature Syndicate, Inc.
I WONDERED WHY YOU'VE BEEN SO NICE TO ME LATELY! I KNEW YOU HAD ULTERIOR MOTIVES!!
8/23
THE ONLY REASON YOU'VE BEEN SO NICE IS BECAUSE YOU WANT ME TO VOTE FOR YOU!
RALPH, THAT'S NOT TRUE
www.comics.com
I ALSO WANT YOU TO PUT THIS SIGN ON YOUR FRONT LAWN!
VOTE
STEINBAUER
FAGAN
DOES THIS MEAN YOU'RE NOT GOING TO VOTE FOR ME FOR PRESIDENT OF THE HOMEOWNERS ASSOCIATION??
© 1999 United Feature Syndicate, Inc.
NOT ONLY WILL I NOT VOTE FOR YOU, I'M GOING TO RUN AGAINST YOU!!
8-24
YOU CAN'T DO THAT!!
OF COURSE I CAN!
www.comics.com
ALL I NEED IS A PLATFORM TO RUN ON!
ANY PLATFORM YOU'RE ON BETTER BE REINFORCED!
FAGAN
WELCOME TO THIS DEBATE BETWEEN THE CANDIDATES FOR PRESIDENT OF THE SUNRISE VALLEY HOME-OWNERS ASSOCIATION.
© 1999 United Feature Syndicate, Inc.
THE CANDIDATES ARE: GEORGE W. STEINBAUER, ENTREPRENEUR AND PHILANTHROPIST.
8-25
...AND RALPH DRABBLE, HIGHLY DECORATED LAW ENFORCEMENT OFFICIAL.
MALL
www.comics.com
WHERE DID DAD GET ALL THOSE MEDALS?
MOST OF THEM ARE COMMEMORATIVE PINS FROM DISNEYLAND.
FAGAN

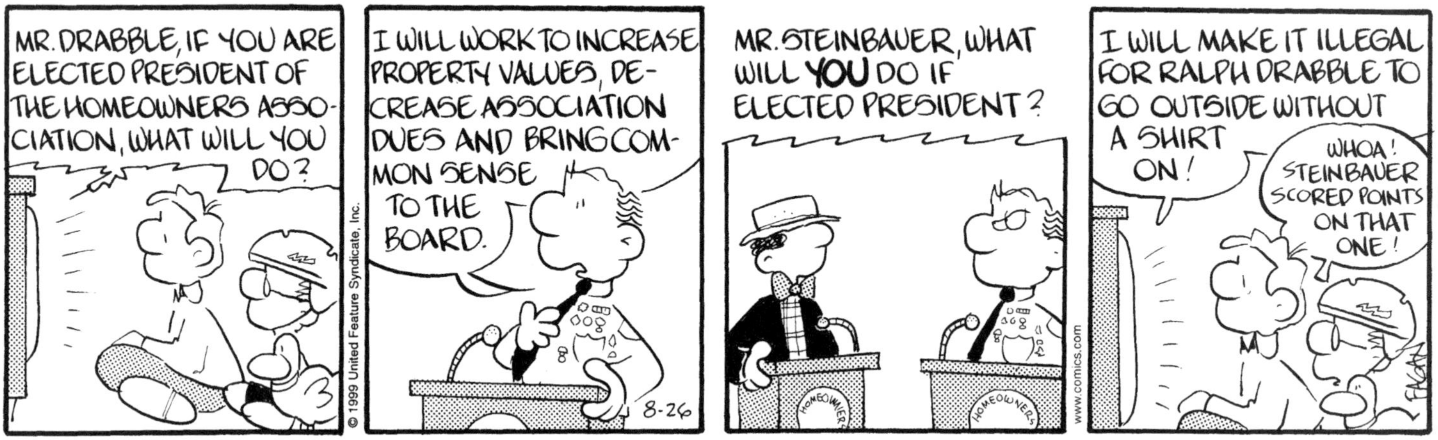
MR. DRABBLE, IF YOU ARE ELECTED PRESIDENT OF THE HOMEOWNERS ASSOCIATION, WHAT WILL YOU DO?
I WILL WORK TO INCREASE PROPERTY VALUES, DECREASE ASSOCIATION DUES AND BRING COMMON SENSE TO THE BOARD.
8-26
© 1999 United Feature Syndicate, Inc.
MR. STEINBAUER, WHAT WILL YOU DO IF ELECTED PRESIDENT?
HOMEOWNERS
HOMEOWNERS
www.comics.com
I WILL MAKE IT ILLEGAL FOR RALPH DRABBLE TO GO OUTSIDE WITHOUT A SHIRT ON!
WHOA! STEINBAUER SCORED POINTS ON THAT ONE!

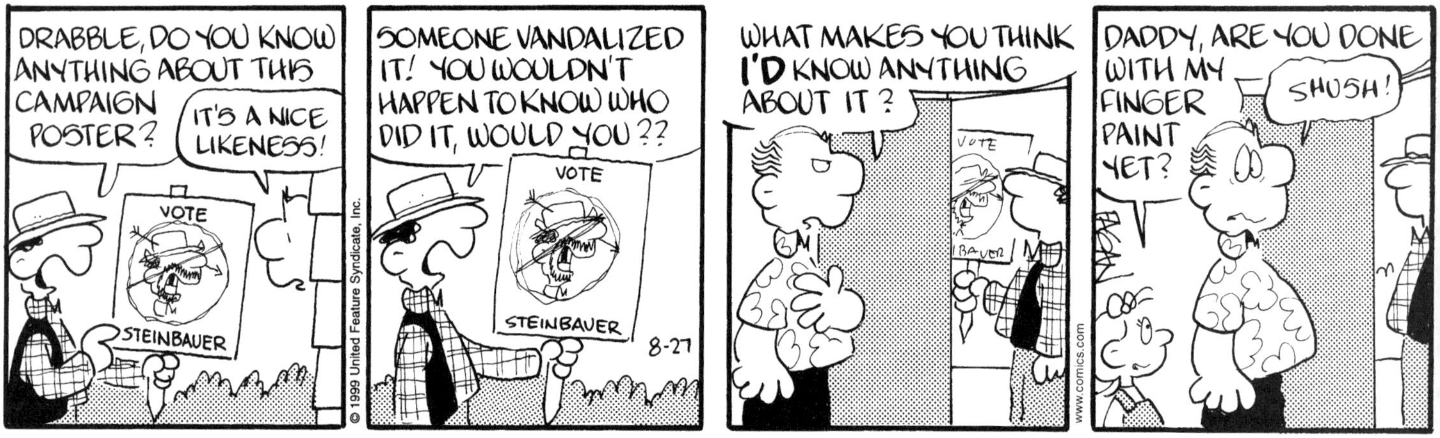
DRABBLE, DO YOU KNOW ANYTHING ABOUT THIS CAMPAIGN POSTER?
IT'S A NICE LIKENESS!
VOTE
STEINBAUER
© 1999 United Feature Syndicate, Inc.
SOMEONE VANDALIZED IT! YOU WOULDN'T HAPPEN TO KNOW WHO DID IT, WOULD YOU??
VOTE
STEINBAUER
8-27
WHAT MAKES YOU THINK I'D KNOW ANYTHING ABOUT IT?
www.comics.com
DADDY, ARE YOU DONE WITH MY FINGER PAINT YET?
SHUSH!

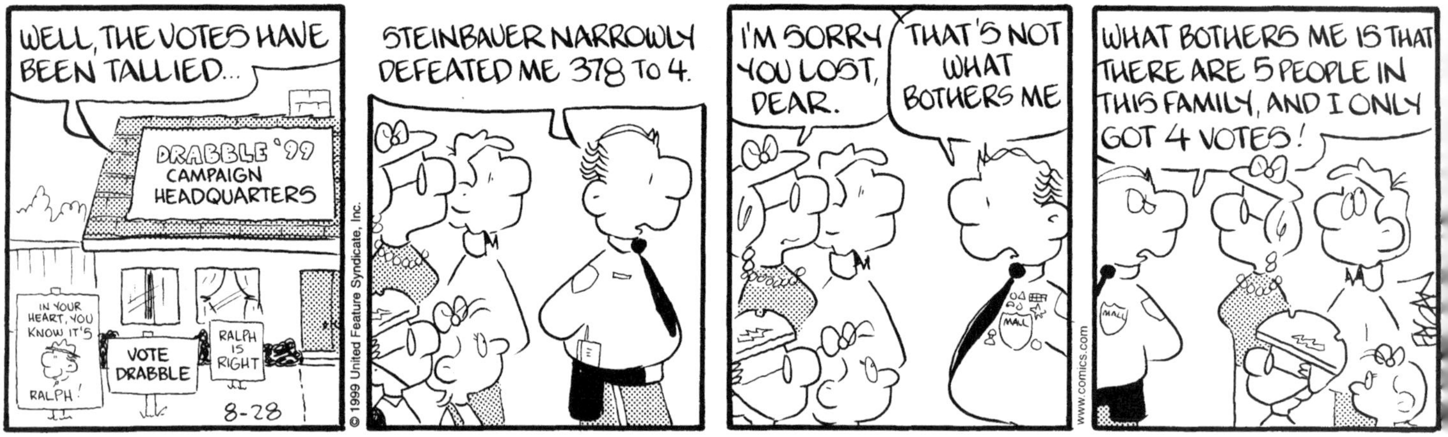
WELL, THE VOTES HAVE BEEN TALLIED...
DRABBLE '99 CAMPAIGN HEADQUARTERS
IN YOUR HEART, YOU KNOW IT'S RALPH!
VOTE DRABBLE
RALPH IS RIGHT
8-28
© 1999 United Feature Syndicate, Inc.
STEINBAUER NARROWLY DEFEATED ME 378 TO 4.
I'M SORRY YOU LOST, DEAR.
THAT'S NOT WHAT BOTHERS ME
MALL
www.comics.com
WHAT BOTHERS ME IS THAT THERE ARE 5 PEOPLE IN THIS FAMILY, AND I ONLY GOT 4 VOTES!
MALL

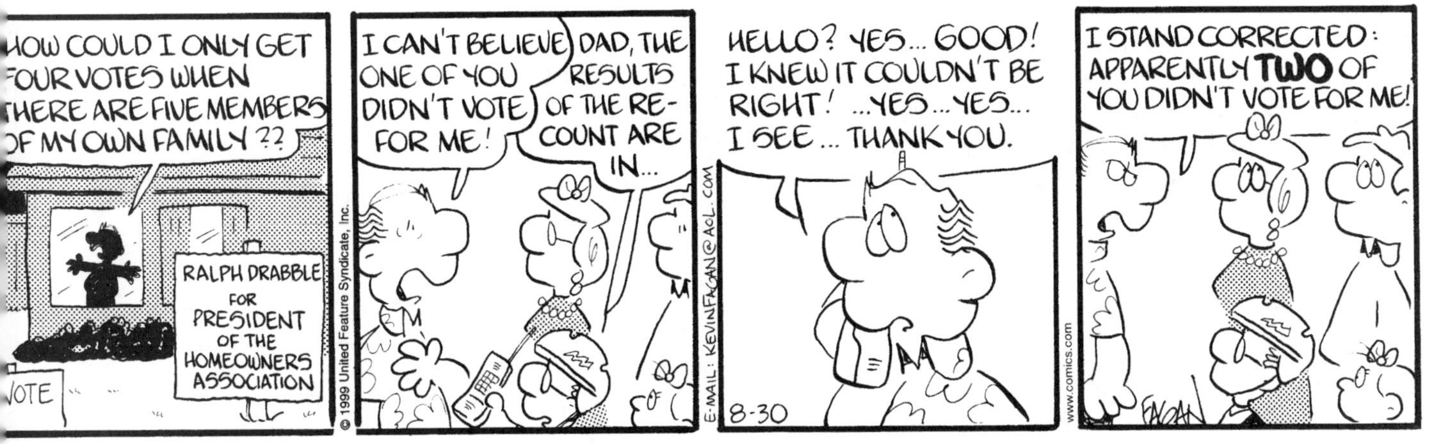
HOW COULD I ONLY GET FOUR VOTES WHEN THERE ARE FIVE MEMBERS OF MY OWN FAMILY ??
RALPH DRABBLE FOR PRESIDENT OF THE HOMEOWNERS ASSOCIATION
VOTE
© 1999 United Feature Syndicate, Inc.
I CAN'T BELIEVE ONE OF YOU DIDN'T VOTE FOR ME!
DAD, THE RESULTS OF THE RE-COUNT ARE IN...
E-MAIL: KEVINFAGAN@AOL.COM
HELLO? YES... GOOD! I KNEW IT COULDN'T BE RIGHT! ...YES... YES... I SEE... THANK YOU.
8-30
www.comics.com
I STAND CORRECTED: APPARENTLY **TWO** OF YOU DIDN'T VOTE FOR ME!
FAGAN

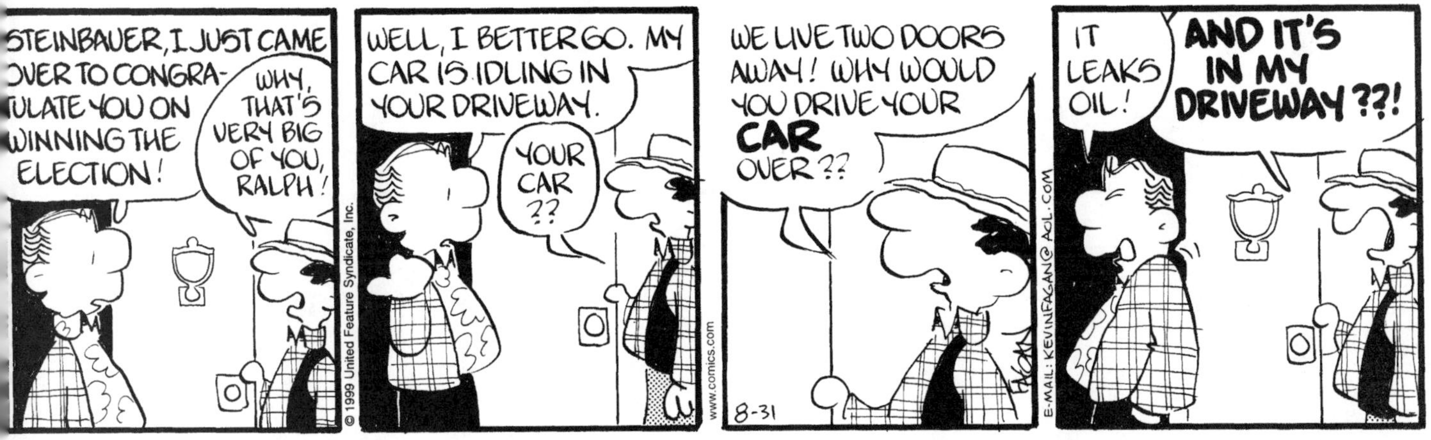
STEINBAUER, I JUST CAME OVER TO CONGRATULATE YOU ON WINNING THE ELECTION!
WHY, THAT'S VERY BIG OF YOU, RALPH!
© 1999 United Feature Syndicate, Inc.
WELL, I BETTER GO. MY CAR IS IDLING IN YOUR DRIVEWAY.
YOUR CAR ??
www.comics.com
WE LIVE TWO DOORS AWAY! WHY WOULD YOU DRIVE YOUR **CAR** OVER??
8-31
FAGAN
E-MAIL: KEVINFAGAN@AOL.COM
IT LEAKS OIL!
AND IT'S IN MY DRIVEWAY ??!

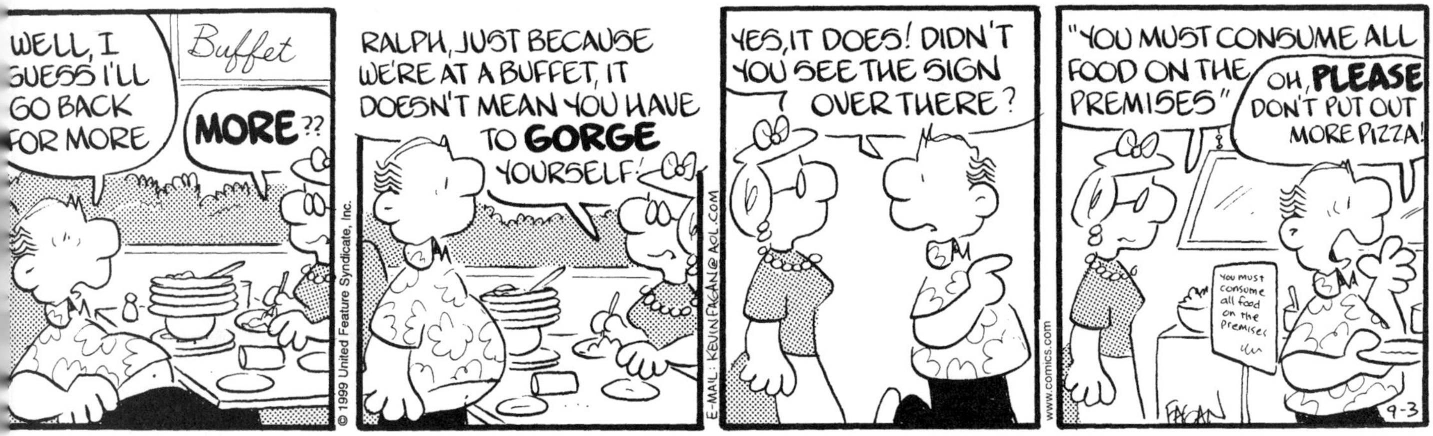
Buffet
WELL, I GUESS I'LL GO BACK FOR MORE
MORE??
© 1999 United Feature Syndicate, Inc.
RALPH, JUST BECAUSE WE'RE AT A BUFFET, IT DOESN'T MEAN YOU HAVE TO **GORGE** YOURSELF!
E-MAIL: KEVINFAGAN@AOL.COM
YES, IT DOES! DIDN'T YOU SEE THE SIGN OVER THERE?
www.comics.com
"YOU MUST CONSUME ALL FOOD ON THE PREMISES"
OH, **PLEASE** DON'T PUT OUT MORE PIZZA!
You must consume all food on the premises
FAGAN
9-3

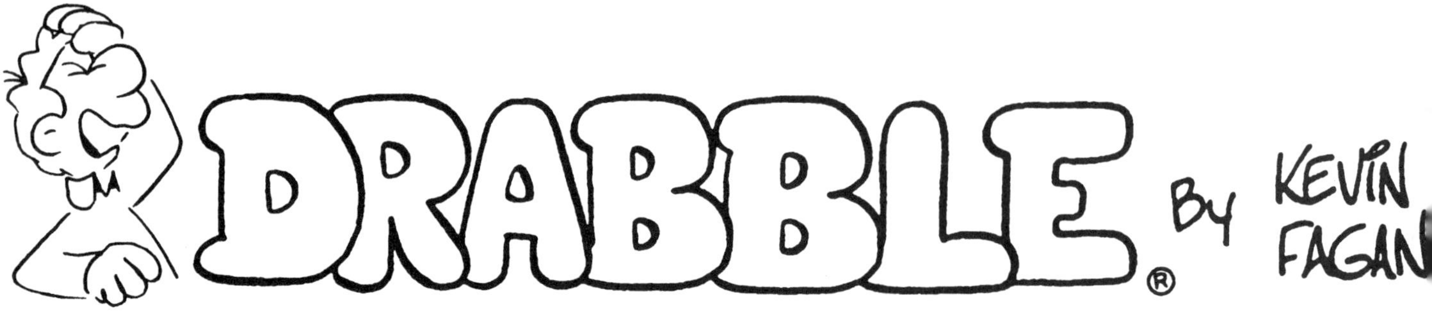
DRABBLE®
By KEVIN FAGAN

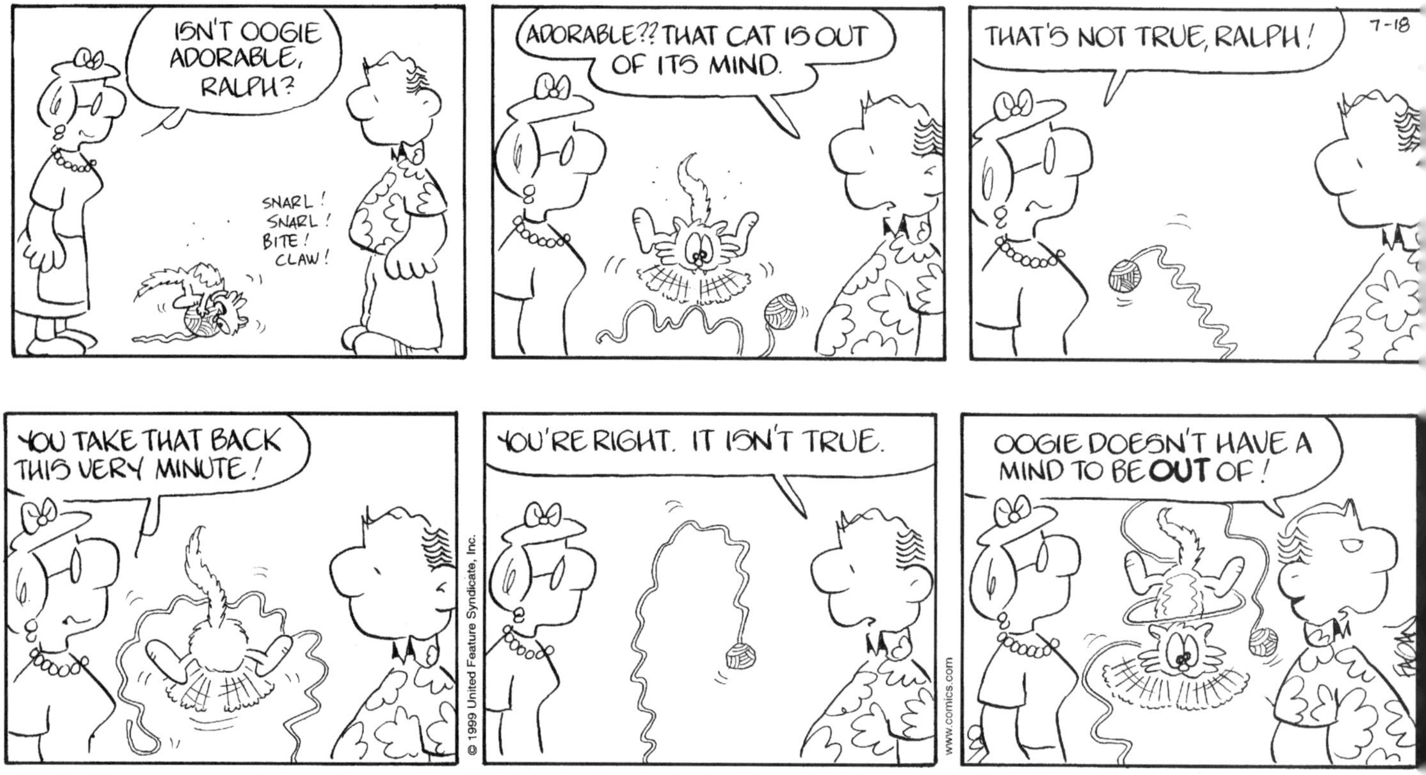
ISN'T OOGIE ADORABLE, RALPH?
SNARL! SNARL! BITE! CLAW!
ADORABLE?? THAT CAT IS OUT OF ITS MIND.
7-18
THAT'S NOT TRUE, RALPH!
YOU TAKE THAT BACK THIS VERY MINUTE!
© 1999 United Feature Syndicate, Inc.
YOU'RE RIGHT. IT ISN'T TRUE.
www.comics.com
OOGIE DOESN'T HAVE A MIND TO BE OUT OF!

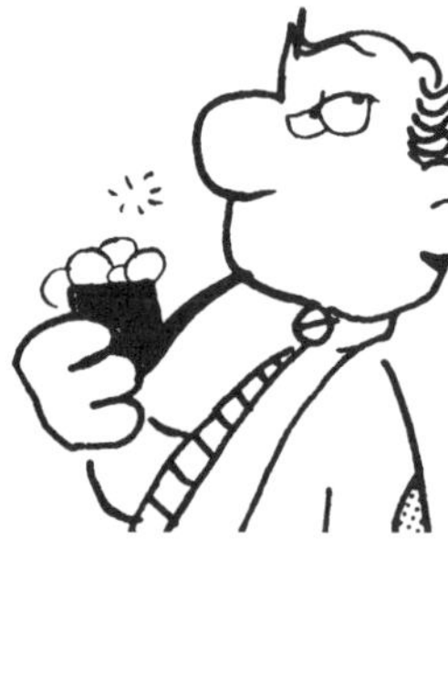

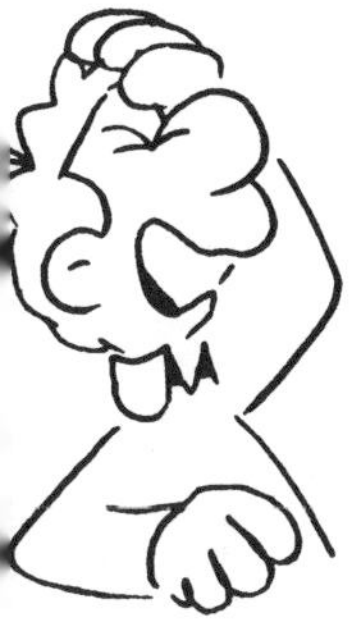

DRABBLE® By KEVIN FAGAN

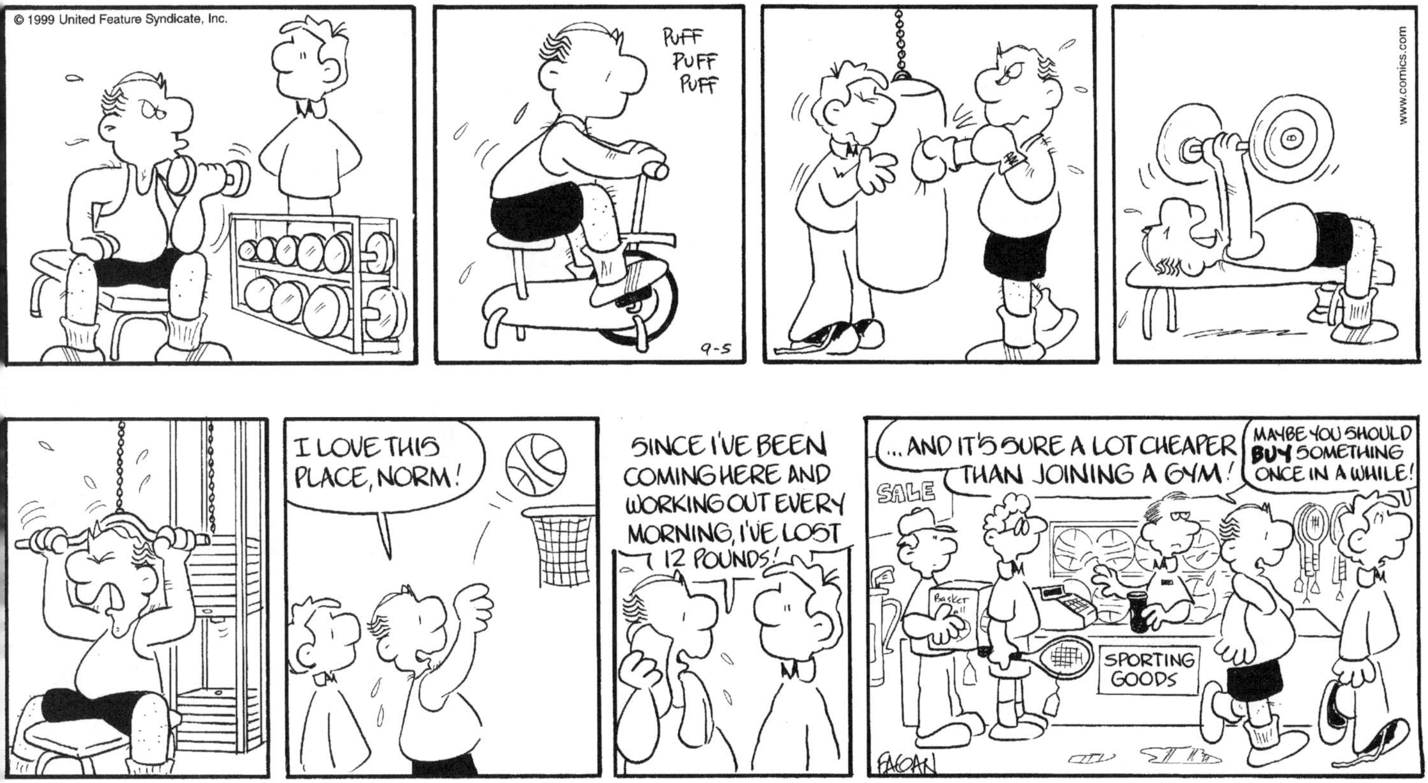
© 1999 United Feature Syndicate, Inc.
PUFF PUFF PUFF
9-5
www.comics.com
I LOVE THIS PLACE, NORM!
SINCE I'VE BEEN COMING HERE AND WORKING OUT EVERY MORNING, I'VE LOST 12 POUNDS!
...AND IT'S SURE A LOT CHEAPER THAN JOINING A GYM!
MAYBE YOU SHOULD BUY SOMETHING ONCE IN A WHILE!
SALE
Basket ball
SPORTING GOODS
FAGAN

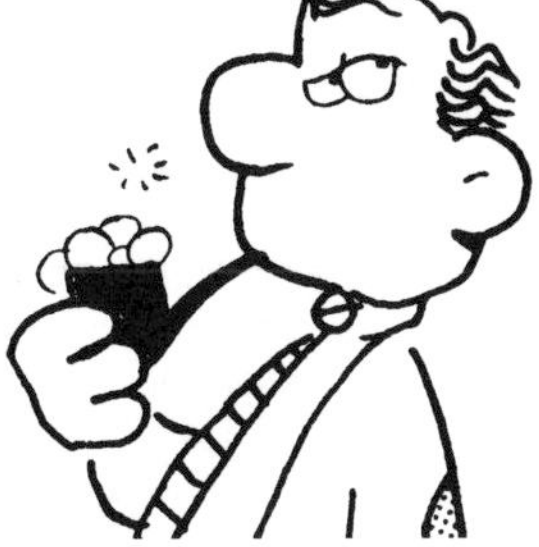

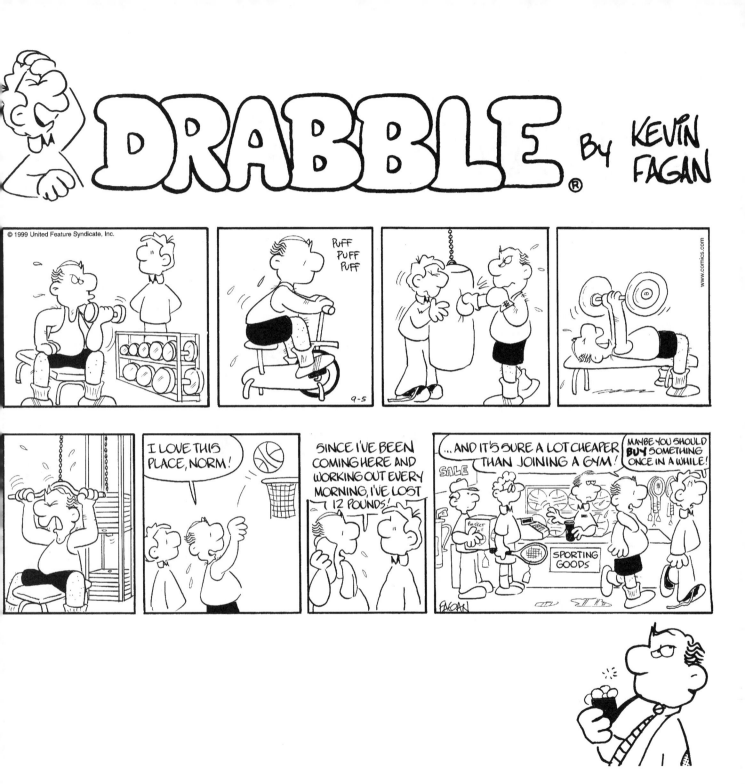

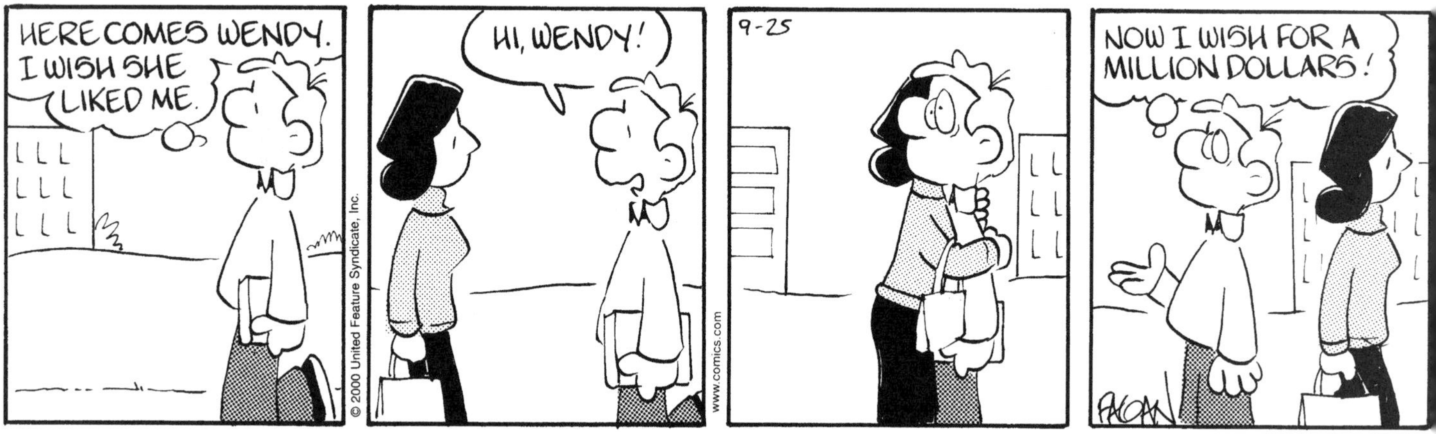
HERE COMES WENDY. I WISH SHE LIKED ME.
HI, WENDY!
9-25
NOW I WISH FOR A MILLION DOLLARS!
© 2000 United Feature Syndicate, Inc.
www.comics.com

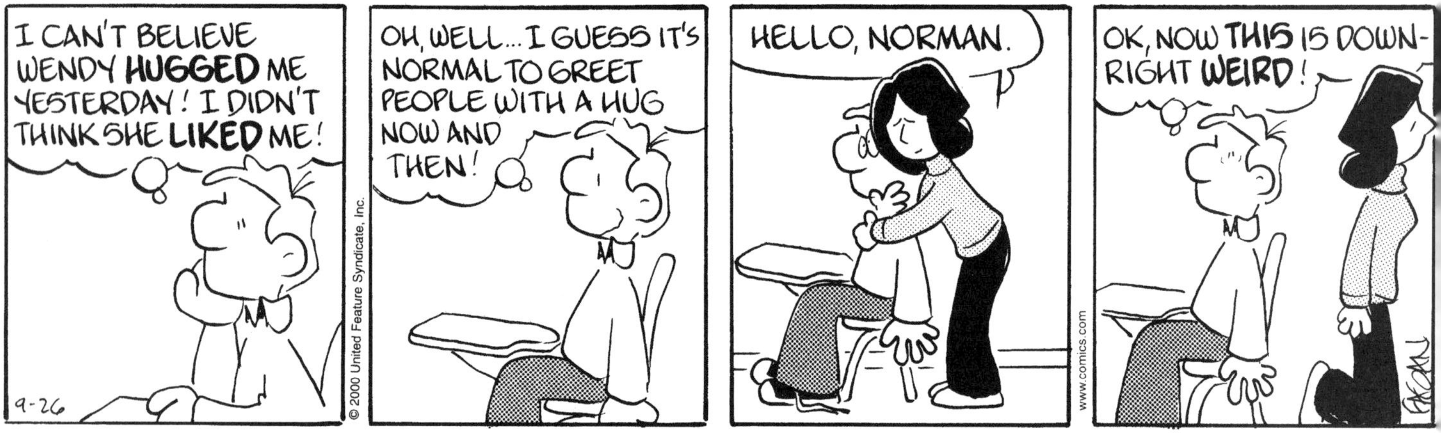
I CAN'T BELIEVE WENDY **HUGGED** ME YESTERDAY! I DIDN'T THINK SHE **LIKED** ME!
9-26
OH, WELL... I GUESS IT'S NORMAL TO GREET PEOPLE WITH A HUG NOW AND THEN!
HELLO, NORMAN.
OK, NOW **THIS** IS DOWN-RIGHT **WEIRD**!
© 2000 United Feature Syndicate, Inc.
www.comics.com

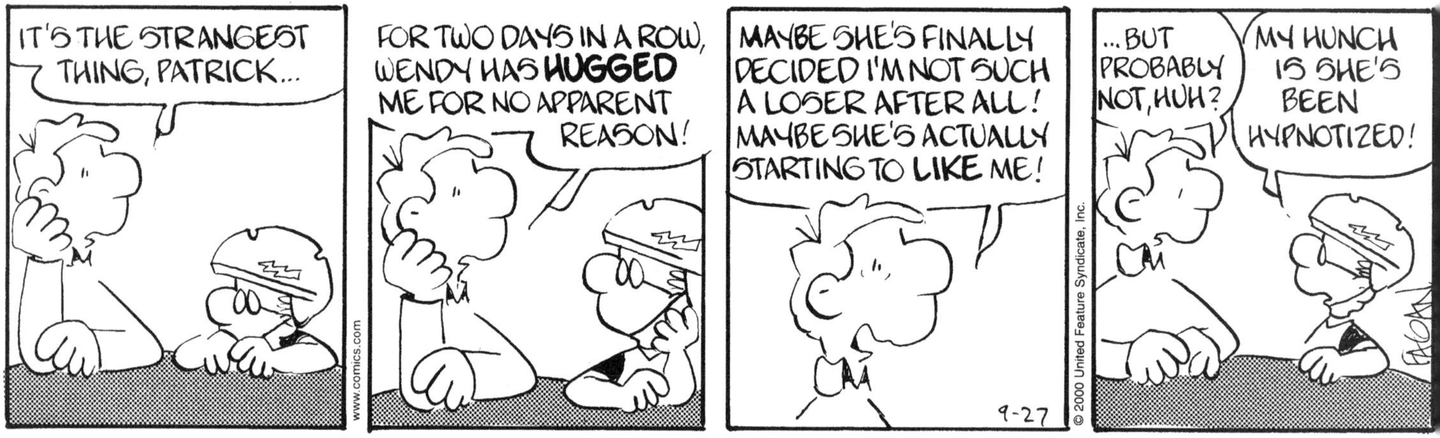
IT'S THE STRANGEST THING, PATRICK...
FOR TWO DAYS IN A ROW, WENDY HAS **HUGGED** ME FOR NO APPARENT REASON!
MAYBE SHE'S FINALLY DECIDED I'M NOT SUCH A LOSER AFTER ALL! MAYBE SHE'S ACTUALLY STARTING TO **LIKE** ME!
9-27
...BUT PROBABLY NOT, HUH?
MY HUNCH IS SHE'S BEEN HYPNOTIZED!
www.comics.com
© 2000 United Feature Syndicate, Inc.

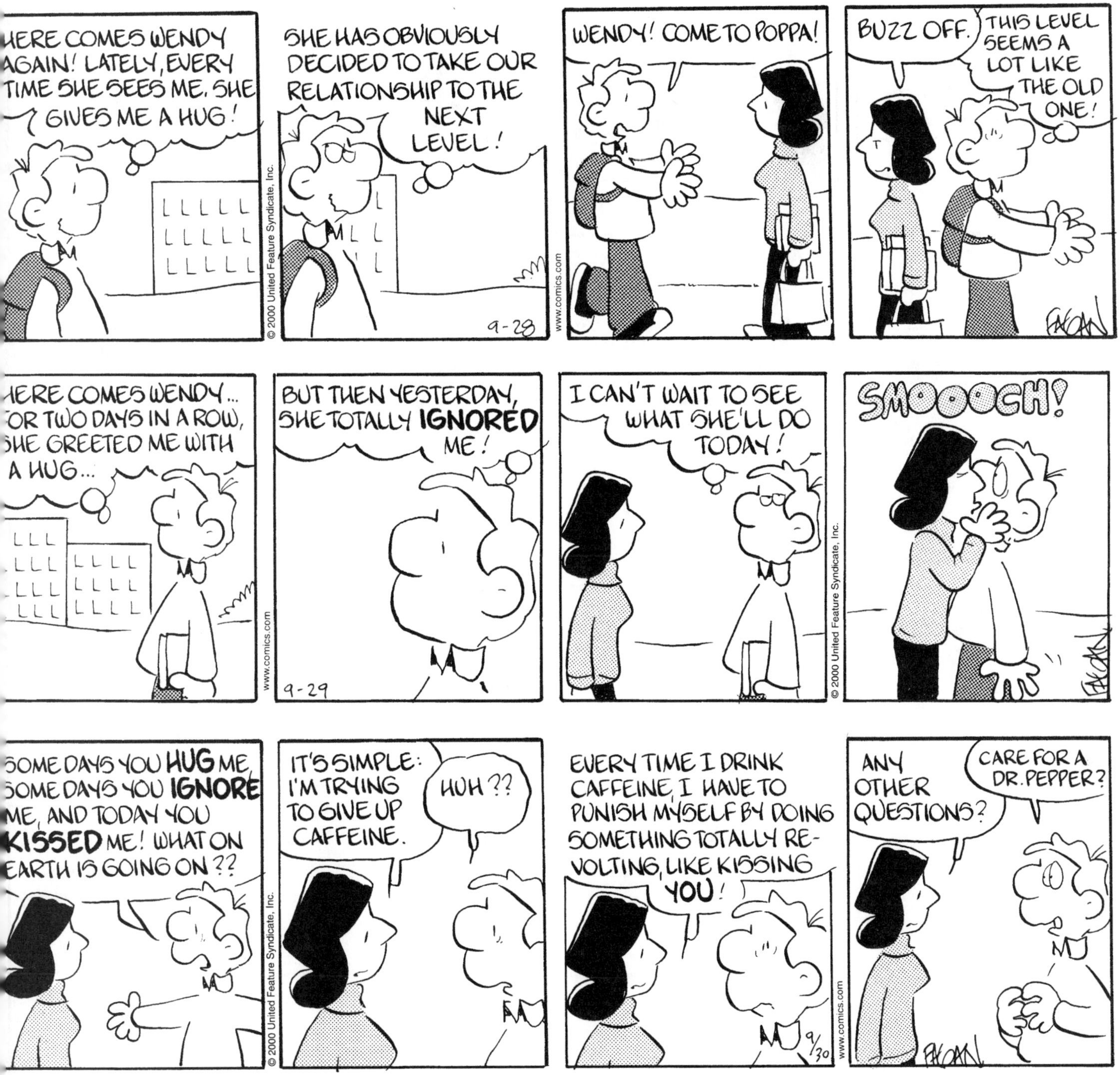
HERE COMES WENDY AGAIN! LATELY, EVERY TIME SHE SEES ME, SHE GIVES ME A HUG!
SHE HAS OBVIOUSLY DECIDED TO TAKE OUR RELATIONSHIP TO THE NEXT LEVEL!
© 2000 United Feature Syndicate, Inc.
9-28
www.comics.com
WENDY! COME TO POPPA!
BUZZ OFF.
THIS LEVEL SEEMS A LOT LIKE THE OLD ONE!
FAGAN
HERE COMES WENDY... FOR TWO DAYS IN A ROW, SHE GREETED ME WITH A HUG...
www.comics.com
BUT THEN YESTERDAY, SHE TOTALLY IGNORED ME!
9-29
I CAN'T WAIT TO SEE WHAT SHE'LL DO TODAY!
© 2000 United Feature Syndicate, Inc.
SMOOOCH!
FAGAN
SOME DAYS YOU HUG ME, SOME DAYS YOU IGNORE ME, AND TODAY YOU KISSED ME! WHAT ON EARTH IS GOING ON??
© 2000 United Feature Syndicate, Inc.
IT'S SIMPLE: I'M TRYING TO GIVE UP CAFFEINE.
HUH??
EVERY TIME I DRINK CAFFEINE, I HAVE TO PUNISH MYSELF BY DOING SOMETHING TOTALLY REVOLTING, LIKE KISSING YOU!
9/30
www.comics.com
ANY OTHER QUESTIONS?
CARE FOR A DR. PEPPER?
FAGAN

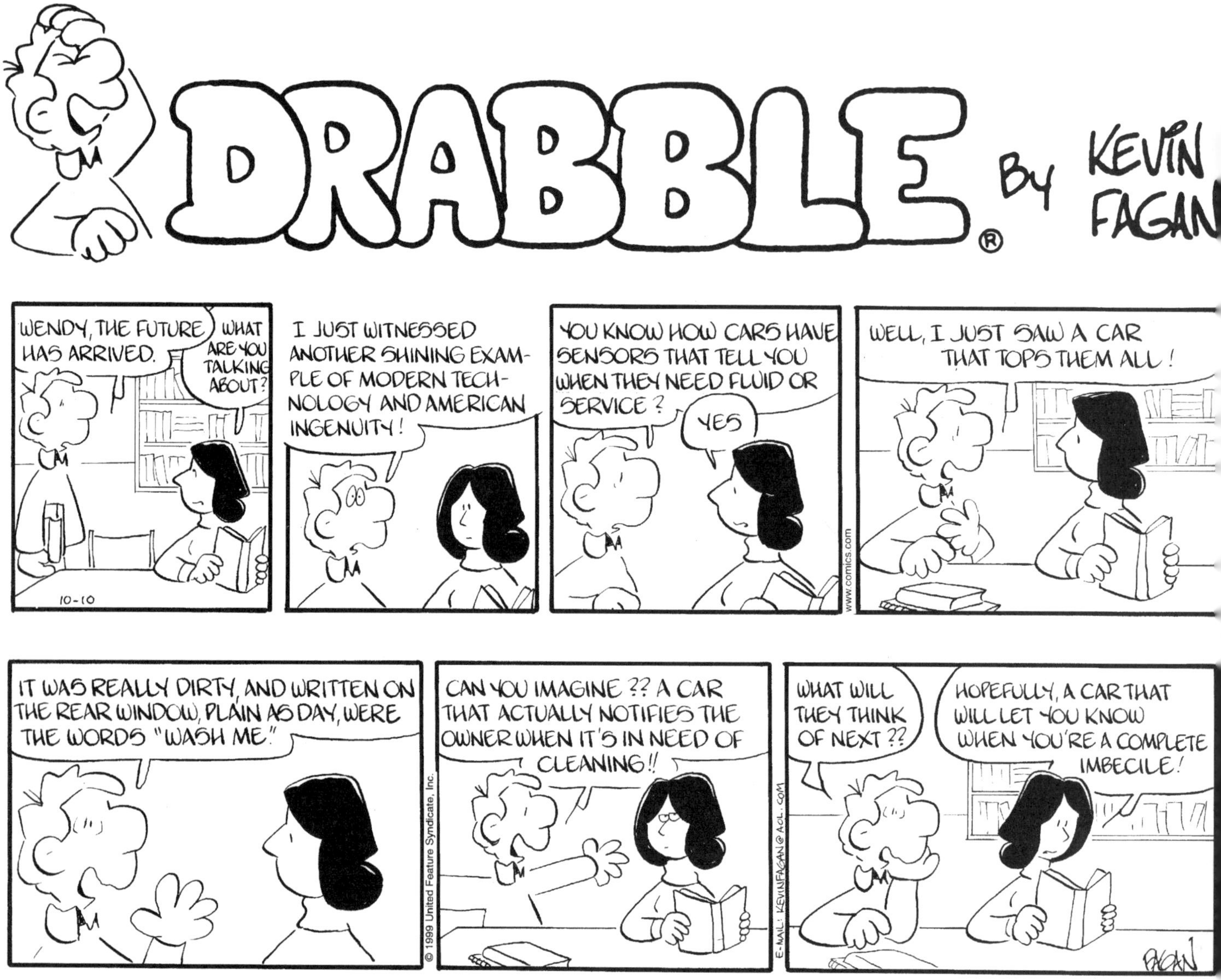
DRABBLE®
By KEVIN FAGAN
WENDY, THE FUTURE HAS ARRIVED.
WHAT ARE YOU TALKING ABOUT?
10-10
I JUST WITNESSED ANOTHER SHINING EXAMPLE OF MODERN TECHNOLOGY AND AMERICAN INGENUITY!
YOU KNOW HOW CARS HAVE SENSORS THAT TELL YOU WHEN THEY NEED FLUID OR SERVICE?
YES
www.comics.com
WELL, I JUST SAW A CAR THAT TOPS THEM ALL!
IT WAS REALLY DIRTY, AND WRITTEN ON THE REAR WINDOW, PLAIN AS DAY, WERE THE WORDS "WASH ME."
© 1999 United Feature Syndicate, Inc.
CAN YOU IMAGINE ?? A CAR THAT ACTUALLY NOTIFIES THE OWNER WHEN IT'S IN NEED OF CLEANING!!
E-MAIL: KEVINFAGAN@AOL.COM
WHAT WILL THEY THINK OF NEXT??
HOPEFULLY, A CAR THAT WILL LET YOU KNOW WHEN YOU'RE A COMPLETE IMBECILE!
FAGAN

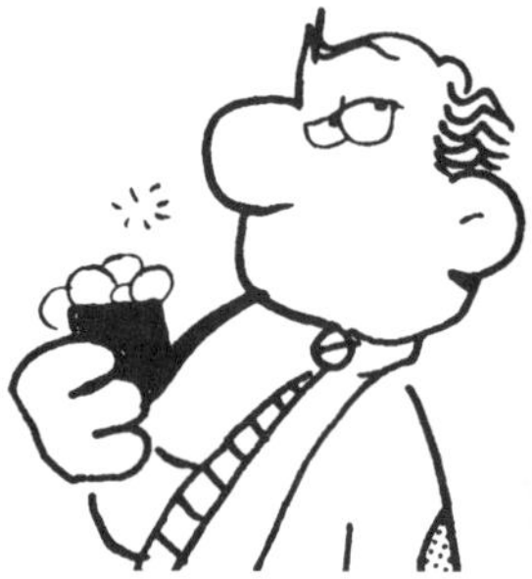

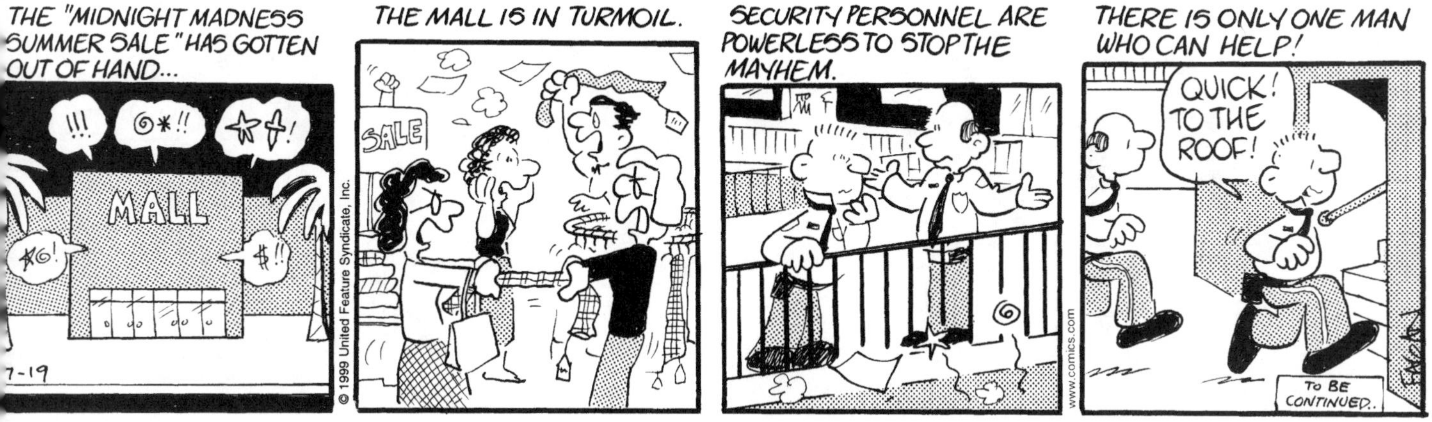
THE "MIDNIGHT MADNESS SUMMER SALE" HAS GOTTEN OUT OF HAND...
!!!
@*!!
!!
MALL
!
$!!
7-19
THE MALL IS IN TURMOIL.
SALE
© 1999 United Feature Syndicate, Inc.
SECURITY PERSONNEL ARE POWERLESS TO STOP THE MAYHEM.
www.comics.com
THERE IS ONLY ONE MAN WHO CAN HELP!
QUICK! TO THE ROOF!
TO BE CONTINUED..

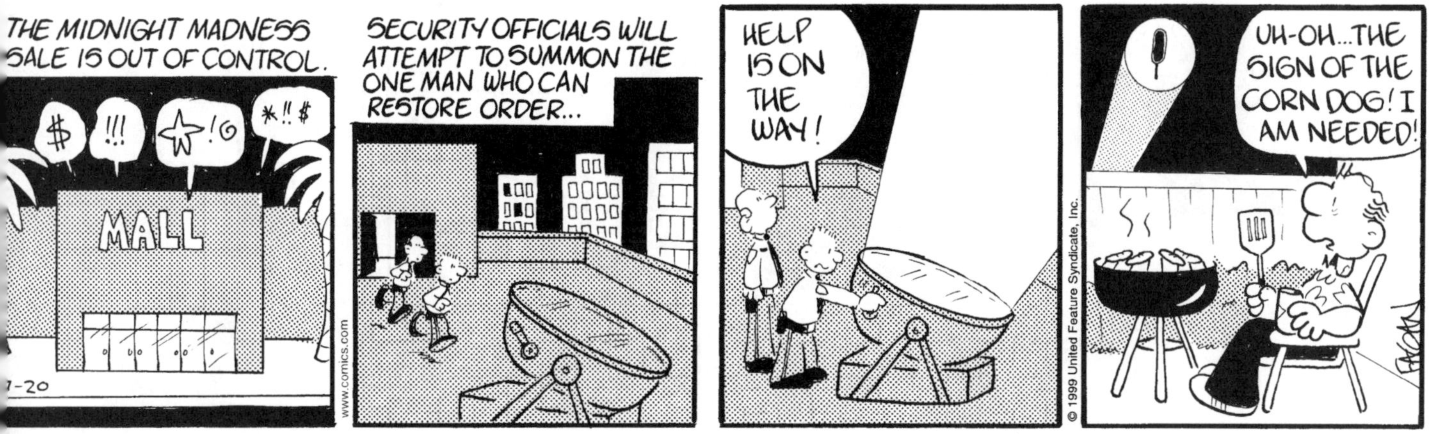
THE MIDNIGHT MADNESS SALE IS OUT OF CONTROL.
$
!!!
!@
*!! $
MALL
7-20
www.comics.com
SECURITY OFFICIALS WILL ATTEMPT TO SUMMON THE ONE MAN WHO CAN RESTORE ORDER...
HELP IS ON THE WAY!
© 1999 United Feature Syndicate, Inc.
UH-OH...THE SIGN OF THE CORN DOG! I AM NEEDED!

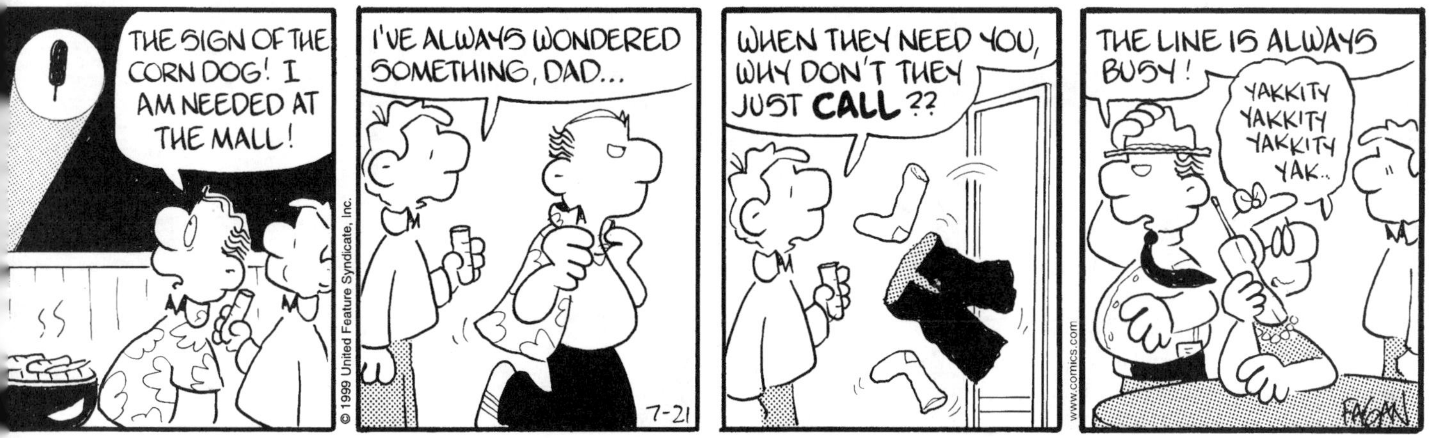
THE SIGN OF THE CORN DOG! I AM NEEDED AT THE MALL!
© 1999 United Feature Syndicate, Inc.
I'VE ALWAYS WONDERED SOMETHING, DAD...
7-21
WHEN THEY NEED YOU, WHY DON'T THEY JUST CALL??
www.comics.com
THE LINE IS ALWAYS BUSY!
YAKKITY YAKKITY YAKKITY YAK..

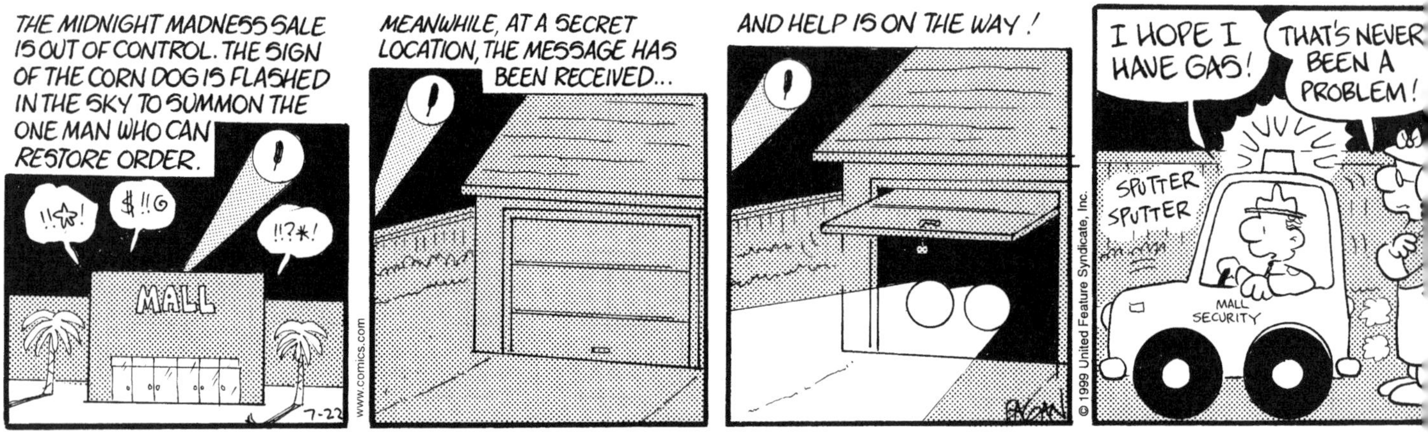
THE MIDNIGHT MADNESS SALE IS OUT OF CONTROL. THE SIGN OF THE CORN DOG IS FLASHED IN THE SKY TO SUMMON THE ONE MAN WHO CAN RESTORE ORDER.
!!☆!
$!!G
!!?*!
MALL
7-22
www.comics.com
MEANWHILE, AT A SECRET LOCATION, THE MESSAGE HAS BEEN RECEIVED...
AND HELP IS ON THE WAY!
© 1999 United Feature Syndicate, Inc.
I HOPE I HAVE GAS!
THAT'S NEVER BEEN A PROBLEM!
SPUTTER SPUTTER
MALL SECURITY

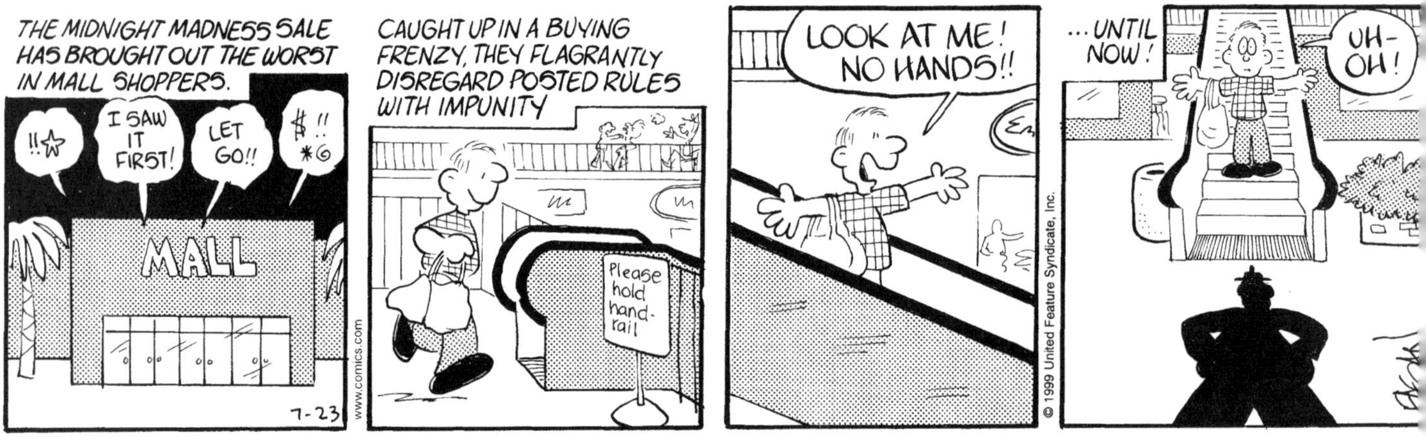
THE MIDNIGHT MADNESS SALE HAS BROUGHT OUT THE WORST IN MALL SHOPPERS.
!!☆
I SAW IT FIRST!
LET GO!!
$!! *G
MALL
7-23
www.comics.com
CAUGHT UP IN A BUYING FRENZY, THEY FLAGRANTLY DISREGARD POSTED RULES WITH IMPUNITY
Please hold hand-rail
LOOK AT ME! NO HANDS!!
© 1999 United Feature Syndicate, Inc.
...UNTIL NOW!
UH-OH!

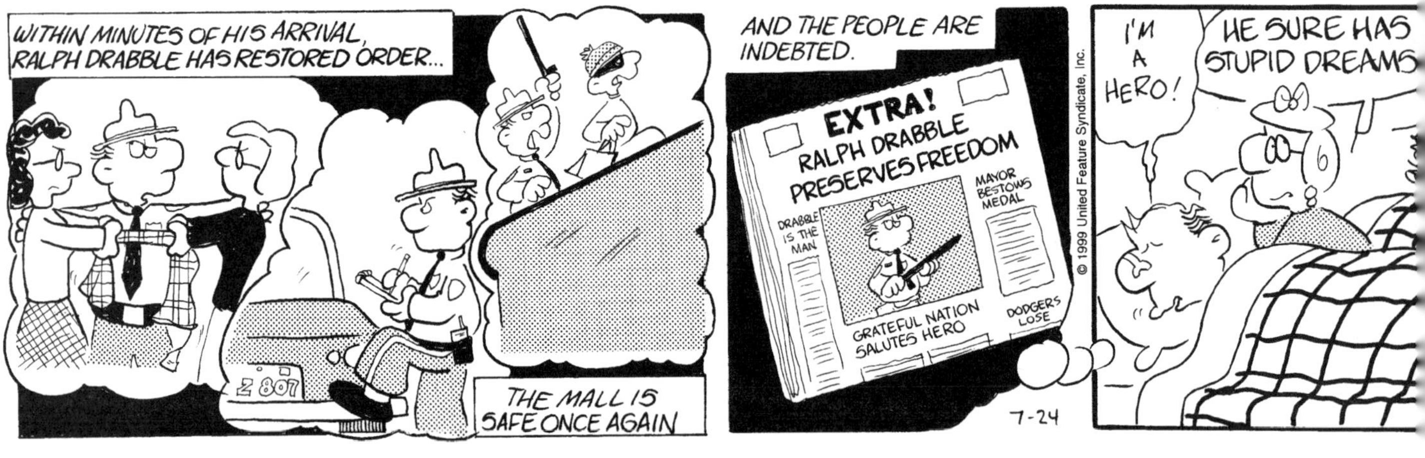
WITHIN MINUTES OF HIS ARRIVAL, RALPH DRABBLE HAS RESTORED ORDER...
Z 807
THE MALL IS SAFE ONCE AGAIN
AND THE PEOPLE ARE INDEBTED.
EXTRA! RALPH DRABBLE PRESERVES FREEDOM
DRABBLE IS THE MAN
MAYOR BESTOWS MEDAL
GRATEFUL NATION SALUTES HERO
DODGERS LOSE
7-24
© 1999 United Feature Syndicate, Inc.
I'M A HERO!
HE SURE HAS STUPID DREAMS

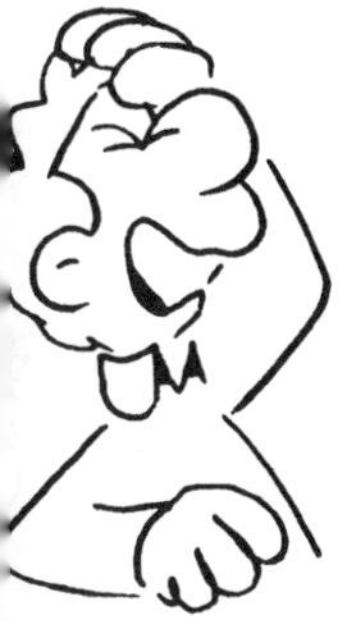

DRABBLE® By KEVIN FAGAN

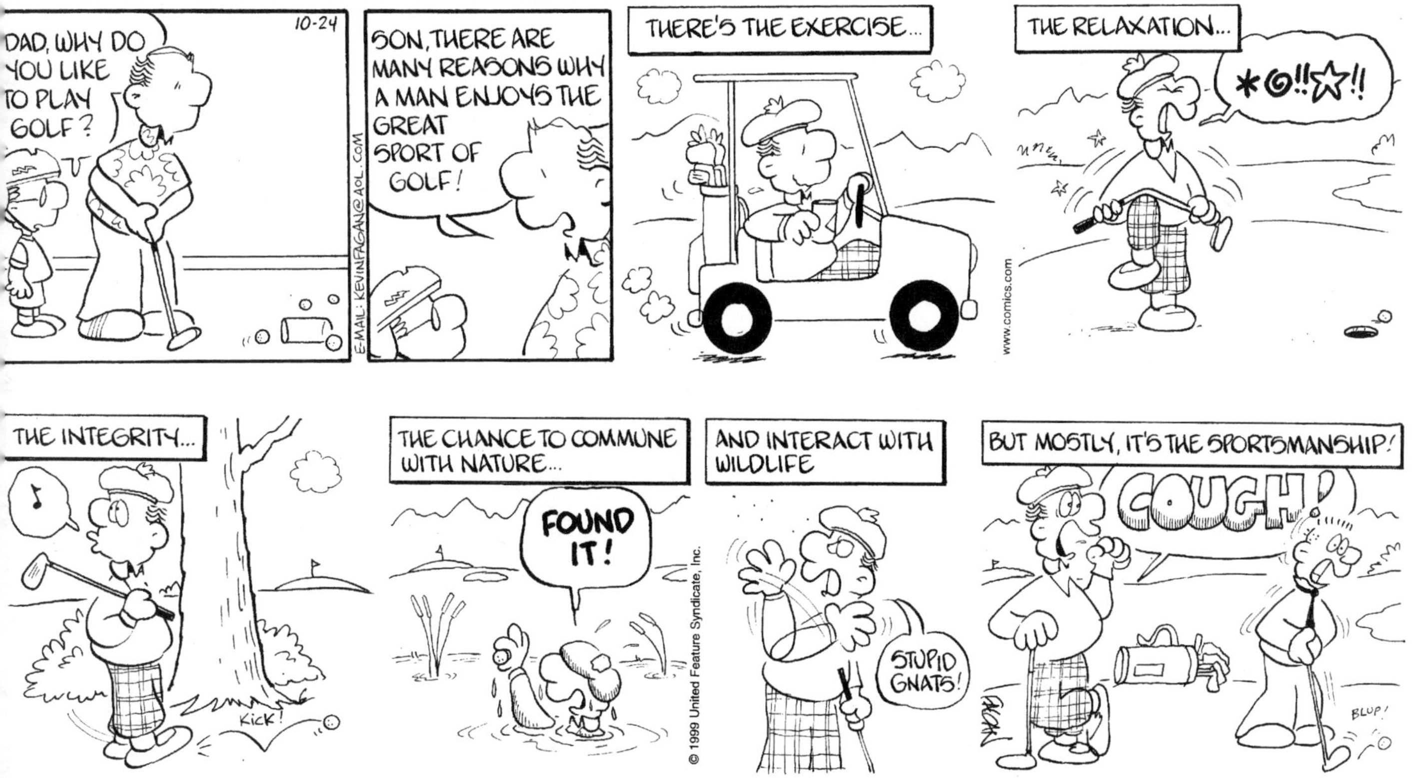
10-24
DAD, WHY DO YOU LIKE TO PLAY GOLF?
E-MAIL: KEVINFAGAN@AOL.COM
SON, THERE ARE MANY REASONS WHY A MAN ENJOYS THE GREAT SPORT OF GOLF!
THERE'S THE EXERCISE...
THE RELAXATION...
*@!!☆!!
www.comics.com
THE INTEGRITY...
♪
KICK!
THE CHANCE TO COMMUNE WITH NATURE...
FOUND IT!
© 1999 United Feature Syndicate, Inc.
AND INTERACT WITH WILDLIFE
STUPID GNATS!
BUT MOSTLY, IT'S THE SPORTSMANSHIP!
COUGH!
BLUP!

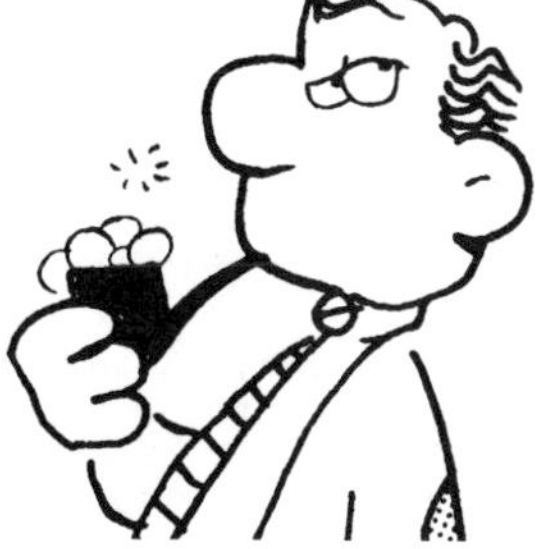

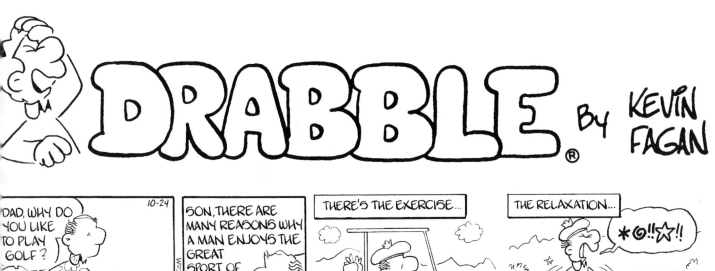

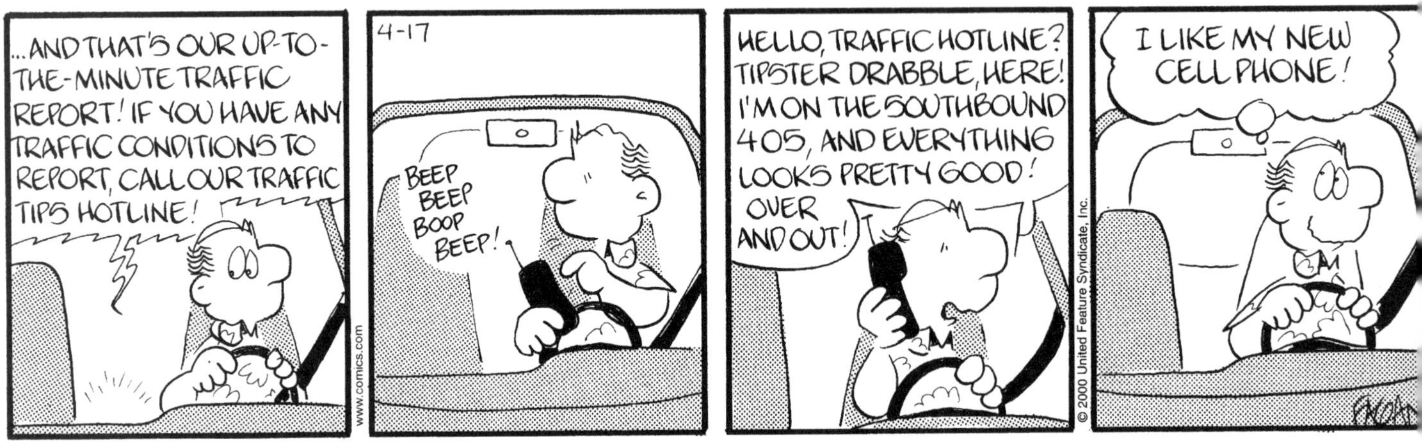
...AND THAT'S OUR UP-TO-THE-MINUTE TRAFFIC REPORT! IF YOU HAVE ANY TRAFFIC CONDITIONS TO REPORT, CALL OUR TRAFFIC TIPS HOTLINE!
4-17
BEEP BEEP BOOP BEEP!
www.comics.com
HELLO, TRAFFIC HOTLINE? TIPSTER DRABBLE, HERE! I'M ON THE SOUTHBOUND 405, AND EVERYTHING LOOKS PRETTY GOOD! OVER AND OUT!
© 2000 United Feature Syndicate, Inc.
I LIKE MY NEW CELL PHONE!

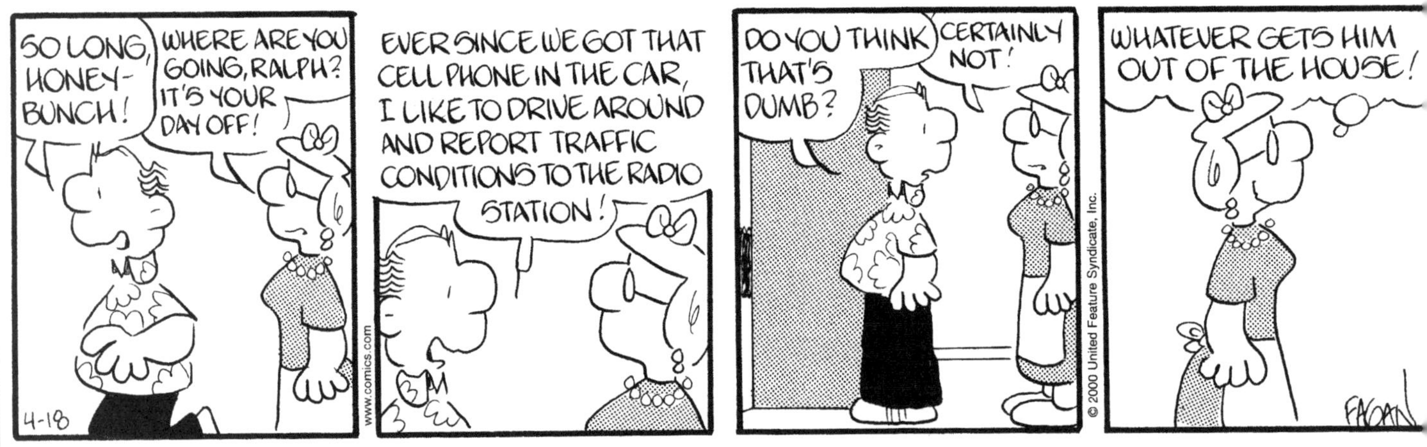
SO LONG, HONEY-BUNCH!
WHERE ARE YOU GOING, RALPH? IT'S YOUR DAY OFF!
4-18
www.comics.com
EVER SINCE WE GOT THAT CELL PHONE IN THE CAR, I LIKE TO DRIVE AROUND AND REPORT TRAFFIC CONDITIONS TO THE RADIO STATION!
DO YOU THINK THAT'S DUMB?
CERTAINLY NOT!
© 2000 United Feature Syndicate, Inc.
WHATEVER GETS HIM OUT OF THE HOUSE!
FAGAN

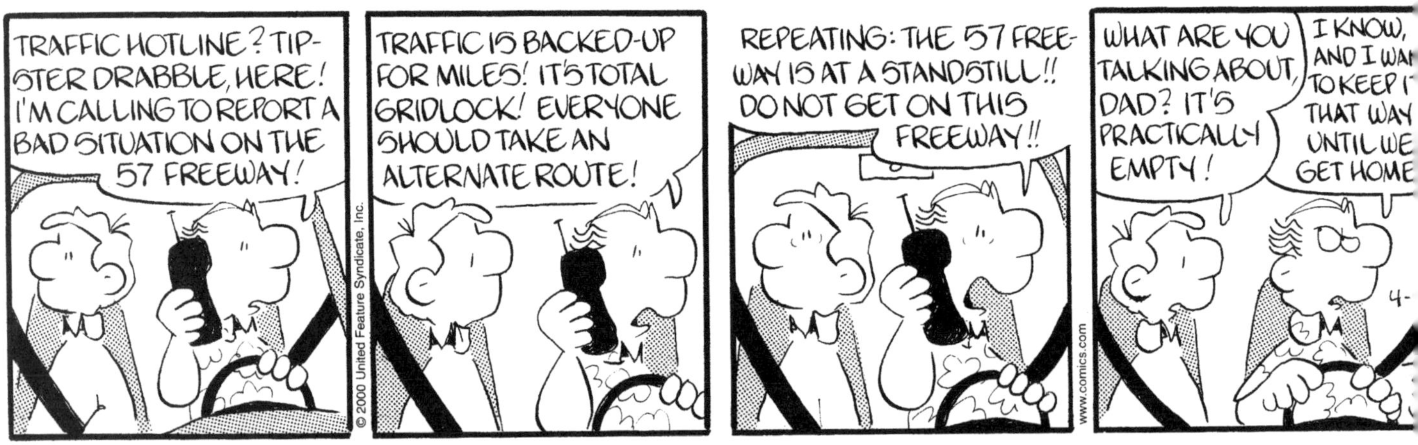
TRAFFIC HOTLINE? TIPSTER DRABBLE, HERE! I'M CALLING TO REPORT A BAD SITUATION ON THE 57 FREEWAY!
© 2000 United Feature Syndicate, Inc.
TRAFFIC IS BACKED-UP FOR MILES! IT'S TOTAL GRIDLOCK! EVERYONE SHOULD TAKE AN ALTERNATE ROUTE!
REPEATING: THE 57 FREEWAY IS AT A STANDSTILL!! DO NOT GET ON THIS FREEWAY!!
www.comics.com
WHAT ARE YOU TALKING ABOUT, DAD? IT'S PRACTICALLY EMPTY!
I KNOW, AND I WA TO KEEP I THAT WAY UNTIL WE GET HOME

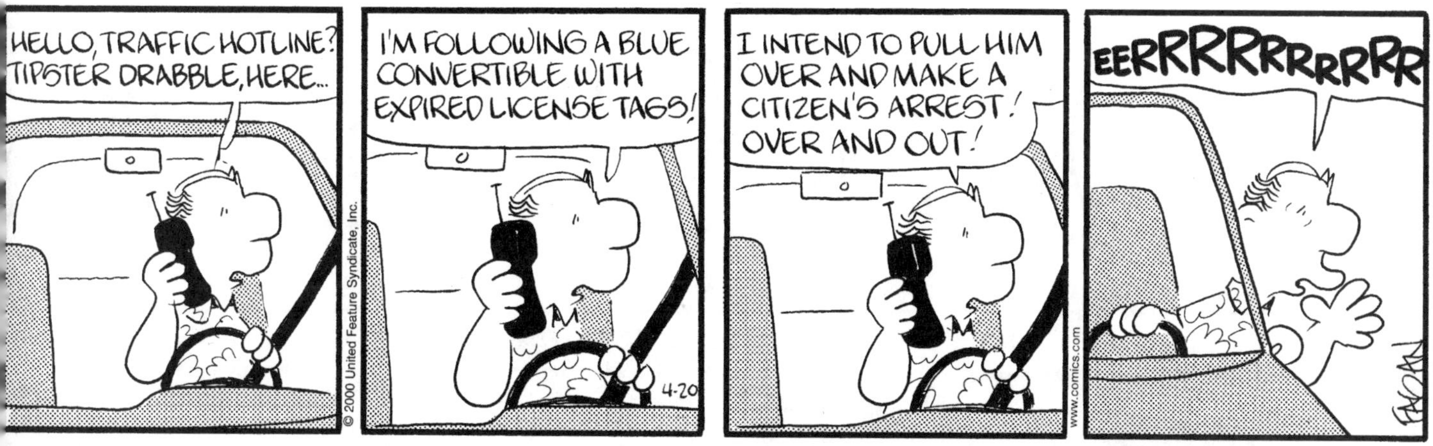
HELLO, TRAFFIC HOTLINE? TIPSTER DRABBLE, HERE...
© 2000 United Feature Syndicate, Inc.
I'M FOLLOWING A BLUE CONVERTIBLE WITH EXPIRED LICENSE TAGS!
4-20
I INTEND TO PULL HIM OVER AND MAKE A CITIZEN'S ARREST! OVER AND OUT!
www.comics.com
EERRRRRRRRRRR
FAGAN

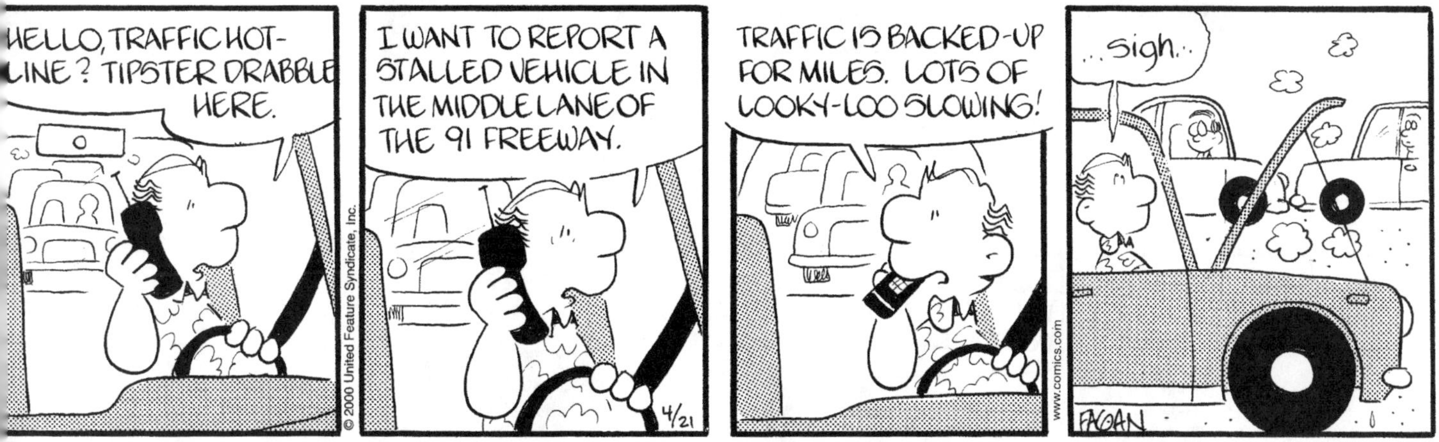
HELLO, TRAFFIC HOT-LINE? TIPSTER DRABBLE HERE.
© 2000 United Feature Syndicate, Inc.
I WANT TO REPORT A STALLED VEHICLE IN THE MIDDLE LANE OF THE 91 FREEWAY.
4/21
TRAFFIC IS BACKED-UP FOR MILES. LOTS OF LOOKY-LOO SLOWING!
www.comics.com
...Sigh...
FAGAN

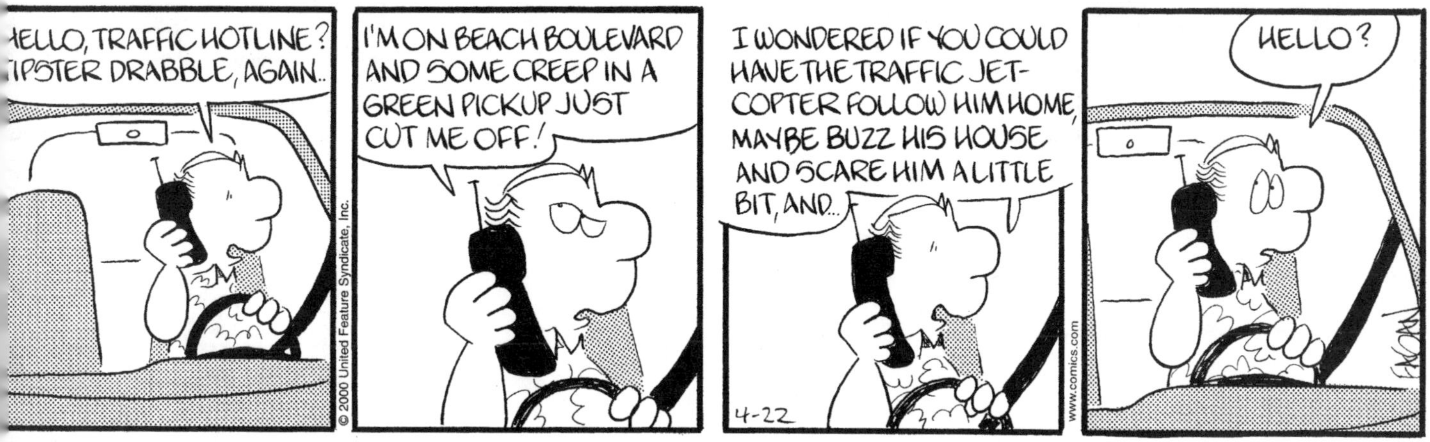
HELLO, TRAFFIC HOTLINE? TIPSTER DRABBLE, AGAIN...
© 2000 United Feature Syndicate, Inc.
I'M ON BEACH BOULEVARD AND SOME CREEP IN A GREEN PICKUP JUST CUT ME OFF!
I WONDERED IF YOU COULD HAVE THE TRAFFIC JET-COPTER FOLLOW HIM HOME, MAYBE BUZZ HIS HOUSE AND SCARE HIM A LITTLE BIT, AND...
4-22
www.comics.com
HELLO?
FAGAN

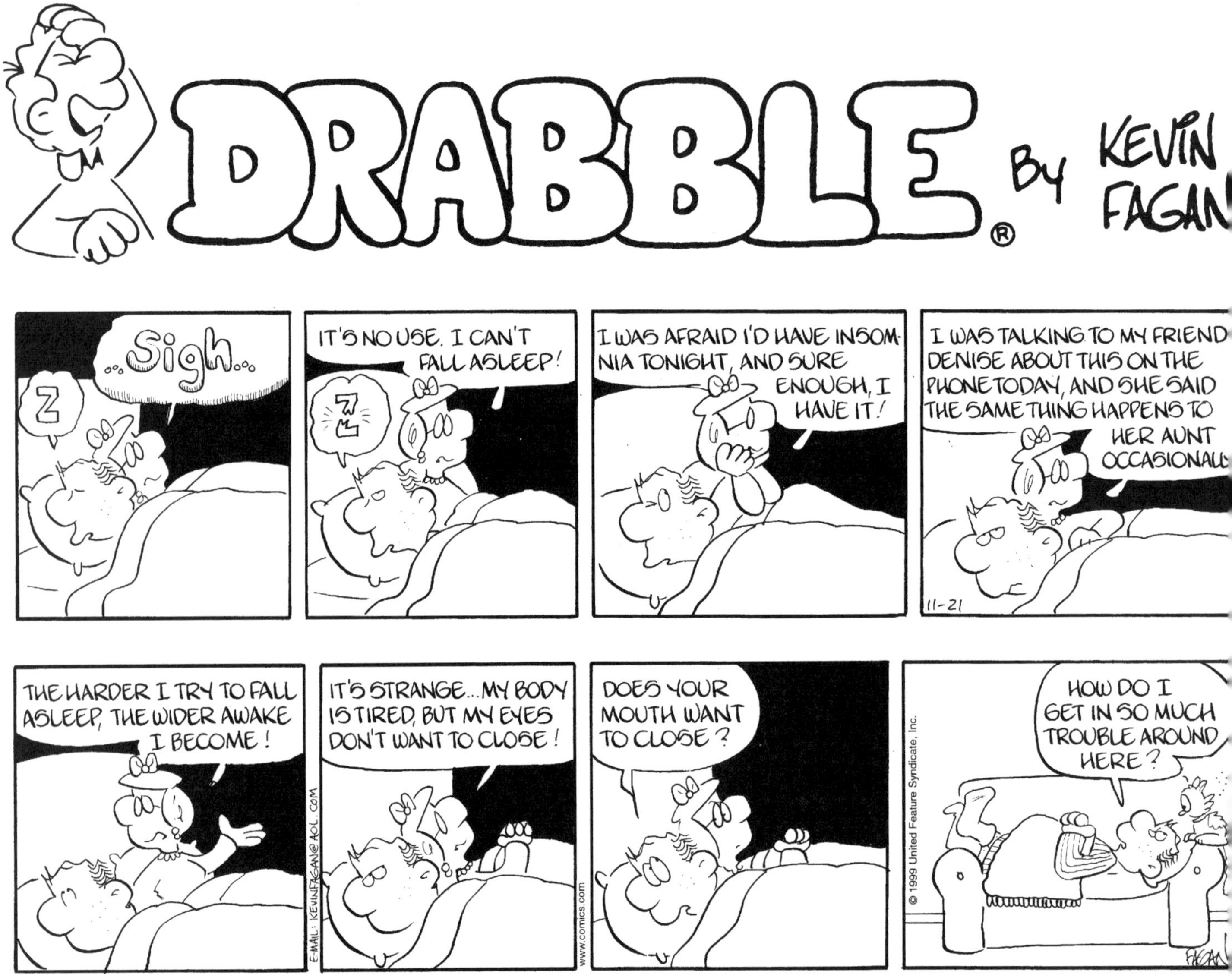
DRABBLE®
By KEVIN FAGAN
Z
...Sigh...
IT'S NO USE. I CAN'T FALL ASLEEP!
I WAS AFRAID I'D HAVE INSOMNIA TONIGHT, AND SURE ENOUGH, I HAVE IT!
I WAS TALKING TO MY FRIEND DENISE ABOUT THIS ON THE PHONE TODAY, AND SHE SAID THE SAME THING HAPPENS TO HER AUNT OCCASIONALLY
11-21
THE HARDER I TRY TO FALL ASLEEP, THE WIDER AWAKE I BECOME!
E-MAIL: KEVINFAGAN@AOL.COM
IT'S STRANGE... MY BODY IS TIRED, BUT MY EYES DON'T WANT TO CLOSE!
www.comics.com
DOES YOUR MOUTH WANT TO CLOSE?
© 1999 United Feature Syndicate, Inc.
HOW DO I GET IN SO MUCH TROUBLE AROUND HERE?
FAGAN

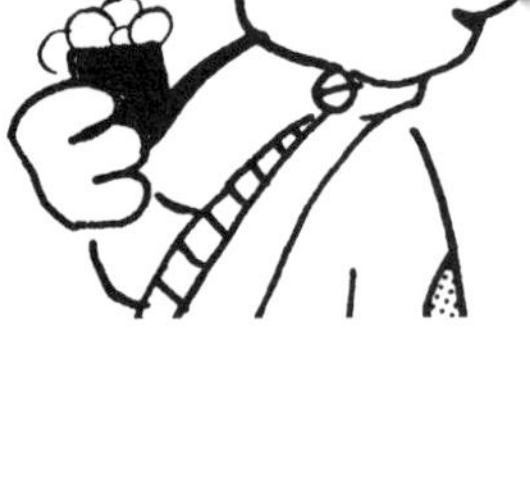

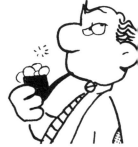

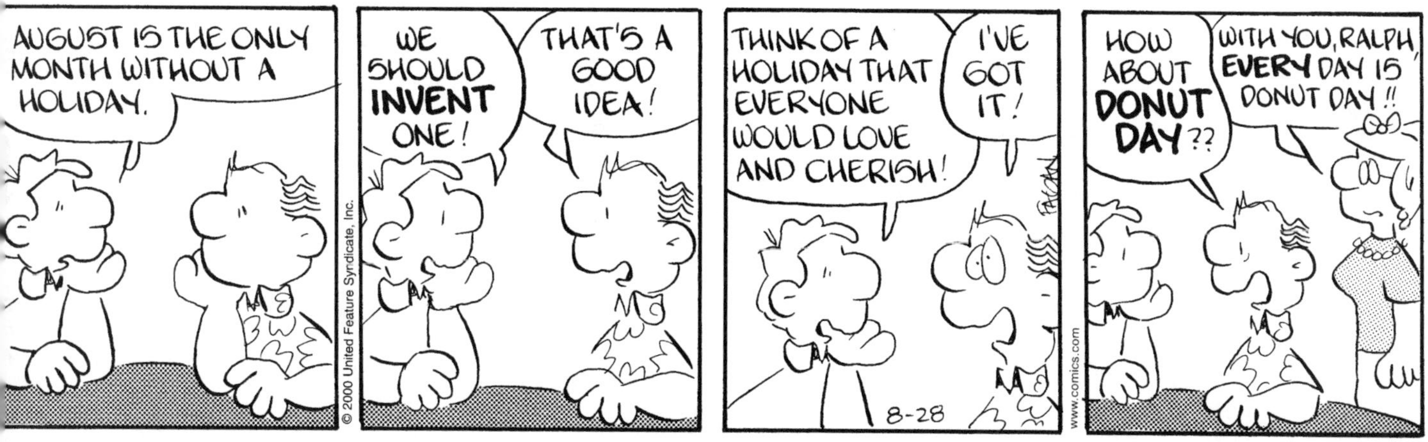
AUGUST IS THE ONLY MONTH WITHOUT A HOLIDAY.
© 2000 United Feature Syndicate, Inc.
WE SHOULD **INVENT** ONE!
THAT'S A GOOD IDEA!
THINK OF A HOLIDAY THAT EVERYONE WOULD LOVE AND CHERISH!
I'VE GOT IT!
FAGAN
8-28
www.comics.com
HOW ABOUT **DONUT DAY**??
WITH YOU, RALPH, **EVERY** DAY IS DONUT DAY!!

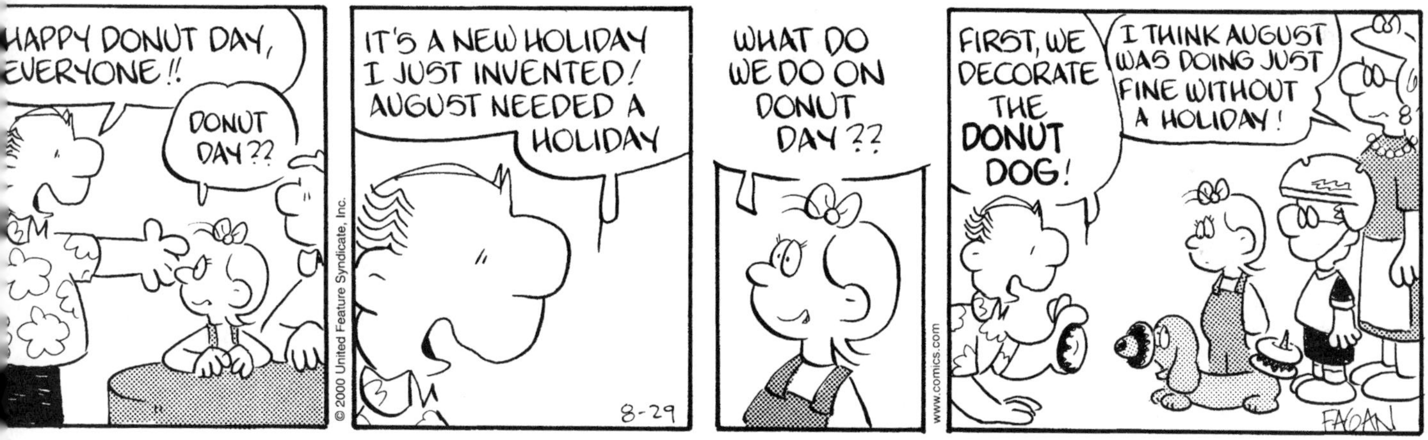
HAPPY DONUT DAY, EVERYONE!!
DONUT DAY??
© 2000 United Feature Syndicate, Inc.
IT'S A NEW HOLIDAY I JUST INVENTED! AUGUST NEEDED A HOLIDAY
8-29
WHAT DO WE DO ON DONUT DAY??
www.comics.com
FIRST, WE DECORATE THE **DONUT DOG**!
I THINK AUGUST WAS DOING JUST FINE WITHOUT A HOLIDAY!
FAGAN

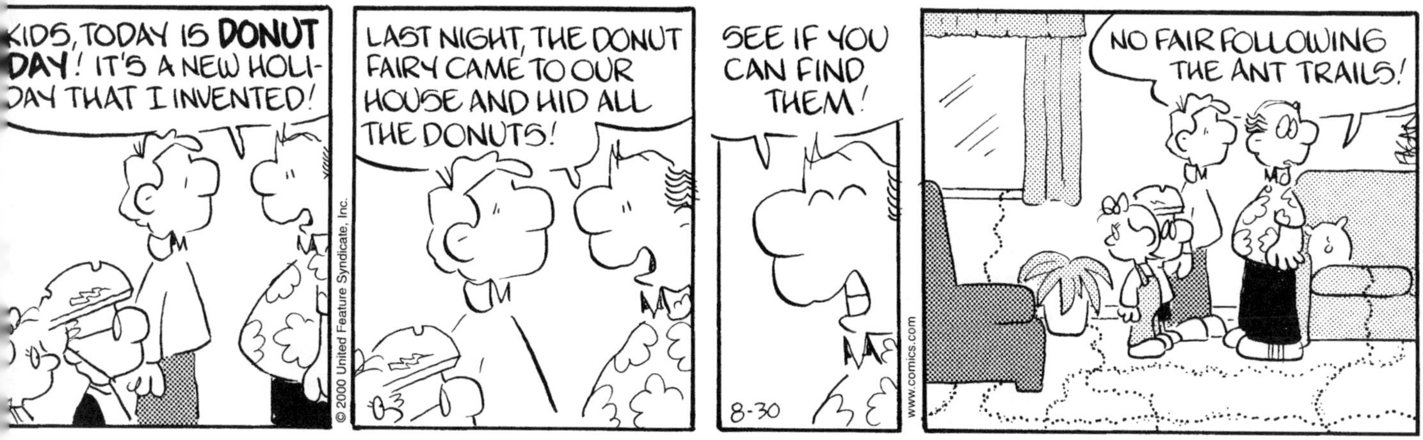
KIDS, TODAY IS **DONUT DAY**! IT'S A NEW HOLIDAY THAT I INVENTED!
© 2000 United Feature Syndicate, Inc.
LAST NIGHT, THE DONUT FAIRY CAME TO OUR HOUSE AND HID ALL THE DONUTS!
SEE IF YOU CAN FIND THEM!
8-30
www.comics.com
NO FAIR FOLLOWING THE ANT TRAILS!
FAGAN

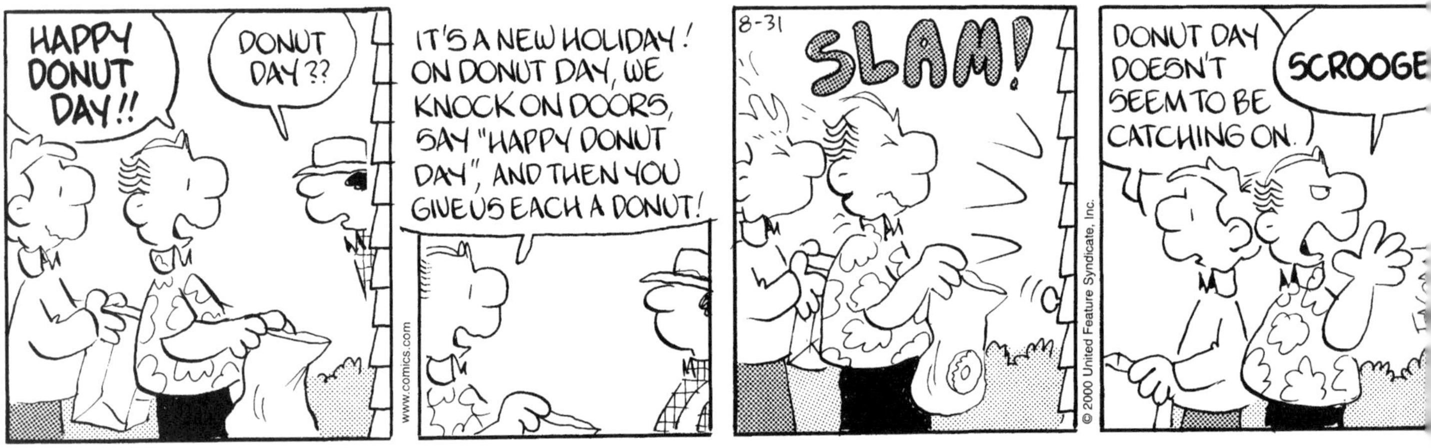
HAPPY DONUT DAY!!
DONUT DAY??
IT'S A NEW HOLIDAY! ON DONUT DAY, WE KNOCK ON DOORS, SAY "HAPPY DONUT DAY", AND THEN YOU GIVE US EACH A DONUT!
www.comics.com
8-31
SLAM!
© 2000 United Feature Syndicate, Inc.
DONUT DAY DOESN'T SEEM TO BE CATCHING ON.
SCROOGE

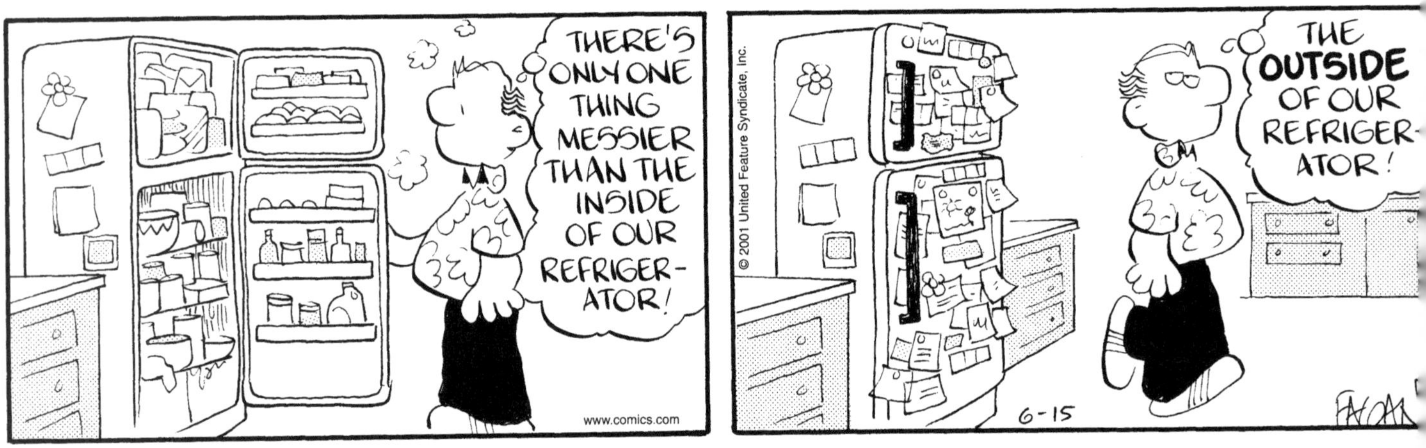
THERE'S ONLY ONE THING MESSIER THAN THE INSIDE OF OUR REFRIGER-ATOR!
www.comics.com
© 2001 United Feature Syndicate, Inc.
THE OUTSIDE OF OUR REFRIGER-ATOR!
6-15

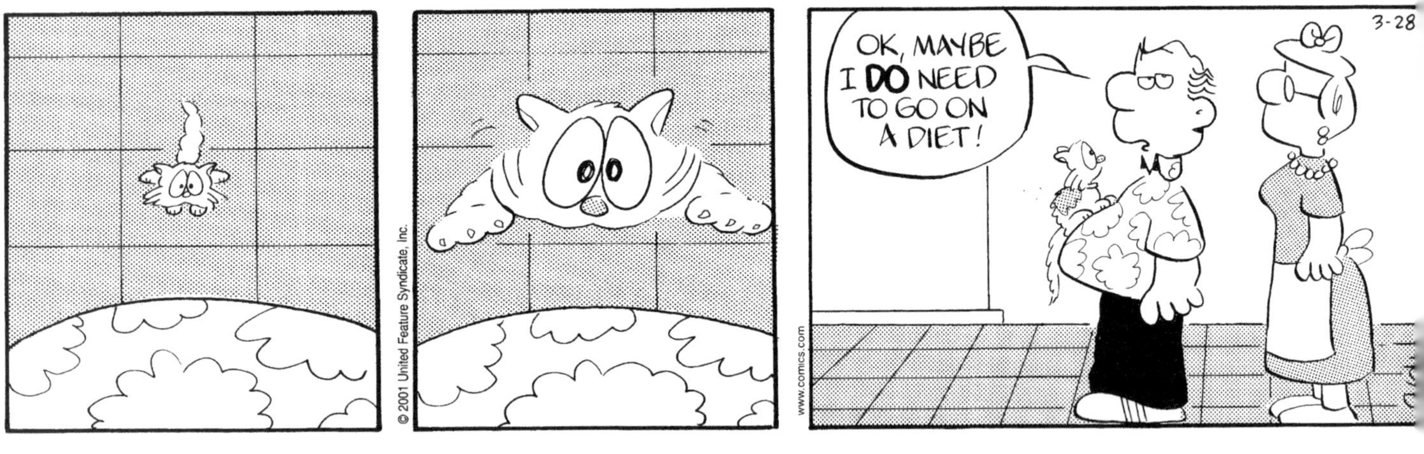
© 2001 United Feature Syndicate, Inc.
www.comics.com
3-28
OK, MAYBE I DO NEED TO GO ON A DIET!

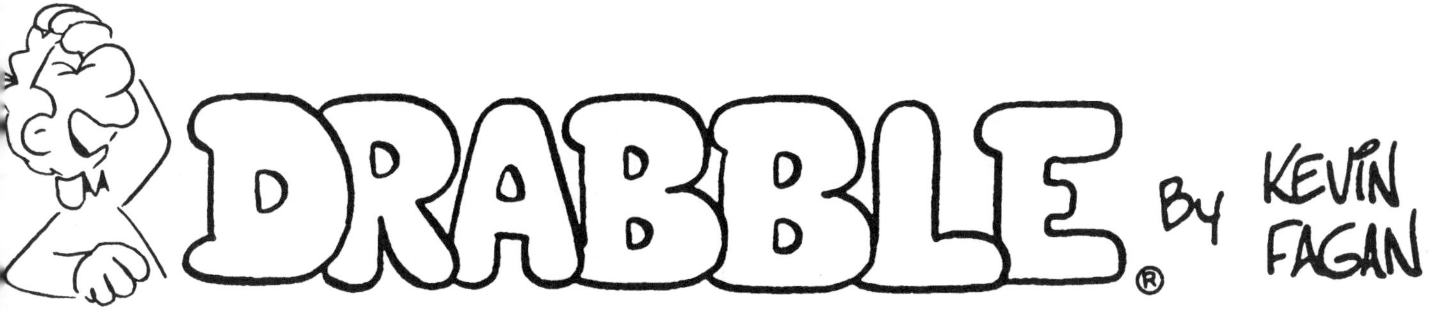
DRABBLE®
By KEVIN FAGAN

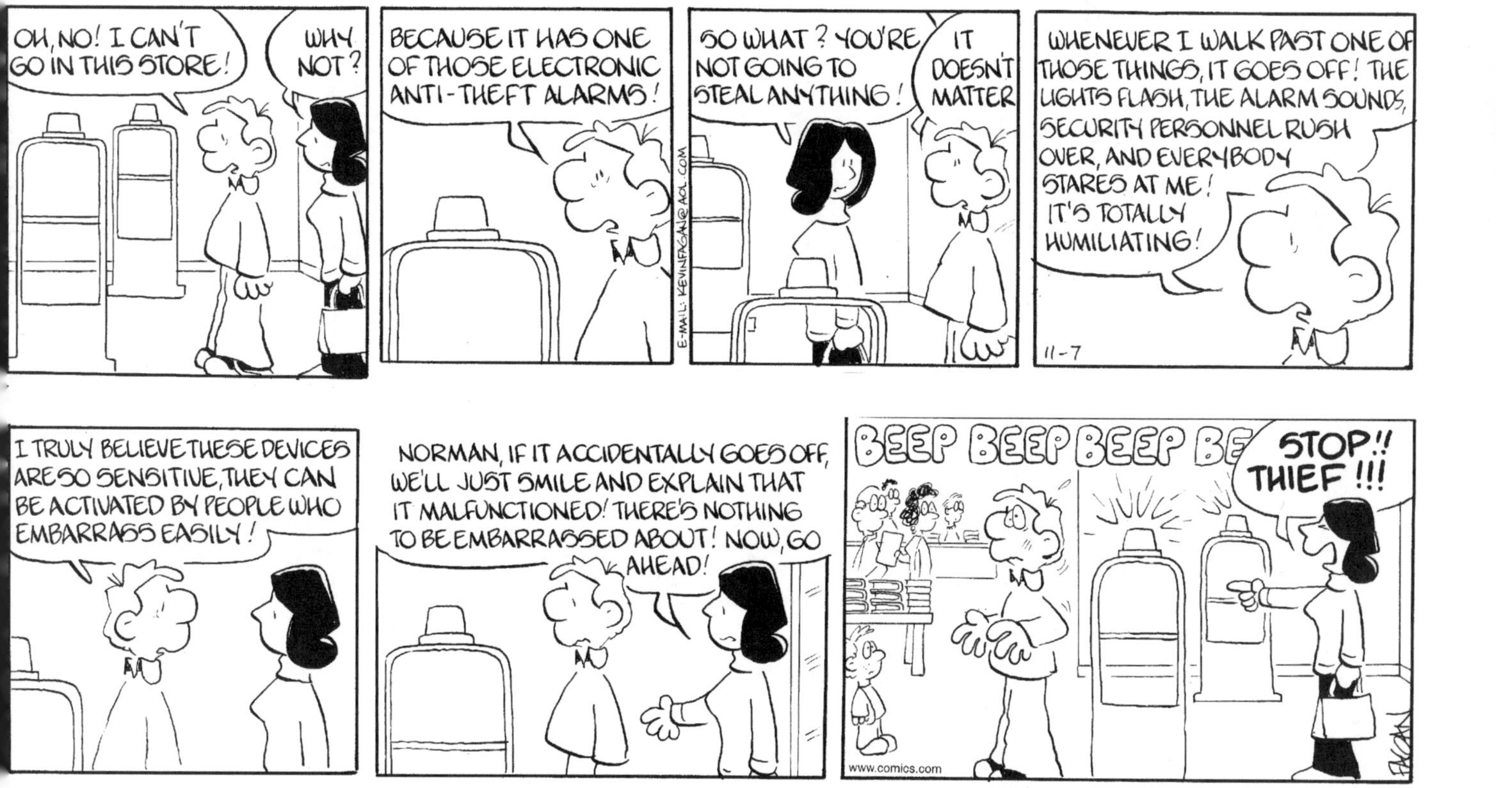
OH, NO! I CAN'T GO IN THIS STORE!
WHY NOT?
BECAUSE IT HAS ONE OF THOSE ELECTRONIC ANTI-THEFT ALARMS!
E-MAIL: KEVINFAGAN@AOL.COM
SO WHAT? YOU'RE NOT GOING TO STEAL ANYTHING!
IT DOESN'T MATTER
WHENEVER I WALK PAST ONE OF THOSE THINGS, IT GOES OFF! THE LIGHTS FLASH, THE ALARM SOUNDS, SECURITY PERSONNEL RUSH OVER, AND EVERYBODY STARES AT ME!
IT'S TOTALLY HUMILIATING!
11-7
I TRULY BELIEVE THESE DEVICES ARE SO SENSITIVE, THEY CAN BE ACTIVATED BY PEOPLE WHO EMBARRASS EASILY!
NORMAN, IF IT ACCIDENTALLY GOES OFF, WE'LL JUST SMILE AND EXPLAIN THAT IT MALFUNCTIONED! THERE'S NOTHING TO BE EMBARRASSED ABOUT! NOW, GO AHEAD!
BEEP BEEP BEEP BEEP BE
STOP!! THIEF!!!
www.comics.com
FAGAN

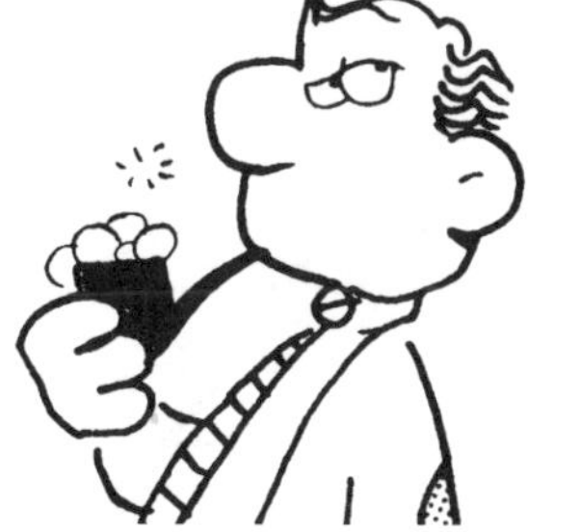

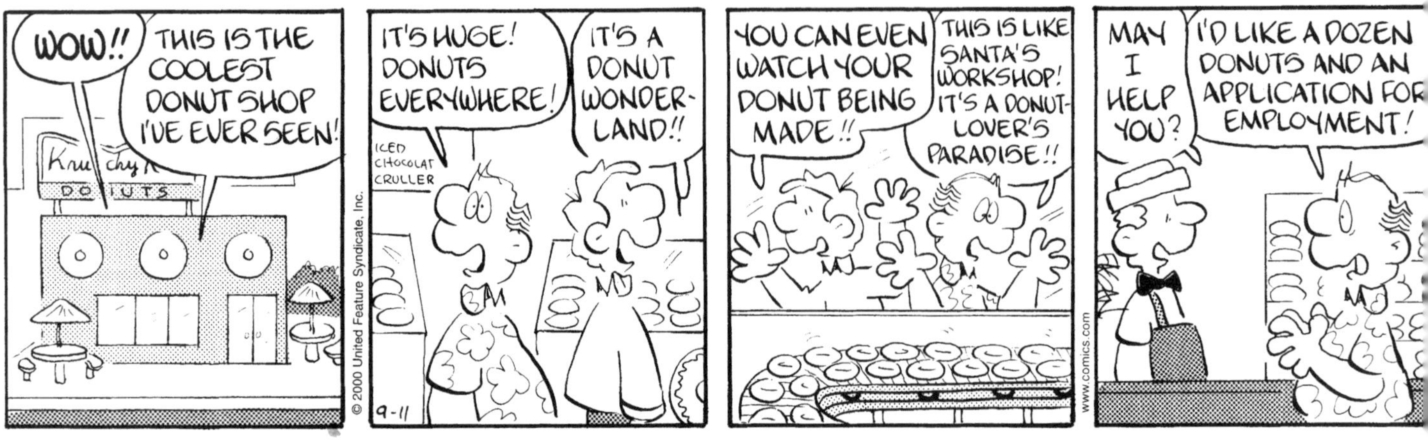
WOW!!
THIS IS THE COOLEST DONUT SHOP I'VE EVER SEEN!
IT'S HUGE! DONUTS EVERYWHERE!
ICED CHOCOLAT CRULLER
IT'S A DONUT WONDERLAND!!
© 2000 United Feature Syndicate, Inc.
9-11
YOU CAN EVEN WATCH YOUR DONUT BEING MADE!!
THIS IS LIKE SANTA'S WORKSHOP! IT'S A DONUT-LOVER'S PARADISE!!
www.comics.com
MAY I HELP YOU?
I'D LIKE A DOZEN DONUTS AND AN APPLICATION FOR EMPLOYMENT!

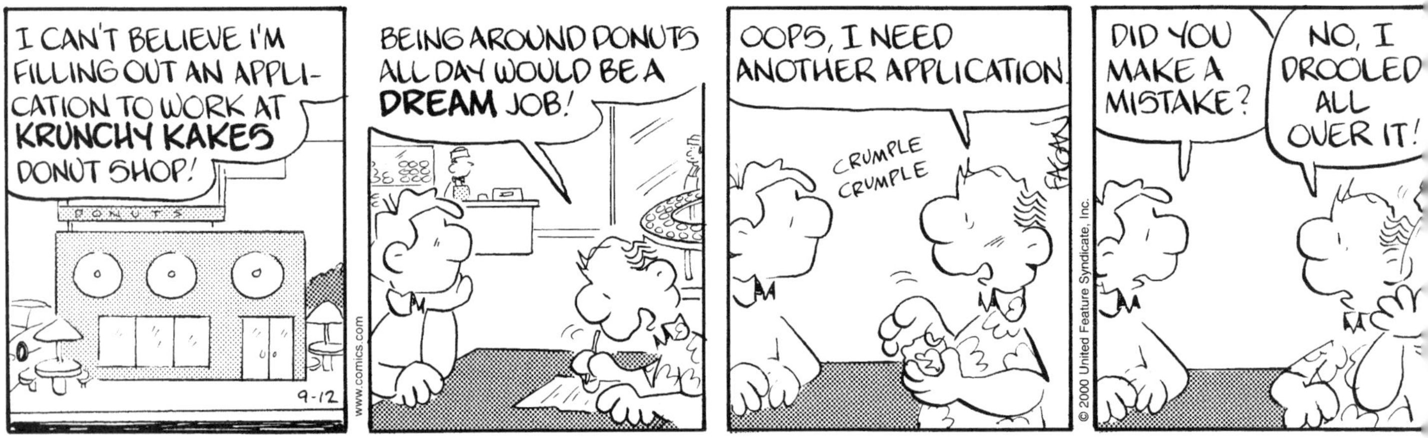
I CAN'T BELIEVE I'M FILLING OUT AN APPLICATION TO WORK AT **KRUNCHY KAKES** DONUT SHOP!
9-12
www.comics.com
BEING AROUND DONUTS ALL DAY WOULD BE A **DREAM** JOB!
OOPS, I NEED ANOTHER APPLICATION!
CRUMPLE CRUMPLE
© 2000 United Feature Syndicate, Inc.
DID YOU MAKE A MISTAKE?
NO, I DROOLED ALL OVER IT!

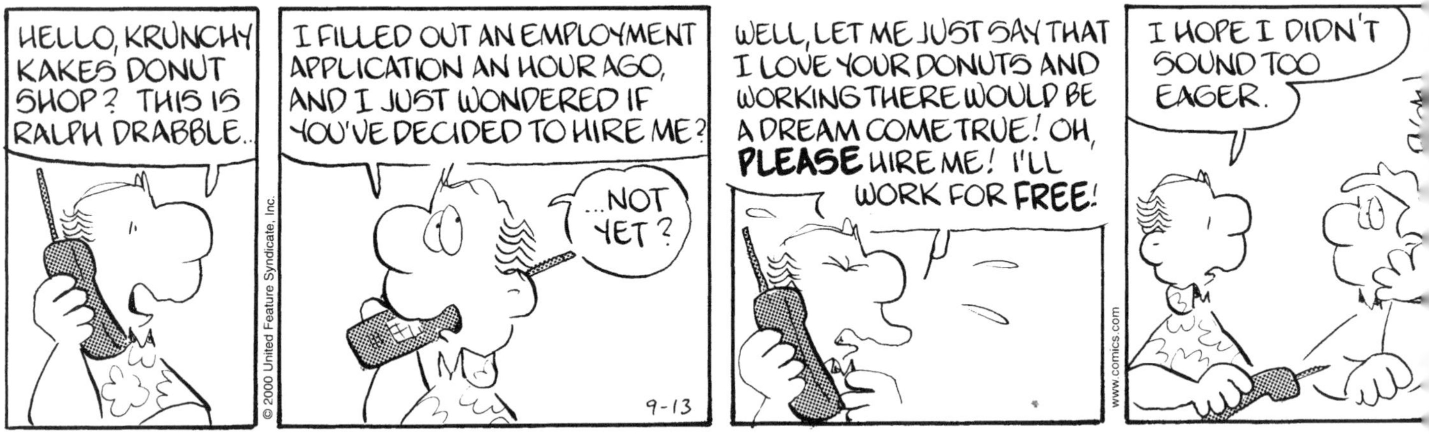
HELLO, KRUNCHY KAKES DONUT SHOP? THIS IS RALPH DRABBLE...
© 2000 United Feature Syndicate, Inc.
I FILLED OUT AN EMPLOYMENT APPLICATION AN HOUR AGO, AND I JUST WONDERED IF YOU'VE DECIDED TO HIRE ME?
...NOT YET?
9-13
WELL, LET ME JUST SAY THAT I LOVE YOUR DONUTS AND WORKING THERE WOULD BE A DREAM COME TRUE! OH, **PLEASE** HIRE ME! I'LL WORK FOR **FREE**!
www.comics.com
I HOPE I DIDN'T SOUND TOO EAGER.

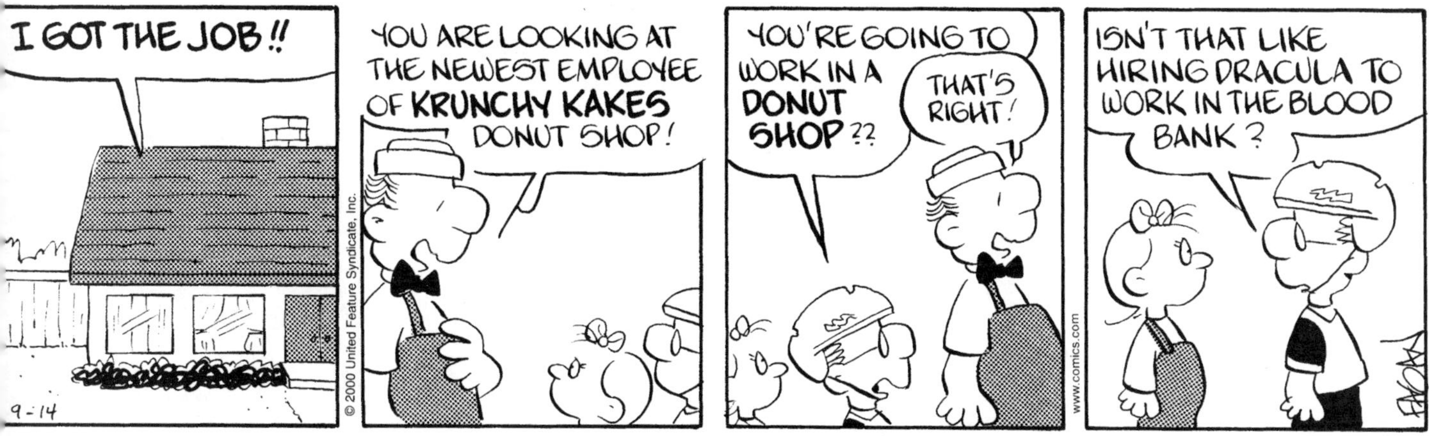
I GOT THE JOB!!
9-14
YOU ARE LOOKING AT THE NEWEST EMPLOYEE OF **KRUNCHY KAKES** DONUT SHOP!
© 2000 United Feature Syndicate, Inc.
YOU'RE GOING TO WORK IN A **DONUT SHOP**??
THAT'S RIGHT!
www.comics.com
ISN'T THAT LIKE HIRING DRACULA TO WORK IN THE BLOOD BANK?

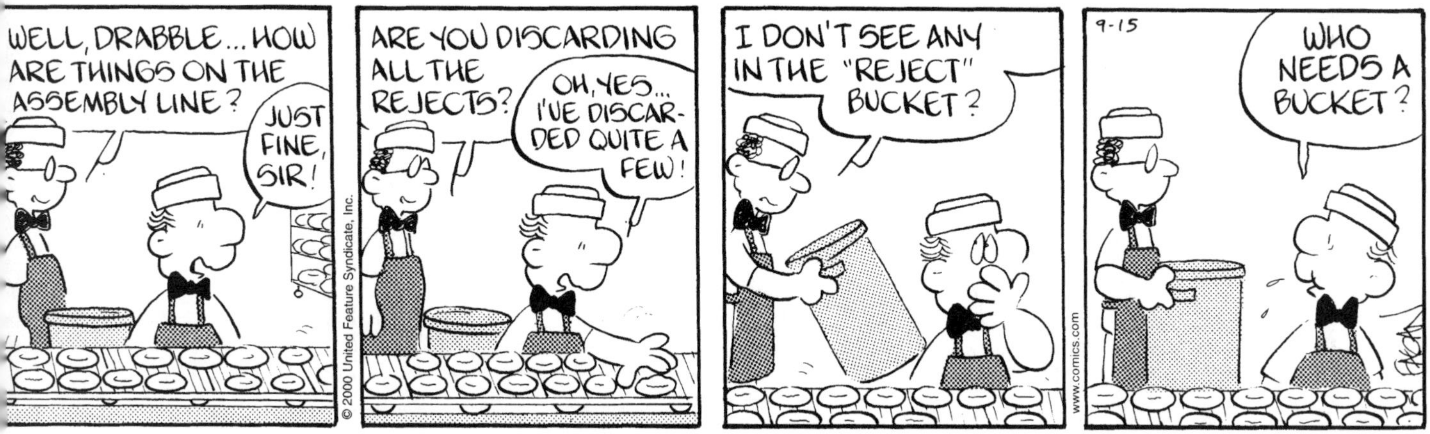
WELL, DRABBLE... HOW ARE THINGS ON THE ASSEMBLY LINE?
JUST FINE, SIR!
© 2000 United Feature Syndicate, Inc.
ARE YOU DISCARDING ALL THE REJECTS?
OH, YES... I'VE DISCARDED QUITE A FEW!
I DON'T SEE ANY IN THE "REJECT" BUCKET?
www.comics.com
9-15
WHO NEEDS A BUCKET?

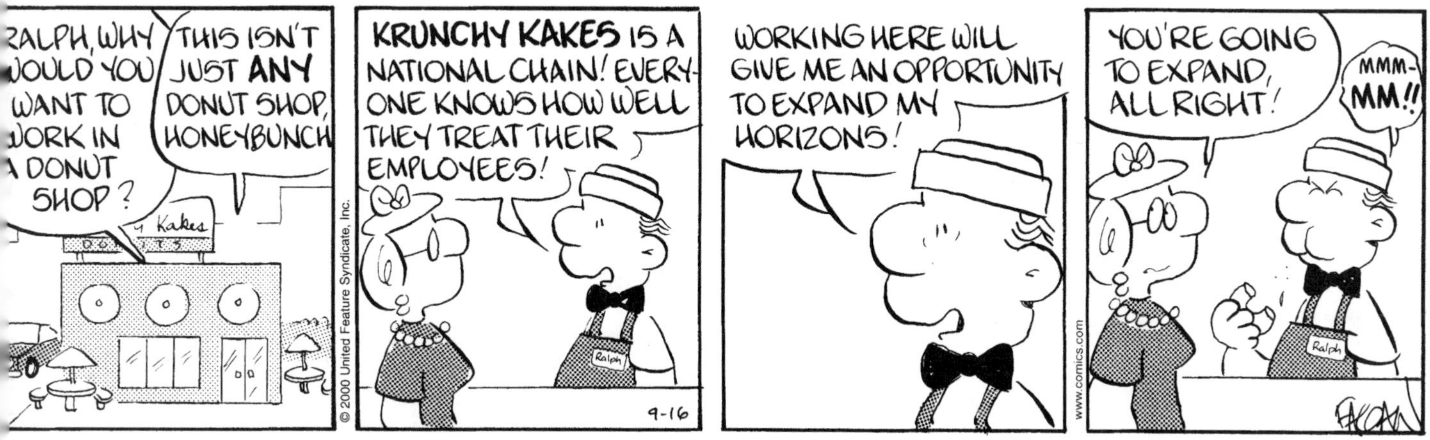
RALPH, WHY WOULD YOU WANT TO WORK IN A DONUT SHOP?
THIS ISN'T JUST **ANY** DONUT SHOP, HONEYBUNCH
Kakes
© 2000 United Feature Syndicate, Inc.
KRUNCHY KAKES IS A NATIONAL CHAIN! EVERYONE KNOWS HOW WELL THEY TREAT THEIR EMPLOYEES!
Ralph
9-16
WORKING HERE WILL GIVE ME AN OPPORTUNITY TO EXPAND MY HORIZONS!
www.comics.com
YOU'RE GOING TO EXPAND, ALL RIGHT!
MMM-**MM!!**
Ralph

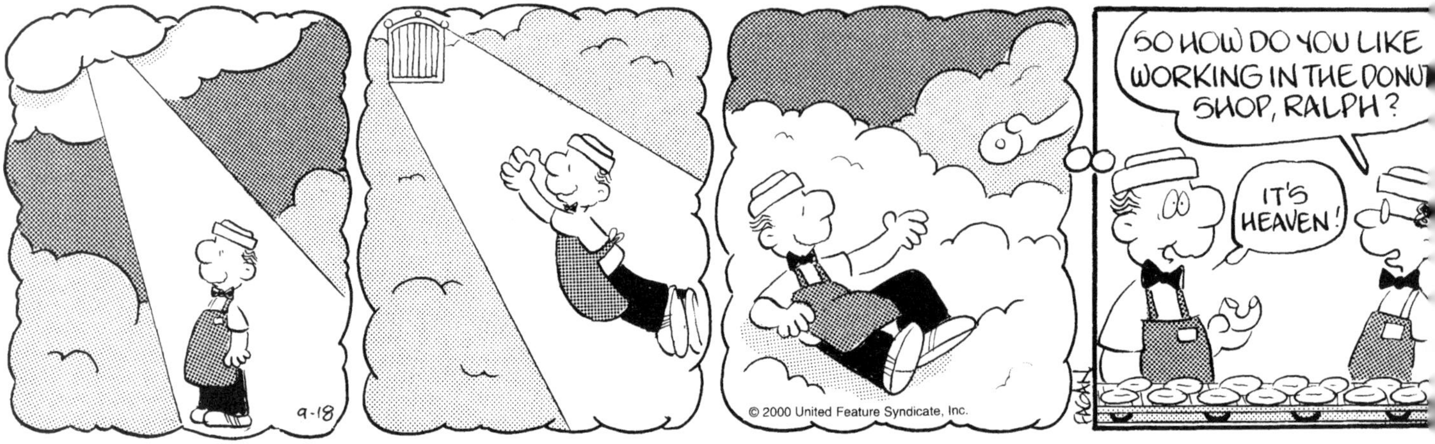
9-18
© 2000 United Feature Syndicate, Inc.
SO HOW DO YOU LIKE WORKING IN THE DONUT SHOP, RALPH?
IT'S HEAVEN!

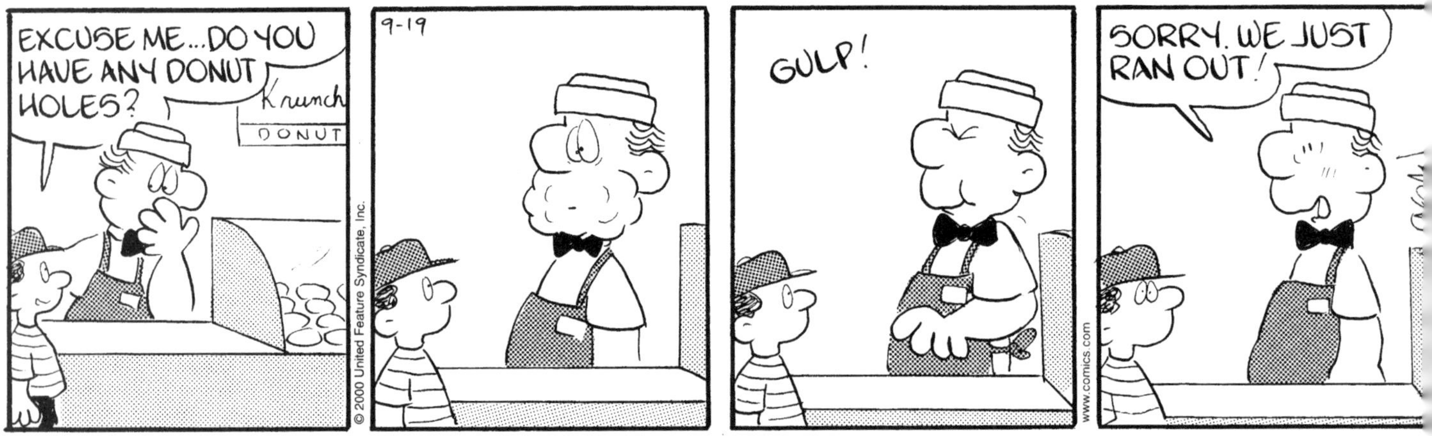
EXCUSE ME...DO YOU HAVE ANY DONUT HOLES?
Krunch
DONUT
© 2000 United Feature Syndicate, Inc.
9-19
GULP!
www.comics.com
SORRY. WE JUST RAN OUT!

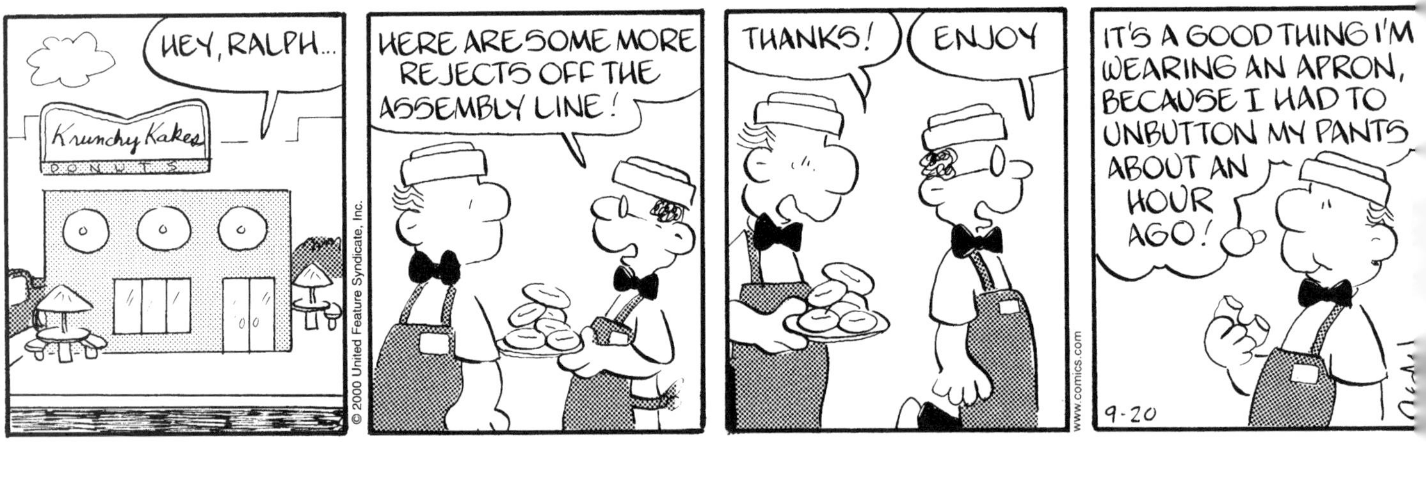
HEY, RALPH...
Krunchy Kakes
DONUTS
© 2000 United Feature Syndicate, Inc.
HERE ARE SOME MORE REJECTS OFF THE ASSEMBLY LINE!
THANKS!
ENJOY
www.comics.com
IT'S A GOOD THING I'M WEARING AN APRON, BECAUSE I HAD TO UNBUTTON MY PANTS ABOUT AN HOUR AGO!
9-20

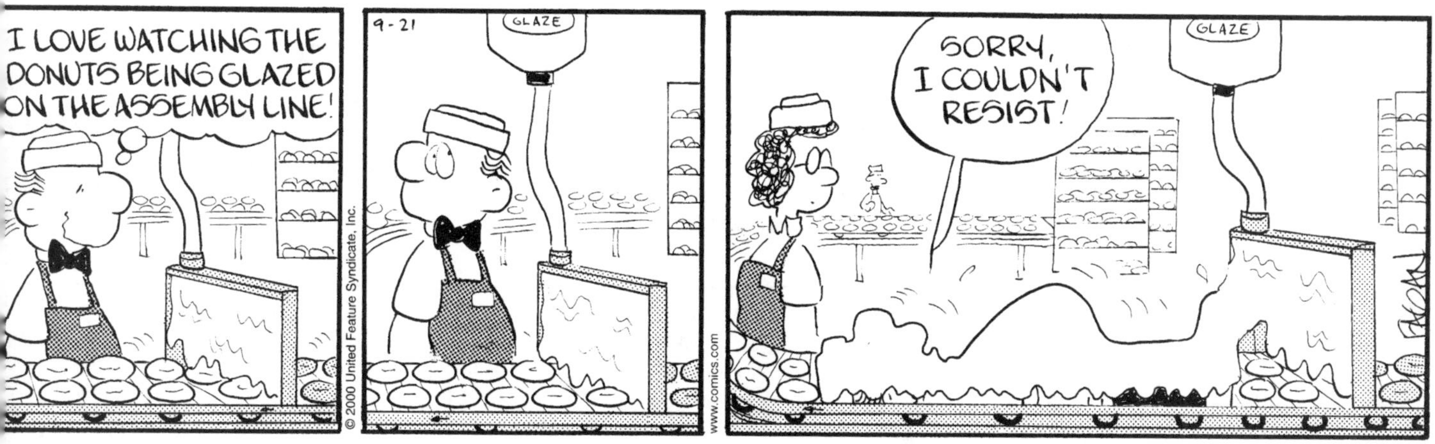
I LOVE WATCHING THE DONUTS BEING GLAZED ON THE ASSEMBLY LINE!
9-21
GLAZE
© 2000 United Feature Syndicate, Inc.
SORRY, I COULDN'T RESIST!
GLAZE
www.comics.com
FAGAN

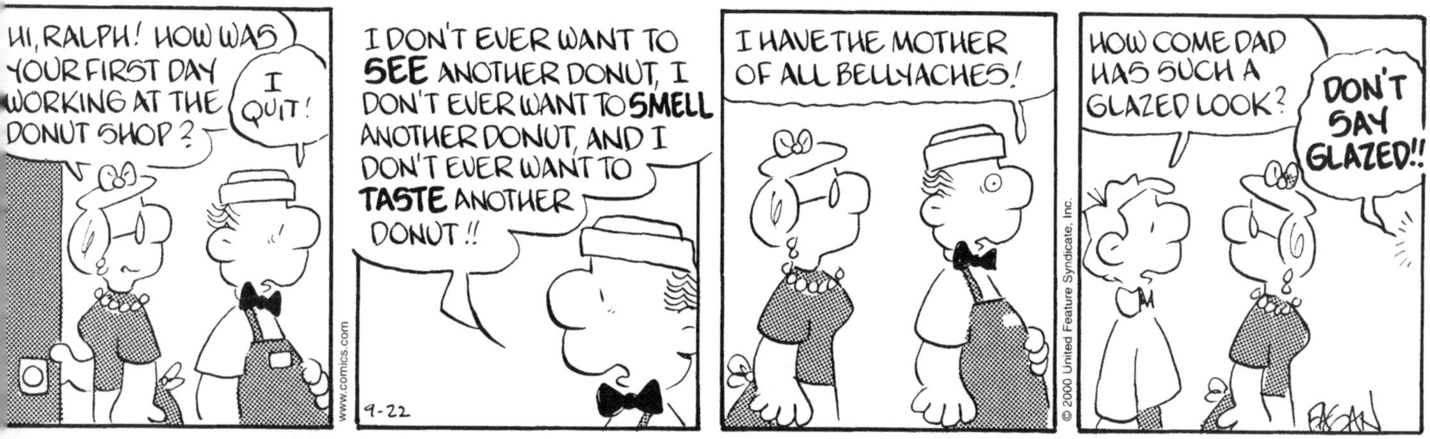
HI, RALPH! HOW WAS YOUR FIRST DAY WORKING AT THE DONUT SHOP?
I QUIT!
www.comics.com
I DON'T EVER WANT TO **SEE** ANOTHER DONUT, I DON'T EVER WANT TO **SMELL** ANOTHER DONUT, AND I DON'T EVER WANT TO **TASTE** ANOTHER DONUT!!
9-22
I HAVE THE MOTHER OF ALL BELLYACHES!
© 2000 United Feature Syndicate, Inc.
HOW COME DAD HAS SUCH A GLAZED LOOK?
DON'T SAY GLAZED!!
FAGAN

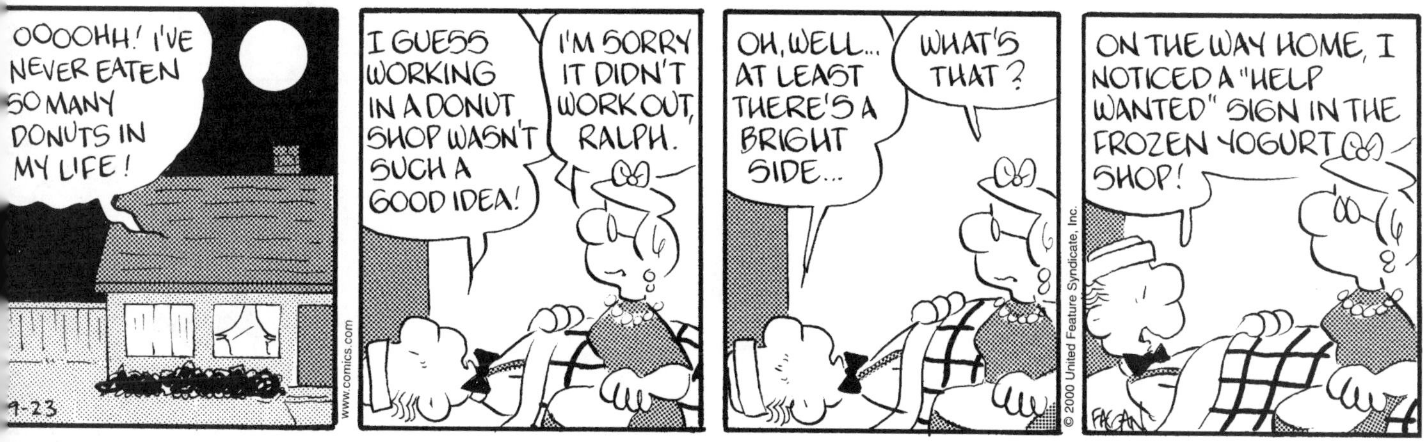
OOOOHH! I'VE NEVER EATEN SO MANY DONUTS IN MY LIFE!
9-23
www.comics.com
I GUESS WORKING IN A DONUT SHOP WASN'T SUCH A GOOD IDEA!
I'M SORRY IT DIDN'T WORK OUT, RALPH.
OH, WELL... AT LEAST THERE'S A BRIGHT SIDE...
WHAT'S THAT?
© 2000 United Feature Syndicate, Inc.
ON THE WAY HOME, I NOTICED A "HELP WANTED" SIGN IN THE FROZEN YOGURT SHOP!
FAGAN

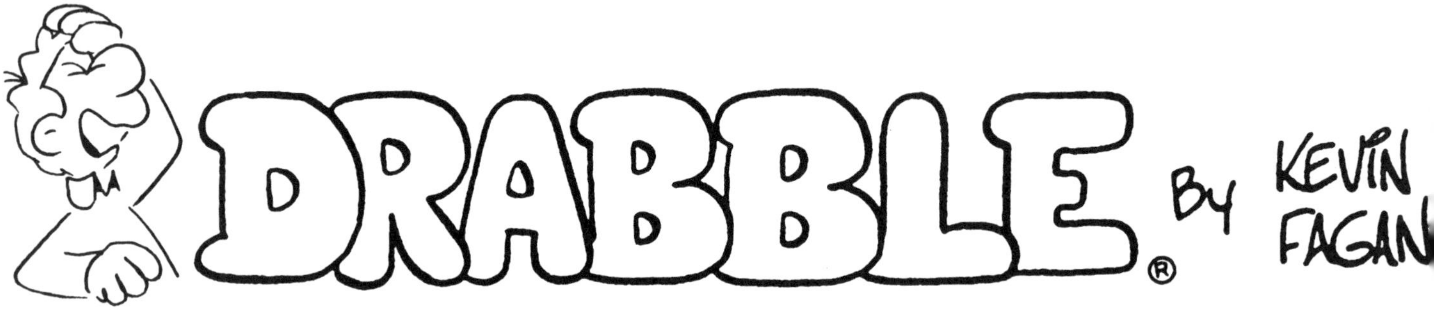
DRABBLE®
By KEVIN FAGAN

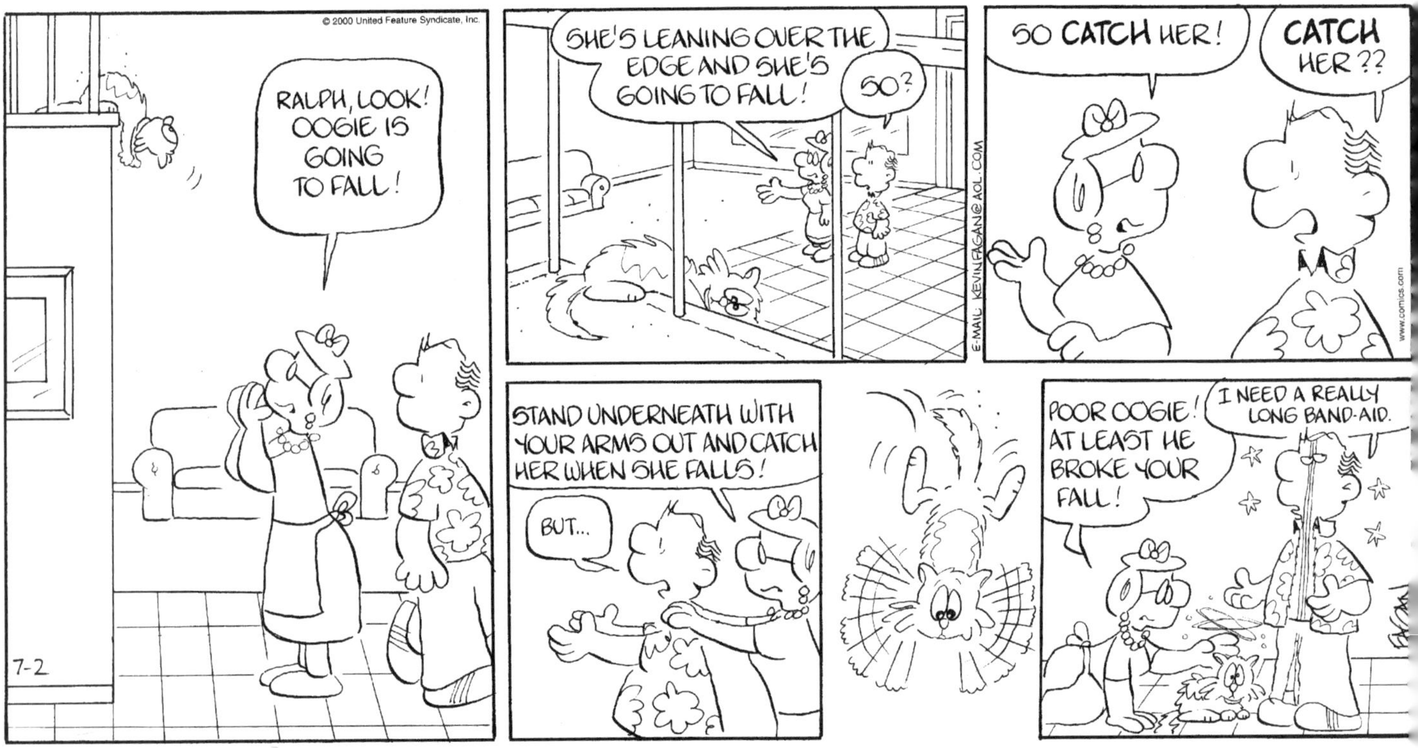
© 2000 United Feature Syndicate, Inc.
RALPH, LOOK! OOGIE IS GOING TO FALL!
7-2
SHE'S LEANING OVER THE EDGE AND SHE'S GOING TO FALL!
SO?
E-MAIL: KEVINFAGAN@AOL.COM
SO CATCH HER!
CATCH HER??
www.comics.com
STAND UNDERNEATH WITH YOUR ARMS OUT AND CATCH HER WHEN SHE FALLS!
BUT...
POOR OOGIE! AT LEAST HE BROKE YOUR FALL!
I NEED A REALLY LONG BAND-AID.

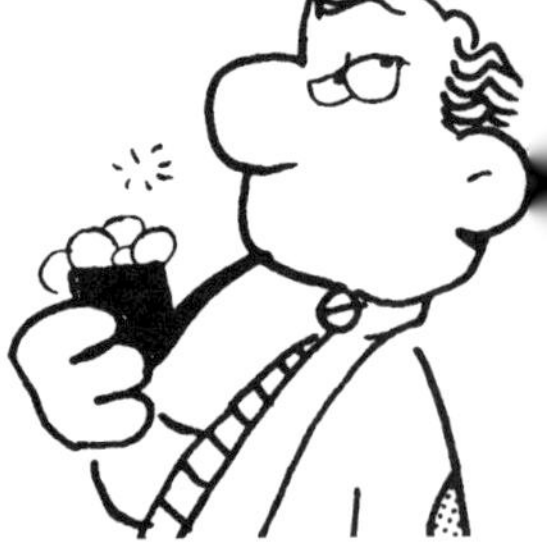

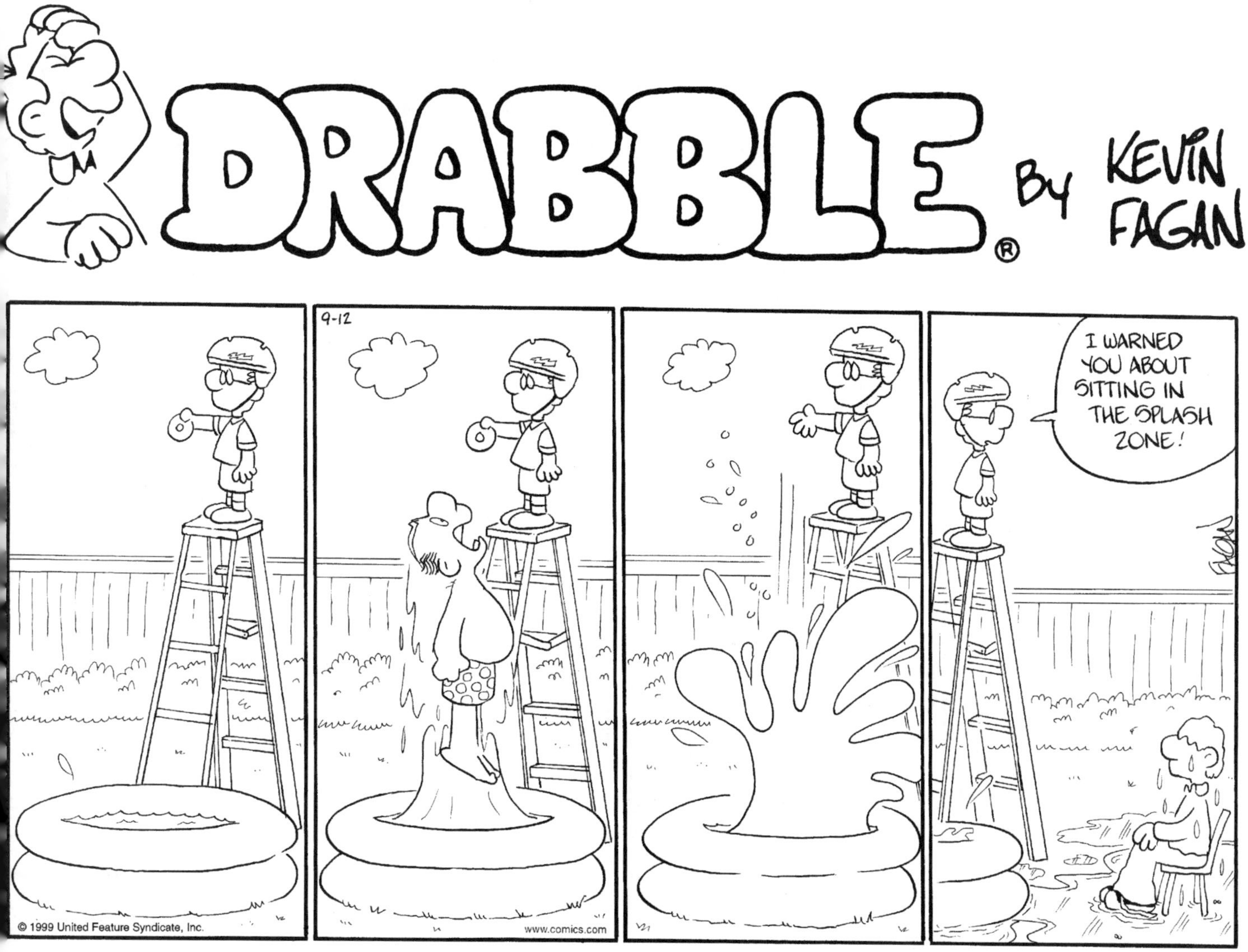
DRABBLE®
By KEVIN FAGAN
9-12
I WARNED YOU ABOUT SITTING IN THE SPLASH ZONE!
© 1999 United Feature Syndicate, Inc.
www.comics.com

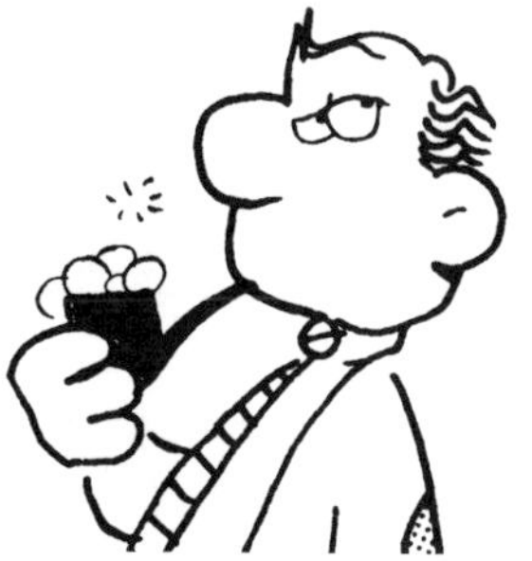

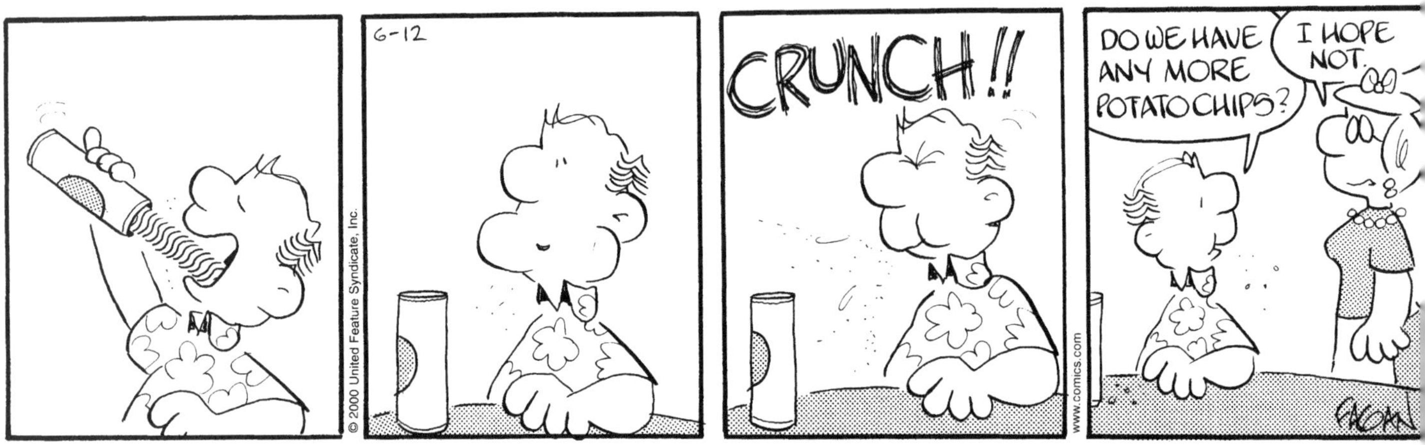
6-12
CRUNCH!!
DO WE HAVE ANY MORE POTATO CHIPS?
I HOPE NOT.
© 2000 United Feature Syndicate, Inc.
www.comics.com
FAGAN

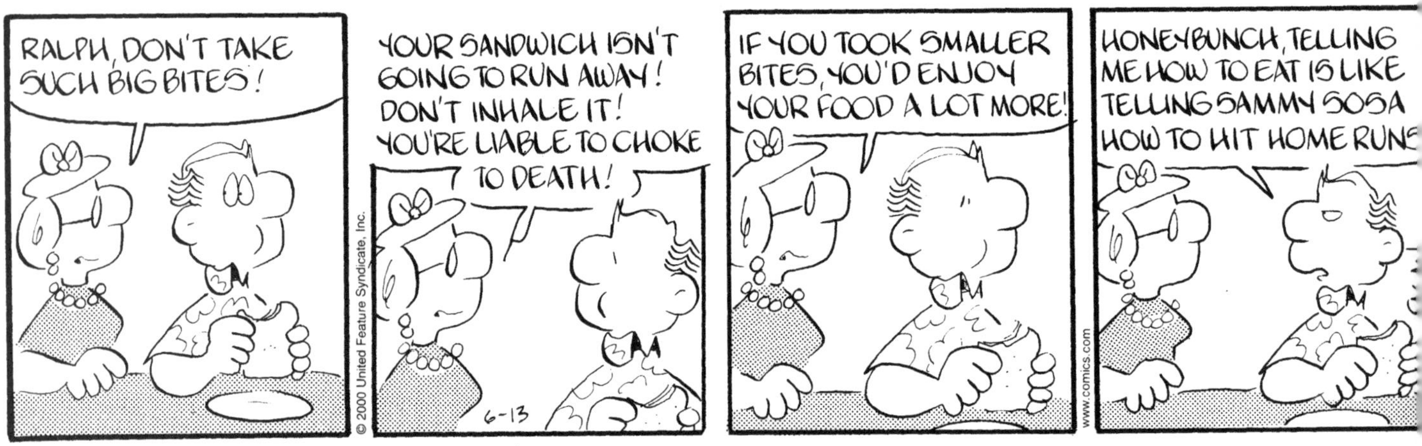
RALPH, DON'T TAKE SUCH BIG BITES!
YOUR SANDWICH ISN'T GOING TO RUN AWAY! DON'T INHALE IT! YOU'RE LIABLE TO CHOKE TO DEATH!
6-13
IF YOU TOOK SMALLER BITES, YOU'D ENJOY YOUR FOOD A LOT MORE!
HONEYBUNCH, TELLING ME HOW TO EAT IS LIKE TELLING SAMMY SOSA HOW TO HIT HOME RUNS
© 2000 United Feature Syndicate, Inc.
www.comics.com

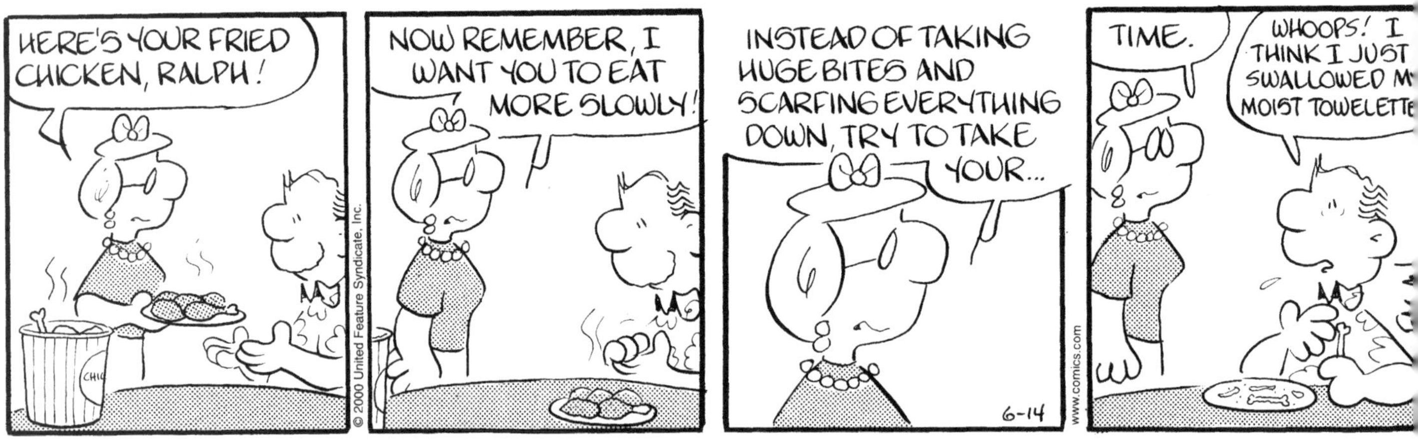
HERE'S YOUR FRIED CHICKEN, RALPH!
NOW REMEMBER, I WANT YOU TO EAT MORE SLOWLY!
INSTEAD OF TAKING HUGE BITES AND SCARFING EVERYTHING DOWN, TRY TO TAKE YOUR...
6-14
TIME.
WHOOPS! I THINK I JUST SWALLOWED M MOIST TOWELETTE
© 2000 United Feature Syndicate, Inc.
www.comics.com

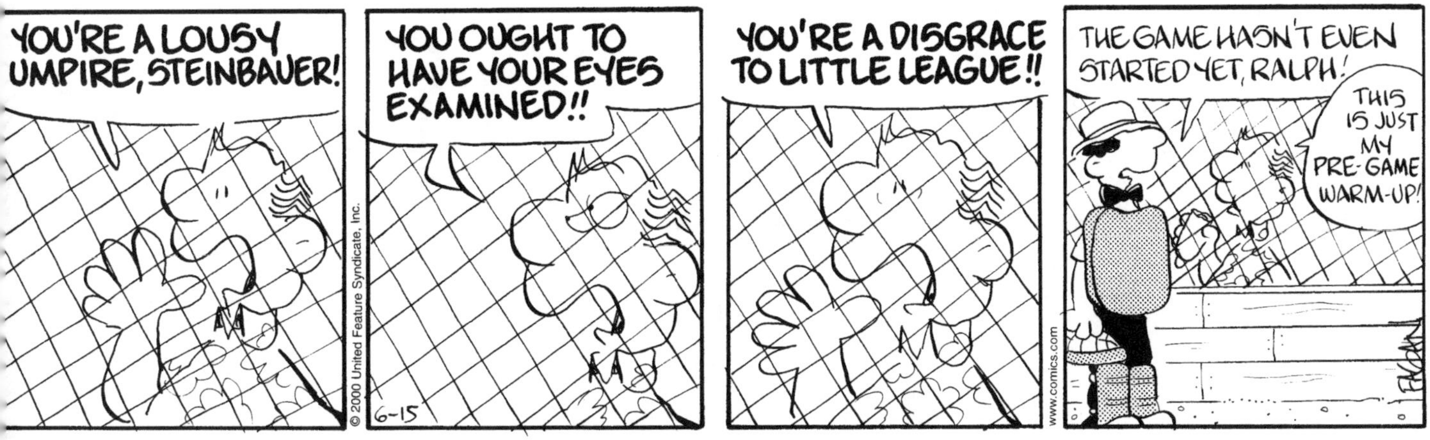
YOU'RE A LOUSY UMPIRE, STEINBAUER!
YOU OUGHT TO HAVE YOUR EYES EXAMINED!!
YOU'RE A DISGRACE TO LITTLE LEAGUE!!
THE GAME HASN'T EVEN STARTED YET, RALPH!
THIS IS JUST MY PRE-GAME WARM-UP!
© 2000 United Feature Syndicate, Inc.
6-15
www.comics.com

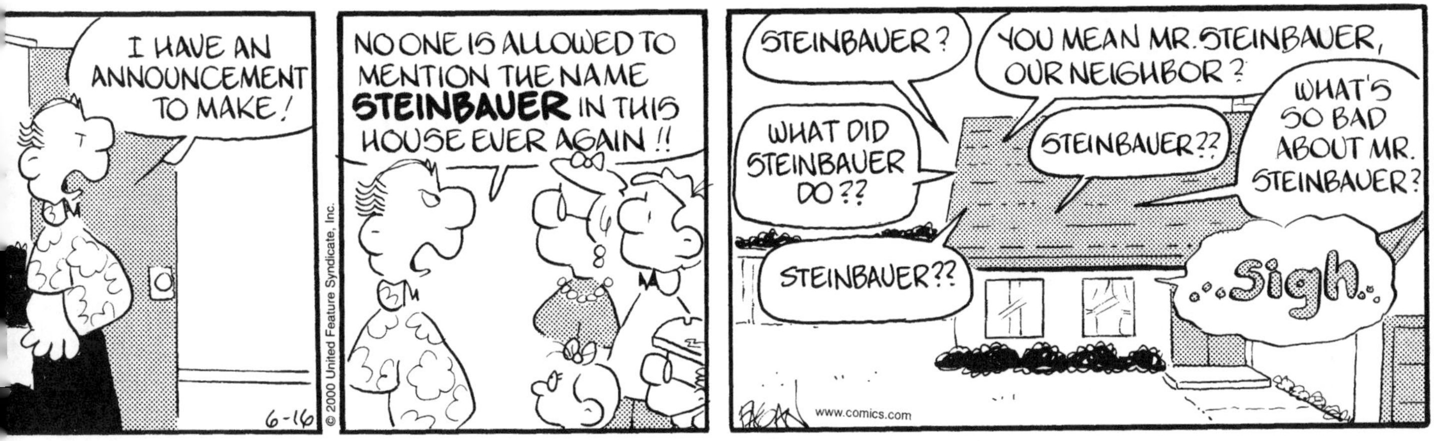
I HAVE AN ANNOUNCEMENT TO MAKE!
NO ONE IS ALLOWED TO MENTION THE NAME STEINBAUER IN THIS HOUSE EVER AGAIN!!
STEINBAUER?
YOU MEAN MR. STEINBAUER, OUR NEIGHBOR?
WHAT DID STEINBAUER DO??
STEINBAUER??
WHAT'S SO BAD ABOUT MR. STEINBAUER?
STEINBAUER??
...Sigh...
6-16
© 2000 United Feature Syndicate, Inc.
www.comics.com

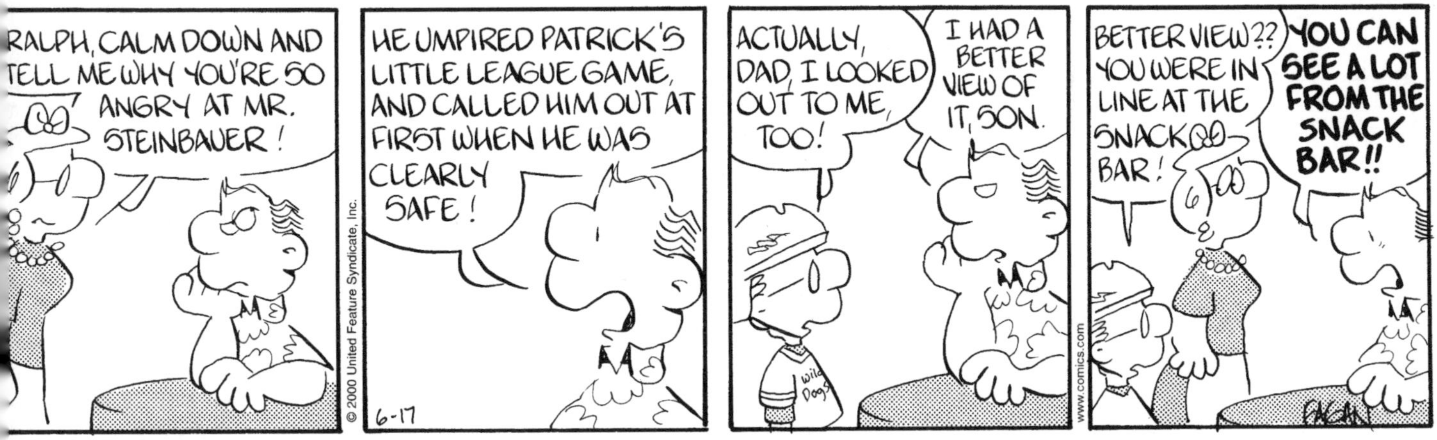
RALPH, CALM DOWN AND TELL ME WHY YOU'RE SO ANGRY AT MR. STEINBAUER!
HE UMPIRED PATRICK'S LITTLE LEAGUE GAME, AND CALLED HIM OUT AT FIRST WHEN HE WAS CLEARLY SAFE!
ACTUALLY, DAD, I LOOKED OUT TO ME, TOO!
I HAD A BETTER VIEW OF IT, SON.
BETTER VIEW?? YOU WERE IN LINE AT THE SNACK BAR!
YOU CAN SEE A LOT FROM THE SNACK BAR!!
© 2000 United Feature Syndicate, Inc.
6-17
www.comics.com

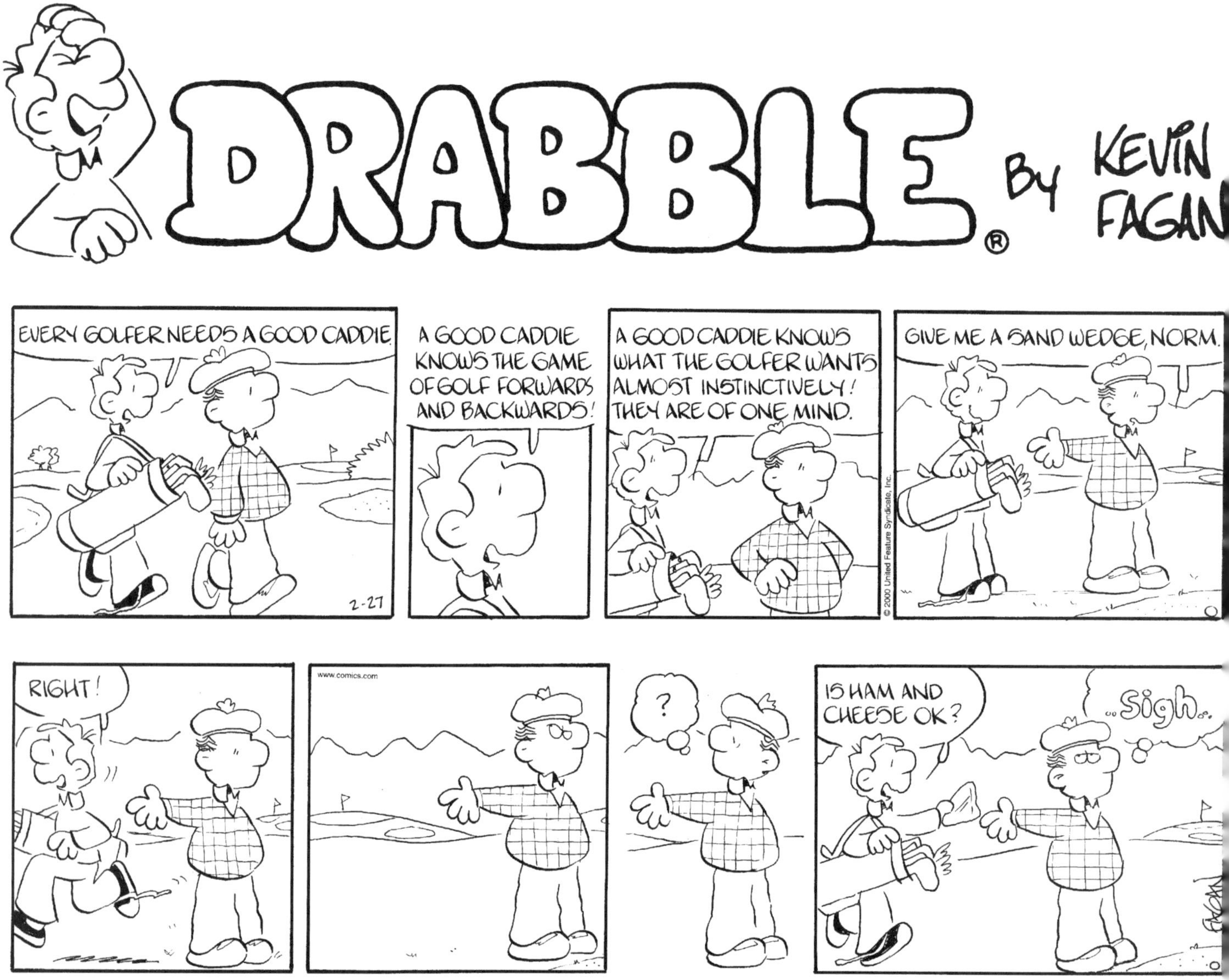
DRABBLE
By KEVIN FAGAN
EVERY GOLFER NEEDS A GOOD CADDIE.
2-27
A GOOD CADDIE KNOWS THE GAME OF GOLF FORWARDS AND BACKWARDS!
A GOOD CADDIE KNOWS WHAT THE GOLFER WANTS ALMOST INSTINCTIVELY! THEY ARE OF ONE MIND.
© 2000 United Feature Syndicate, Inc.
GIVE ME A SAND WEDGE, NORM.
RIGHT!
www.comics.com
?
IS HAM AND CHEESE OK?
..Sigh..

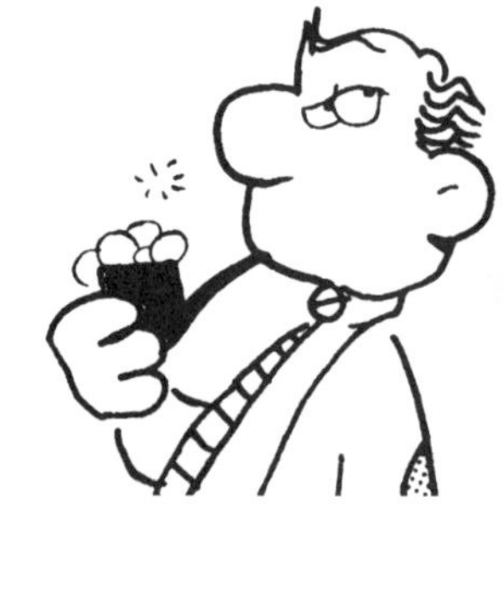

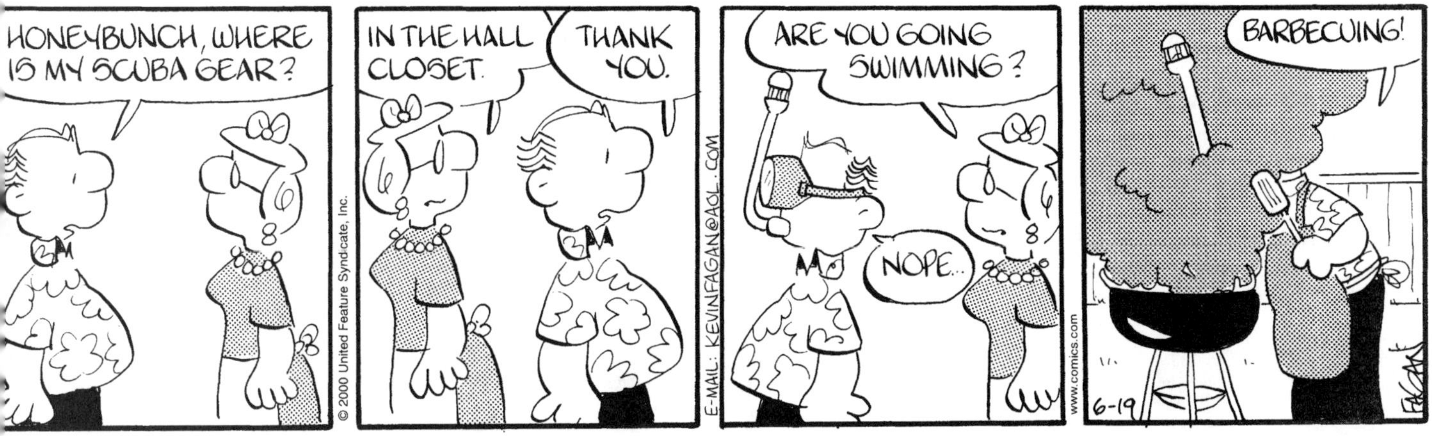
HONEYBUNCH, WHERE IS MY SCUBA GEAR?
© 2000 United Feature Syndicate, Inc.
IN THE HALL CLOSET.
THANK YOU.
E-MAIL: KEVINFAGAN@AOL.COM
ARE YOU GOING SWIMMING?
NOPE...
www.comics.com
BARBECUING!
6-19
FAGAN

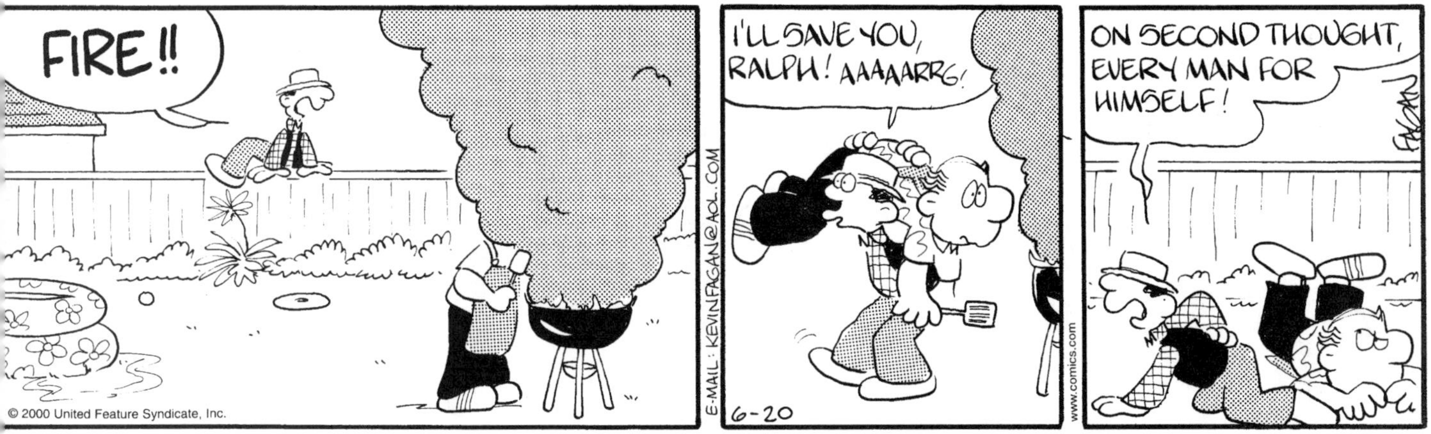
FIRE!!
© 2000 United Feature Syndicate, Inc.
E-MAIL: KEVINFAGAN@AOL.COM
I'LL SAVE YOU, RALPH! AAAAARRG!
6-20
www.comics.com
ON SECOND THOUGHT, EVERY MAN FOR HIMSELF!
FAGAN

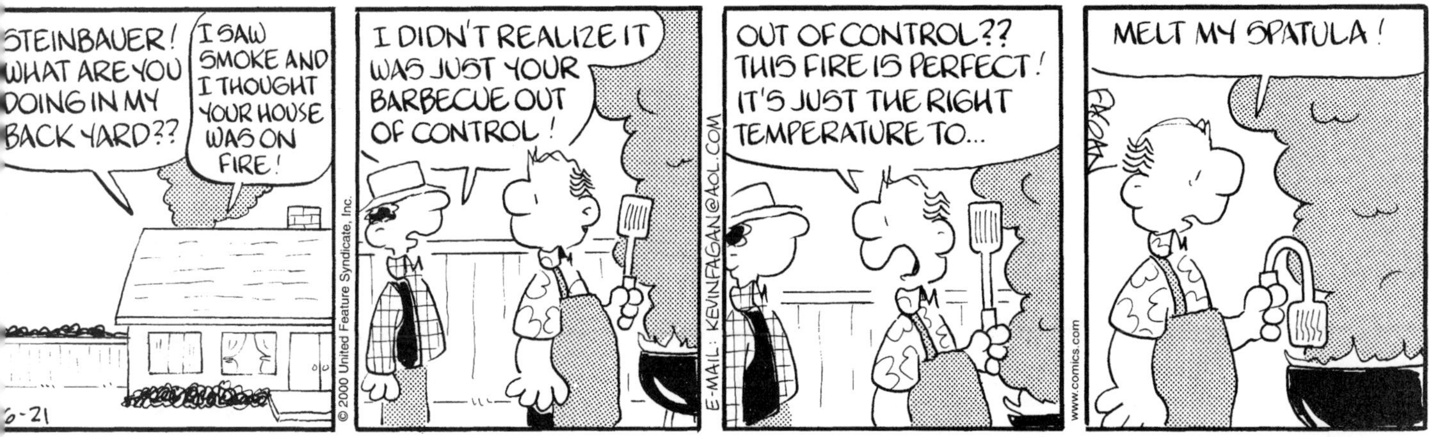
STEINBAUER! WHAT ARE YOU DOING IN MY BACK YARD??
I SAW SMOKE AND I THOUGHT YOUR HOUSE WAS ON FIRE!
6-21
© 2000 United Feature Syndicate, Inc.
I DIDN'T REALIZE IT WAS JUST YOUR BARBECUE OUT OF CONTROL!
E-MAIL: KEVINFAGAN@AOL.COM
OUT OF CONTROL?? THIS FIRE IS PERFECT! IT'S JUST THE RIGHT TEMPERATURE TO...
www.comics.com
MELT MY SPATULA!
FAGAN

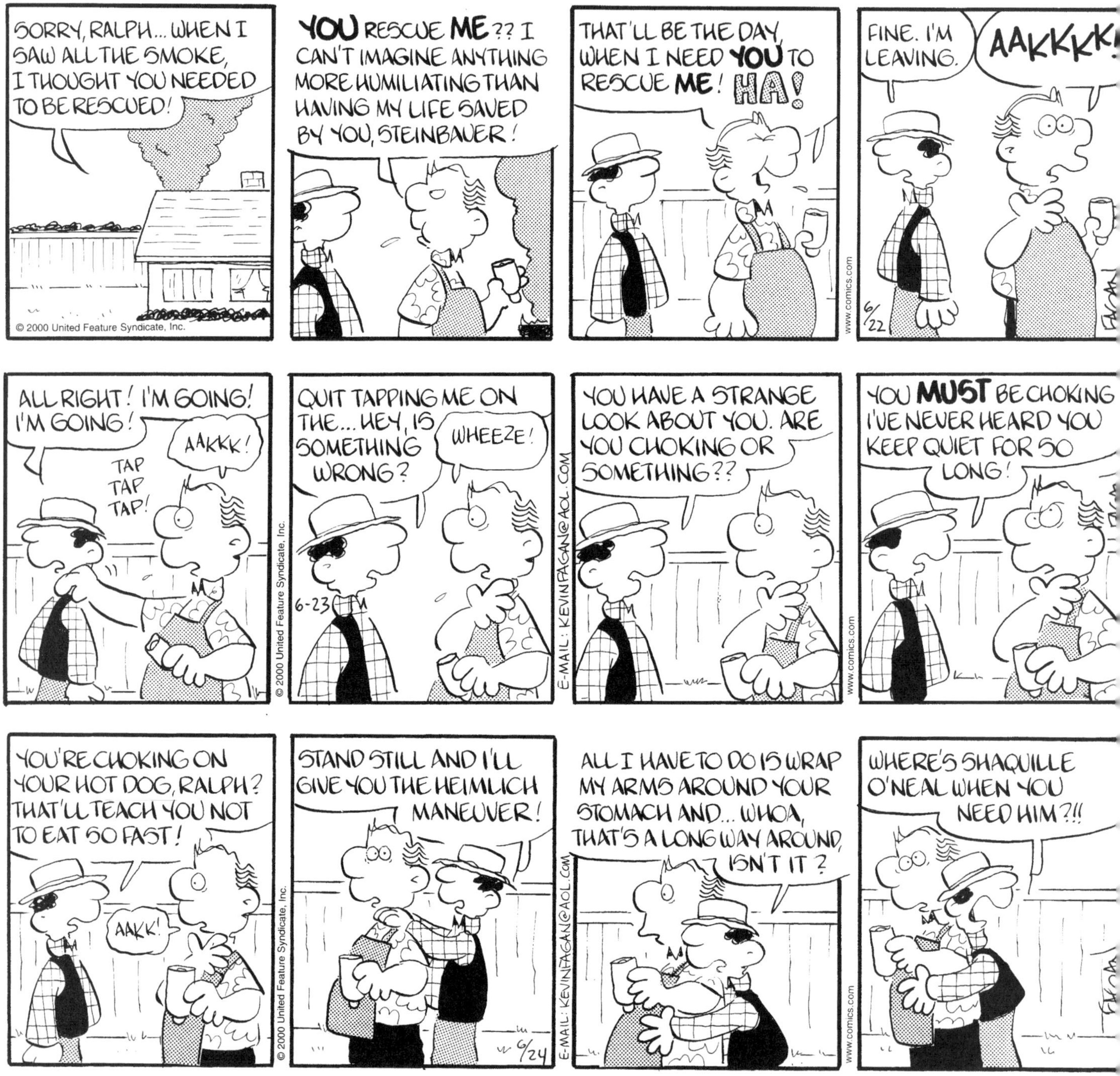
SORRY, RALPH... WHEN I SAW ALL THE SMOKE, I THOUGHT YOU NEEDED TO BE RESCUED!
© 2000 United Feature Syndicate, Inc.
YOU RESCUE ME?? I CAN'T IMAGINE ANYTHING MORE HUMILIATING THAN HAVING MY LIFE SAVED BY YOU, STEINBAUER!
THAT'LL BE THE DAY, WHEN I NEED YOU TO RESCUE ME! HA!
www.comics.com
6/22
FINE. I'M LEAVING.
AAKKKK!
ALL RIGHT! I'M GOING! I'M GOING!
AAKKK!
TAP TAP TAP!
© 2000 United Feature Syndicate, Inc.
QUIT TAPPING ME ON THE... HEY, IS SOMETHING WRONG?
WHEEZE!
6-23
E-MAIL: KEVINFAGAN@AOL.COM
YOU HAVE A STRANGE LOOK ABOUT YOU. ARE YOU CHOKING OR SOMETHING??
www.comics.com
YOU MUST BE CHOKING. I'VE NEVER HEARD YOU KEEP QUIET FOR SO LONG!
YOU'RE CHOKING ON YOUR HOT DOG, RALPH? THAT'LL TEACH YOU NOT TO EAT SO FAST!
AAKK!
© 2000 United Feature Syndicate, Inc.
STAND STILL AND I'LL GIVE YOU THE HEIMLICH MANEUVER!
6/24
E-MAIL: KEVINFAGAN@AOL.COM
ALL I HAVE TO DO IS WRAP MY ARMS AROUND YOUR STOMACH AND... WHOA, THAT'S A LONG WAY AROUND, ISN'T IT?
www.comics.com
WHERE'S SHAQUILLE O'NEAL WHEN YOU NEED HIM?!!

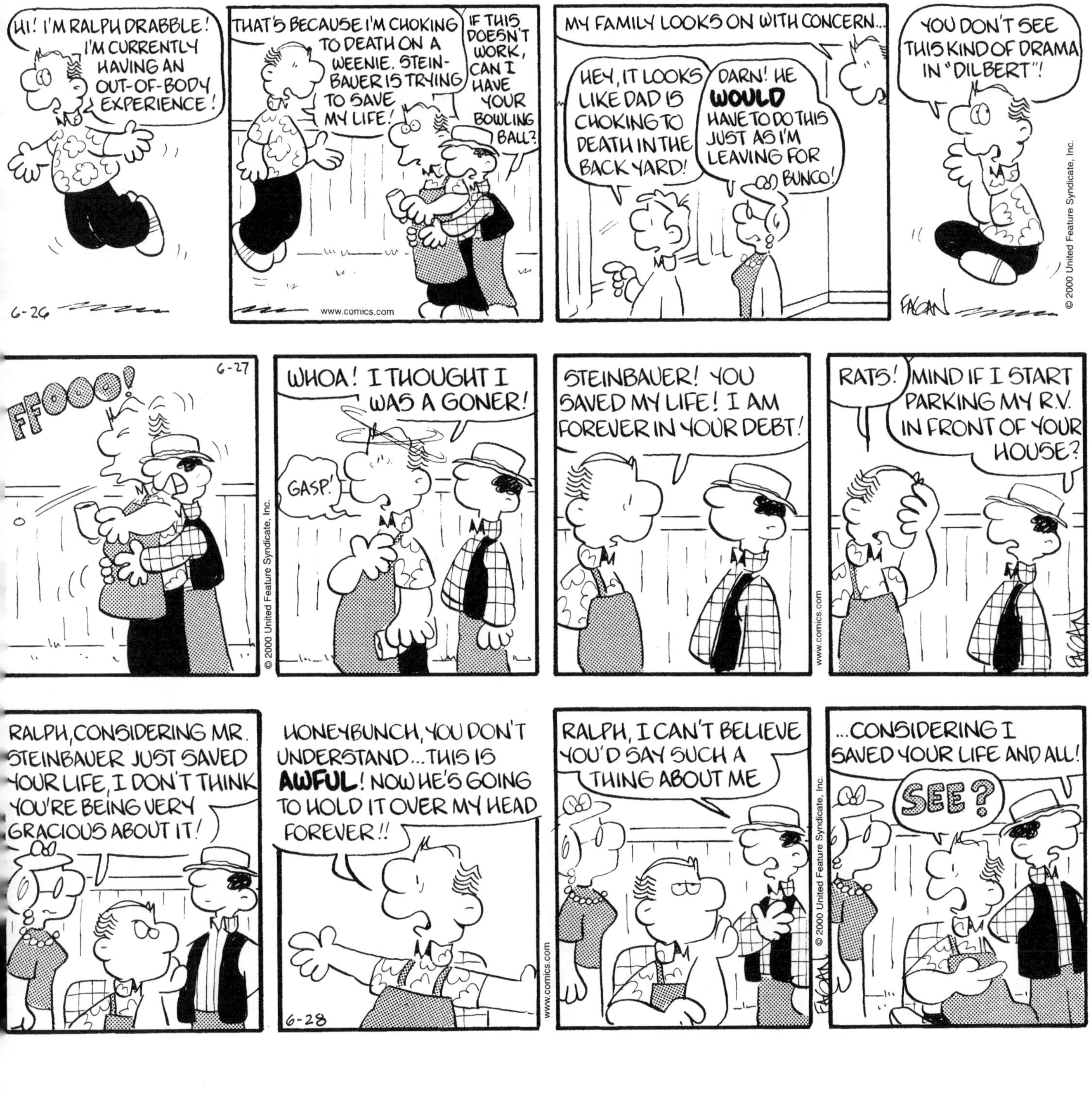
HI! I'M RALPH DRABBLE! I'M CURRENTLY HAVING AN OUT-OF-BODY EXPERIENCE!
6-26
THAT'S BECAUSE I'M CHOKING TO DEATH ON A WEENIE. STEINBAUER IS TRYING TO SAVE MY LIFE!
IF THIS DOESN'T WORK, CAN I HAVE YOUR BOWLING BALL?
www.comics.com
MY FAMILY LOOKS ON WITH CONCERN...
HEY, IT LOOKS LIKE DAD IS CHOKING TO DEATH IN THE BACK YARD!
DARN! HE **WOULD** HAVE TO DO THIS JUST AS I'M LEAVING FOR BUNCO!
YOU DON'T SEE THIS KIND OF DRAMA IN "DILBERT"!
FAGAN
© 2000 United Feature Syndicate, Inc.
6-27
FFOOOO!
© 2000 United Feature Syndicate, Inc.
WHOA! I THOUGHT I WAS A GONER!
GASP!
STEINBAUER! YOU SAVED MY LIFE! I AM FOREVER IN YOUR DEBT!
www.comics.com
RATS!
MIND IF I START PARKING MY R.V. IN FRONT OF YOUR HOUSE?
FAGAN
RALPH, CONSIDERING MR. STEINBAUER JUST SAVED YOUR LIFE, I DON'T THINK YOU'RE BEING VERY GRACIOUS ABOUT IT!
HONEYBUNCH, YOU DON'T UNDERSTAND... THIS IS **AWFUL**! NOW HE'S GOING TO HOLD IT OVER MY HEAD FOREVER!!
6-28
www.comics.com
RALPH, I CAN'T BELIEVE YOU'D SAY SUCH A THING ABOUT ME
FAGAN
© 2000 United Feature Syndicate, Inc.
...CONSIDERING I SAVED YOUR LIFE AND ALL!
SEE?

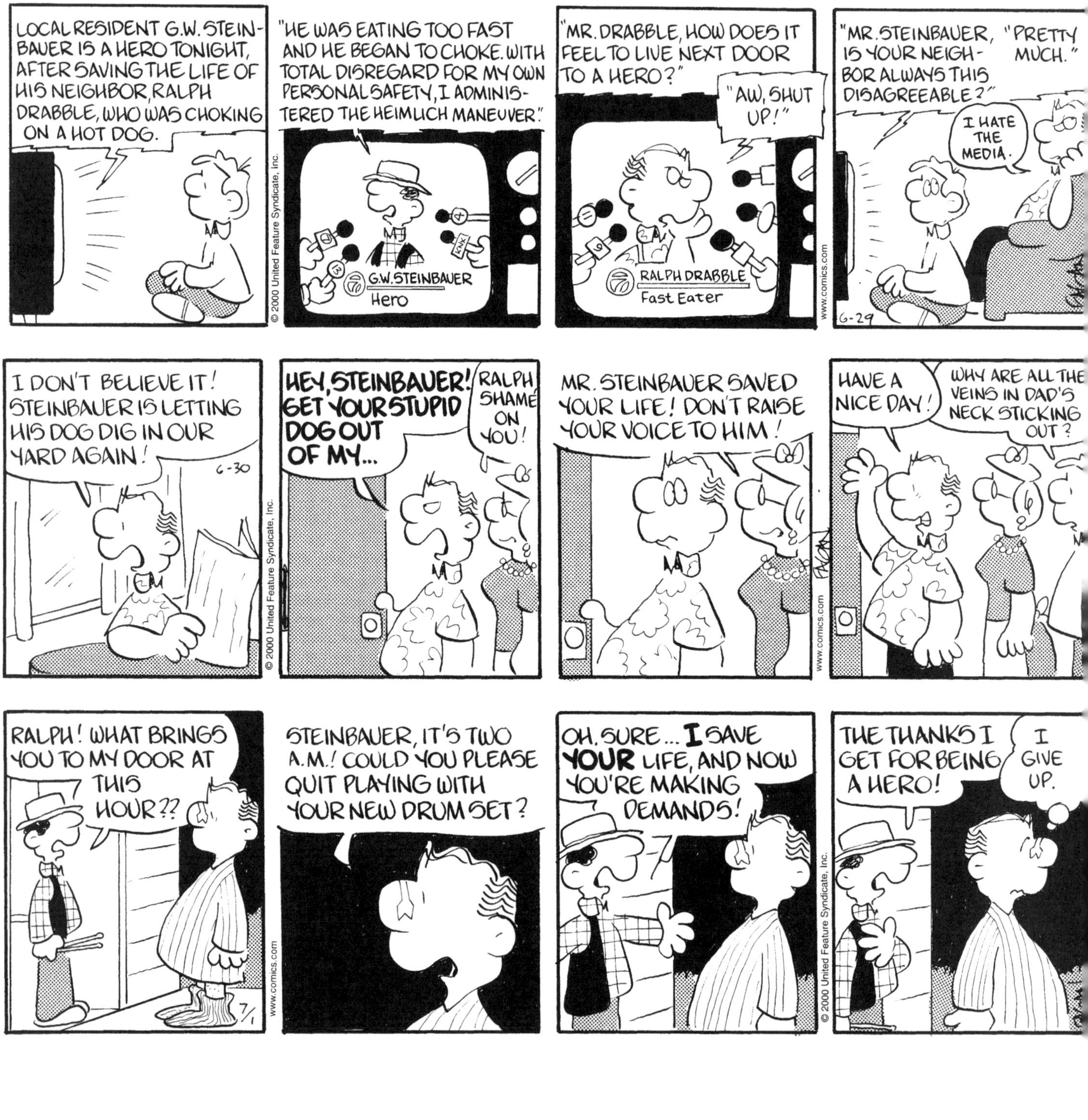
LOCAL RESIDENT G.W. STEINBAUER IS A HERO TONIGHT, AFTER SAVING THE LIFE OF HIS NEIGHBOR, RALPH DRABBLE, WHO WAS CHOKING ON A HOT DOG.
"HE WAS EATING TOO FAST AND HE BEGAN TO CHOKE. WITH TOTAL DISREGARD FOR MY OWN PERSONAL SAFETY, I ADMINISTERED THE HEIMLICH MANEUVER."
G.W. STEINBAUER
Hero
"MR. DRABBLE, HOW DOES IT FEEL TO LIVE NEXT DOOR TO A HERO?"
"AW, SHUT UP!"
RALPH DRABBLE
Fast Eater
"MR. STEINBAUER, IS YOUR NEIGHBOR ALWAYS THIS DISAGREEABLE?"
"PRETTY MUCH."
I HATE THE MEDIA.
© 2000 United Feature Syndicate, Inc.
www.comics.com
6-29
I DON'T BELIEVE IT! STEINBAUER IS LETTING HIS DOG DIG IN OUR YARD AGAIN!
6-30
HEY, STEINBAUER! GET YOUR STUPID DOG OUT OF MY...
RALPH SHAME ON YOU!
MR. STEINBAUER SAVED YOUR LIFE! DON'T RAISE YOUR VOICE TO HIM!
HAVE A NICE DAY!
WHY ARE ALL THE VEINS IN DAD'S NECK STICKING OUT?
© 2000 United Feature Syndicate, Inc.
www.comics.com
RALPH! WHAT BRINGS YOU TO MY DOOR AT THIS HOUR??
7/1
STEINBAUER, IT'S TWO A.M.! COULD YOU PLEASE QUIT PLAYING WITH YOUR NEW DRUM SET?
OH, SURE... I SAVE YOUR LIFE, AND NOW YOU'RE MAKING DEMANDS!
THE THANKS I GET FOR BEING A HERO!
I GIVE UP.
www.comics.com
© 2000 United Feature Syndicate, Inc.

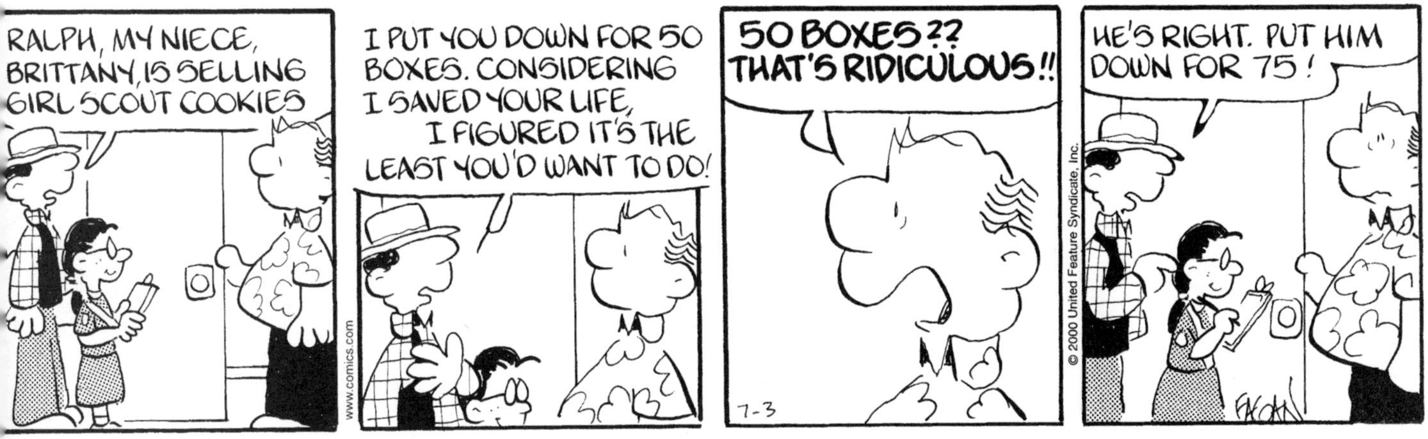
RALPH, MY NIECE, BRITTANY, IS SELLING GIRL SCOUT COOKIES
www.comics.com
I PUT YOU DOWN FOR 50 BOXES. CONSIDERING I SAVED YOUR LIFE, I FIGURED IT'S THE LEAST YOU'D WANT TO DO!
50 BOXES?? THAT'S RIDICULOUS!!
7-3
© 2000 United Feature Syndicate, Inc.
HE'S RIGHT. PUT HIM DOWN FOR 75!
FAGAN

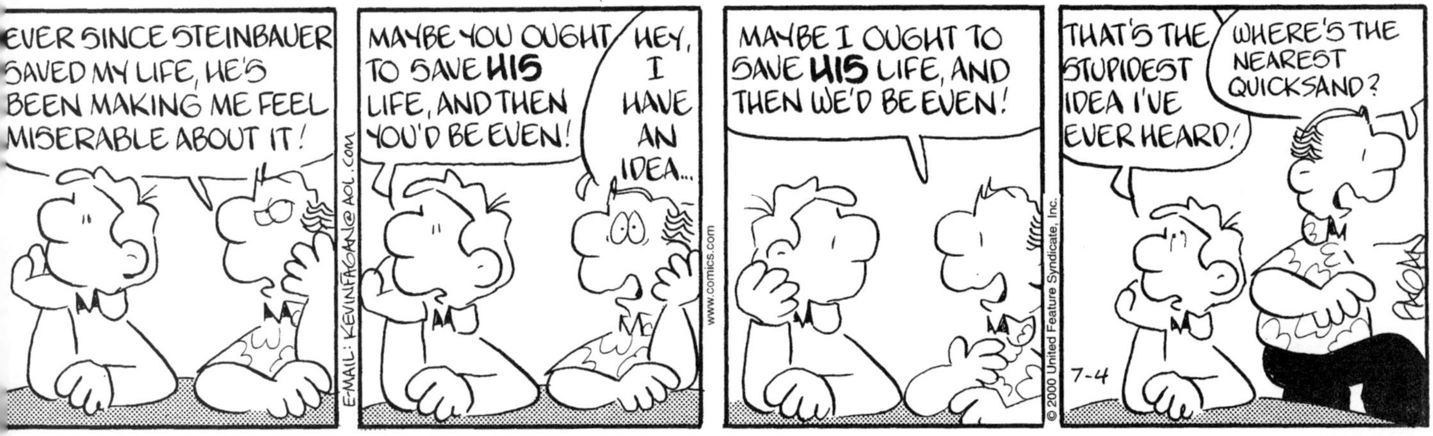
EVER SINCE STEINBAUER SAVED MY LIFE, HE'S BEEN MAKING ME FEEL MISERABLE ABOUT IT!
E-MAIL: KEVINFAGAN@AOL.COM
MAYBE YOU OUGHT TO SAVE HIS LIFE, AND THEN YOU'D BE EVEN!
HEY, I HAVE AN IDEA...
www.comics.com
MAYBE I OUGHT TO SAVE HIS LIFE, AND THEN WE'D BE EVEN!
© 2000 United Feature Syndicate, Inc.
THAT'S THE STUPIDEST IDEA I'VE EVER HEARD!
WHERE'S THE NEAREST QUICKSAND?
7-4
FAGAN

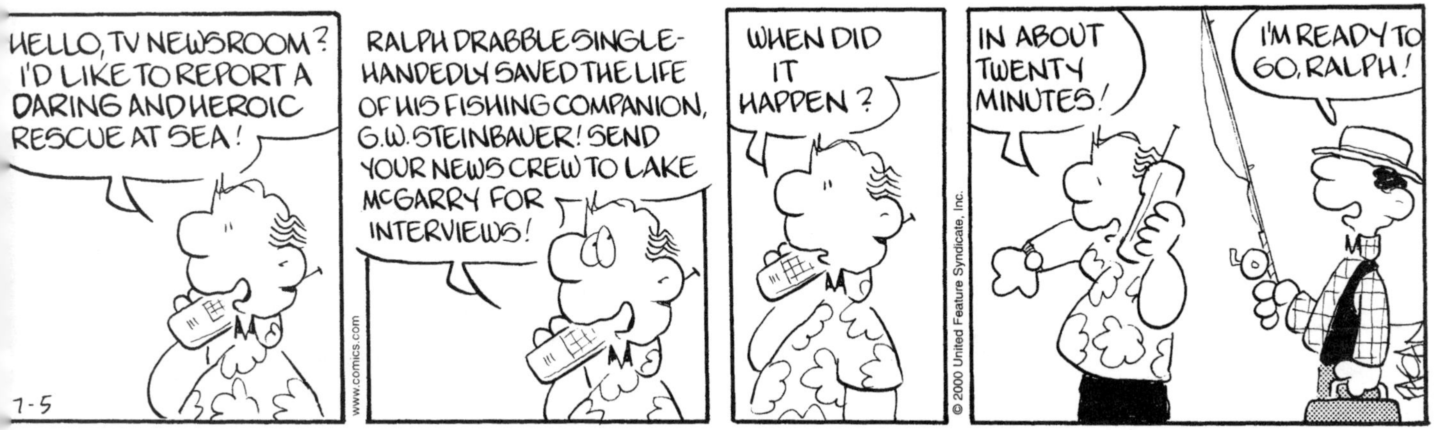
HELLO, TV NEWSROOM? I'D LIKE TO REPORT A DARING AND HEROIC RESCUE AT SEA!
7-5
www.comics.com
RALPH DRABBLE SINGLE-HANDEDLY SAVED THE LIFE OF HIS FISHING COMPANION, G.W. STEINBAUER! SEND YOUR NEWS CREW TO LAKE McGARRY FOR INTERVIEWS!
WHEN DID IT HAPPEN?
© 2000 United Feature Syndicate, Inc.
IN ABOUT TWENTY MINUTES!
I'M READY TO GO, RALPH!

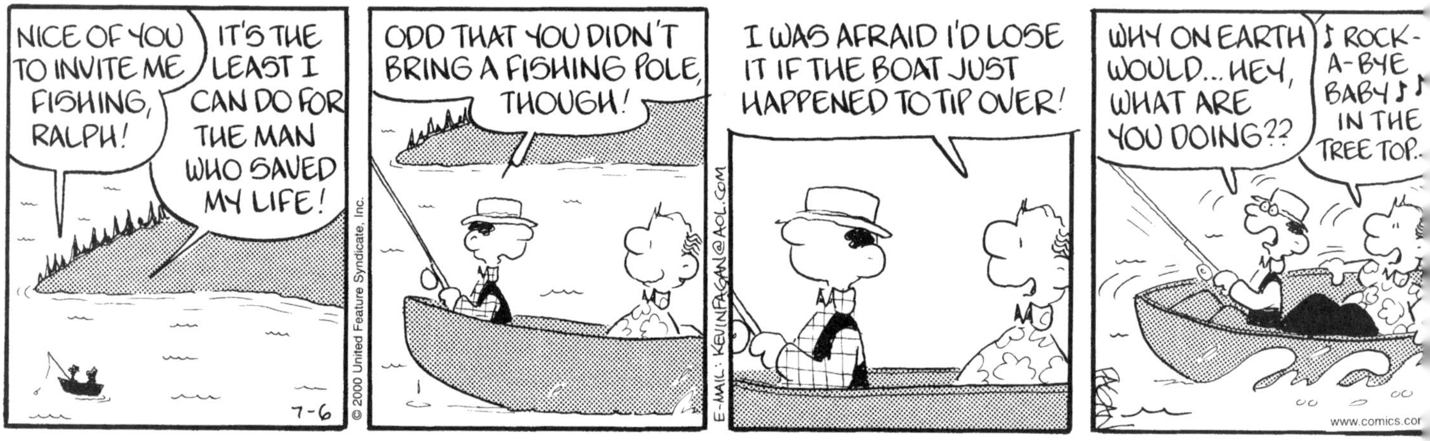
NICE OF YOU TO INVITE ME FISHING, RALPH!
IT'S THE LEAST I CAN DO FOR THE MAN WHO SAVED MY LIFE!
7-6
© 2000 United Feature Syndicate, Inc.
ODD THAT YOU DIDN'T BRING A FISHING POLE, THOUGH!
E-MAIL: KEVINFAGAN@AOL.COM
I WAS AFRAID I'D LOSE IT IF THE BOAT JUST HAPPENED TO TIP OVER!
WHY ON EARTH WOULD... HEY, WHAT ARE YOU DOING??
♪ ROCK-A-BYE BABY ♪♪ IN THE TREE TOP...
www.comics.co

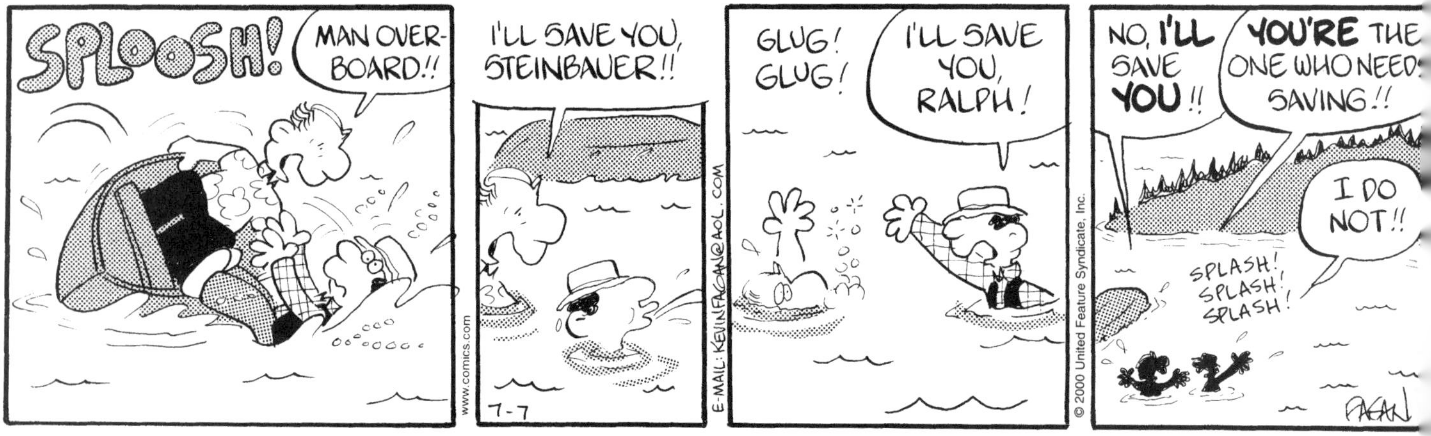
SPLOOSH!
MAN OVERBOARD!!
I'LL SAVE YOU, STEINBAUER!!
www.comics.com
7-7
E-MAIL: KEVINFAGAN@AOL.COM
GLUG! GLUG!
I'LL SAVE YOU, RALPH!
© 2000 United Feature Syndicate, Inc.
NO, I'LL SAVE YOU!!
YOU'RE THE ONE WHO NEEDS SAVING!!
I DO NOT!!
SPLASH! SPLASH! SPLASH!
FAGAN

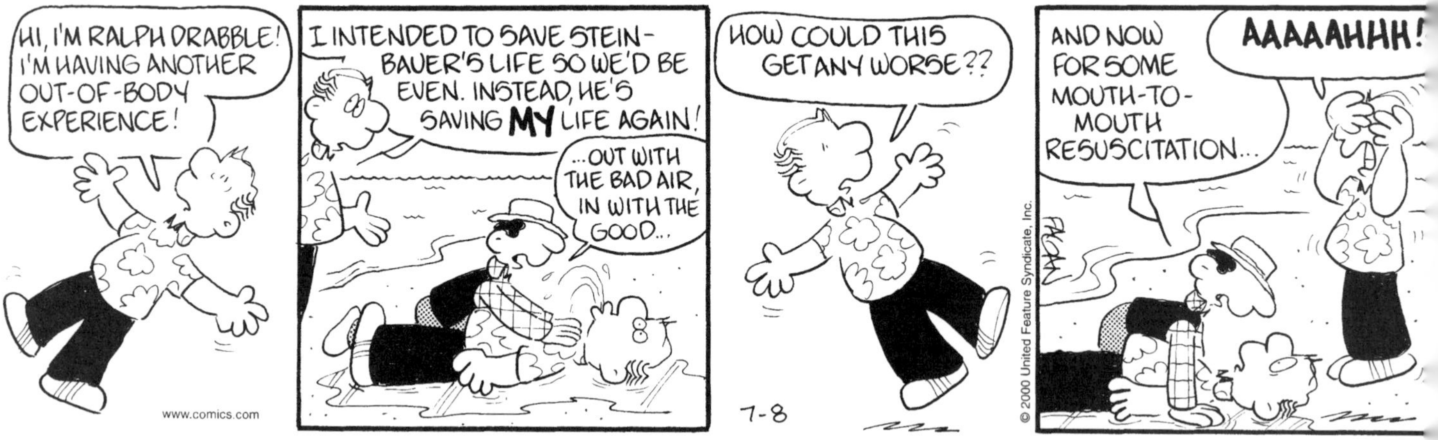
HI, I'M RALPH DRABBLE! I'M HAVING ANOTHER OUT-OF-BODY EXPERIENCE!
www.comics.com
I INTENDED TO SAVE STEINBAUER'S LIFE SO WE'D BE EVEN. INSTEAD, HE'S SAVING MY LIFE AGAIN!
...OUT WITH THE BAD AIR, IN WITH THE GOOD...
7-8
HOW COULD THIS GET ANY WORSE??
© 2000 United Feature Syndicate, Inc.
FAGAN
AND NOW FOR SOME MOUTH-TO-MOUTH RESUSCITATION...
AAAAAHHH!

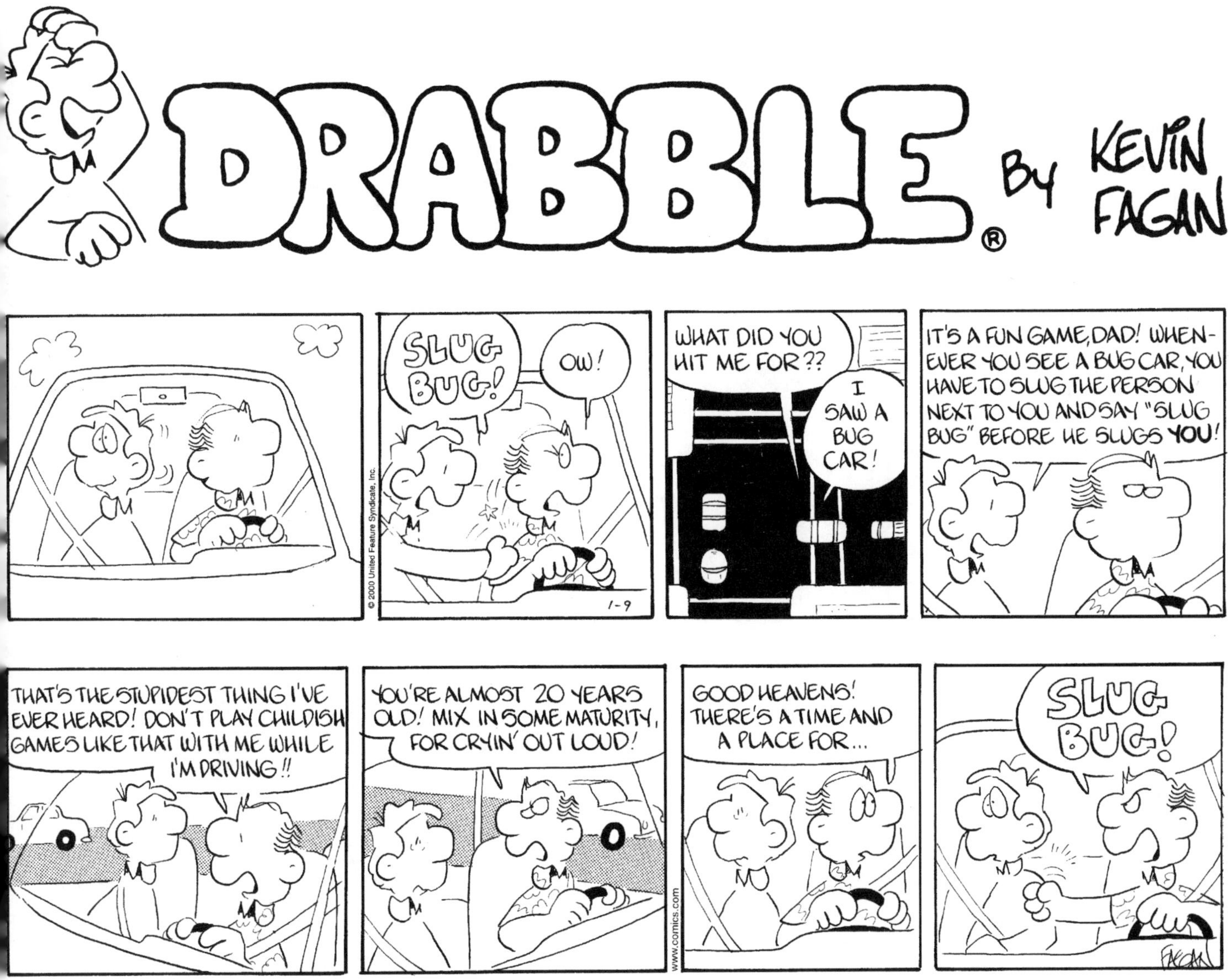
DRABBLE® By KEVIN FAGAN
SLUG BUG!
OW!
© 2000 United Feature Syndicate, Inc.
1-9
WHAT DID YOU HIT ME FOR??
I SAW A BUG CAR!
IT'S A FUN GAME, DAD! WHENEVER YOU SEE A BUG CAR, YOU HAVE TO SLUG THE PERSON NEXT TO YOU AND SAY "SLUG BUG" BEFORE HE SLUGS **YOU**!
THAT'S THE STUPIDEST THING I'VE EVER HEARD! DON'T PLAY CHILDISH GAMES LIKE THAT WITH ME WHILE I'M DRIVING!!
YOU'RE ALMOST 20 YEARS OLD! MIX IN SOME MATURITY, FOR CRYIN' OUT LOUD!
www.comics.com
GOOD HEAVENS! THERE'S A TIME AND A PLACE FOR...
SLUG BUG!
FAGAN

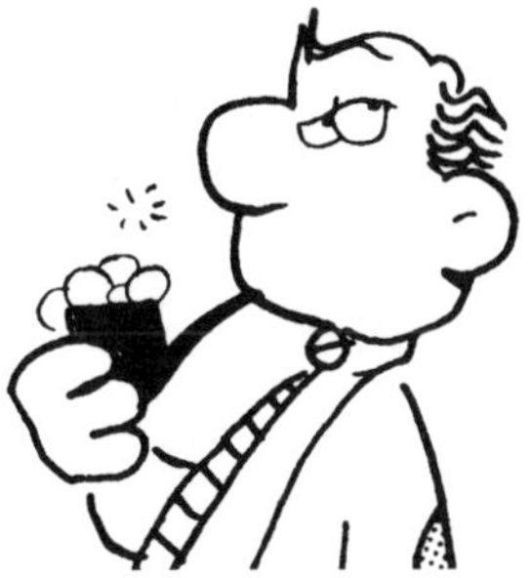

DRABBLE

By KEVIN FAGAN

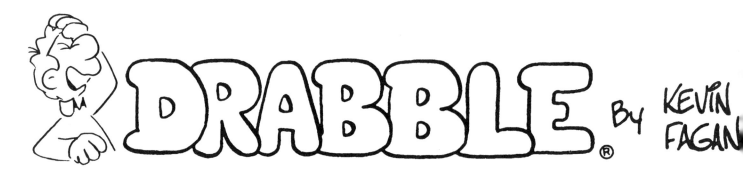

Panel 1: MY WIFE IS TALKING ABOUT SOMETHING, BUT I HAVE NO IDEA WHAT.

www.comics.com 3-19

Panel 2: THAT'S BECAUSE I TUNED OUT A WHILE BACK. THE TRICK IS TO MAKE IT LOOK LIKE I'M STILL LISTENING.

Panel 3: THERE ARE SEVERAL METHODS... FOR EXAMPLE, IF SHE SMILES, I SMILE!

Panel 4: IF SHE FROWNS, I FROWN.

Panel 5: STROKING MY CHIN WHILE STARING INTO SPACE GIVES THE IMPRESSION THAT I'M PONDERING HER WORDS.

Panel 6: A FEW NON-COMMITTAL VERBAL REACTIONS ARE ALSO HELPFUL.

IS THAT RIGHT?

YOU DON'T SAY!

UH-HUH...

Panel 7: FINALLY, GOOD EYE CONTACT IS A MUST!

Panel 8: THE KEY TO A SUCCESSFUL RELATIONSHIP IS TO ALWAYS ACT LIKE YOU'RE PAYING ATTENTION!

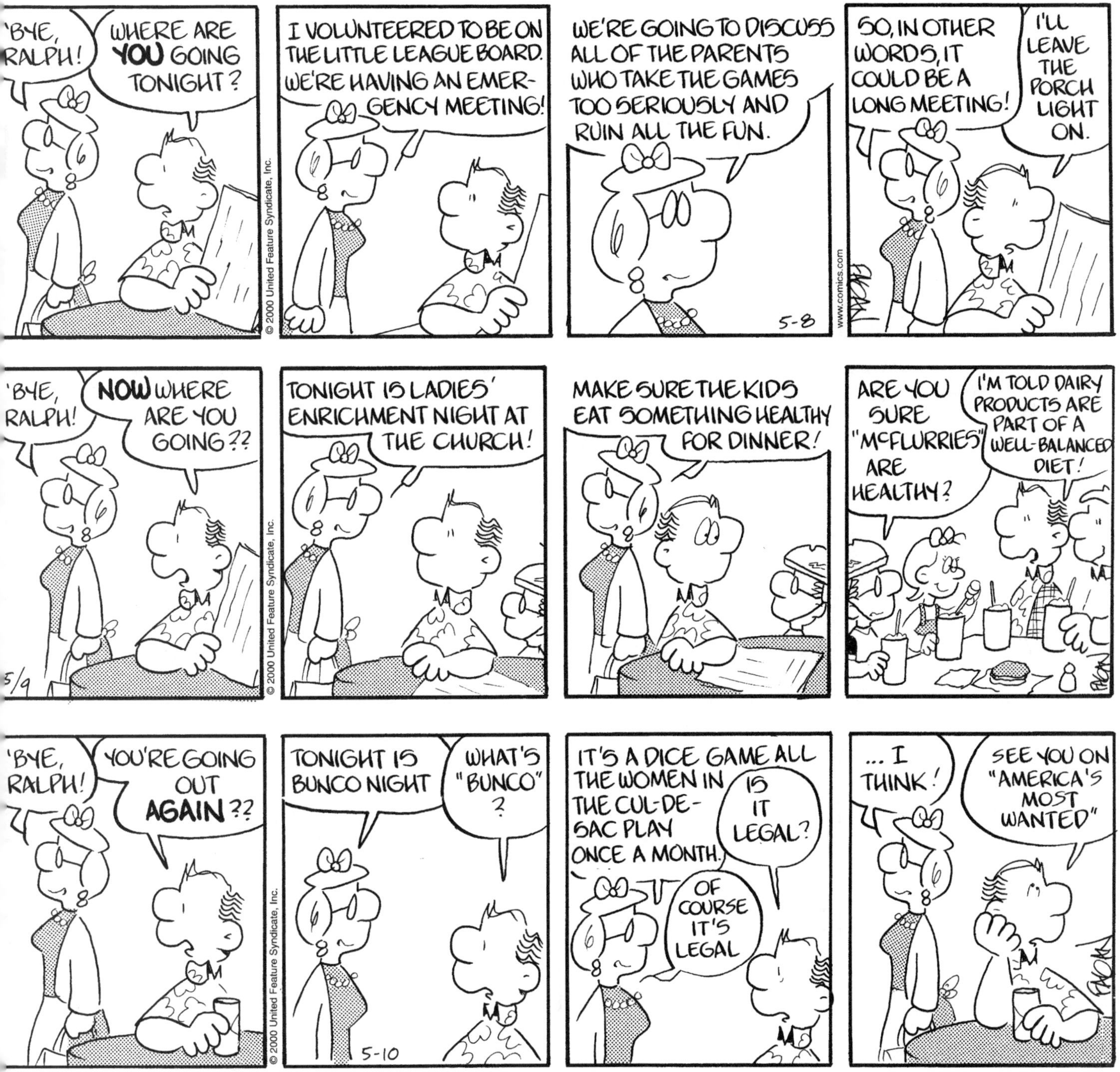
'BYE, RALPH!
WHERE ARE **YOU** GOING TONIGHT?
I VOLUNTEERED TO BE ON THE LITTLE LEAGUE BOARD. WE'RE HAVING AN EMERGENCY MEETING!
WE'RE GOING TO DISCUSS ALL OF THE PARENTS WHO TAKE THE GAMES TOO SERIOUSLY AND RUIN ALL THE FUN.
SO, IN OTHER WORDS, IT COULD BE A LONG MEETING!
I'LL LEAVE THE PORCH LIGHT ON.
© 2000 United Feature Syndicate, Inc.
5-8
www.comics.com
'BYE, RALPH!
NOW WHERE ARE YOU GOING??
TONIGHT IS LADIES' ENRICHMENT NIGHT AT THE CHURCH!
MAKE SURE THE KIDS EAT SOMETHING HEALTHY FOR DINNER!
ARE YOU SURE "McFLURRIES" ARE HEALTHY?
I'M TOLD DAIRY PRODUCTS ARE PART OF A WELL-BALANCED DIET!
5/9
© 2000 United Feature Syndicate, Inc.
'BYE, RALPH!
YOU'RE GOING OUT **AGAIN**??
TONIGHT IS BUNCO NIGHT
WHAT'S "BUNCO"?
IT'S A DICE GAME ALL THE WOMEN IN THE CUL-DE-SAC PLAY ONCE A MONTH.
IS IT LEGAL?
OF COURSE IT'S LEGAL
... I THINK!
SEE YOU ON "AMERICA'S MOST WANTED"
© 2000 United Feature Syndicate, Inc.
5-10

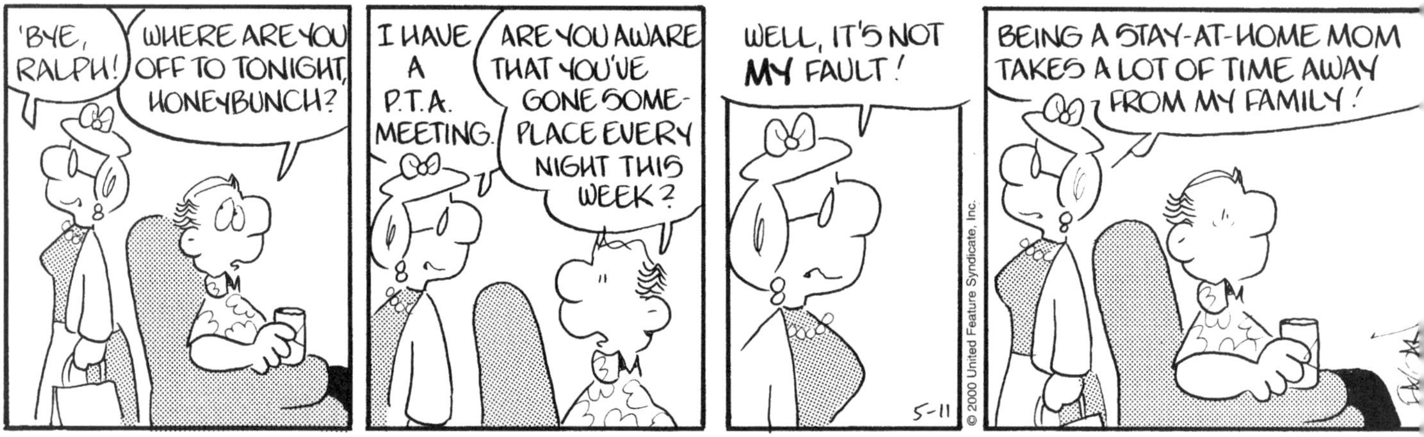
'BYE, RALPH!
WHERE ARE YOU OFF TO TONIGHT, HONEYBUNCH?
I HAVE A P.T.A. MEETING.
ARE YOU AWARE THAT YOU'VE GONE SOMEPLACE EVERY NIGHT THIS WEEK?
WELL, IT'S NOT **MY** FAULT!
5-11
© 2000 United Feature Syndicate, Inc.
BEING A STAY-AT-HOME MOM TAKES A LOT OF TIME AWAY FROM MY FAMILY!

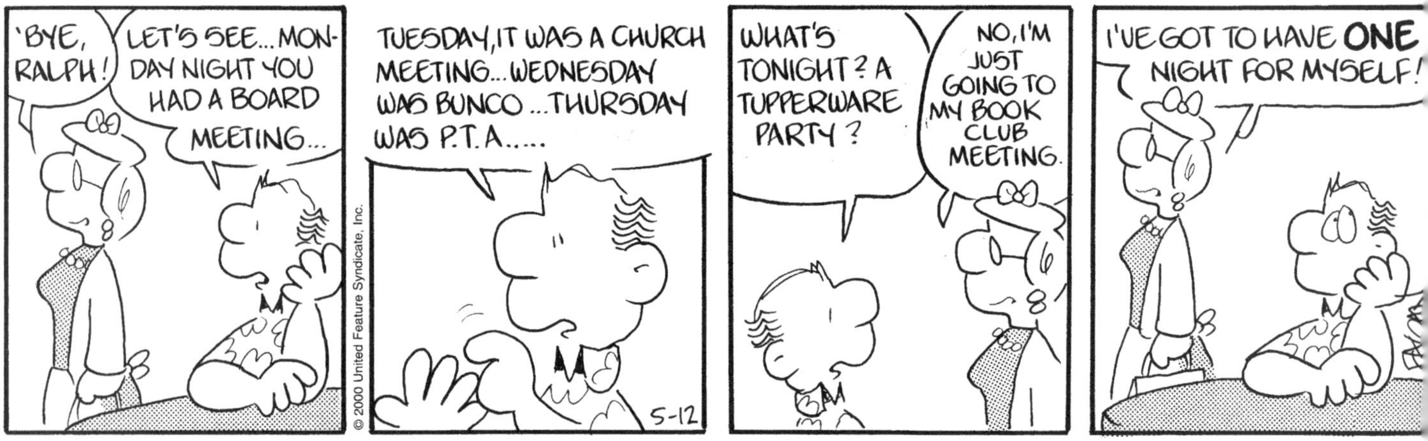
'BYE, RALPH!
LET'S SEE... MONDAY NIGHT YOU HAD A BOARD MEETING...
© 2000 United Feature Syndicate, Inc.
TUESDAY, IT WAS A CHURCH MEETING... WEDNESDAY WAS BUNCO ... THURSDAY WAS P.T.A.....
5-12
WHAT'S TONIGHT? A TUPPERWARE PARTY?
NO, I'M JUST GOING TO MY BOOK CLUB MEETING.
I'VE GOT TO HAVE **ONE** NIGHT FOR MYSELF!

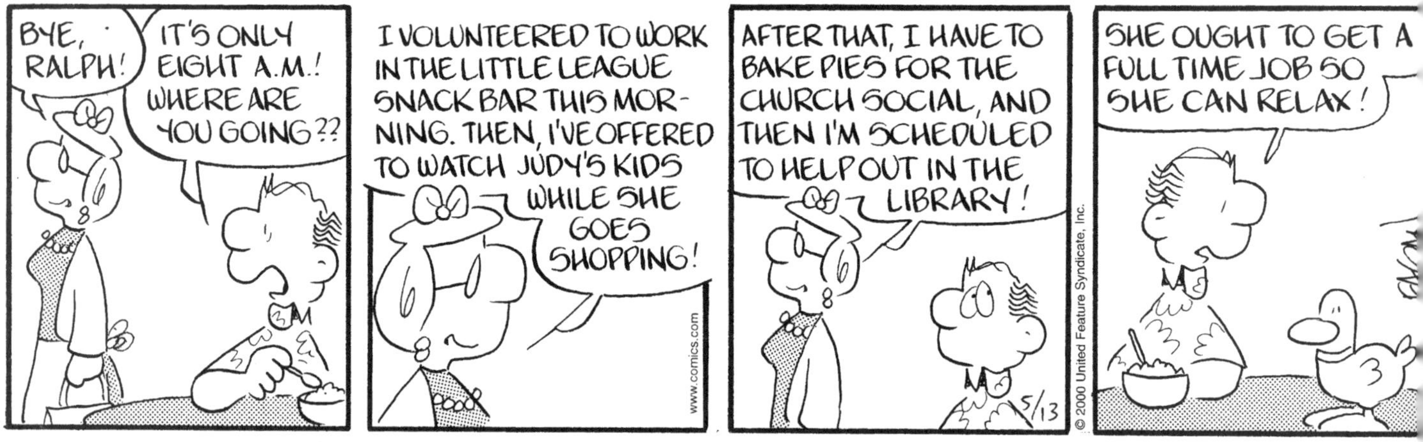
BYE, RALPH!
IT'S ONLY EIGHT A.M.! WHERE ARE YOU GOING??
I VOLUNTEERED TO WORK IN THE LITTLE LEAGUE SNACK BAR THIS MORNING. THEN, I'VE OFFERED TO WATCH JUDY'S KIDS WHILE SHE GOES SHOPPING!
www.comics.com
AFTER THAT, I HAVE TO BAKE PIES FOR THE CHURCH SOCIAL, AND THEN I'M SCHEDULED TO HELP OUT IN THE LIBRARY!
5/13
© 2000 United Feature Syndicate, Inc.
SHE OUGHT TO GET A FULL TIME JOB SO SHE CAN RELAX!

DRABBLE® By KEVIN FAGAN

HEY, NO-NECK, CHECK OUT MY NEW CAR ALARM SYSTEM!
1-21
RATTLE THE DOOR AND SEE WHAT HAPPENS!
HONK HONK HONK
RRRRRRRRRRRRRRRRRRRRRRRRRR!
WHOOOP WHOOOP WHOOOP
BEEEEP BEEEEP BEEEEP BEEEEP
AH OOOO GUH!
© 2001 United Feature Syndicate, Inc.
THAT'S PRETTY GOOD! WHERE CAN I GET A SYSTEM LIKE THAT?
SORRY. IT'S A ONE-OF-A-KIND!
www.comics.com
DAD, CAN I HAVE THE REST OF THE DAY OFF? I'M GETTING A LITTLE HOARSE!
FAGAN

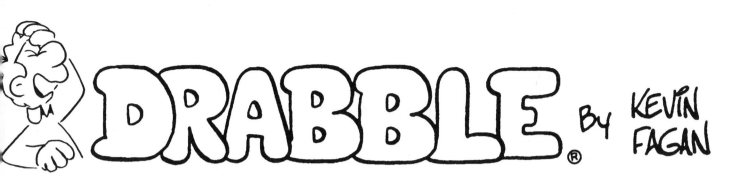

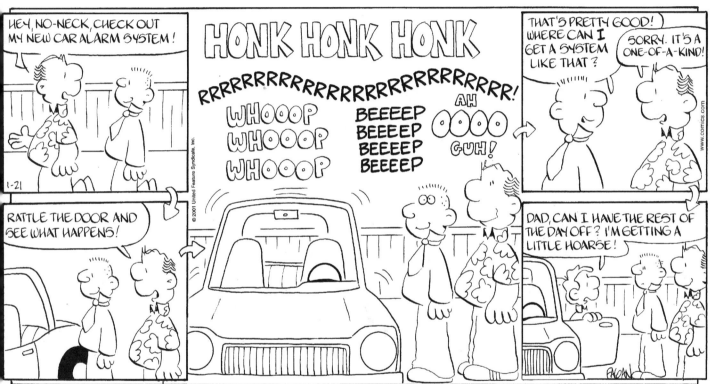

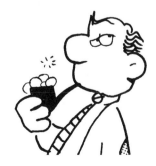

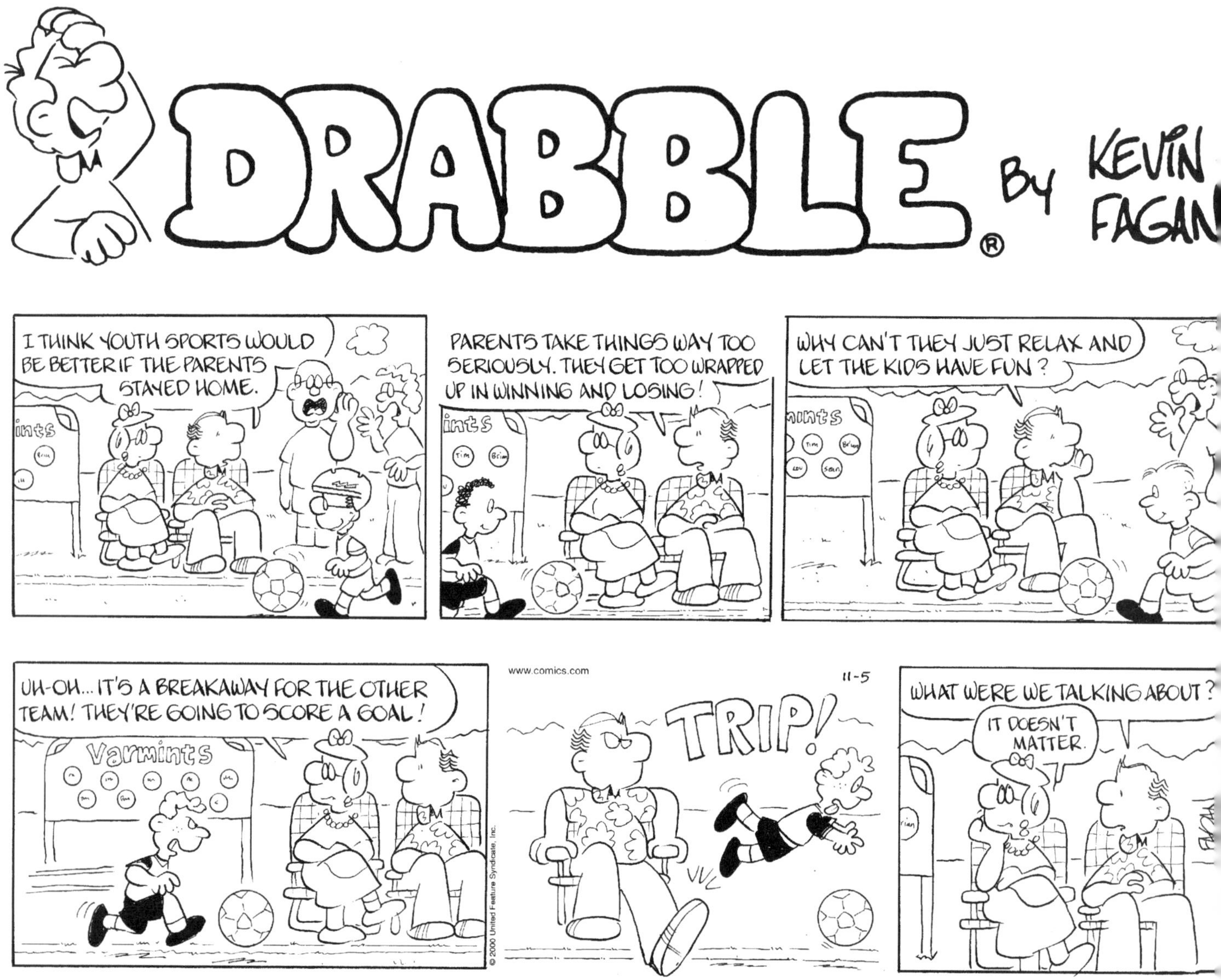
DRABBLE®
By KEVIN FAGAN
I THINK YOUTH SPORTS WOULD BE BETTER IF THE PARENTS STAYED HOME.
PARENTS TAKE THINGS WAY TOO SERIOUSLY. THEY GET TOO WRAPPED UP IN WINNING AND LOSING!
WHY CAN'T THEY JUST RELAX AND LET THE KIDS HAVE FUN?
UH-OH... IT'S A BREAKAWAY FOR THE OTHER TEAM! THEY'RE GOING TO SCORE A GOAL!
Varmints
www.comics.com
11-5
© 2000 United Feature Syndicate, Inc.
TRIP!
WHAT WERE WE TALKING ABOUT?
IT DOESN'T MATTER.

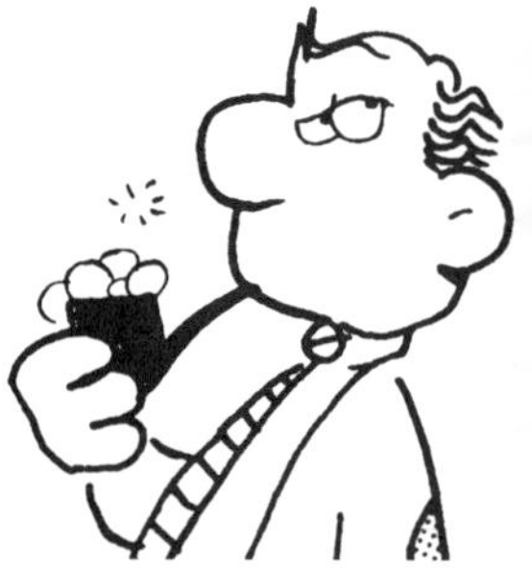

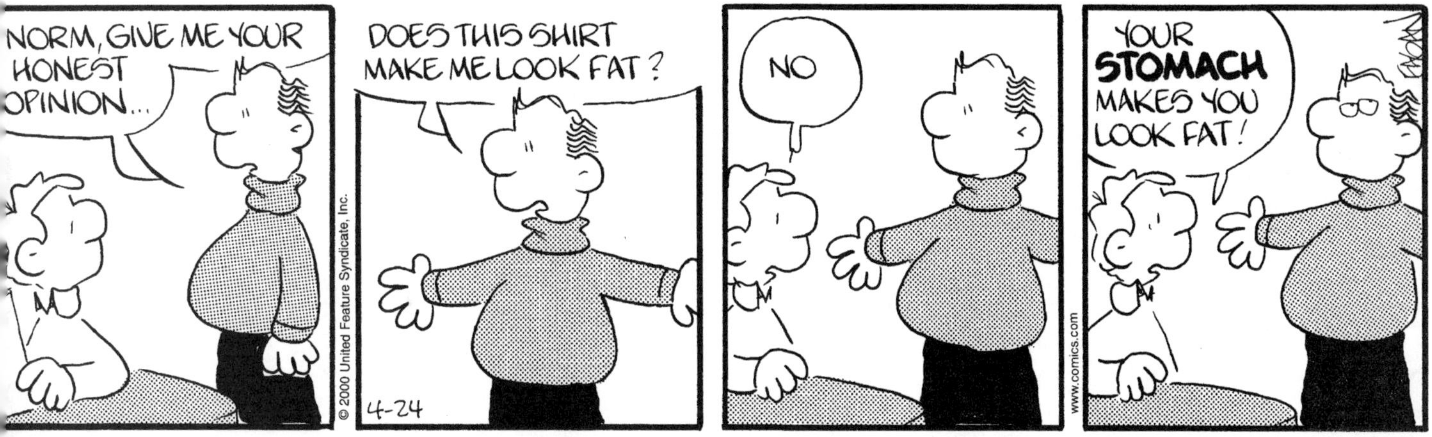
NORM, GIVE ME YOUR HONEST OPINION...
DOES THIS SHIRT MAKE ME LOOK FAT?
© 2000 United Feature Syndicate, Inc.
4-24
NO
YOUR STOMACH MAKES YOU LOOK FAT!
www.comics.com

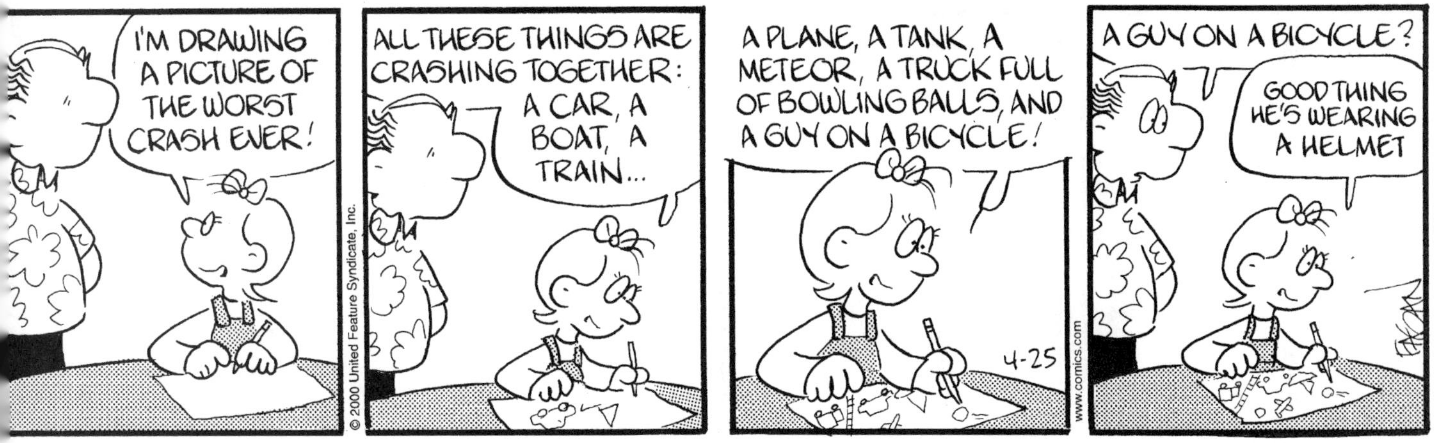
I'M DRAWING A PICTURE OF THE WORST CRASH EVER!
© 2000 United Feature Syndicate, Inc.
ALL THESE THINGS ARE CRASHING TOGETHER:
A CAR, A BOAT, A TRAIN...
A PLANE, A TANK, A METEOR, A TRUCK FULL OF BOWLING BALLS, AND A GUY ON A BICYCLE!
4-25
www.comics.com
A GUY ON A BICYCLE?
GOOD THING HE'S WEARING A HELMET

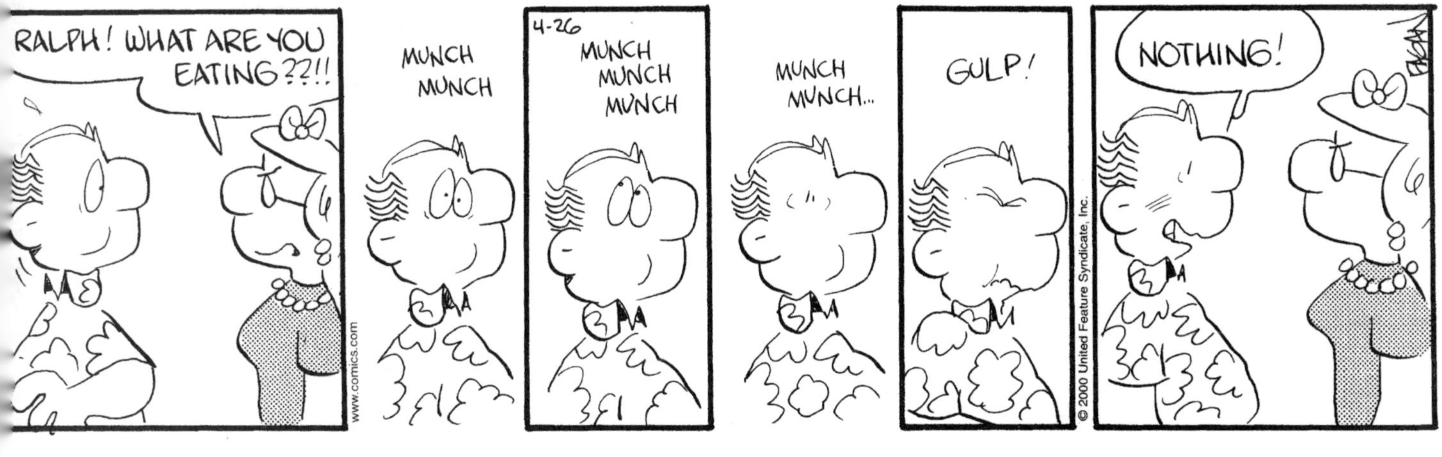
RALPH! WHAT ARE YOU EATING??!!
www.comics.com
MUNCH MUNCH
4-26
MUNCH MUNCH MUNCH
MUNCH MUNCH...
GULP!
© 2000 United Feature Syndicate, Inc.
NOTHING!

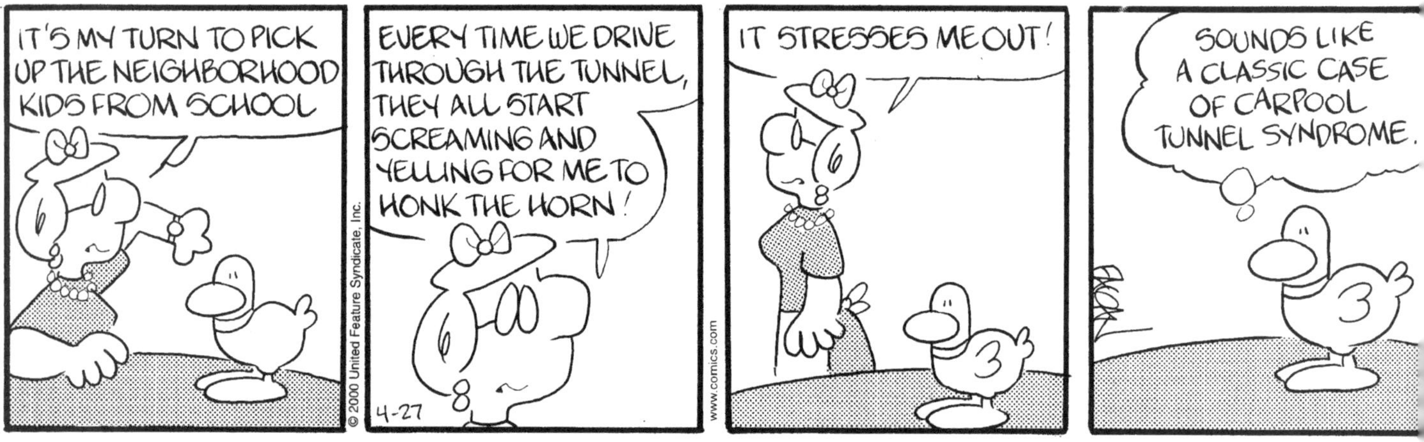
IT'S MY TURN TO PICK UP THE NEIGHBORHOOD KIDS FROM SCHOOL
EVERY TIME WE DRIVE THROUGH THE TUNNEL, THEY ALL START SCREAMING AND YELLING FOR ME TO HONK THE HORN!
© 2000 United Feature Syndicate, Inc.
4-27
IT STRESSES ME OUT!
www.comics.com
SOUNDS LIKE A CLASSIC CASE OF CARPOOL TUNNEL SYNDROME.

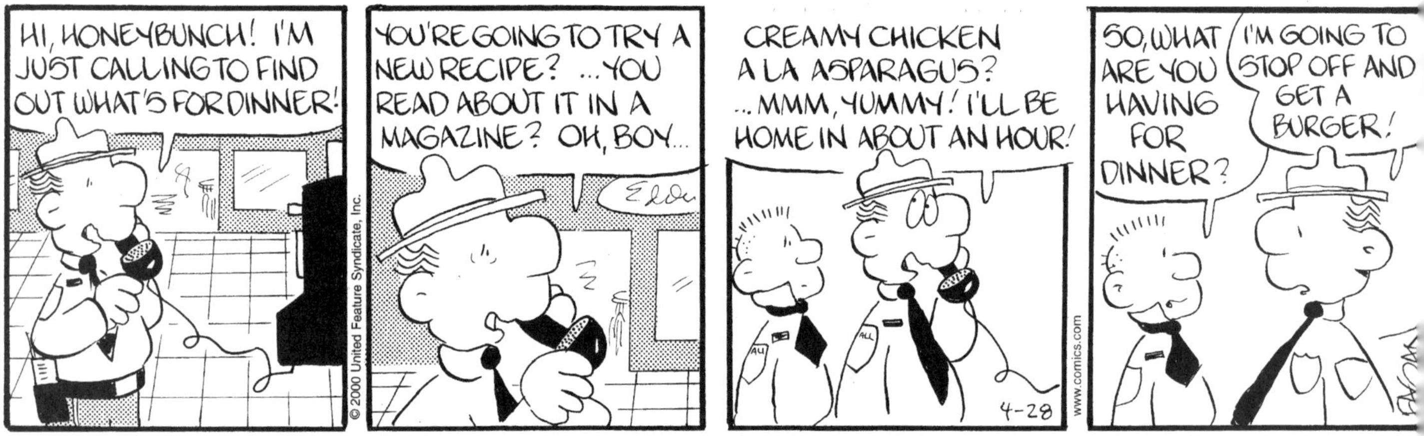
HI, HONEYBUNCH! I'M JUST CALLING TO FIND OUT WHAT'S FOR DINNER!
YOU'RE GOING TO TRY A NEW RECIPE? ...YOU READ ABOUT IT IN A MAGAZINE? OH, BOY...
© 2000 United Feature Syndicate, Inc.
CREAMY CHICKEN A LA ASPARAGUS? ...MMM, YUMMY! I'LL BE HOME IN ABOUT AN HOUR!
4-28
www.comics.com
SO, WHAT ARE YOU HAVING FOR DINNER?
I'M GOING TO STOP OFF AND GET A BURGER!

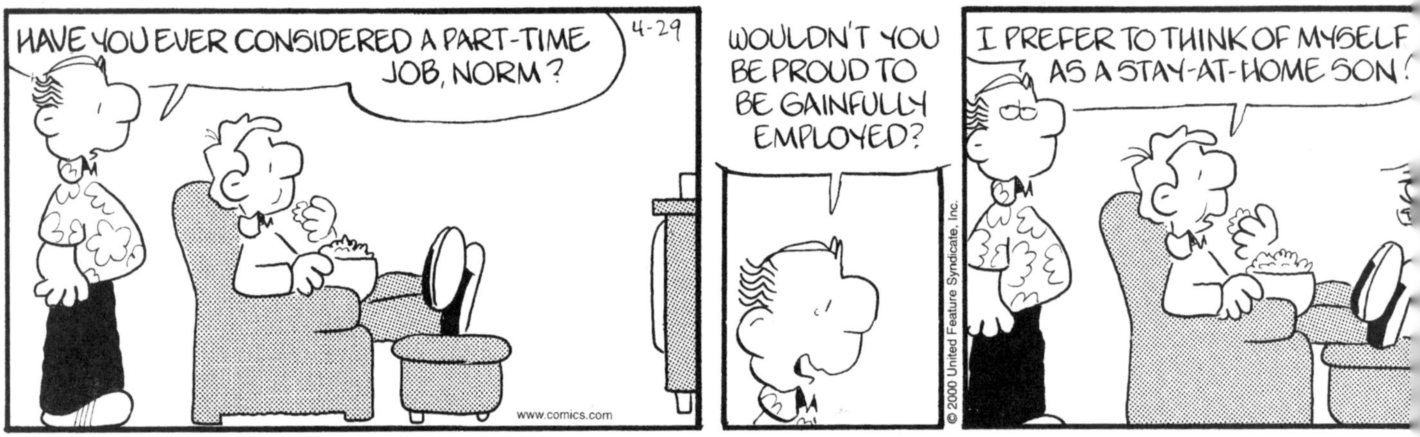
HAVE YOU EVER CONSIDERED A PART-TIME JOB, NORM?
4-29
www.comics.com
WOULDN'T YOU BE PROUD TO BE GAINFULLY EMPLOYED?
© 2000 United Feature Syndicate, Inc.
I PREFER TO THINK OF MYSELF AS A STAY-AT-HOME SON!

DRABBLE ® BY KEVIN FAGAN

Panel 1: HELLO, IS THIS NEWSRADIO'S TRAFFIC HOTLINE? TIPSTER DRABBLE, HERE!

Panel 2: I JUST TURNED ONTO MAIN STREET, AND I FIND MYSELF IN THE MIDDLE OF A SERIOUS TRAFFIC PROBLEM!

Panel 3: THERE'S BEDLAM IN THE STREET! PEOPLE ARE SITTING ATOP THEIR CARS, ANIMALS RUNNING LOOSE... I EVEN SEE A LARGE BAND OF TEENAGERS ON FOOT! TRAFFIC IS MOVING AT A SNAIL'S PACE!

www.comics.com

Panel 4: ...THAT'S RIGHT, MAIN STREET! ...YES... OH, REALLY? ...I AM? ...OH... OK... NEVER MIND... `BYE.

11-19

© 2000 United Feature Syndicate, Inc.

MAYOR JOHNSON

Panel 5: STUPID PARADE!

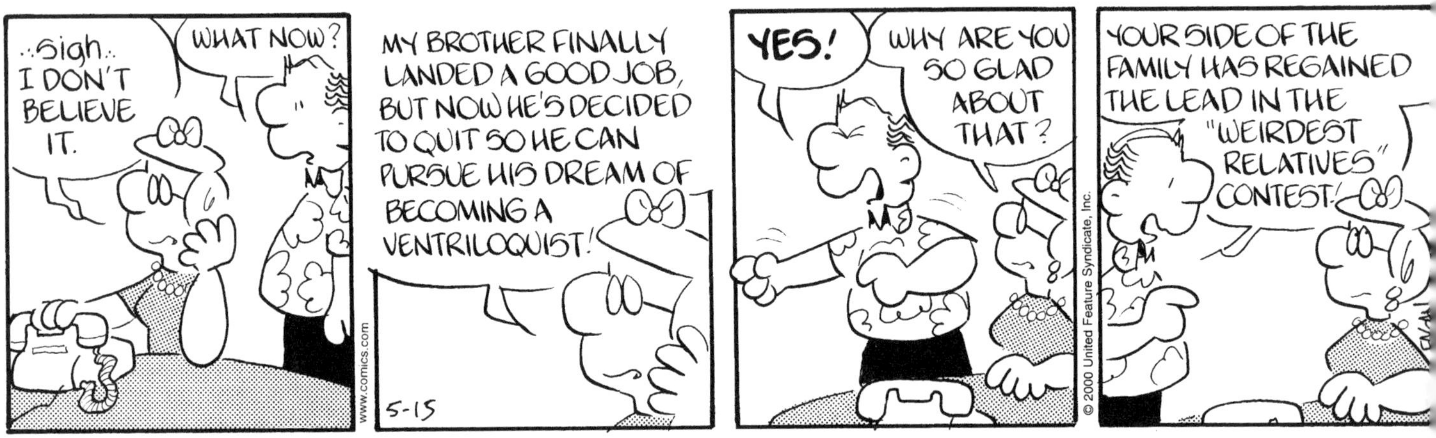
..sigh.. I DON'T BELIEVE IT.
WHAT NOW?
www.comics.com
MY BROTHER FINALLY LANDED A GOOD JOB, BUT NOW HE'S DECIDED TO QUIT SO HE CAN PURSUE HIS DREAM OF BECOMING A VENTRILOQUIST!
5-15
YES!
WHY ARE YOU SO GLAD ABOUT THAT?
© 2000 United Feature Syndicate, Inc.
YOUR SIDE OF THE FAMILY HAS REGAINED THE LEAD IN THE "WEIRDEST RELATIVES" CONTEST!

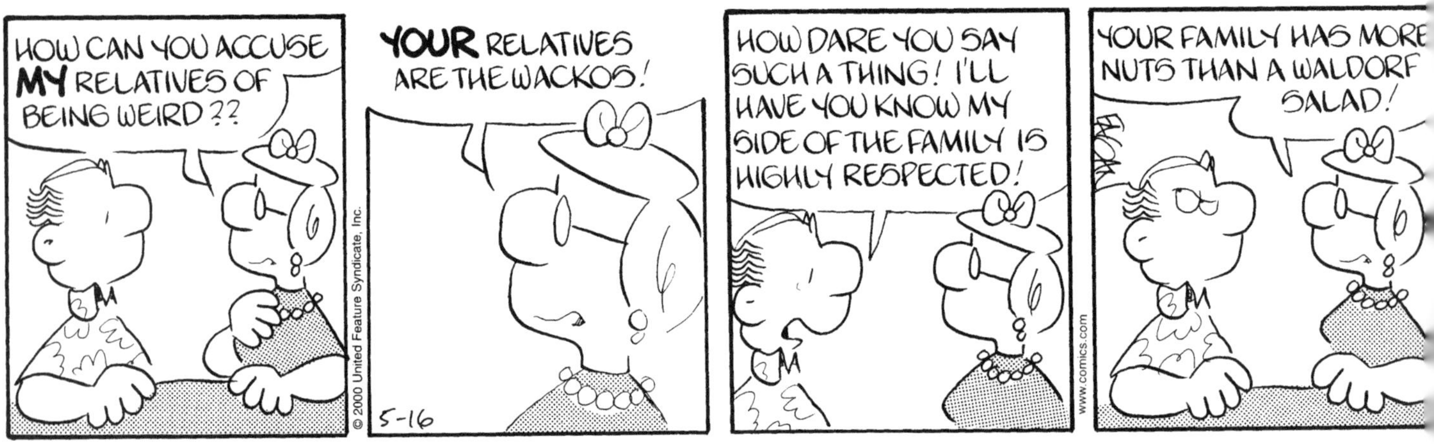
HOW CAN YOU ACCUSE **MY** RELATIVES OF BEING WEIRD??
© 2000 United Feature Syndicate, Inc.
YOUR RELATIVES ARE THE WACKOS!
5-16
HOW DARE YOU SAY SUCH A THING! I'LL HAVE YOU KNOW MY SIDE OF THE FAMILY IS HIGHLY RESPECTED!
www.comics.com
YOUR FAMILY HAS MORE NUTS THAN A WALDORF SALAD!

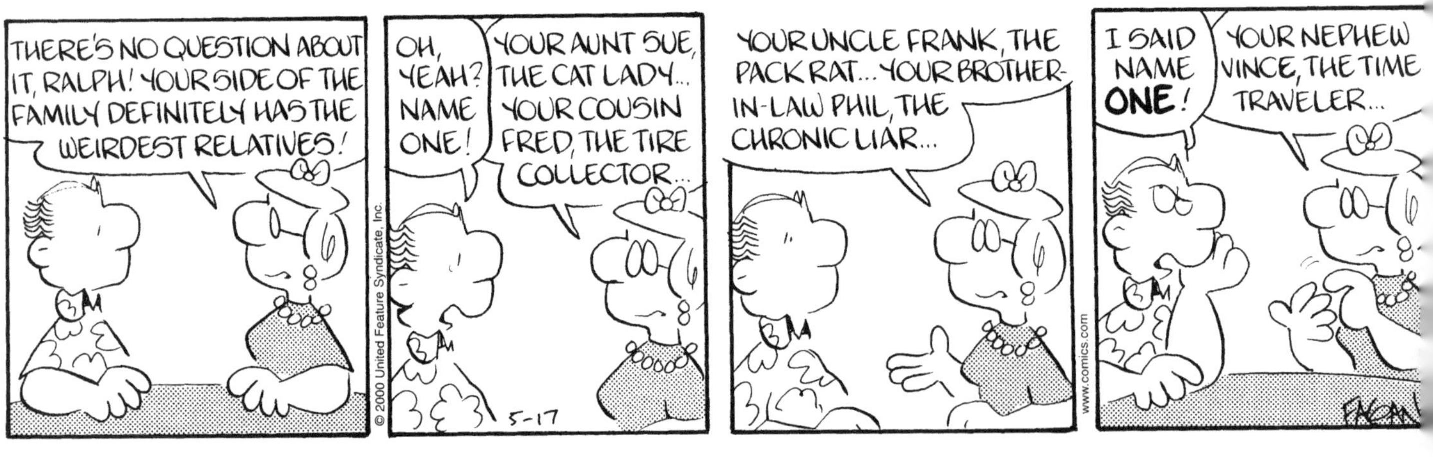
THERE'S NO QUESTION ABOUT IT, RALPH! YOUR SIDE OF THE FAMILY DEFINITELY HAS THE WEIRDEST RELATIVES!
© 2000 United Feature Syndicate, Inc.
OH, YEAH? NAME ONE!
YOUR AUNT SUE, THE CAT LADY... YOUR COUSIN FRED, THE TIRE COLLECTOR...
5-17
YOUR UNCLE FRANK, THE PACK RAT... YOUR BROTHER-IN-LAW PHIL, THE CHRONIC LIAR...
www.comics.com
I SAID NAME **ONE**!
YOUR NEPHEW VINCE, THE TIME TRAVELER...
FAGAN

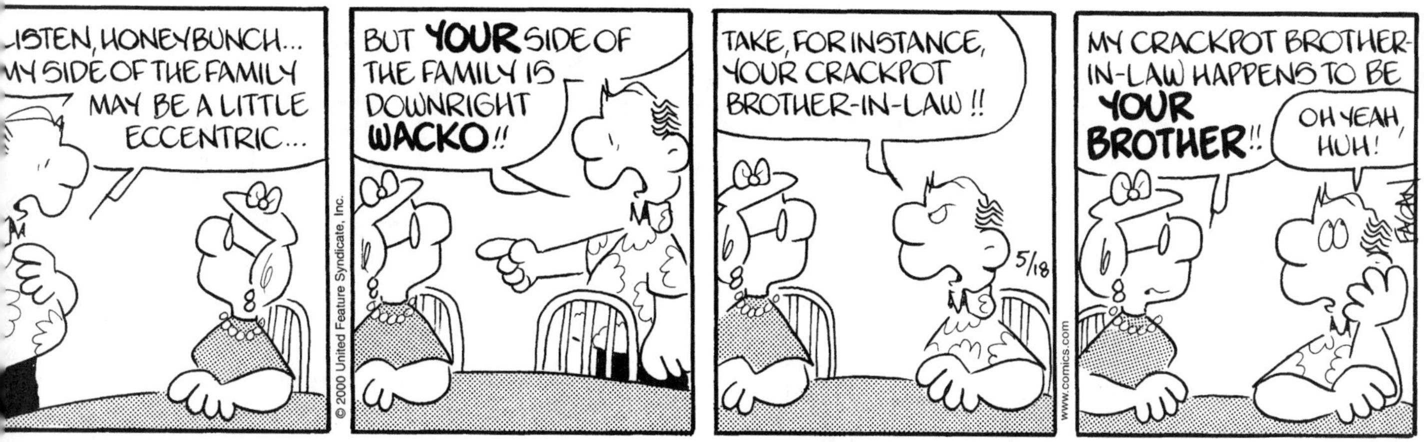
ISTEN, HONEYBUNCH... MY SIDE OF THE FAMILY MAY BE A LITTLE ECCENTRIC...
© 2000 United Feature Syndicate, Inc.
BUT YOUR SIDE OF THE FAMILY IS DOWNRIGHT WACKO!!
TAKE, FOR INSTANCE, YOUR CRACKPOT BROTHER-IN-LAW!!
5/18
www.comics.com
MY CRACKPOT BROTHER-IN-LAW HAPPENS TO BE YOUR BROTHER!!
OH YEAH, HUH!

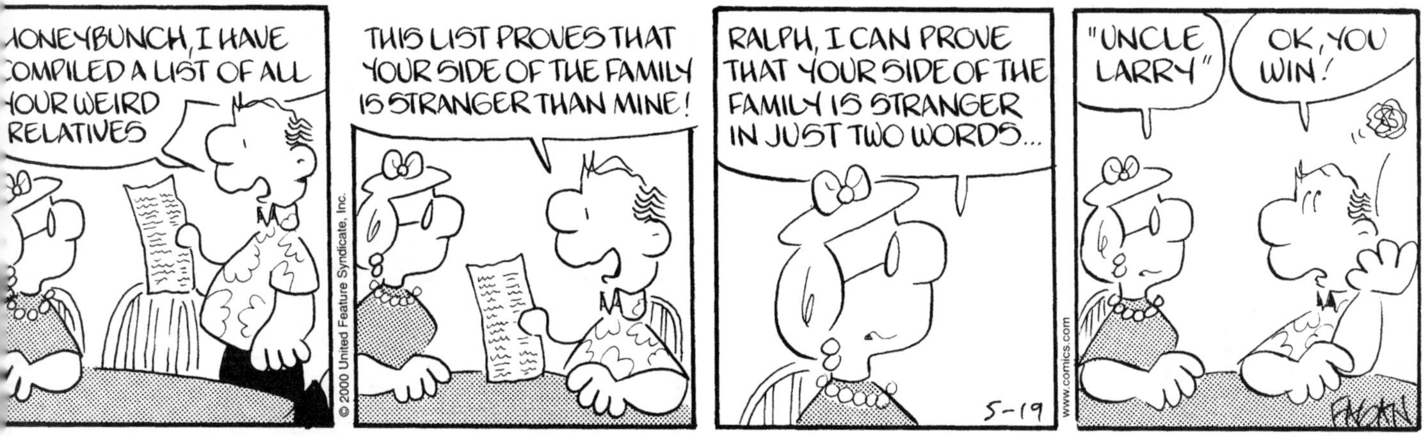
ONEYBUNCH, I HAVE COMPILED A LIST OF ALL YOUR WEIRD RELATIVES
© 2000 United Feature Syndicate, Inc.
THIS LIST PROVES THAT YOUR SIDE OF THE FAMILY IS STRANGER THAN MINE!
RALPH, I CAN PROVE THAT YOUR SIDE OF THE FAMILY IS STRANGER IN JUST TWO WORDS...
5-19
www.comics.com
"UNCLE LARRY"
OK, YOU WIN!

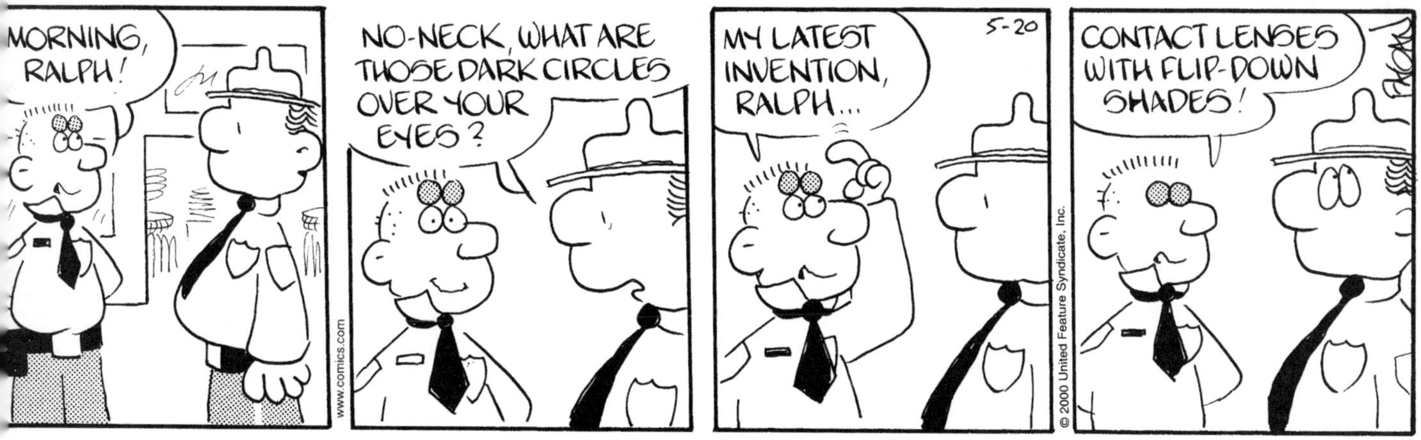
MORNING, RALPH!
www.comics.com
NO-NECK, WHAT ARE THOSE DARK CIRCLES OVER YOUR EYES?
MY LATEST INVENTION, RALPH...
5-20
© 2000 United Feature Syndicate, Inc.
CONTACT LENSES WITH FLIP-DOWN SHADES!

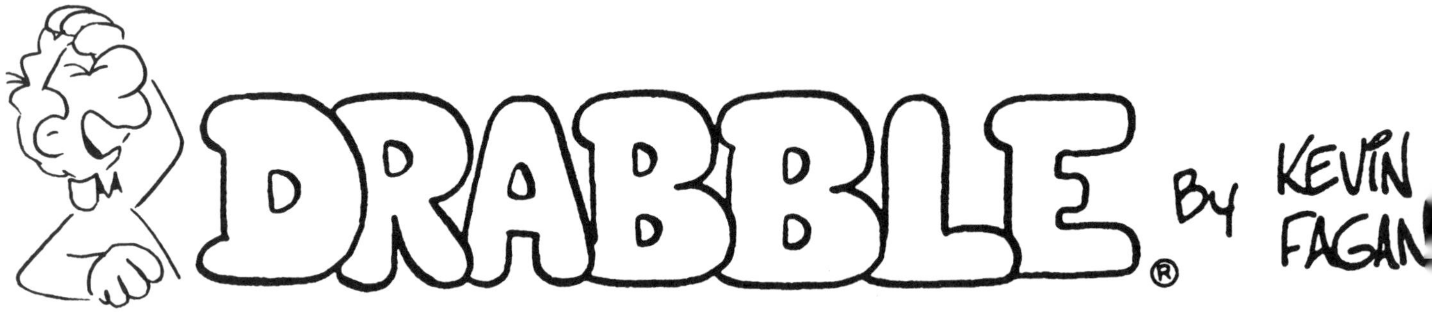
DRABBLE®
BY KEVIN FAGAN

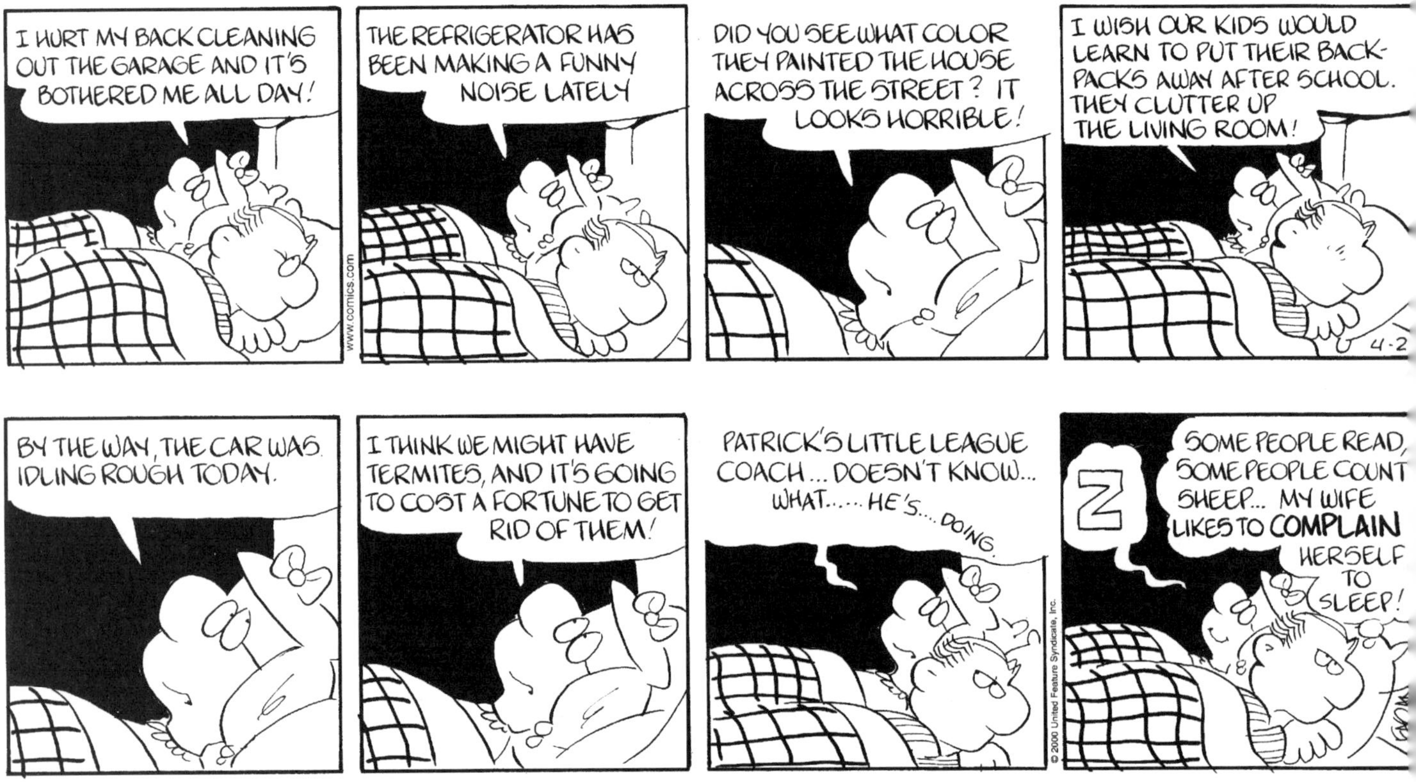
I HURT MY BACK CLEANING OUT THE GARAGE AND IT'S BOTHERED ME ALL DAY!
www.comics.com
THE REFRIGERATOR HAS BEEN MAKING A FUNNY NOISE LATELY
DID YOU SEE WHAT COLOR THEY PAINTED THE HOUSE ACROSS THE STREET? IT LOOKS HORRIBLE!
I WISH OUR KIDS WOULD LEARN TO PUT THEIR BACK-PACKS AWAY AFTER SCHOOL. THEY CLUTTER UP THE LIVING ROOM!
4-2
BY THE WAY, THE CAR WAS IDLING ROUGH TODAY.
I THINK WE MIGHT HAVE TERMITES, AND IT'S GOING TO COST A FORTUNE TO GET RID OF THEM!
PATRICK'S LITTLE LEAGUE COACH ... DOESN'T KNOW... WHAT...... HE'S..... DOING.
© 2000 United Feature Syndicate, Inc.
Z
SOME PEOPLE READ, SOME PEOPLE COUNT SHEEP... MY WIFE LIKES TO COMPLAIN HERSELF TO SLEEP!

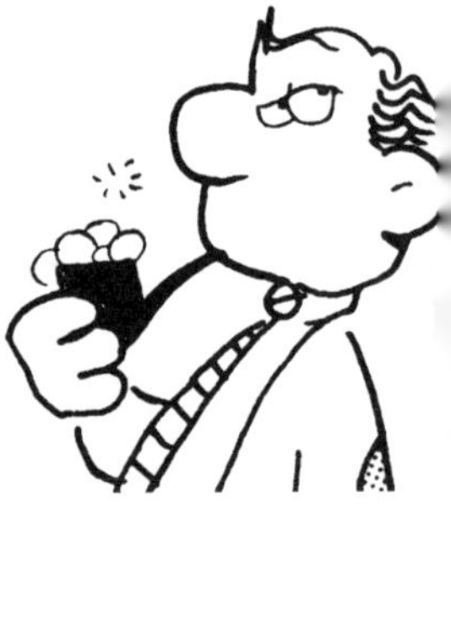

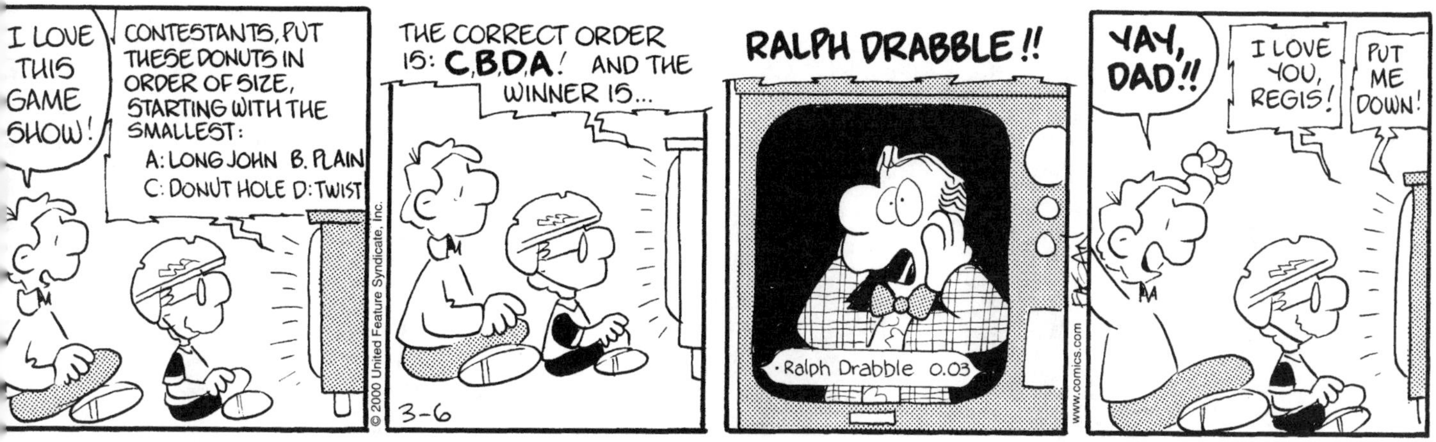
I LOVE THIS GAME SHOW!
CONTESTANTS, PUT THESE DONUTS IN ORDER OF SIZE, STARTING WITH THE SMALLEST:
A: LONG JOHN B. PLAIN
C: DONUT HOLE D: TWIST
© 2000 United Feature Syndicate, Inc.
THE CORRECT ORDER IS: C,B,D,A! AND THE WINNER IS...
3-6
RALPH DRABBLE!!
• Ralph Drabble 0.03
www.comics.com
YAY, DAD!!
I LOVE YOU, REGIS!
PUT ME DOWN!

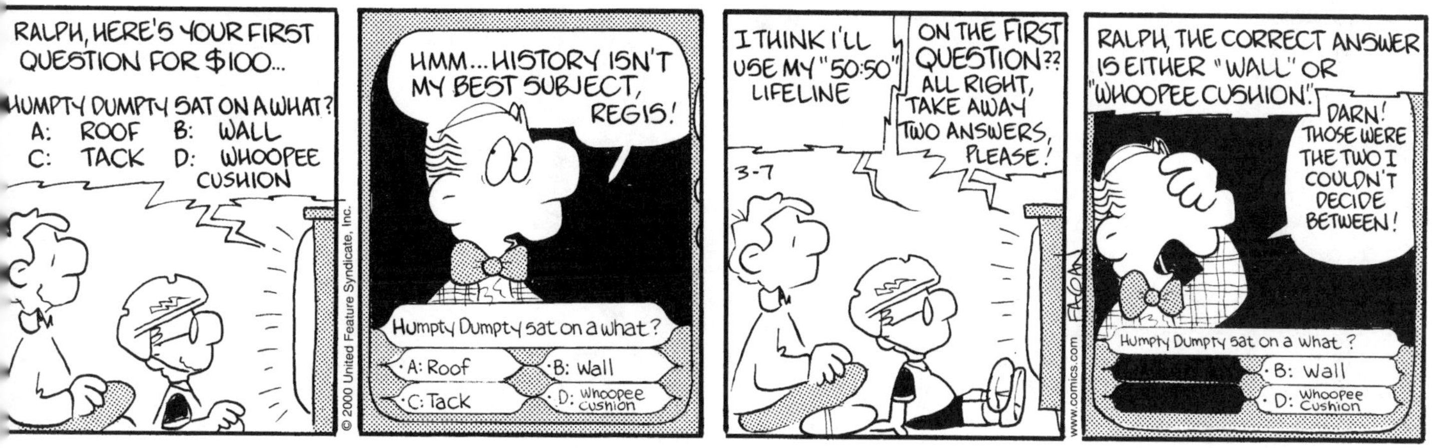
RALPH, HERE'S YOUR FIRST QUESTION FOR $100...
HUMPTY DUMPTY SAT ON A WHAT?
A: ROOF B: WALL
C: TACK D: WHOOPEE CUSHION
© 2000 United Feature Syndicate, Inc.
HMM... HISTORY ISN'T MY BEST SUBJECT, REGIS!
Humpty Dumpty sat on a what?
• A: Roof
• B: Wall
• C: Tack
• D: Whoopee Cushion
I THINK I'LL USE MY "50:50" LIFELINE
ON THE FIRST QUESTION?? ALL RIGHT, TAKE AWAY TWO ANSWERS, PLEASE!
3-7
www.comics.com
RALPH, THE CORRECT ANSWER IS EITHER "WALL" OR "WHOOPEE CUSHION".
DARN! THOSE WERE THE TWO I COULDN'T DECIDE BETWEEN!
Humpty Dumpty sat on a what?
• B: Wall
• D: Whoopee Cushion

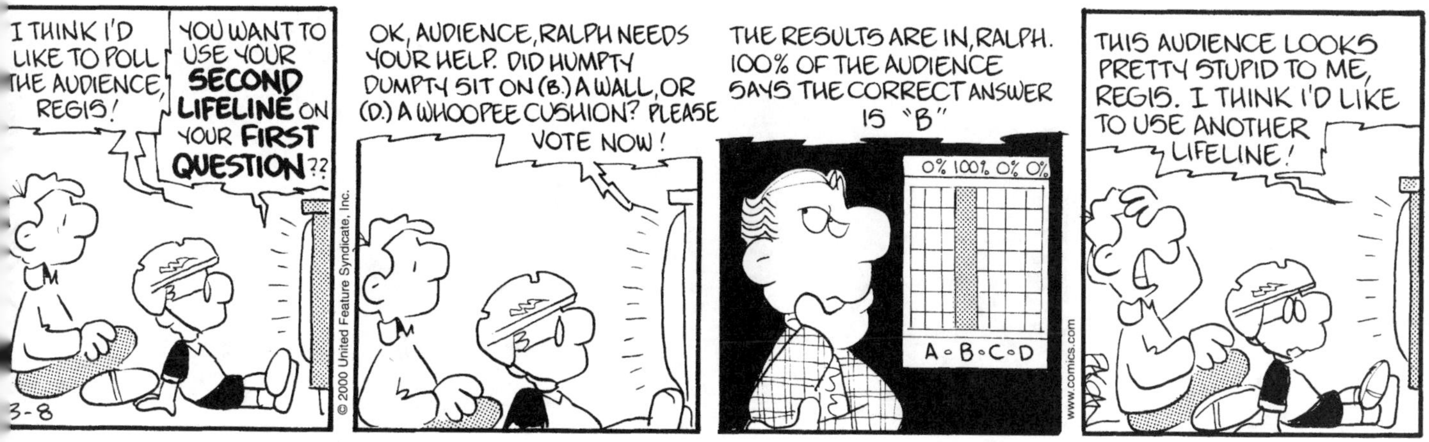
I THINK I'D LIKE TO POLL THE AUDIENCE, REGIS!
YOU WANT TO USE YOUR SECOND LIFELINE ON YOUR FIRST QUESTION??
3-8
© 2000 United Feature Syndicate, Inc.
OK, AUDIENCE, RALPH NEEDS YOUR HELP. DID HUMPTY DUMPTY SIT ON (B.) A WALL, OR (D.) A WHOOPEE CUSHION? PLEASE VOTE NOW!
THE RESULTS ARE IN, RALPH. 100% OF THE AUDIENCE SAYS THE CORRECT ANSWER IS "B"
0% 100% 0% 0%
A B C D
www.comics.com
THIS AUDIENCE LOOKS PRETTY STUPID TO ME, REGIS. I THINK I'D LIKE TO USE ANOTHER LIFELINE!

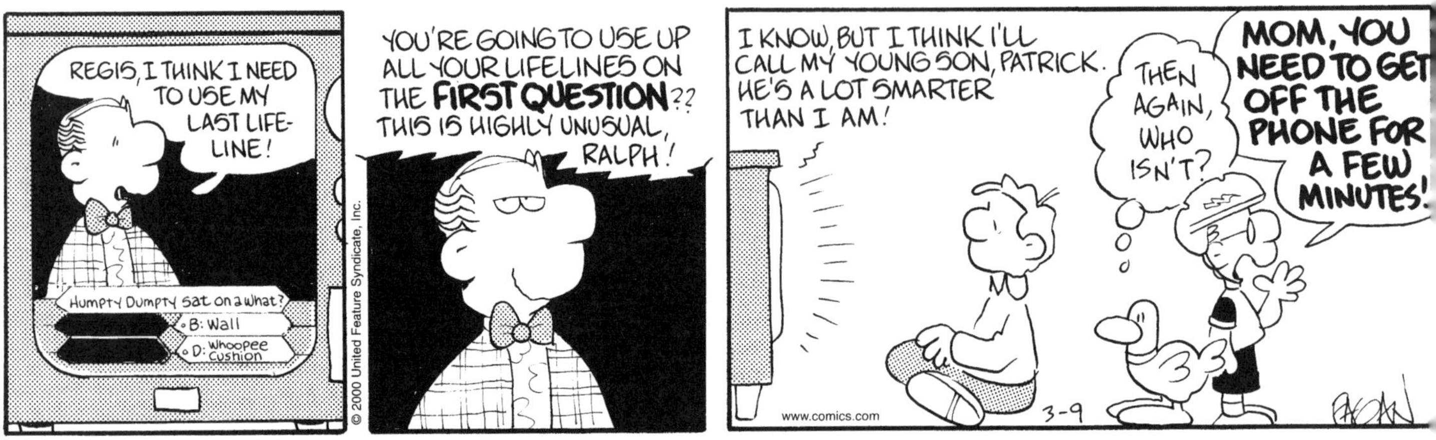
REGIS, I THINK I NEED TO USE MY LAST LIFE-LINE!
Humpty Dumpty sat on a what?
B: Wall
D: Whoopee Cushion
© 2000 United Feature Syndicate, Inc.
YOU'RE GOING TO USE UP ALL YOUR LIFELINES ON THE **FIRST QUESTION**?? THIS IS HIGHLY UNUSUAL, RALPH!
I KNOW, BUT I THINK I'LL CALL MY YOUNG SON, PATRICK. HE'S A LOT SMARTER THAN I AM!
THEN AGAIN, WHO ISN'T?
MOM, YOU NEED TO GET OFF THE PHONE FOR A FEW MINUTES!
www.comics.com
3-9
FAGAN

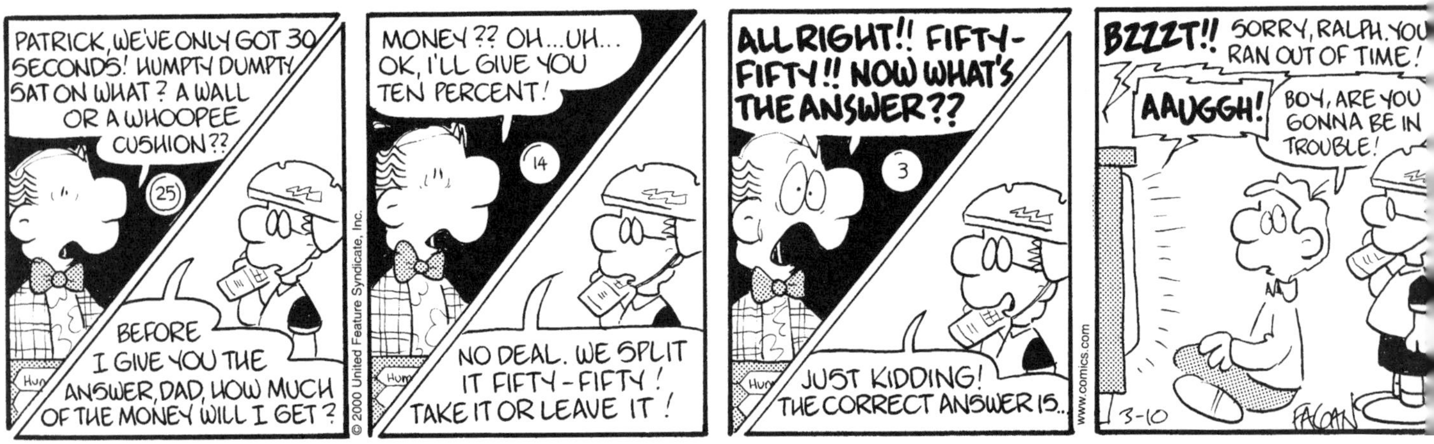
PATRICK, WE'VE ONLY GOT 30 SECONDS! HUMPTY DUMPTY SAT ON WHAT? A WALL OR A WHOOPEE CUSHION??
25
BEFORE I GIVE YOU THE ANSWER, DAD, HOW MUCH OF THE MONEY WILL I GET?
© 2000 United Feature Syndicate, Inc.
MONEY?? OH...UH... OK, I'LL GIVE YOU TEN PERCENT!
14
NO DEAL. WE SPLIT IT FIFTY-FIFTY! TAKE IT OR LEAVE IT!
ALL RIGHT!! FIFTY-FIFTY!! NOW WHAT'S THE ANSWER??
3
JUST KIDDING! THE CORRECT ANSWER IS...
www.comics.com
BZZZT!!
SORRY, RALPH. YOU RAN OUT OF TIME!
AAUGGH!
BOY, ARE YOU GONNA BE IN TROUBLE!
3-10
FAGAN

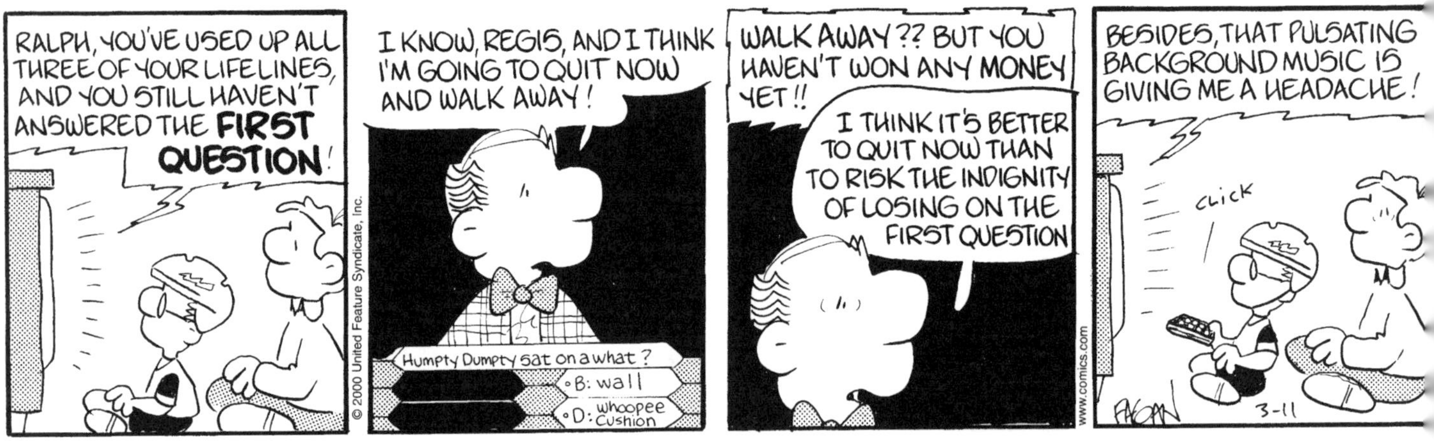
RALPH, YOU'VE USED UP ALL THREE OF YOUR LIFELINES, AND YOU STILL HAVEN'T ANSWERED THE **FIRST QUESTION**!
© 2000 United Feature Syndicate, Inc.
I KNOW, REGIS, AND I THINK I'M GOING TO QUIT NOW AND WALK AWAY!
Humpty Dumpty sat on a what?
B: wall
D: whoopee Cushion
WALK AWAY?? BUT YOU HAVEN'T WON ANY MONEY YET!!
I THINK IT'S BETTER TO QUIT NOW THAN TO RISK THE INDIGNITY OF LOSING ON THE FIRST QUESTION
www.comics.com
BESIDES, THAT PULSATING BACKGROUND MUSIC IS GIVING ME A HEADACHE!
CLICK
FAGAN
3-11

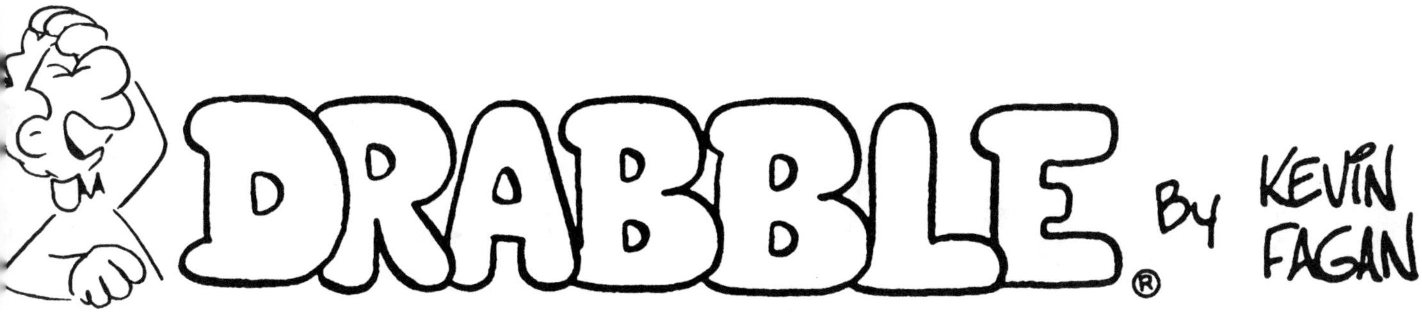
DRABBLE®
By KEVIN FAGAN

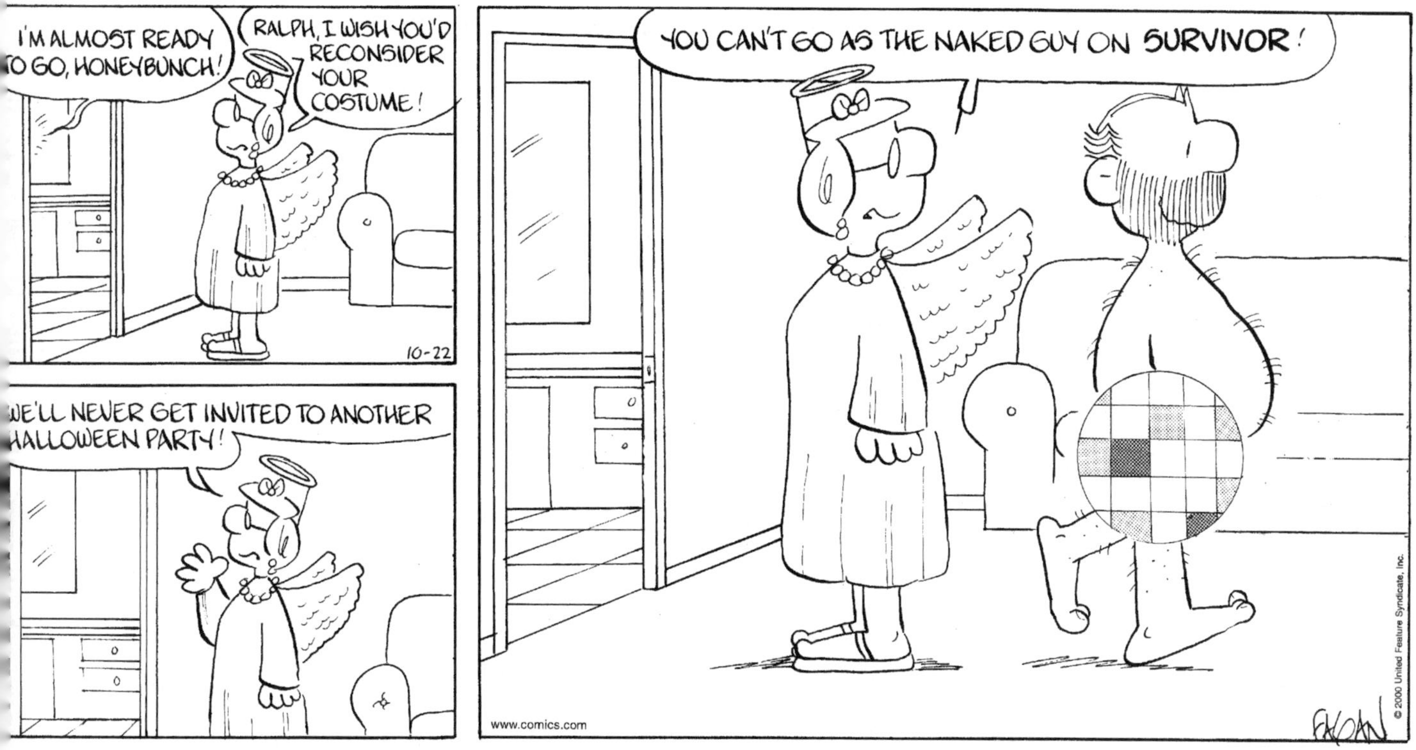
I'M ALMOST READY TO GO, HONEYBUNCH!
RALPH, I WISH YOU'D RECONSIDER YOUR COSTUME!
10-22
WE'LL NEVER GET INVITED TO ANOTHER HALLOWEEN PARTY!
YOU CAN'T GO AS THE NAKED GUY ON SURVIVOR!
www.comics.com
FAGAN
© 2000 United Feature Syndicate, Inc.

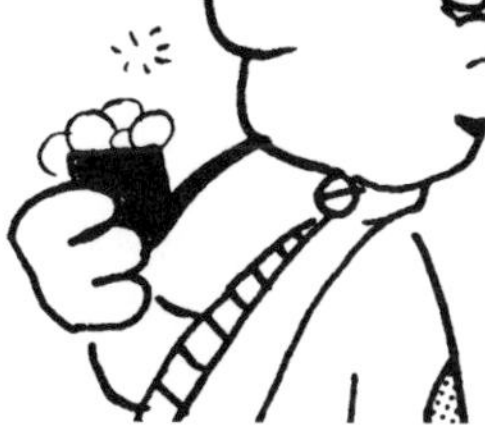

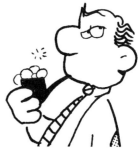

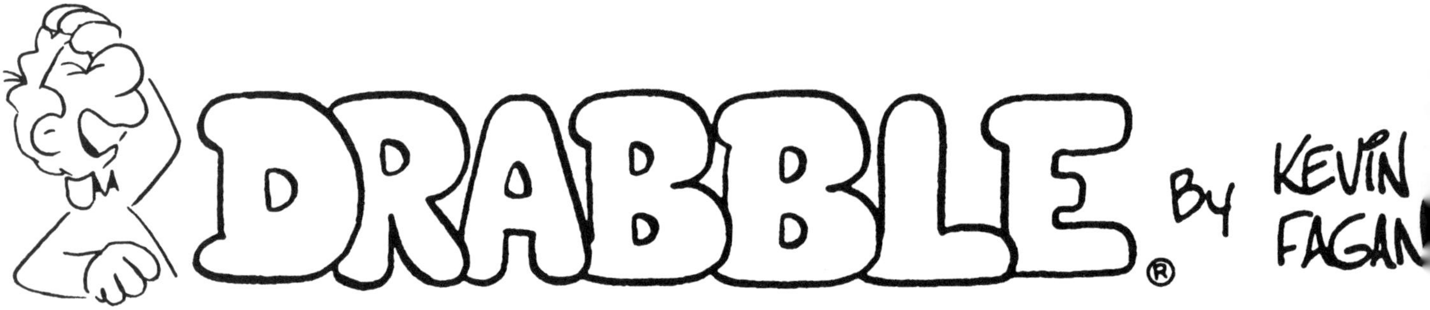
DRABBLE®
By KEVIN FAGAN

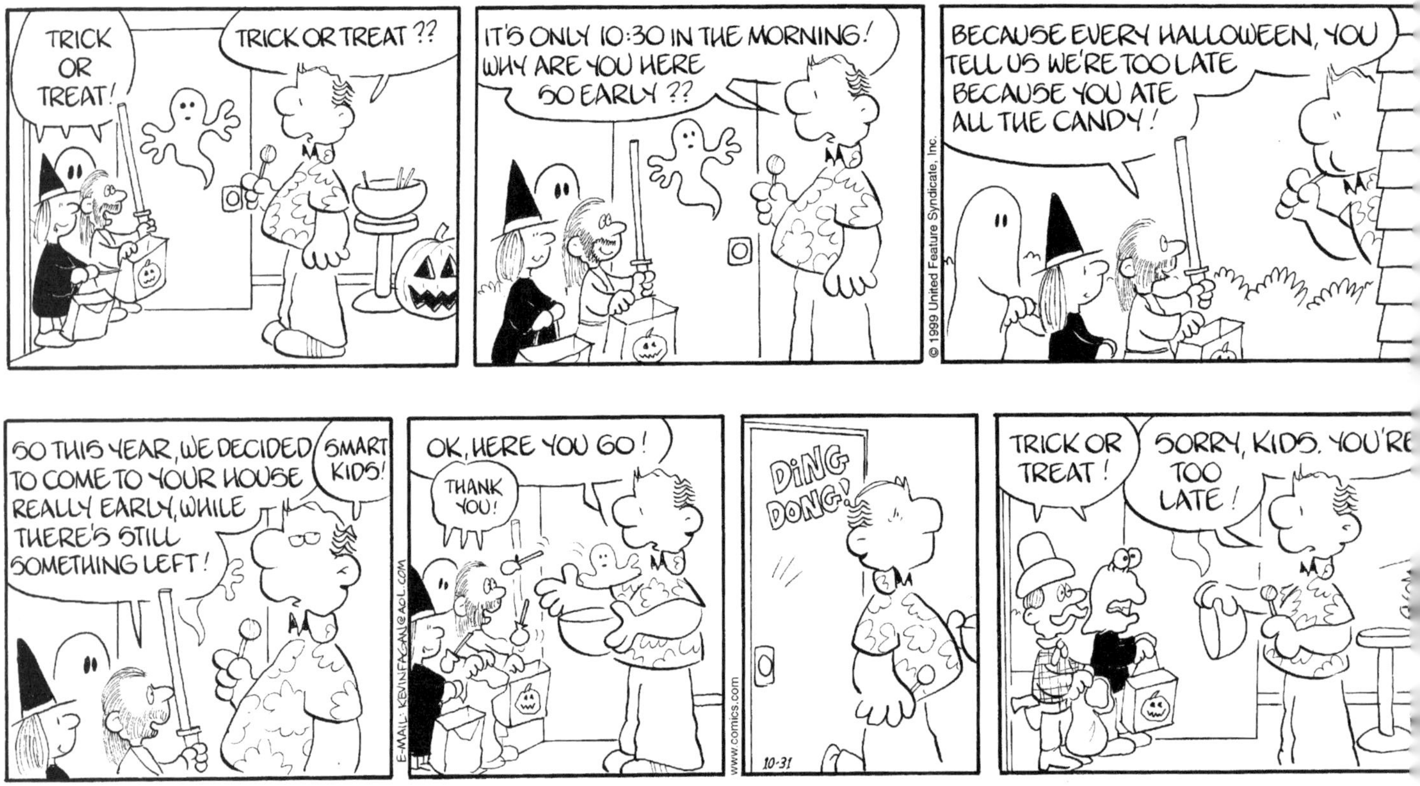
TRICK OR TREAT!
TRICK OR TREAT ??
IT'S ONLY 10:30 IN THE MORNING! WHY ARE YOU HERE SO EARLY ??
© 1999 United Feature Syndicate, Inc.
BECAUSE EVERY HALLOWEEN, YOU TELL US WE'RE TOO LATE BECAUSE YOU ATE ALL THE CANDY!
SO THIS YEAR, WE DECIDED TO COME TO YOUR HOUSE REALLY EARLY, WHILE THERE'S STILL SOMETHING LEFT!
SMART KIDS!
E-MAIL: KEVINFAGAN@AOL.COM
OK, HERE YOU GO!
THANK YOU!
www.comics.com
DING DONG!
10-31
TRICK OR TREAT!
SORRY, KIDS. YOU'RE TOO LATE!

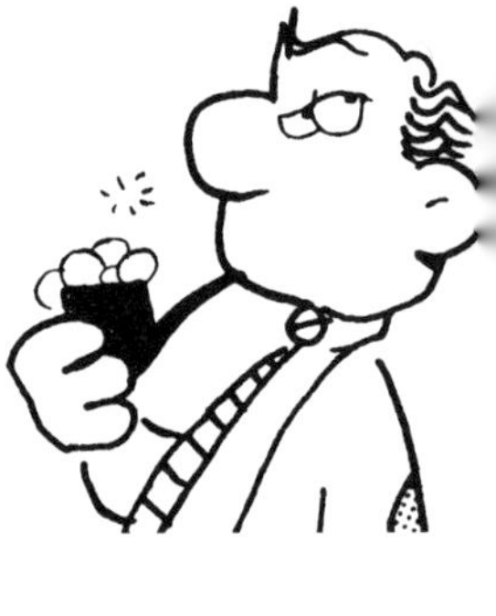

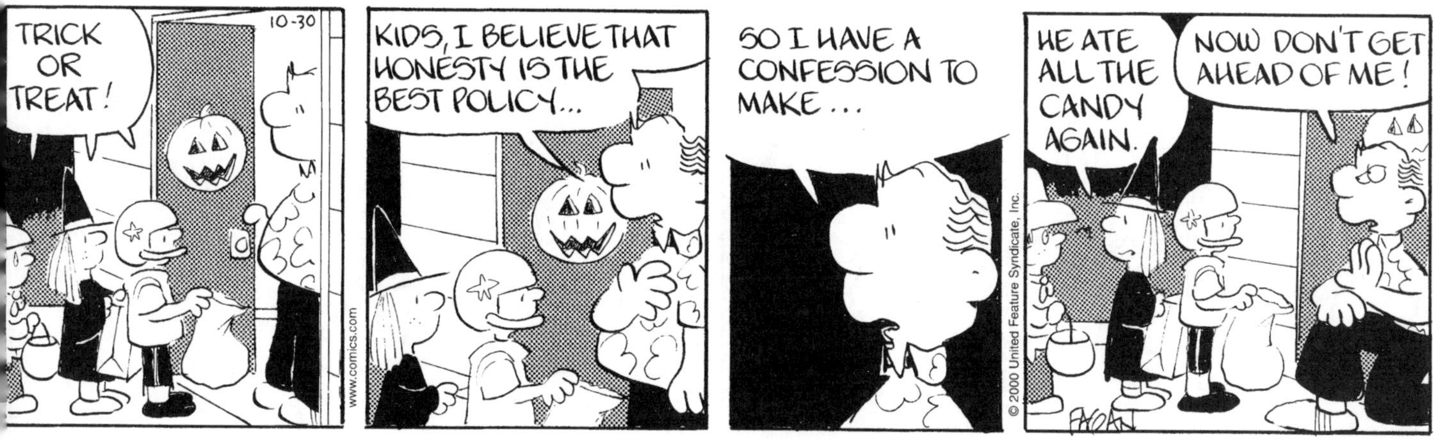
10-30
TRICK OR TREAT!
KIDS, I BELIEVE THAT HONESTY IS THE BEST POLICY...
SO I HAVE A CONFESSION TO MAKE...
HE ATE ALL THE CANDY AGAIN.
NOW DON'T GET AHEAD OF ME!
www.comics.com
© 2000 United Feature Syndicate, Inc.
FAGAN

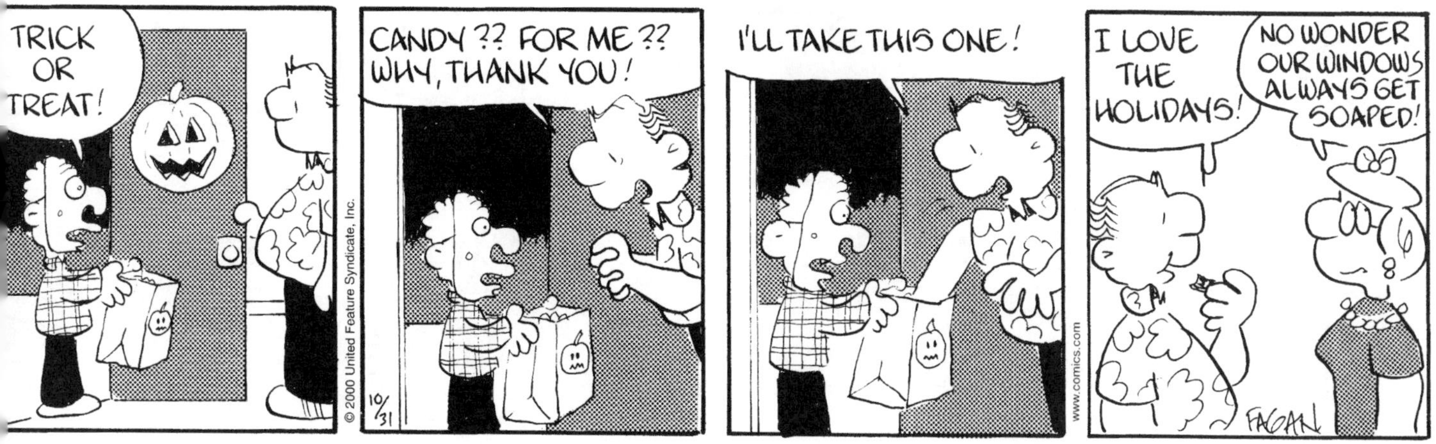
TRICK OR TREAT!
CANDY ?? FOR ME ?? WHY, THANK YOU!
I'LL TAKE THIS ONE!
I LOVE THE HOLIDAYS!
NO WONDER OUR WINDOWS ALWAYS GET SOAPED!
10/31
© 2000 United Feature Syndicate, Inc.
www.comics.com
FAGAN

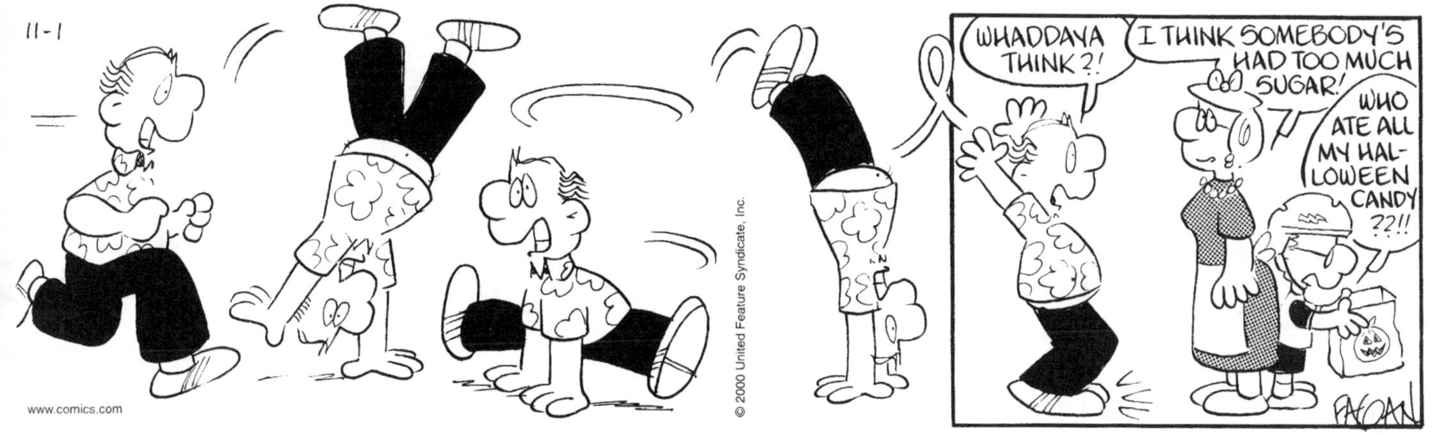
11-1
WHADDAYA THINK?!
I THINK SOMEBODY'S HAD TOO MUCH SUGAR!
WHO ATE ALL MY HALLOWEEN CANDY ??!!
www.comics.com
© 2000 United Feature Syndicate, Inc.
FAGAN

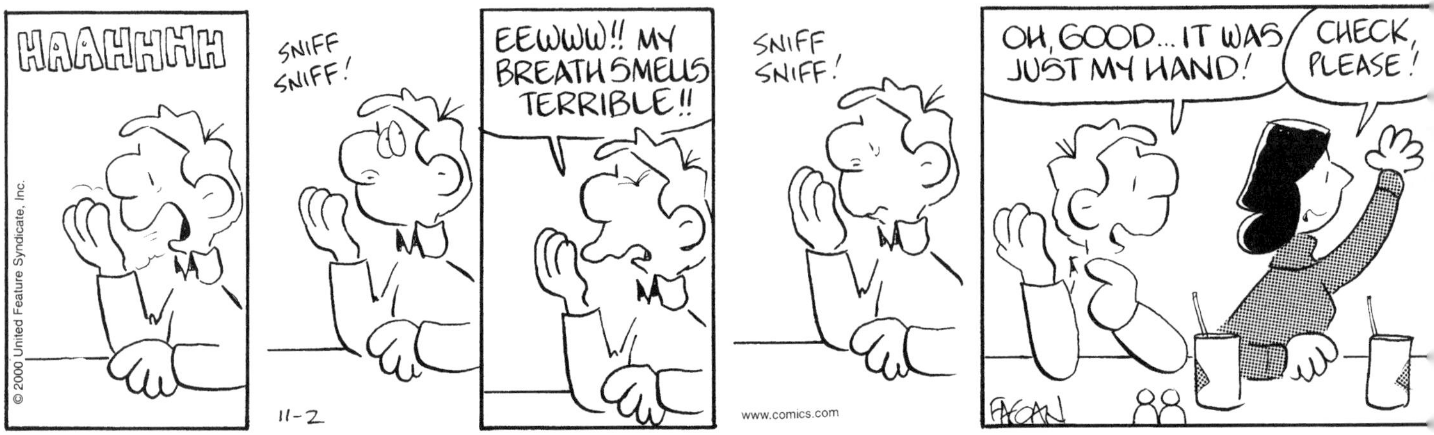
© 2000 United Feature Syndicate, Inc.
HAAHHHH
SNIFF SNIFF!
11-2
EEWWW!! MY BREATH SMELLS TERRIBLE!!
SNIFF SNIFF!
www.comics.com
OH, GOOD... IT WAS JUST MY HAND!
CHECK, PLEASE!
FAGAN

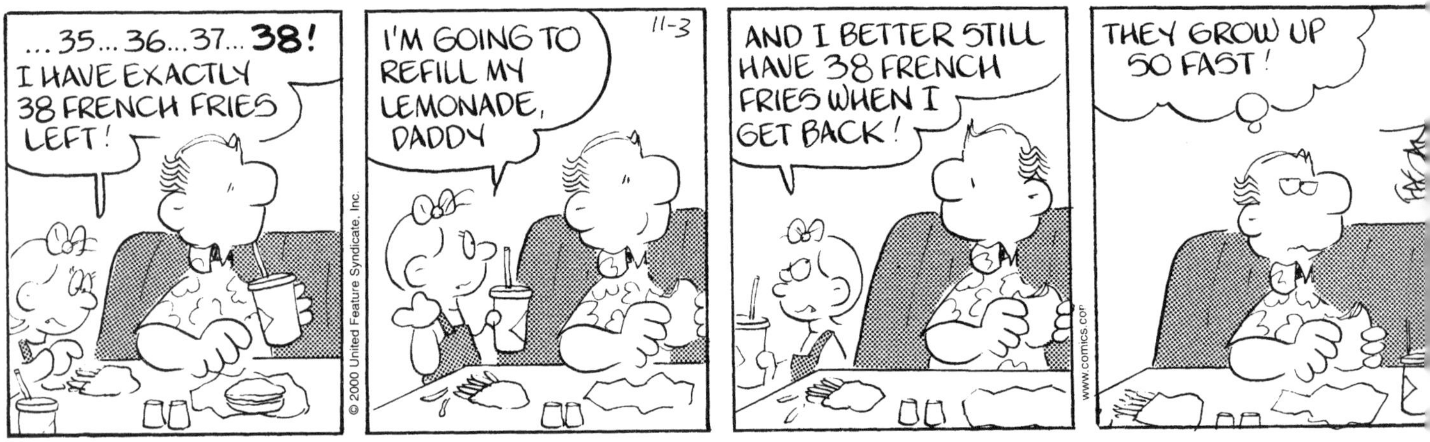
...35...36...37...38! I HAVE EXACTLY 38 FRENCH FRIES LEFT!
11-3
I'M GOING TO REFILL MY LEMONADE, DADDY
© 2000 United Feature Syndicate, Inc.
AND I BETTER STILL HAVE 38 FRENCH FRIES WHEN I GET BACK!
www.comics.com
THEY GROW UP SO FAST!

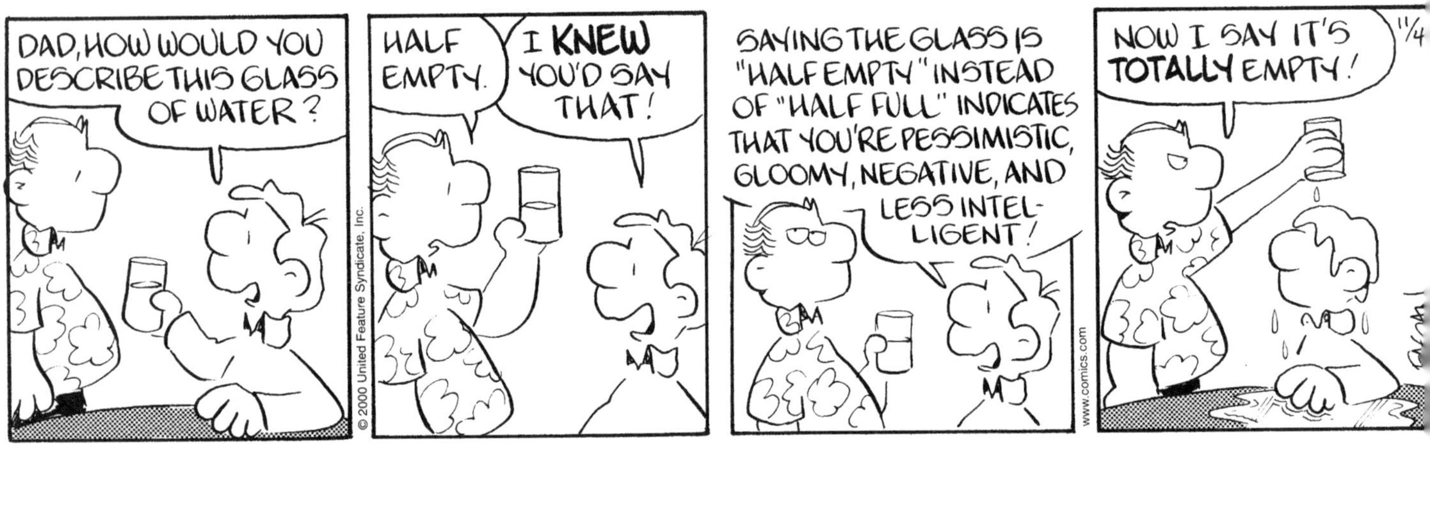
DAD, HOW WOULD YOU DESCRIBE THIS GLASS OF WATER?
HALF EMPTY.
I KNEW YOU'D SAY THAT!
© 2000 United Feature Syndicate, Inc.
SAYING THE GLASS IS "HALF EMPTY" INSTEAD OF "HALF FULL" INDICATES THAT YOU'RE PESSIMISTIC, GLOOMY, NEGATIVE, AND LESS INTELLIGENT!
www.comics.com
NOW I SAY IT'S TOTALLY EMPTY!

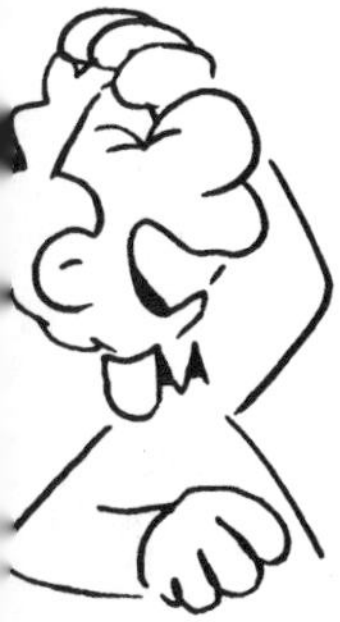

DRABBLE® By KEVIN FAGAN

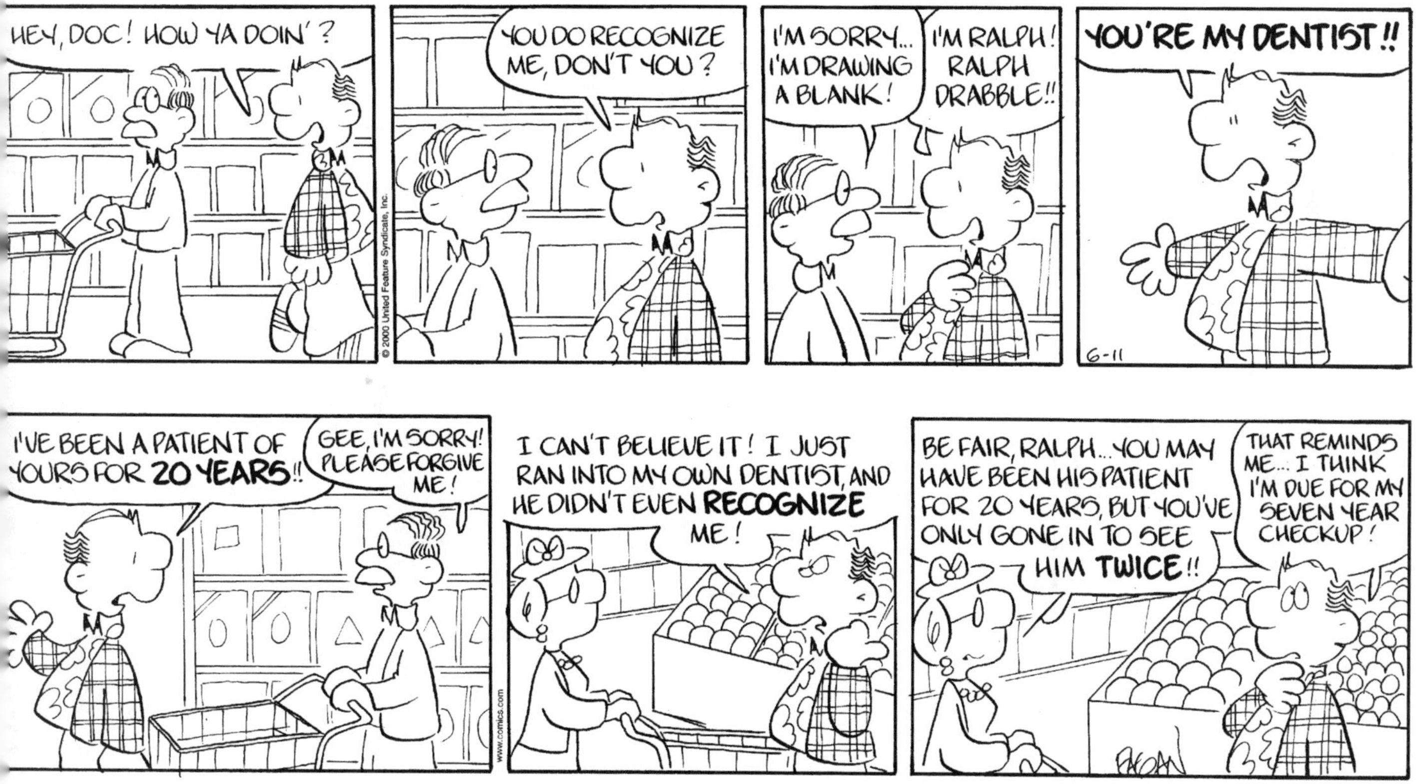

HEY, DOC! HOW YA DOIN'?
YOU DO RECOGNIZE ME, DON'T YOU?
I'M SORRY... I'M DRAWING A BLANK!
I'M RALPH! RALPH DRABBLE!!
YOU'RE MY DENTIST!!
6-11
© 2000 United Feature Syndicate, Inc.
I'VE BEEN A PATIENT OF YOURS FOR 20 YEARS!!
GEE, I'M SORRY! PLEASE FORGIVE ME!
www.comics.com
I CAN'T BELIEVE IT! I JUST RAN INTO MY OWN DENTIST, AND HE DIDN'T EVEN RECOGNIZE ME!
BE FAIR, RALPH... YOU MAY HAVE BEEN HIS PATIENT FOR 20 YEARS, BUT YOU'VE ONLY GONE IN TO SEE HIM TWICE!!
THAT REMINDS ME... I THINK I'M DUE FOR MY SEVEN YEAR CHECKUP!
FAGAN

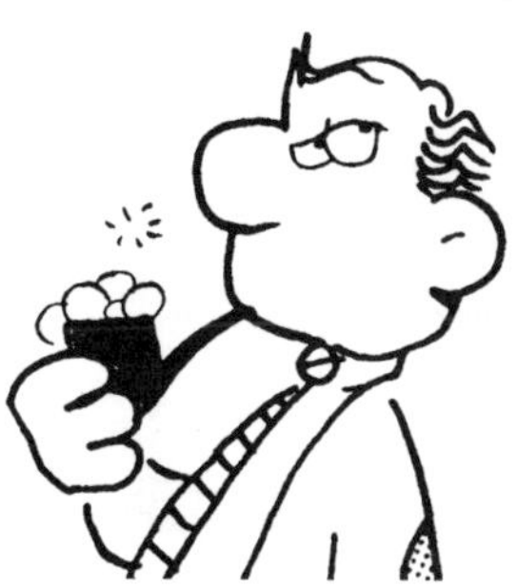

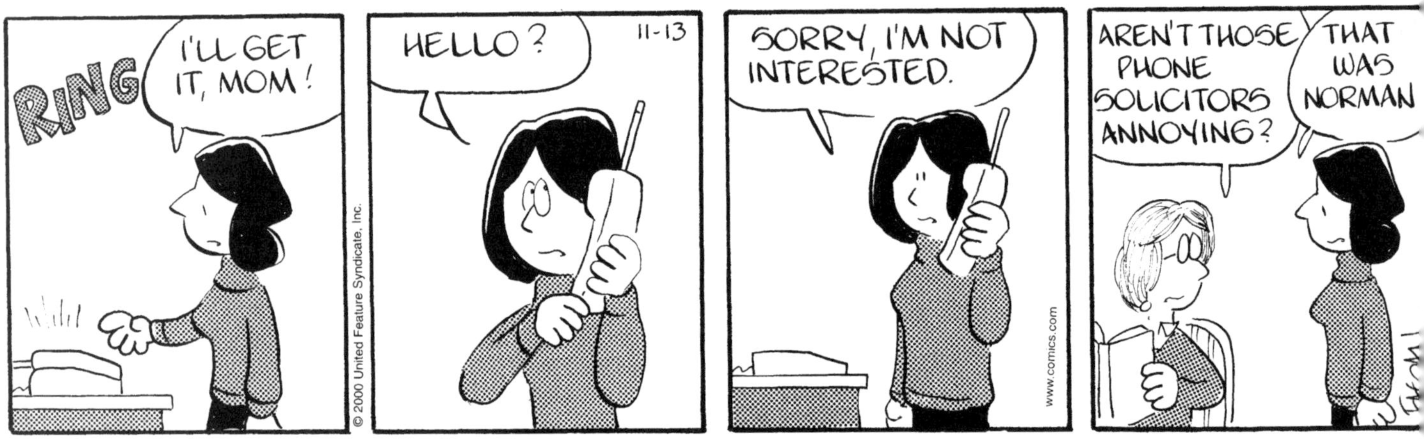
RING
I'LL GET IT, MOM!
HELLO?
11-13
© 2000 United Feature Syndicate, Inc.
SORRY, I'M NOT INTERESTED.
www.comics.com
AREN'T THOSE PHONE SOLICITORS ANNOYING?
THAT WAS NORMAN

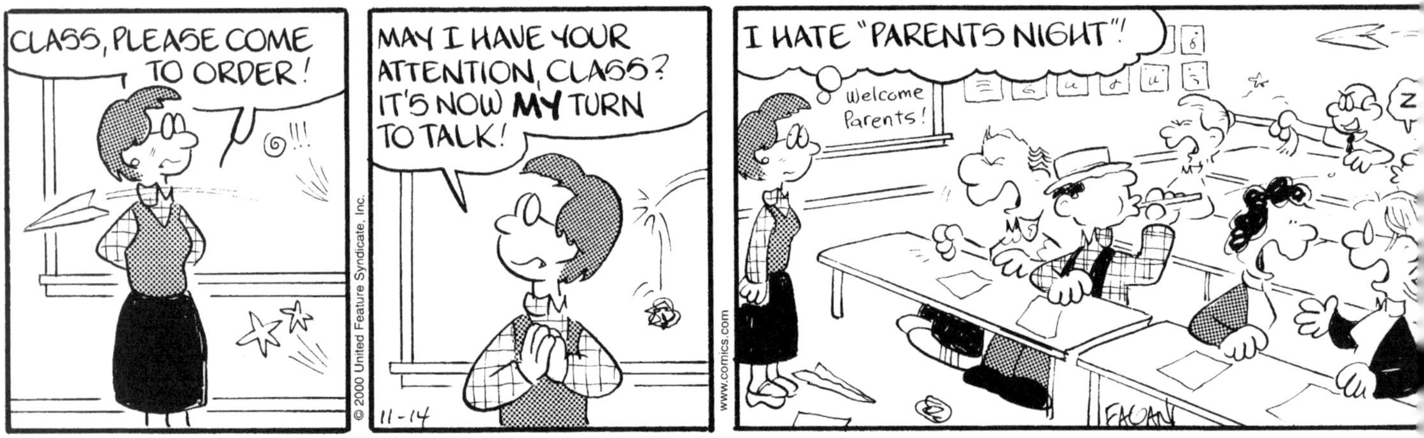
CLASS, PLEASE COME TO ORDER!
MAY I HAVE YOUR ATTENTION, CLASS? IT'S NOW **MY** TURN TO TALK!
© 2000 United Feature Syndicate, Inc.
11-14
I HATE "PARENTS NIGHT"!
Welcome Parents!
www.comics.com
FAGAN

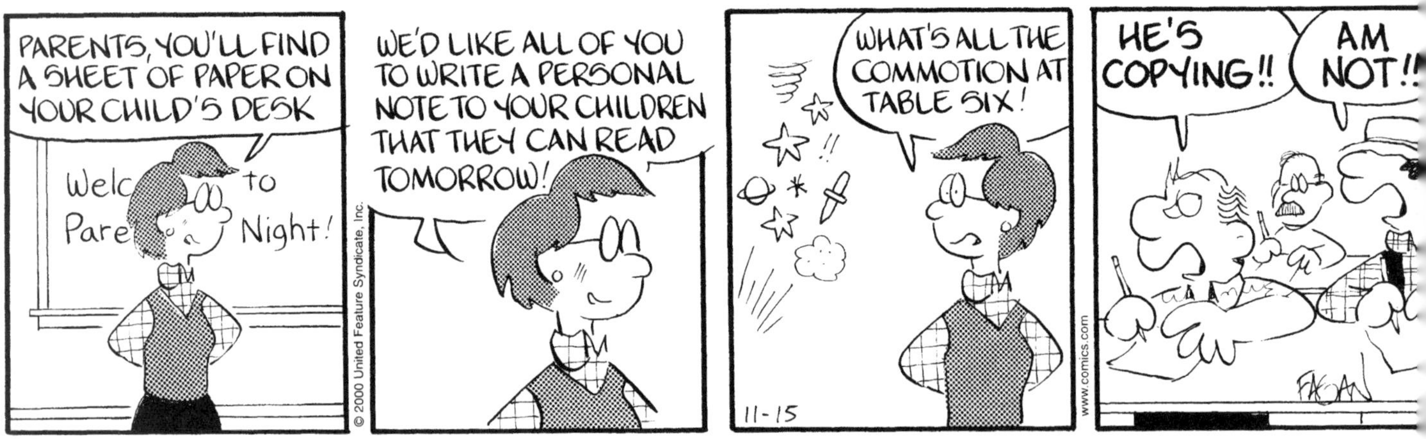
PARENTS, YOU'LL FIND A SHEET OF PAPER ON YOUR CHILD'S DESK
Welc to
Pare Night!
WE'D LIKE ALL OF YOU TO WRITE A PERSONAL NOTE TO YOUR CHILDREN THAT THEY CAN READ TOMORROW!
© 2000 United Feature Syndicate, Inc.
WHAT'S ALL THE COMMOTION AT TABLE SIX!
11-15
www.comics.com
HE'S COPYING!!
AM NOT!!
FAGAN

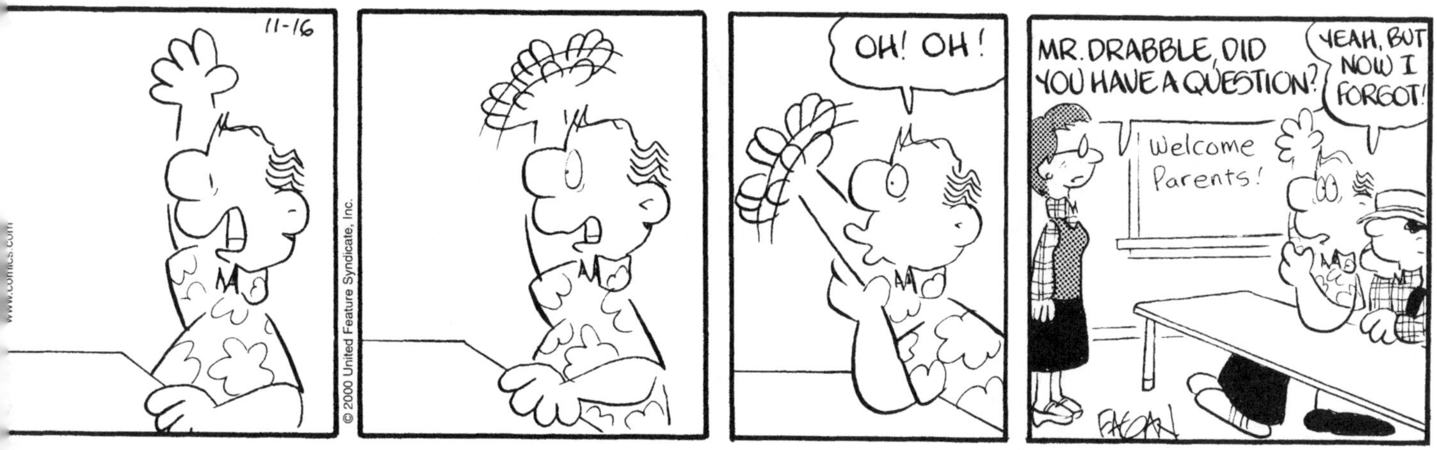
11-16
© 2000 United Feature Syndicate, Inc.
OH! OH!
MR. DRABBLE, DID YOU HAVE A QUESTION?
YEAH, BUT NOW I FORGOT!
Welcome Parents!
FAGAN

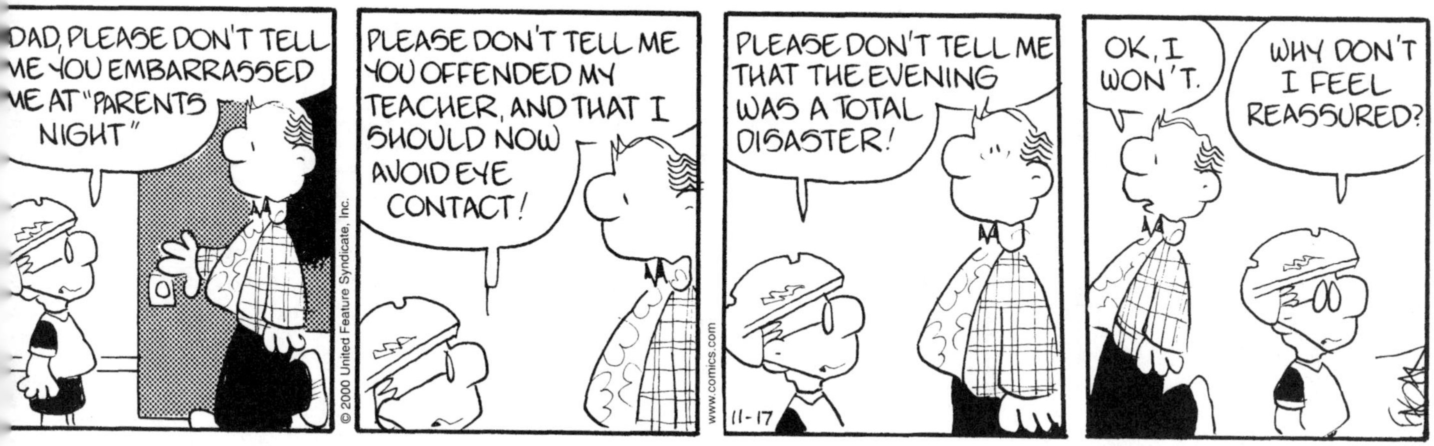
DAD, PLEASE DON'T TELL ME YOU EMBARRASSED ME AT "PARENTS NIGHT"
© 2000 United Feature Syndicate, Inc.
PLEASE DON'T TELL ME YOU OFFENDED MY TEACHER, AND THAT I SHOULD NOW AVOID EYE CONTACT!
www.comics.com
PLEASE DON'T TELL ME THAT THE EVENING WAS A TOTAL DISASTER!
11-17
OK, I WON'T.
WHY DON'T I FEEL REASSURED?

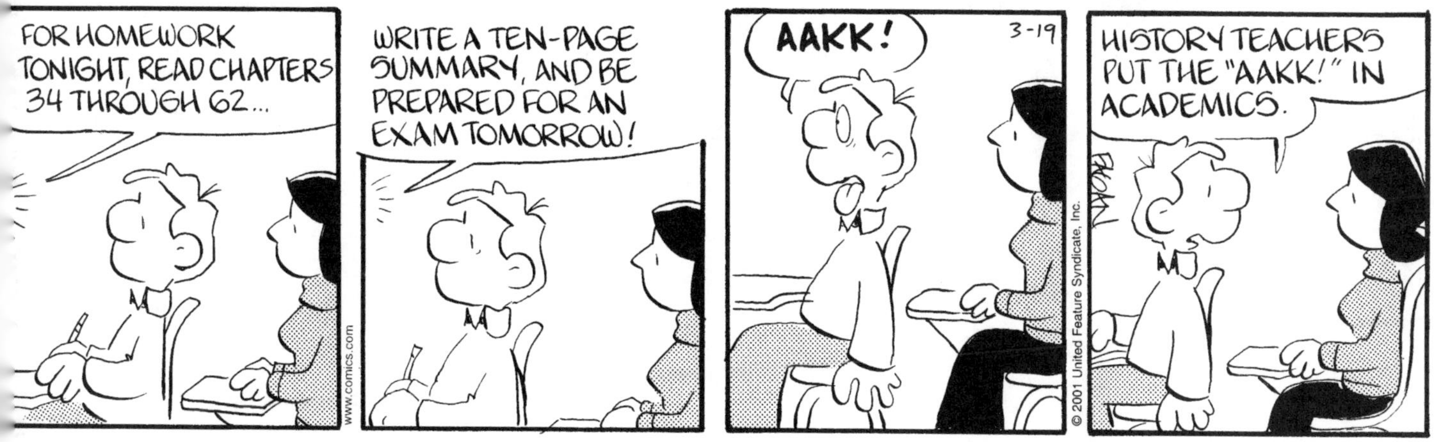
FOR HOMEWORK TONIGHT, READ CHAPTERS 34 THROUGH 62...
www.comics.com
WRITE A TEN-PAGE SUMMARY, AND BE PREPARED FOR AN EXAM TOMORROW!
AAKK!
3-19
© 2001 United Feature Syndicate, Inc.
HISTORY TEACHERS PUT THE "AAKK!" IN ACADEMICS.

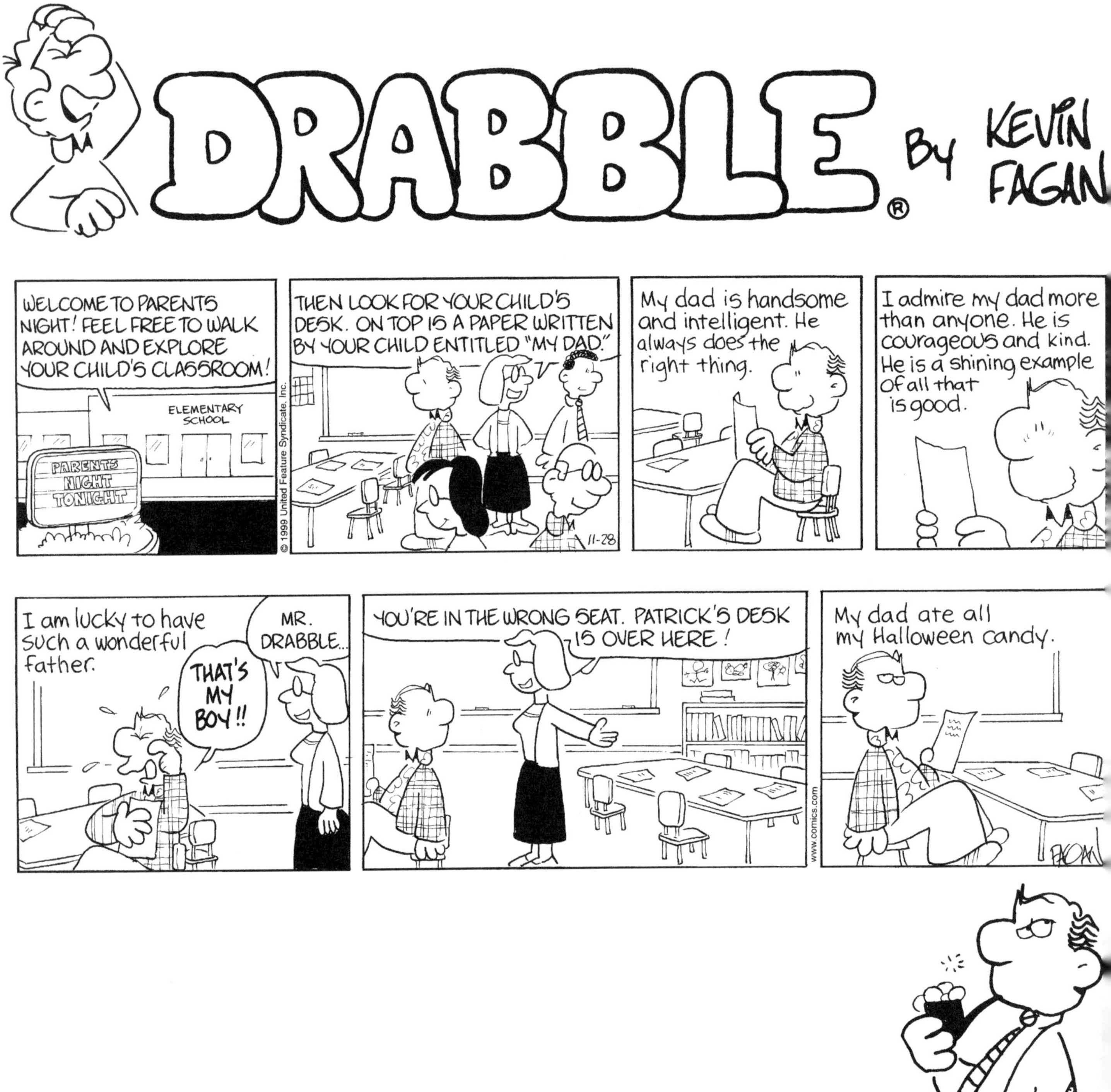
DRABBLE®
By KEVIN FAGAN
WELCOME TO PARENTS NIGHT! FEEL FREE TO WALK AROUND AND EXPLORE YOUR CHILD'S CLASSROOM!
ELEMENTARY SCHOOL
PARENTS NIGHT TONIGHT
THEN LOOK FOR YOUR CHILD'S DESK. ON TOP IS A PAPER WRITTEN BY YOUR CHILD ENTITLED "MY DAD."
© 1999 United Feature Syndicate, Inc.
11-28
My dad is handsome and intelligent. He always does the right thing.
I admire my dad more than anyone. He is courageous and kind. He is a shining example of all that is good.
I am lucky to have such a wonderful father.
THAT'S MY BOY!!
MR. DRABBLE...
YOU'RE IN THE WRONG SEAT. PATRICK'S DESK IS OVER HERE!
www.comics.com
My dad ate all my Halloween candy.
FAGAN

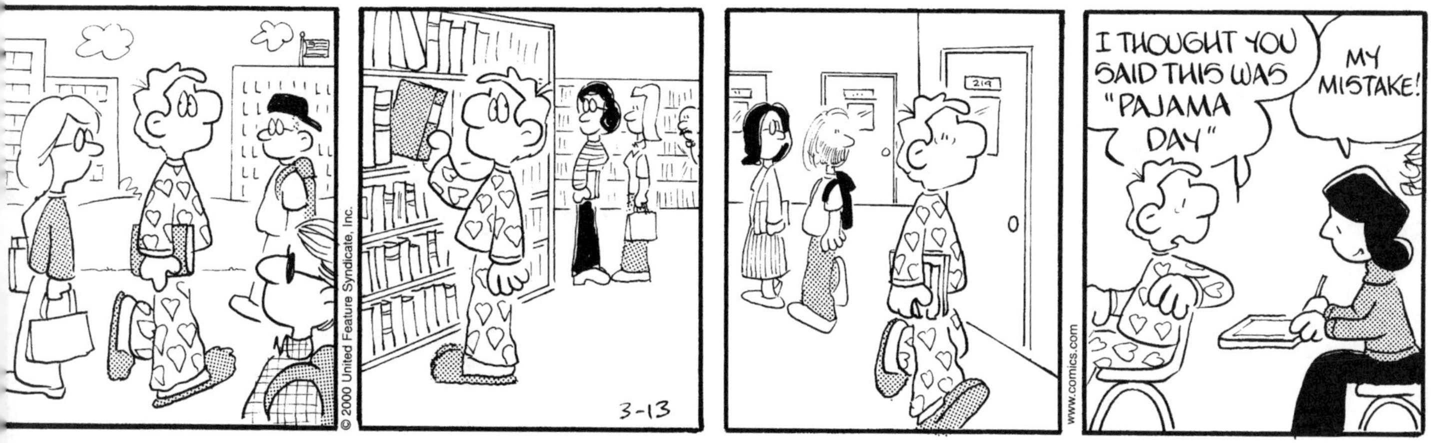
3-13
I THOUGHT YOU SAID THIS WAS "PAJAMA DAY"
MY MISTAKE!

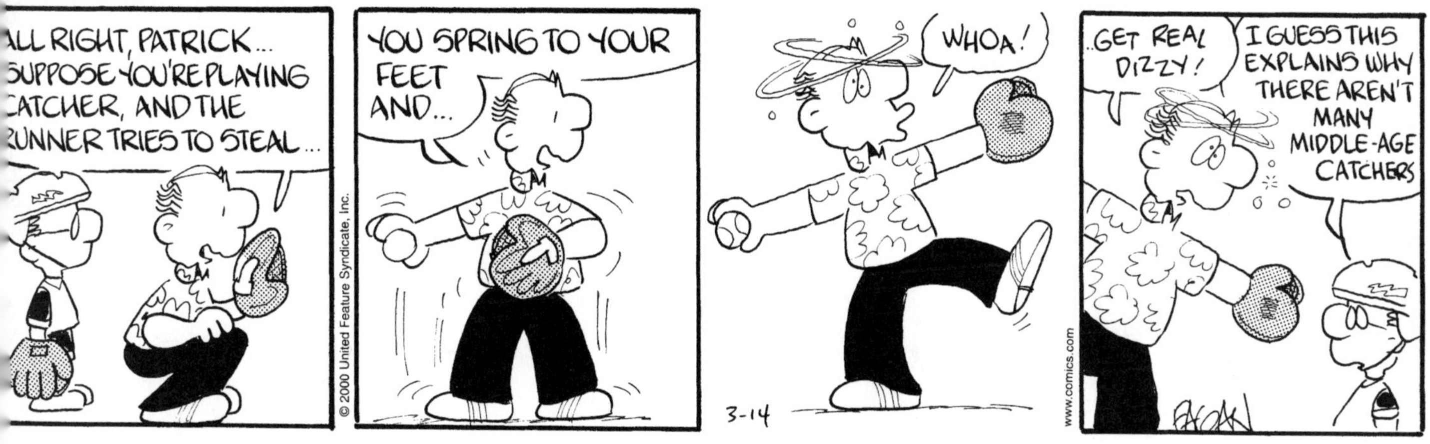
LL RIGHT, PATRICK... SUPPOSE YOU'RE PLAYING CATCHER, AND THE RUNNER TRIES TO STEAL...
YOU SPRING TO YOUR FEET AND...
WHOA!
3-14
...GET REAL DIZZY!
I GUESS THIS EXPLAINS WHY THERE AREN'T MANY MIDDLE-AGE CATCHERS

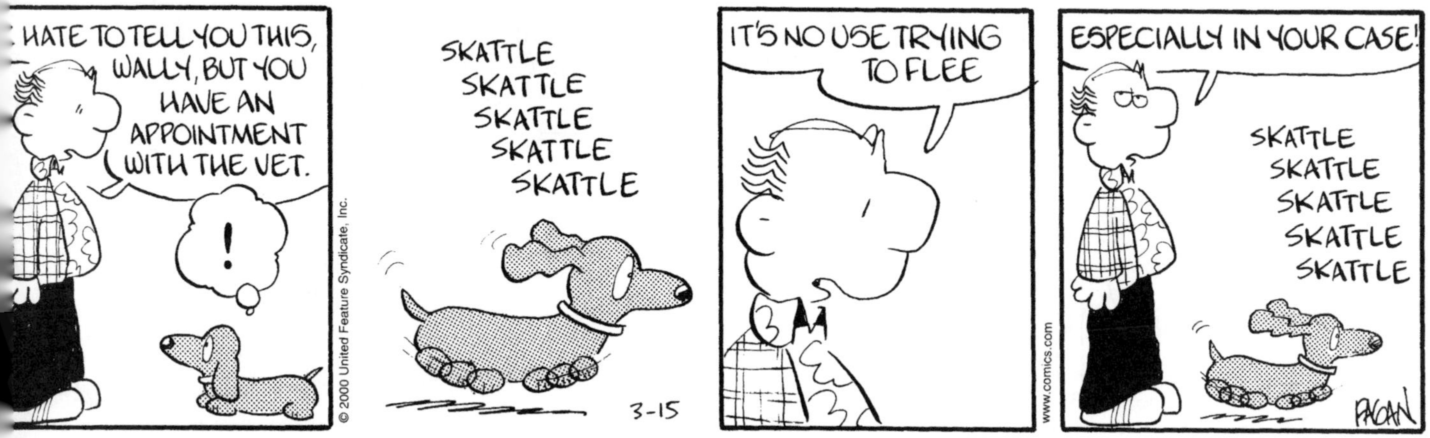
HATE TO TELL YOU THIS, WALLY, BUT YOU HAVE AN APPOINTMENT WITH THE VET.
!
SKATTLE SKATTLE SKATTLE SKATTLE SKATTLE
3-15
IT'S NO USE TRYING TO FLEE
ESPECIALLY IN YOUR CASE!
SKATTLE SKATTLE SKATTLE SKATTLE SKATTLE

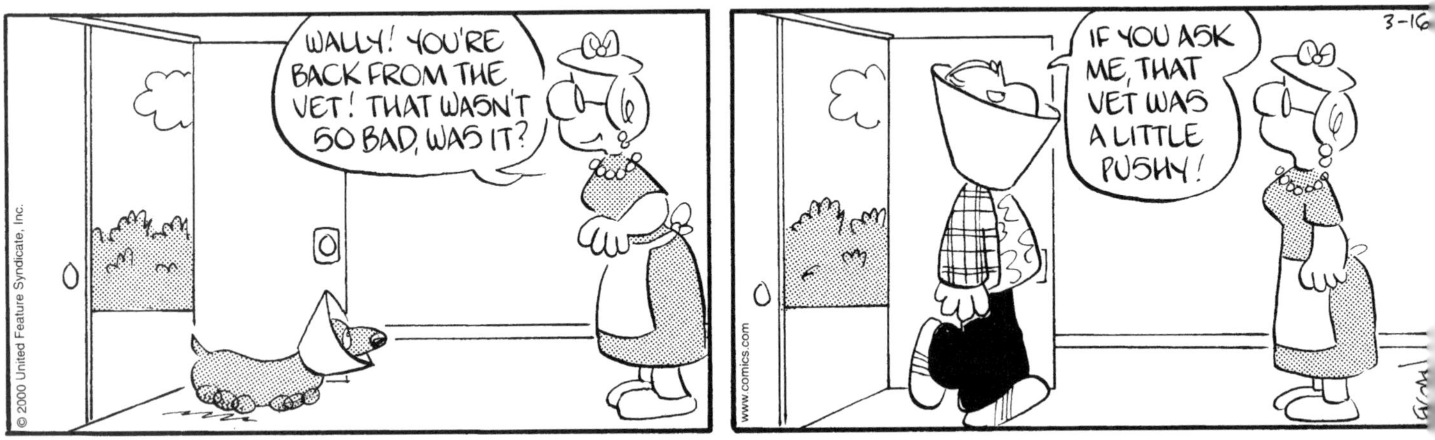
WALLY! YOU'RE BACK FROM THE VET! THAT WASN'T SO BAD, WAS IT?
IF YOU ASK ME, THAT VET WAS A LITTLE PUSHY!
3-16
www.comics.com

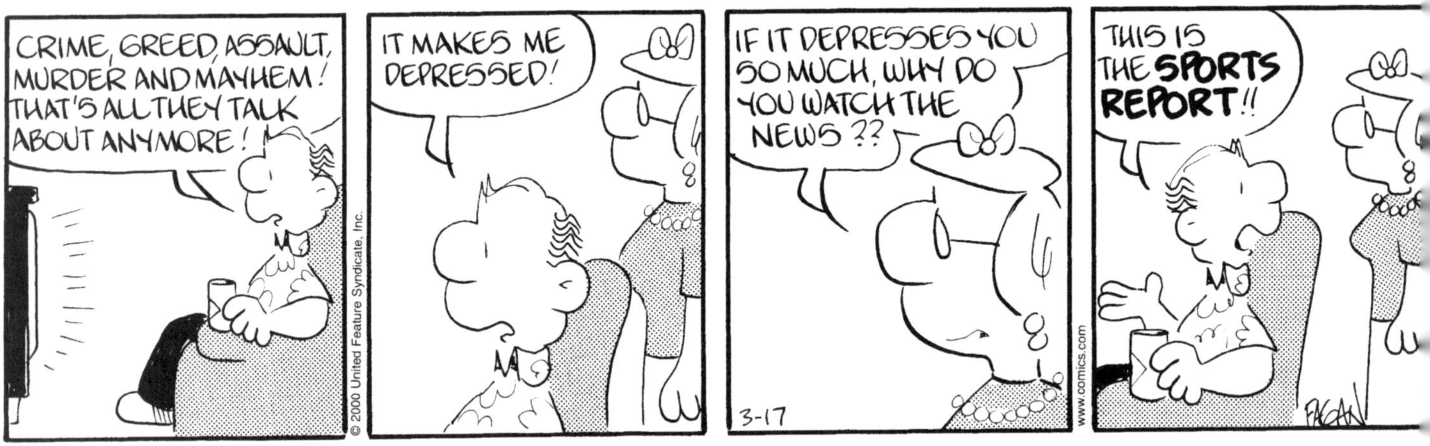
CRIME, GREED, ASSAULT, MURDER AND MAYHEM! THAT'S ALL THEY TALK ABOUT ANYMORE!
IT MAKES ME DEPRESSED!
IF IT DEPRESSES YOU SO MUCH, WHY DO YOU WATCH THE NEWS ??
3-17
THIS IS THE **SPORTS REPORT**!!
FAGAN
www.comics.com

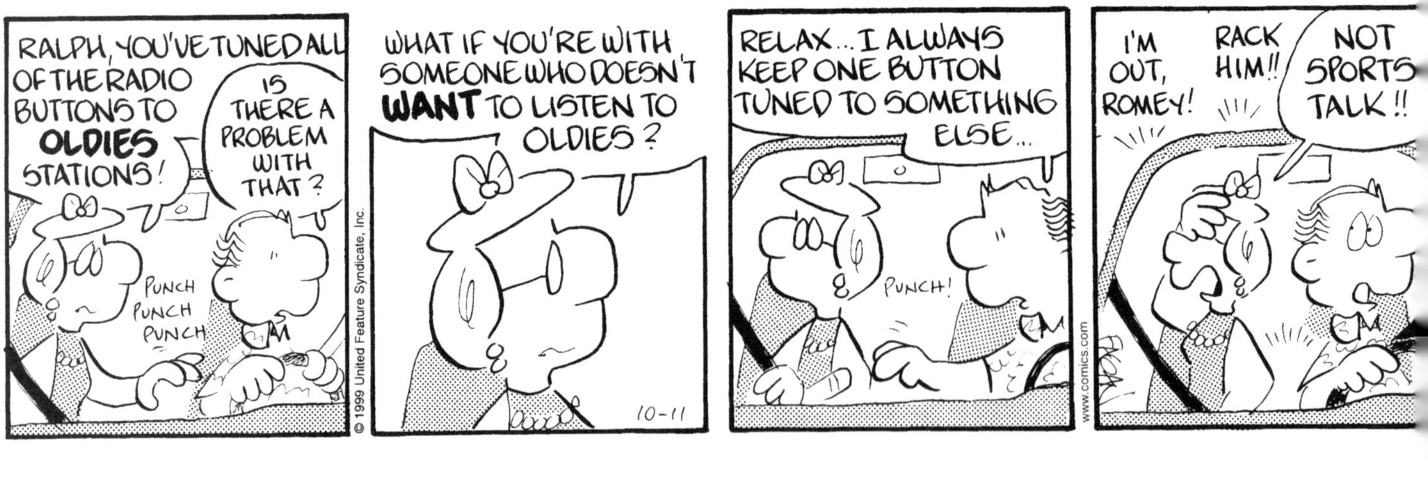
RALPH, YOU'VE TUNED ALL OF THE RADIO BUTTONS TO **OLDIES** STATIONS!
IS THERE A PROBLEM WITH THAT?
PUNCH PUNCH PUNCH
WHAT IF YOU'RE WITH SOMEONE WHO DOESN'T **WANT** TO LISTEN TO OLDIES?
10-11
RELAX... I ALWAYS KEEP ONE BUTTON TUNED TO SOMETHING ELSE...
PUNCH!
I'M OUT, ROMEY!
RACK HIM!!
NOT SPORTS TALK!!
www.comics.com

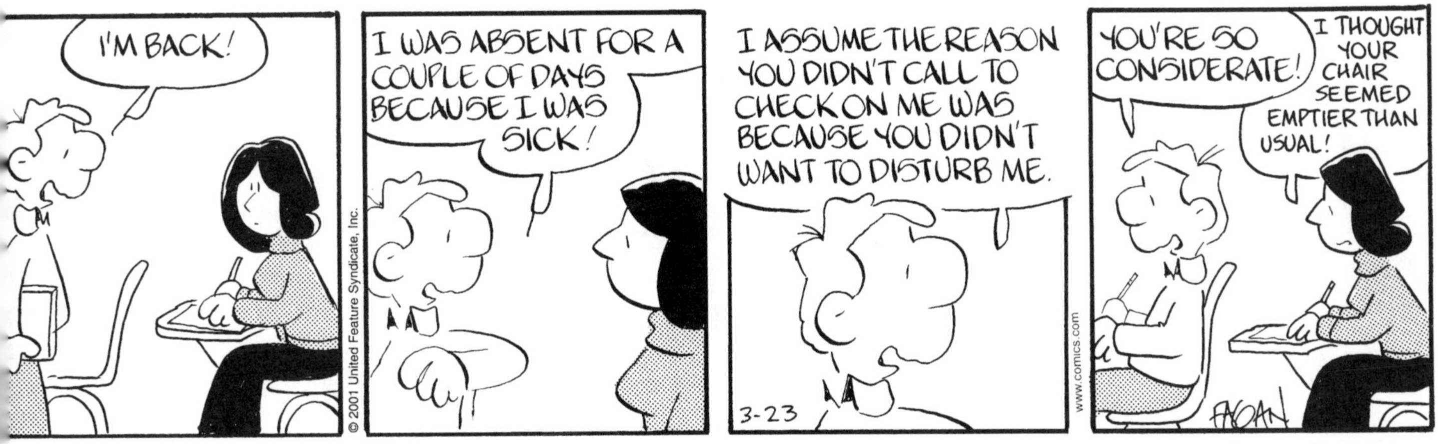
I'M BACK!
© 2001 United Feature Syndicate, Inc.
I WAS ABSENT FOR A COUPLE OF DAYS BECAUSE I WAS SICK!
I ASSUME THE REASON YOU DIDN'T CALL TO CHECK ON ME WAS BECAUSE YOU DIDN'T WANT TO DISTURB ME.
3-23
www.comics.com
YOU'RE SO CONSIDERATE!
I THOUGHT YOUR CHAIR SEEMED EMPTIER THAN USUAL!
FAGAN

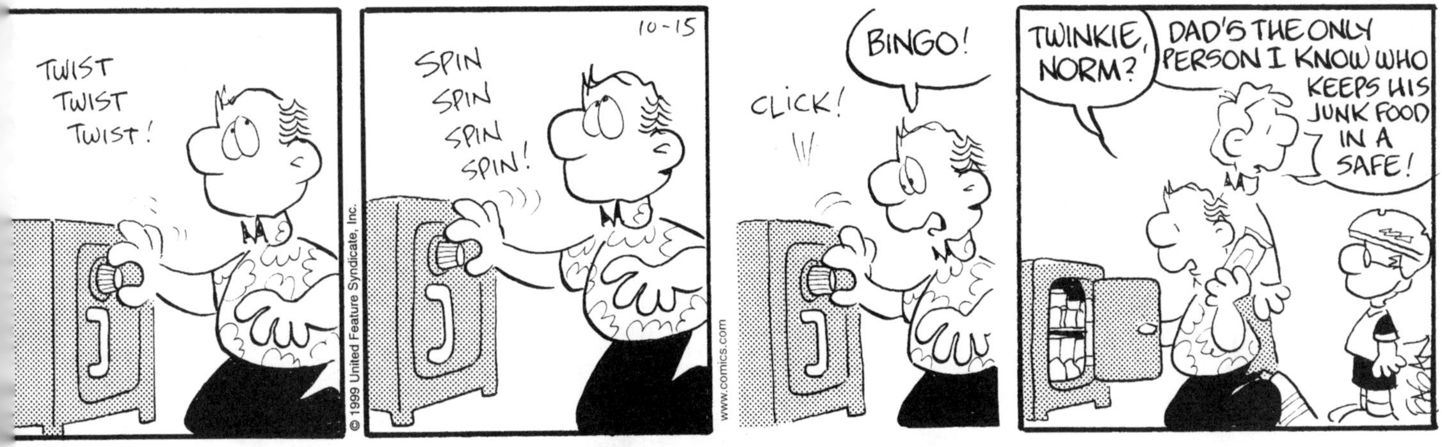
TWIST TWIST TWIST!
© 1999 United Feature Syndicate, Inc.
10-15
SPIN SPIN SPIN SPIN!
www.comics.com
CLICK!
BINGO!
TWINKIE, NORM?
DAD'S THE ONLY PERSON I KNOW WHO KEEPS HIS JUNK FOOD IN A SAFE!

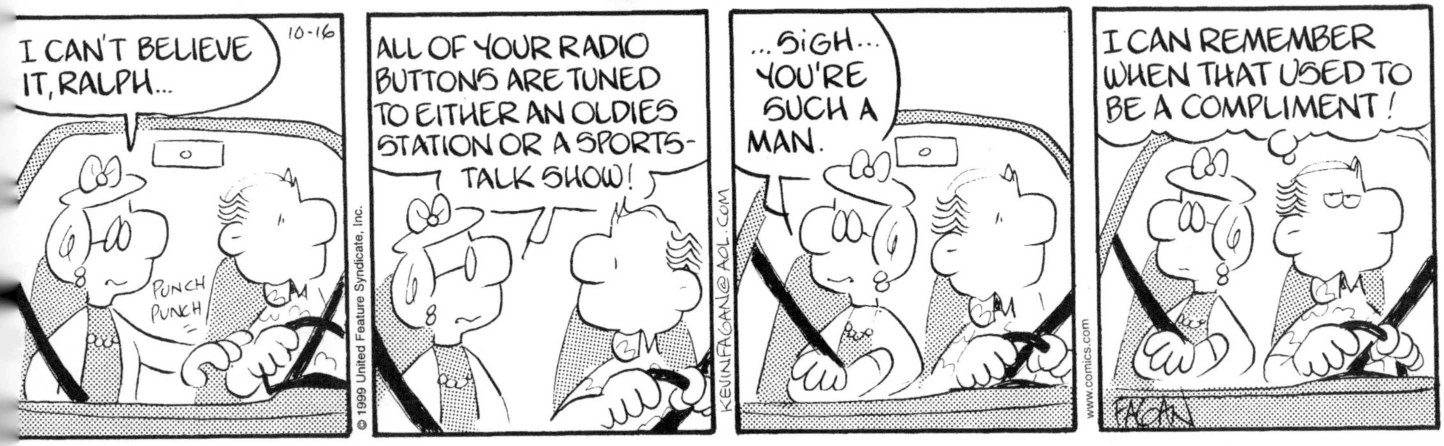
10-16
I CAN'T BELIEVE IT, RALPH...
PUNCH PUNCH
© 1999 United Feature Syndicate, Inc.
ALL OF YOUR RADIO BUTTONS ARE TUNED TO EITHER AN OLDIES STATION OR A SPORTS-TALK SHOW!
KEVINFAGAN@AOL.COM
...SIGH... YOU'RE SUCH A MAN.
www.comics.com
I CAN REMEMBER WHEN THAT USED TO BE A COMPLIMENT!
FAGAN

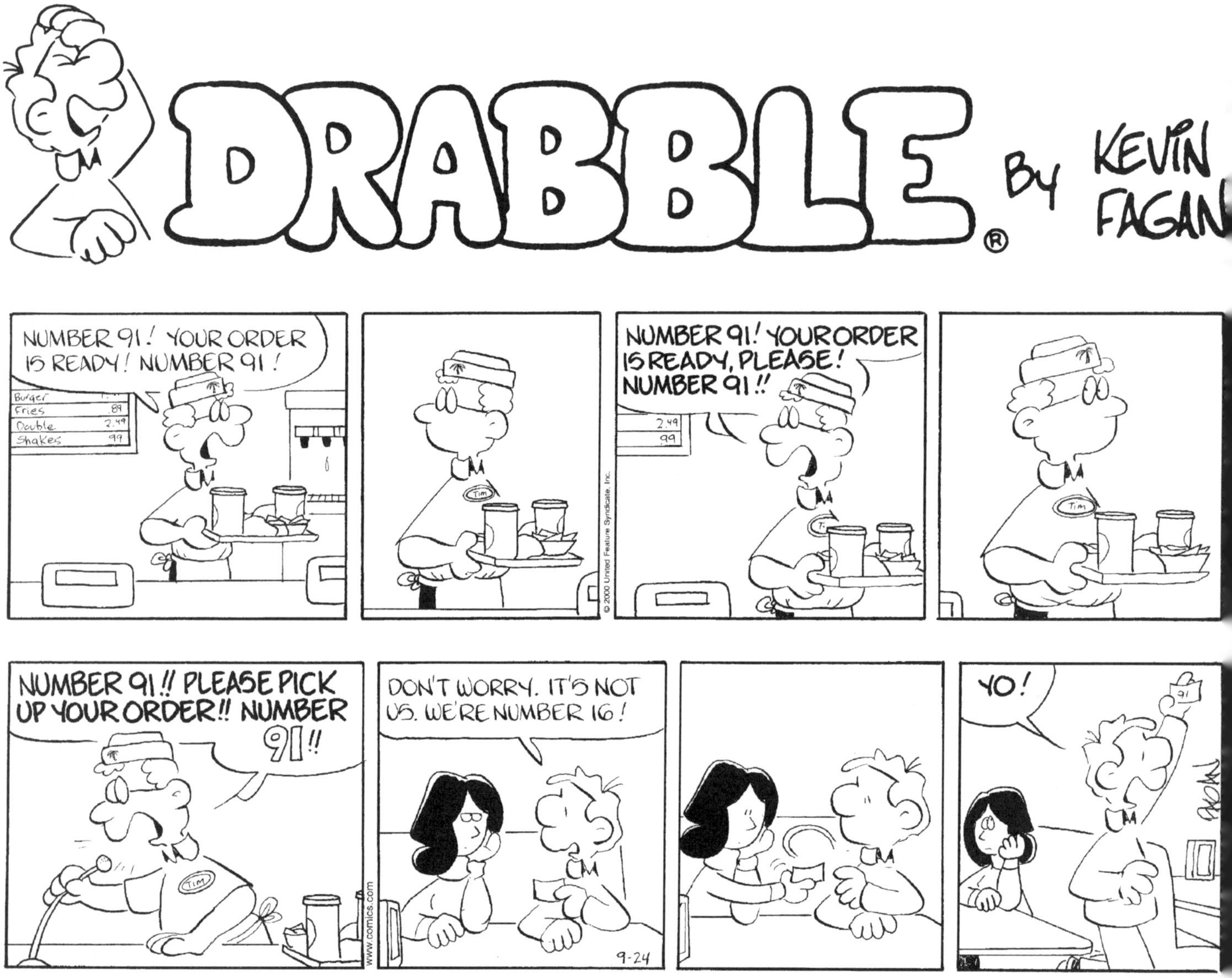
DRABBLE
By KEVIN FAGAN
NUMBER 91! YOUR ORDER IS READY! NUMBER 91!
Burger
Fries .89
Double 2.49
Shakes .99
NUMBER 91! YOUR ORDER IS READY, PLEASE! NUMBER 91!!
© 2000 United Feature Syndicate, Inc.
NUMBER 91!! PLEASE PICK UP YOUR ORDER!! NUMBER 91!!
www.comics.com
DON'T WORRY. IT'S NOT US. WE'RE NUMBER 16!
9-24
YO!
91

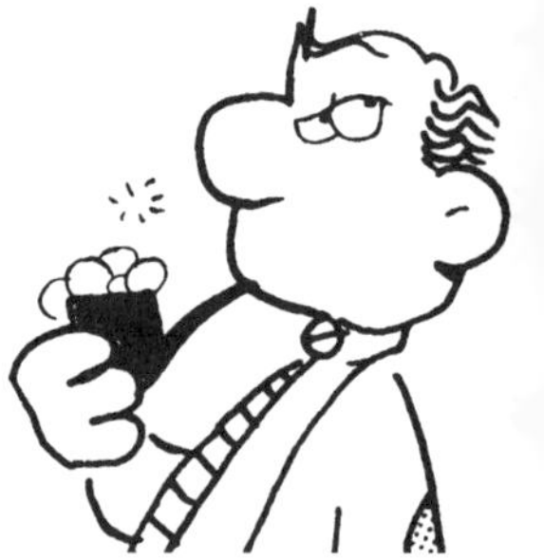

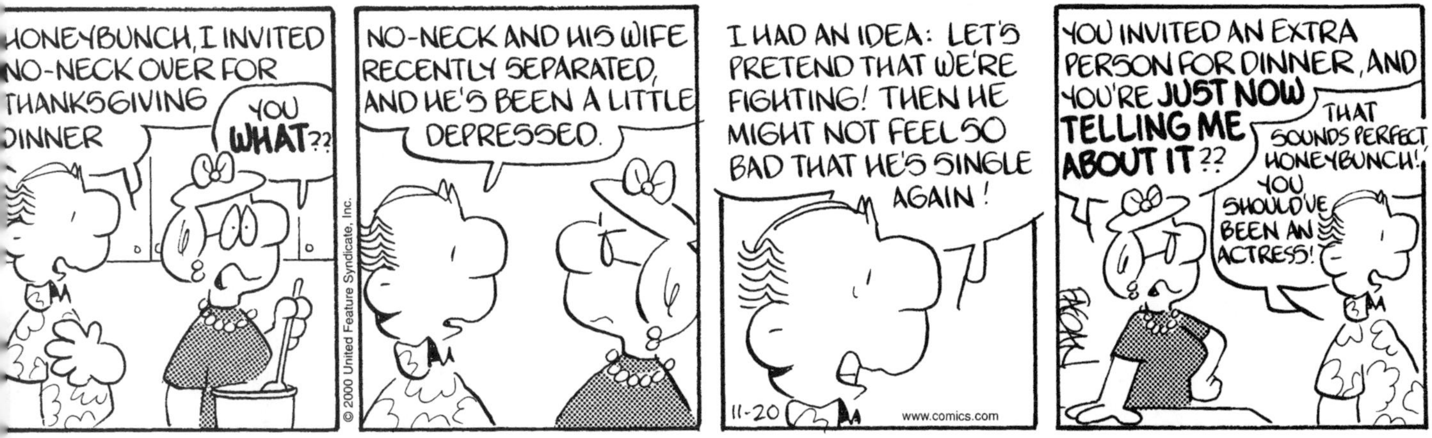
HONEYBUNCH, I INVITED NO-NECK OVER FOR THANKSGIVING DINNER
YOU WHAT??
© 2000 United Feature Syndicate, Inc.
NO-NECK AND HIS WIFE RECENTLY SEPARATED, AND HE'S BEEN A LITTLE DEPRESSED.
I HAD AN IDEA: LET'S PRETEND THAT WE'RE FIGHTING! THEN HE MIGHT NOT FEEL SO BAD THAT HE'S SINGLE AGAIN!
11-20
www.comics.com
YOU INVITED AN EXTRA PERSON FOR DINNER, AND YOU'RE JUST NOW TELLING ME ABOUT IT??
THAT SOUNDS PERFECT, HONEYBUNCH!
YOU SHOULD'VE BEEN AN ACTRESS!

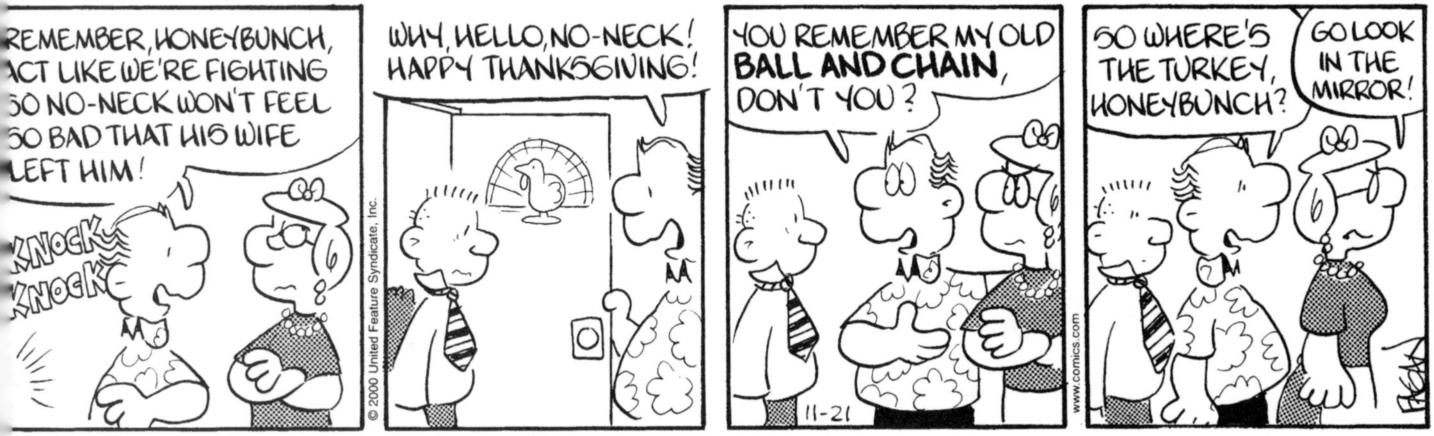
REMEMBER, HONEYBUNCH, ACT LIKE WE'RE FIGHTING SO NO-NECK WON'T FEEL SO BAD THAT HIS WIFE LEFT HIM!
KNOCK KNOCK
© 2000 United Feature Syndicate, Inc.
WHY, HELLO, NO-NECK! HAPPY THANKSGIVING!
YOU REMEMBER MY OLD BALL AND CHAIN, DON'T YOU?
11-21
www.comics.com
SO WHERE'S THE TURKEY, HONEYBUNCH?
GO LOOK IN THE MIRROR!

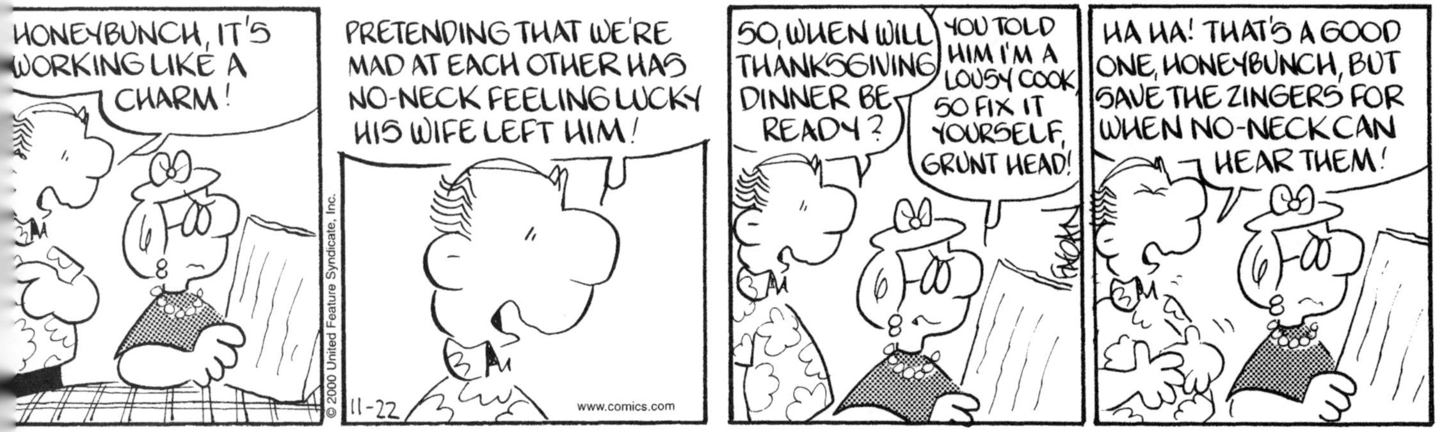
HONEYBUNCH, IT'S WORKING LIKE A CHARM!
© 2000 United Feature Syndicate, Inc.
PRETENDING THAT WE'RE MAD AT EACH OTHER HAS NO-NECK FEELING LUCKY HIS WIFE LEFT HIM!
11-22
www.comics.com
SO, WHEN WILL THANKSGIVING DINNER BE READY?
YOU TOLD HIM I'M A LOUSY COOK, SO FIX IT YOURSELF, GRUNT HEAD!
HA HA! THAT'S A GOOD ONE, HONEYBUNCH, BUT SAVE THE ZINGERS FOR WHEN NO-NECK CAN HEAR THEM!

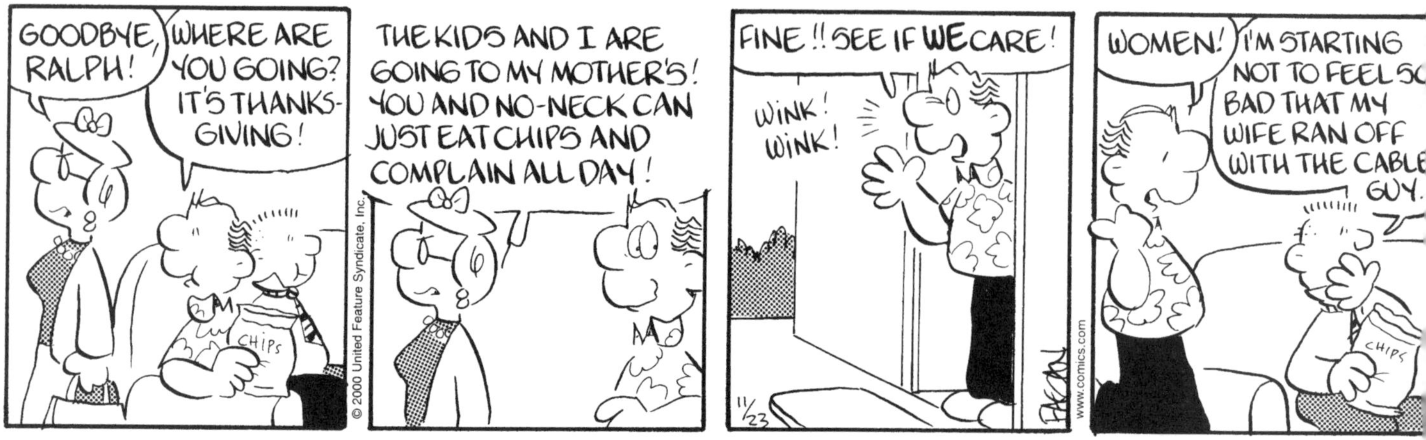
GOODBYE, RALPH!
WHERE ARE YOU GOING? IT'S THANKS-GIVING!
CHIPS
© 2000 United Feature Syndicate, Inc.
THE KIDS AND I ARE GOING TO MY MOTHER'S! YOU AND NO-NECK CAN JUST EAT CHIPS AND COMPLAIN ALL DAY!
FINE!! SEE IF **WE** CARE!
WINK! WINK!
11/23
www.comics.com
WOMEN!
I'M STARTING NOT TO FEEL S BAD THAT MY WIFE RAN OFF WITH THE CABLE GUY.
CHIPS

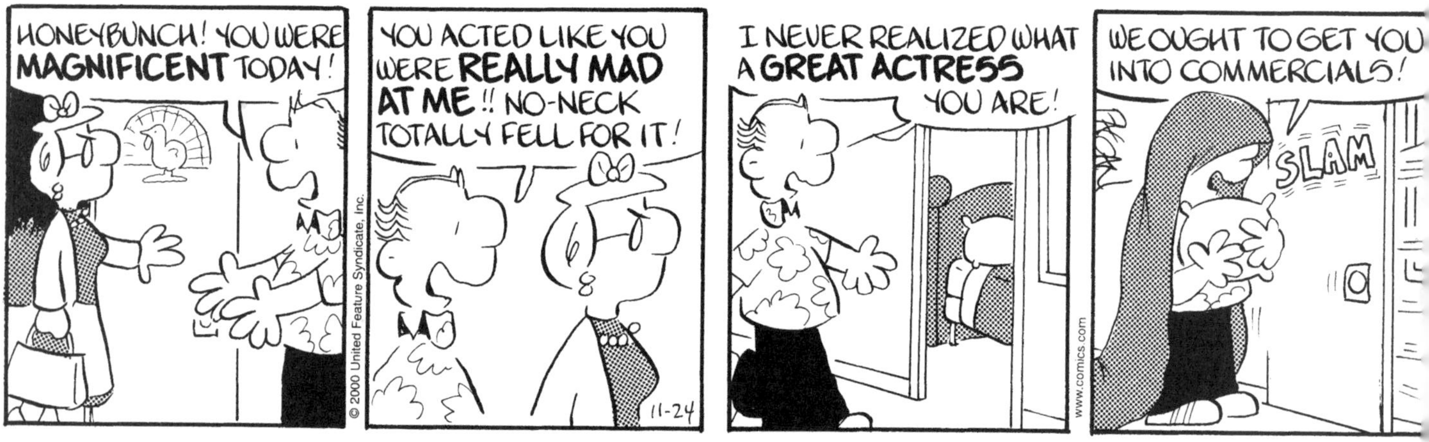
HONEYBUNCH! YOU WERE **MAGNIFICENT** TODAY!
© 2000 United Feature Syndicate, Inc.
YOU ACTED LIKE YOU WERE **REALLY MAD AT ME**!! NO-NECK TOTALLY FELL FOR IT!
11-24
I NEVER REALIZED WHAT A **GREAT ACTRESS** YOU ARE!
www.comics.com
WE OUGHT TO GET YOU INTO COMMERCIALS!
SLAM

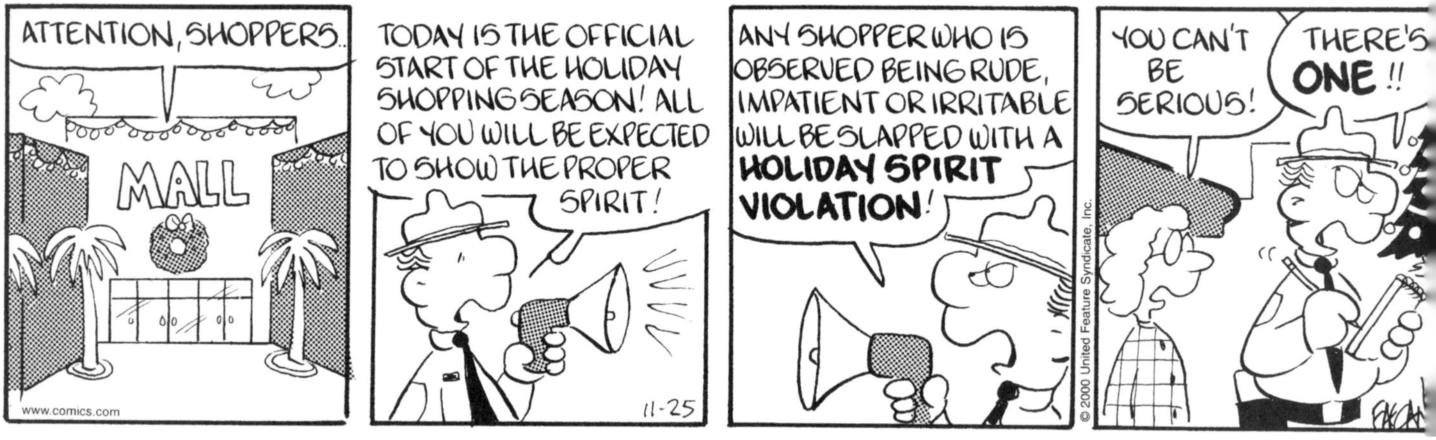
ATTENTION, SHOPPERS...
MALL
www.comics.com
TODAY IS THE OFFICIAL START OF THE HOLIDAY SHOPPING SEASON! ALL OF YOU WILL BE EXPECTED TO SHOW THE PROPER SPIRIT!
11-25
ANY SHOPPER WHO IS OBSERVED BEING RUDE, IMPATIENT OR IRRITABLE WILL BE SLAPPED WITH A **HOLIDAY SPIRIT VIOLATION**!
© 2000 United Feature Syndicate, Inc.
YOU CAN'T BE SERIOUS!
THERE'S **ONE**!!

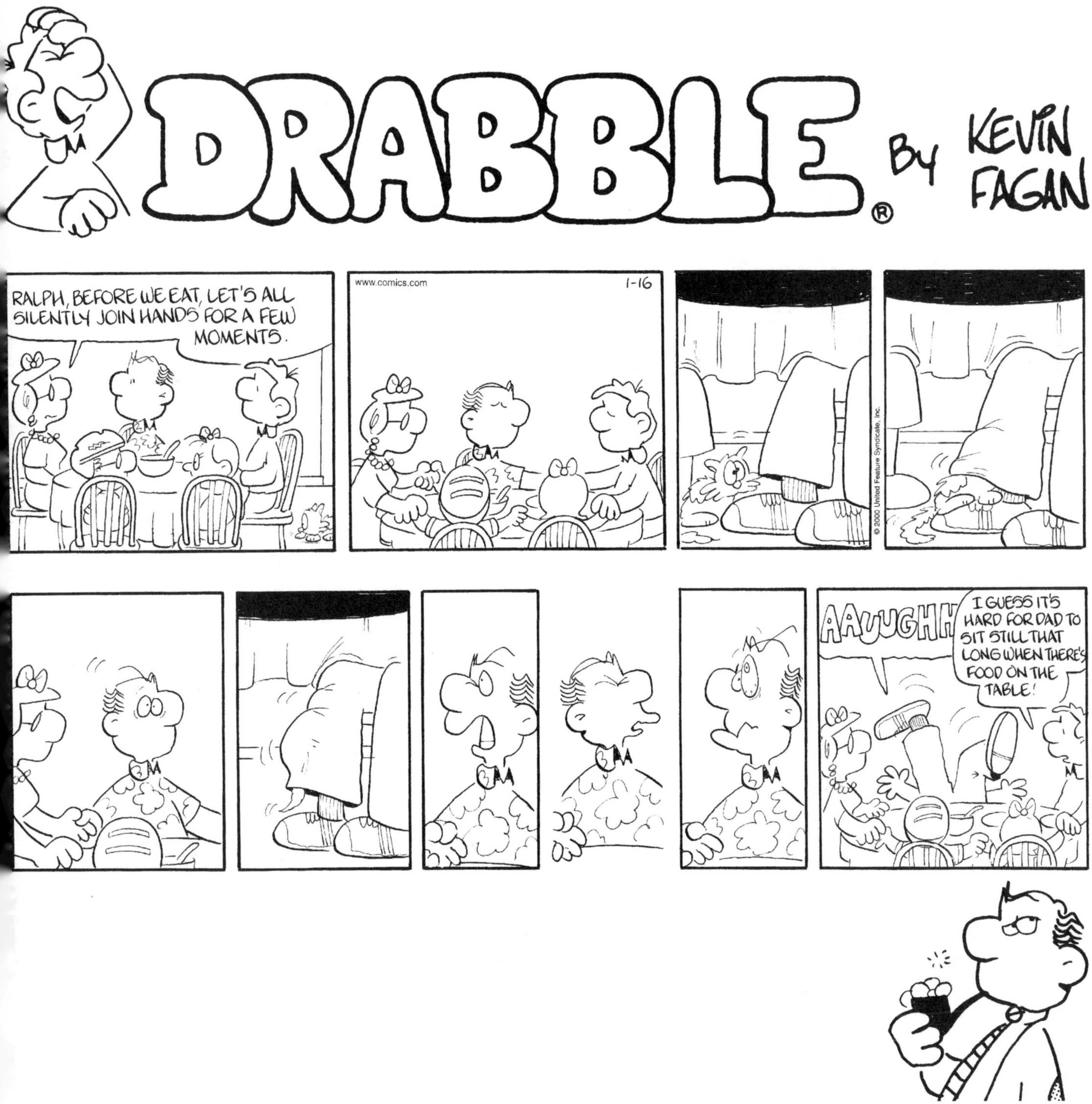
DRABBLE
By KEVIN FAGAN
RALPH, BEFORE WE EAT, LET'S ALL SILENTLY JOIN HANDS FOR A FEW MOMENTS.
www.comics.com
1-16
© 2000 United Feature Syndicate, Inc.
AAUUGHH
I GUESS IT'S HARD FOR DAD TO SIT STILL THAT LONG WHEN THERE'S FOOD ON THE TABLE!

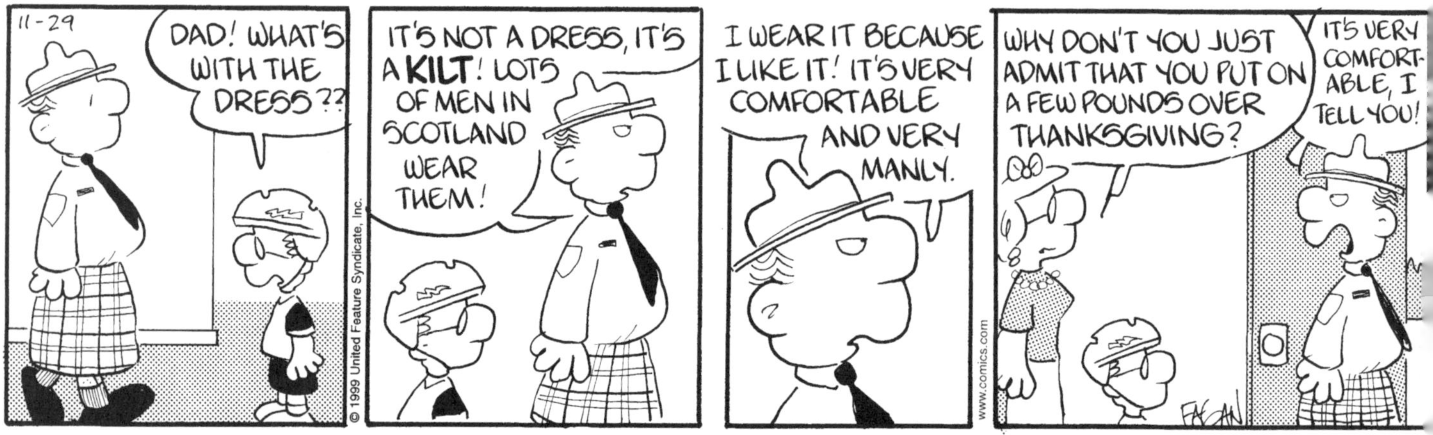
11-29
DAD! WHAT'S WITH THE DRESS??
IT'S NOT A DRESS, IT'S A **KILT**! LOTS OF MEN IN SCOTLAND WEAR THEM!
© 1999 United Feature Syndicate, Inc.
I WEAR IT BECAUSE I LIKE IT! IT'S VERY COMFORTABLE
AND VERY MANLY.
www.comics.com
WHY DON'T YOU JUST ADMIT THAT YOU PUT ON A FEW POUNDS OVER THANKSGIVING?
IT'S VERY COMFORTABLE, I TELL YOU!
FAGAN

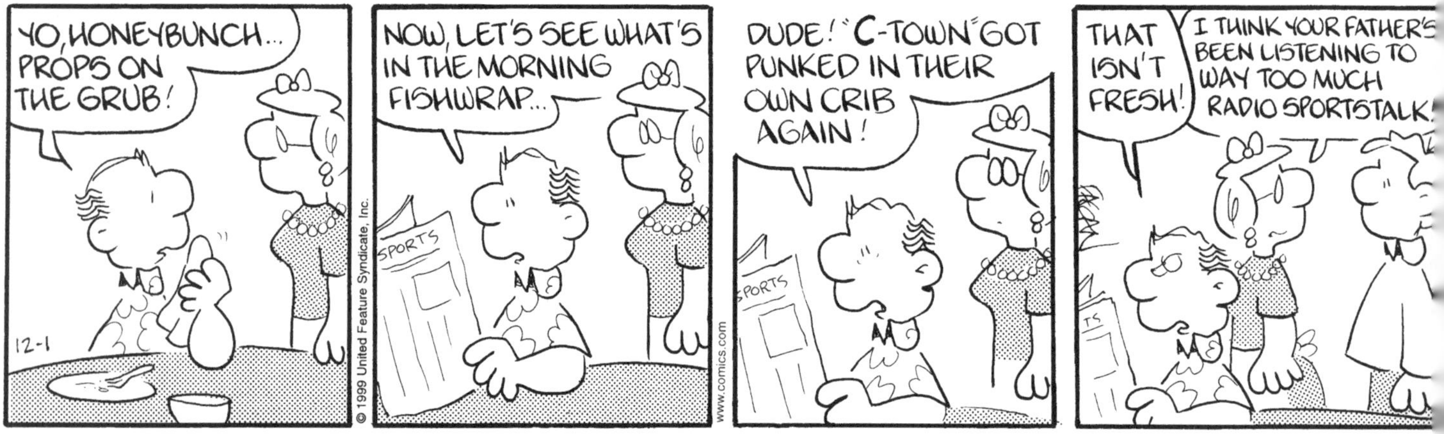
YO, HONEYBUNCH... PROPS ON THE GRUB!
12-1
© 1999 United Feature Syndicate, Inc.
NOW, LET'S SEE WHAT'S IN THE MORNING FISHWRAP...
SPORTS
DUDE! "**C**-TOWN" GOT PUNKED IN THEIR OWN CRIB AGAIN!
SPORTS
www.comics.com
THAT ISN'T FRESH!
I THINK YOUR FATHER'S BEEN LISTENING TO WAY TOO MUCH RADIO SPORTSTALK!

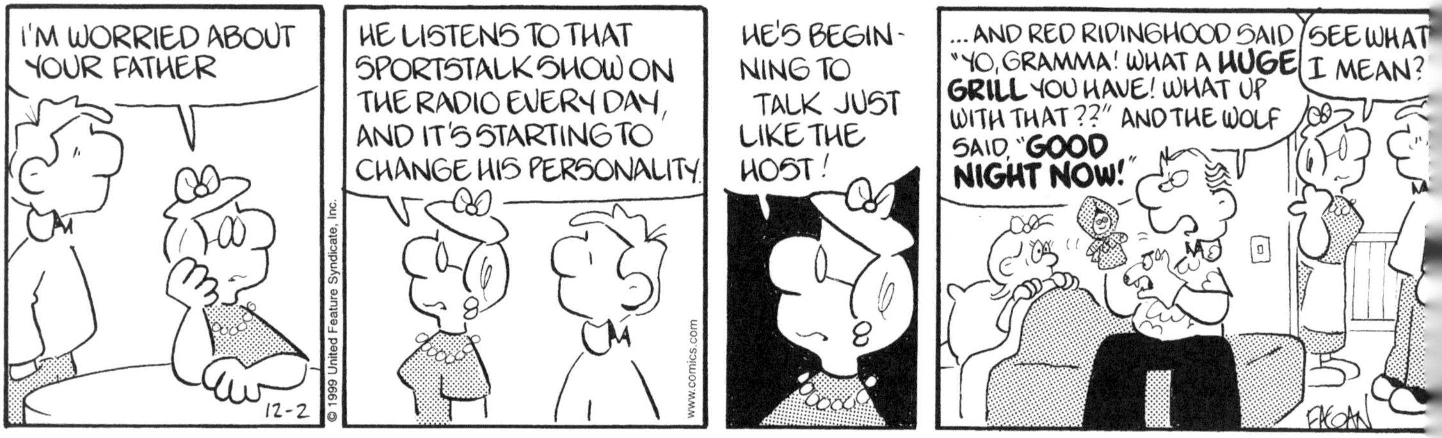
I'M WORRIED ABOUT YOUR FATHER
12-2
© 1999 United Feature Syndicate, Inc.
HE LISTENS TO THAT SPORTSTALK SHOW ON THE RADIO EVERY DAY, AND IT'S STARTING TO CHANGE HIS PERSONALITY.
www.comics.com
HE'S BEGINNING TO TALK JUST LIKE THE HOST!
...AND RED RIDINGHOOD SAID "YO, GRAMMA! WHAT A **HUGE GRILL** YOU HAVE! WHAT UP WITH THAT??" AND THE WOLF SAID, "**GOOD NIGHT NOW!**"
SEE WHAT I MEAN?
FAGAN

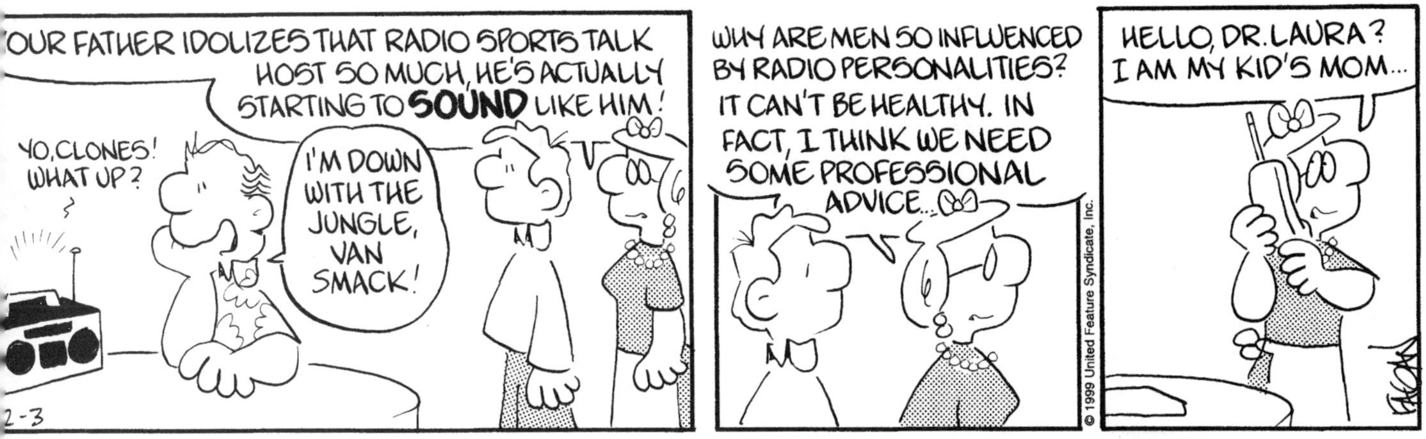
OUR FATHER IDOLIZES THAT RADIO SPORTS TALK HOST SO MUCH, HE'S ACTUALLY STARTING TO **SOUND** LIKE HIM!
YO, CLONES! WHAT UP?
I'M DOWN WITH THE JUNGLE, VAN SMACK!
WHY ARE MEN SO INFLUENCED BY RADIO PERSONALITIES? IT CAN'T BE HEALTHY. IN FACT, I THINK WE NEED SOME PROFESSIONAL ADVICE...
HELLO, DR. LAURA? I AM MY KID'S MOM...
2-3
© 1999 United Feature Syndicate, Inc.

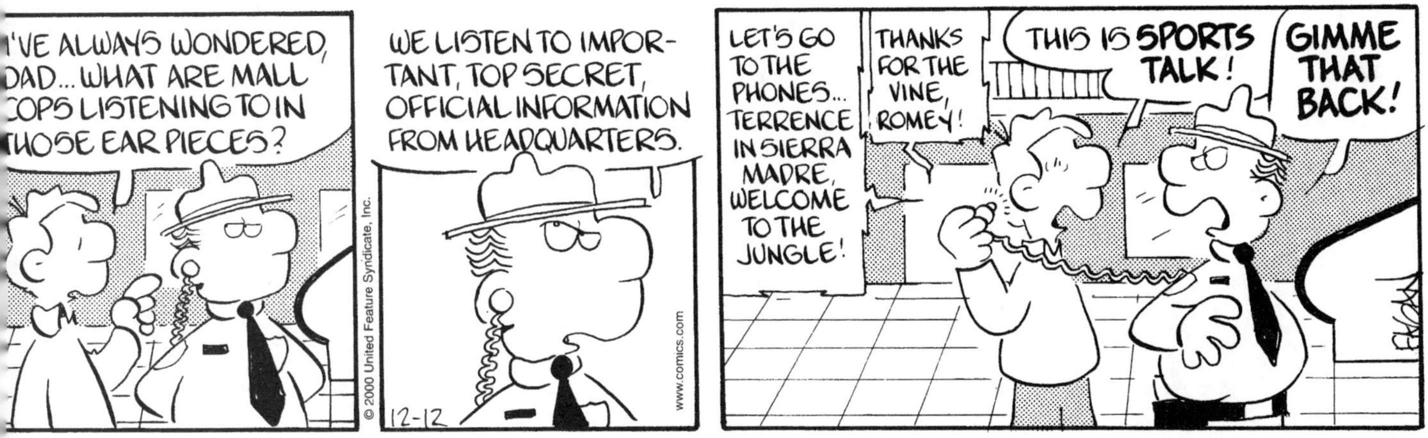
I'VE ALWAYS WONDERED, DAD... WHAT ARE MALL COPS LISTENING TO IN THOSE EAR PIECES?
© 2000 United Feature Syndicate, Inc.
WE LISTEN TO IMPORTANT, TOP SECRET, OFFICIAL INFORMATION FROM HEADQUARTERS.
12-12
www.comics.com
LET'S GO TO THE PHONES... TERRENCE IN SIERRA MADRE, WELCOME TO THE JUNGLE!
THANKS FOR THE VINE, ROMEY!
THIS IS **SPORTS TALK**!
GIMME THAT BACK!

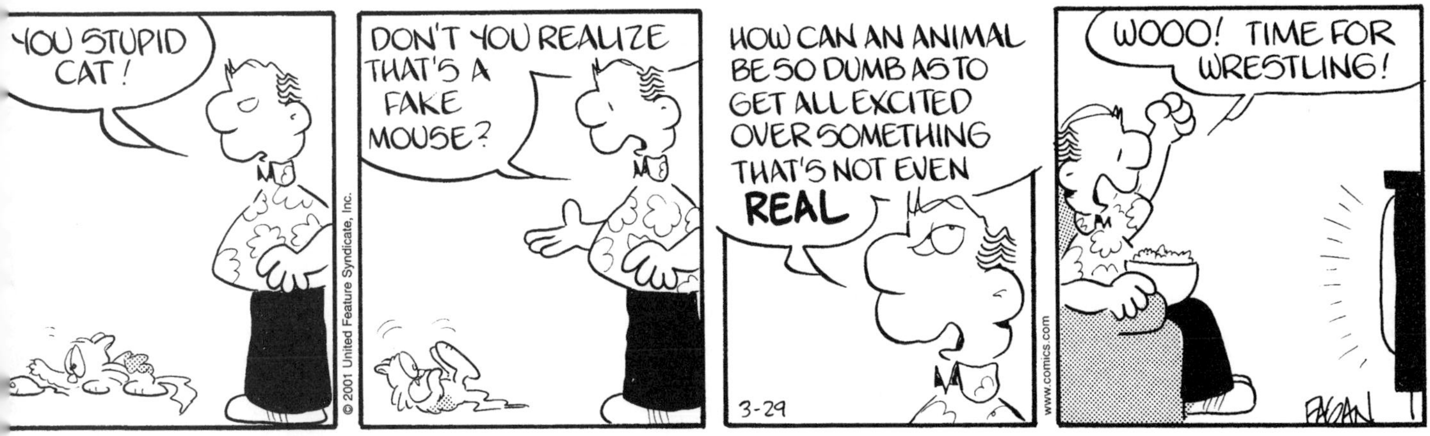
YOU STUPID CAT!
© 2001 United Feature Syndicate, Inc.
DON'T YOU REALIZE THAT'S A FAKE MOUSE?
HOW CAN AN ANIMAL BE SO DUMB AS TO GET ALL EXCITED OVER SOMETHING THAT'S NOT EVEN **REAL**
3-29
www.comics.com
WOOO! TIME FOR WRESTLING!

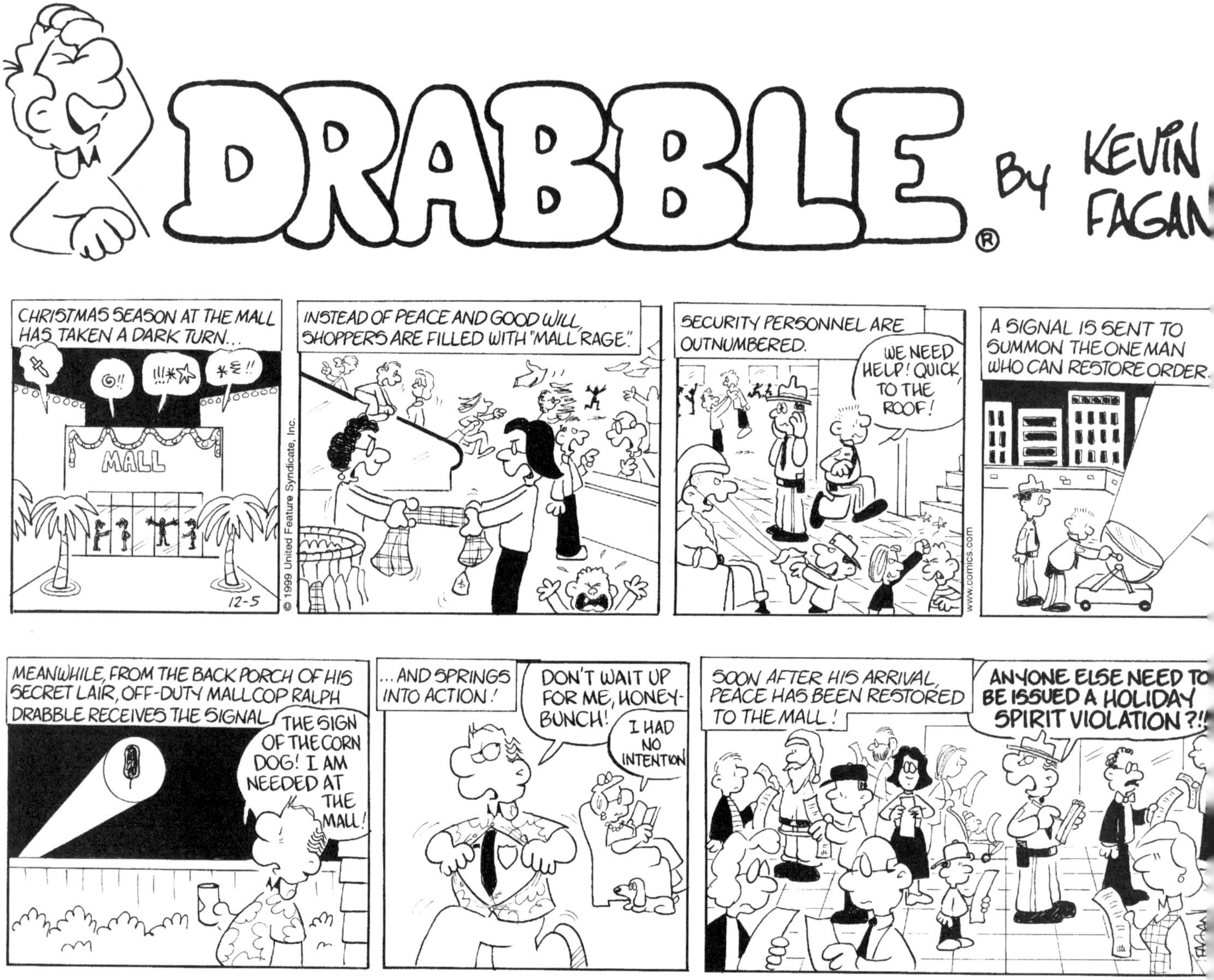
DRABBLE®
By KEVIN FAGAN
CHRISTMAS SEASON AT THE MALL HAS TAKEN A DARK TURN...
MALL
12-5
© 1999 United Feature Syndicate, Inc.
INSTEAD OF PEACE AND GOOD WILL, SHOPPERS ARE FILLED WITH "MALL RAGE."
SECURITY PERSONNEL ARE OUTNUMBERED.
WE NEED HELP! QUICK, TO THE ROOF!
www.comics.com
A SIGNAL IS SENT TO SUMMON THE ONE MAN WHO CAN RESTORE ORDER.
MEANWHILE, FROM THE BACK PORCH OF HIS SECRET LAIR, OFF-DUTY MALLCOP RALPH DRABBLE RECEIVES THE SIGNAL.
THE SIGN OF THE CORN DOG! I AM NEEDED AT THE MALL!
...AND SPRINGS INTO ACTION!
DON'T WAIT UP FOR ME, HONEY-BUNCH!
I HAD NO INTENTION
SOON AFTER HIS ARRIVAL, PEACE HAS BEEN RESTORED TO THE MALL!
ANYONE ELSE NEED TO BE ISSUED A HOLIDAY SPIRIT VIOLATION?!
FAGAN

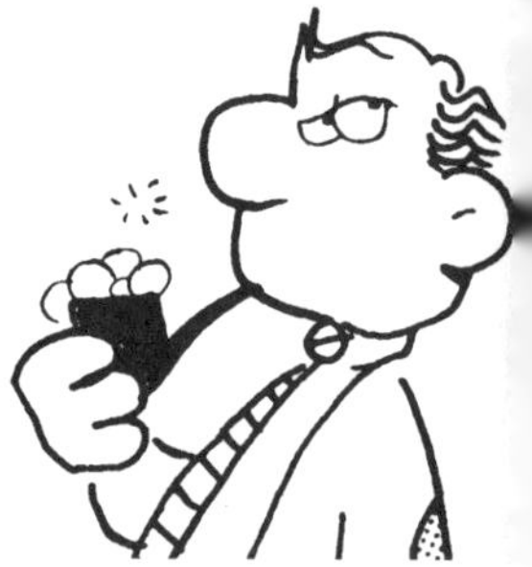

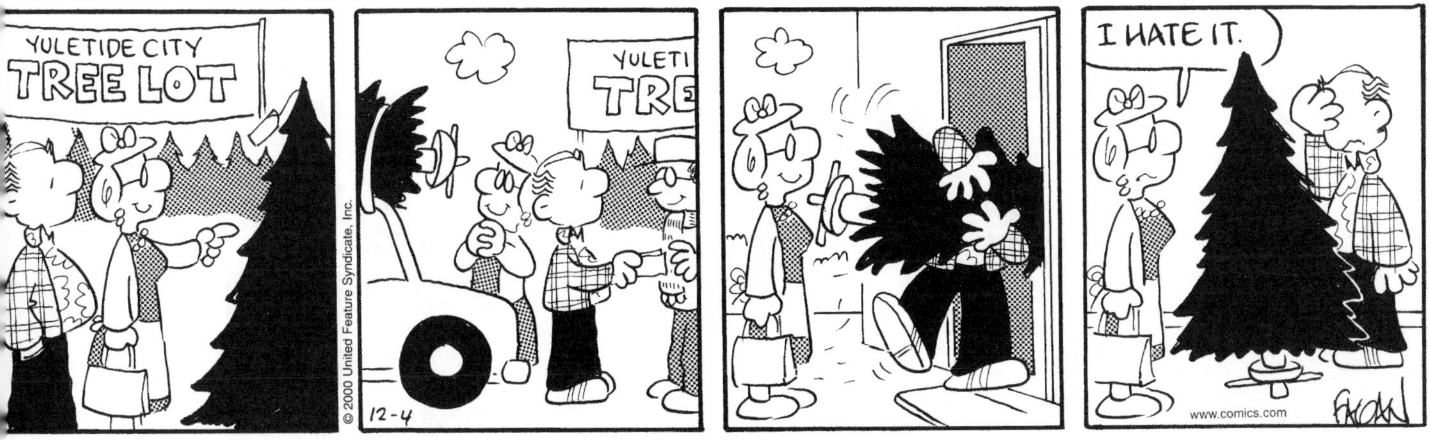
YULETIDE CITY
TREE LOT
© 2000 United Feature Syndicate, Inc.
YULETI
TRE
12-4
I HATE IT.
www.comics.com
FAGAN

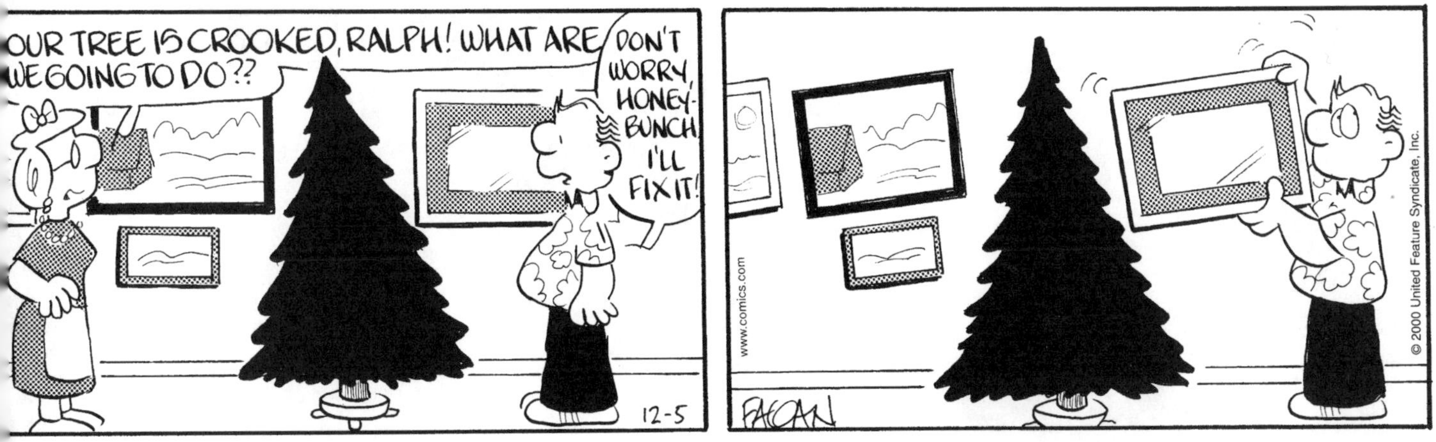
OUR TREE IS CROOKED, RALPH! WHAT ARE WE GOING TO DO??
DON'T WORRY, HONEY-BUNCH. I'LL FIX IT!
12-5
www.comics.com
FAGAN
© 2000 United Feature Syndicate, Inc.

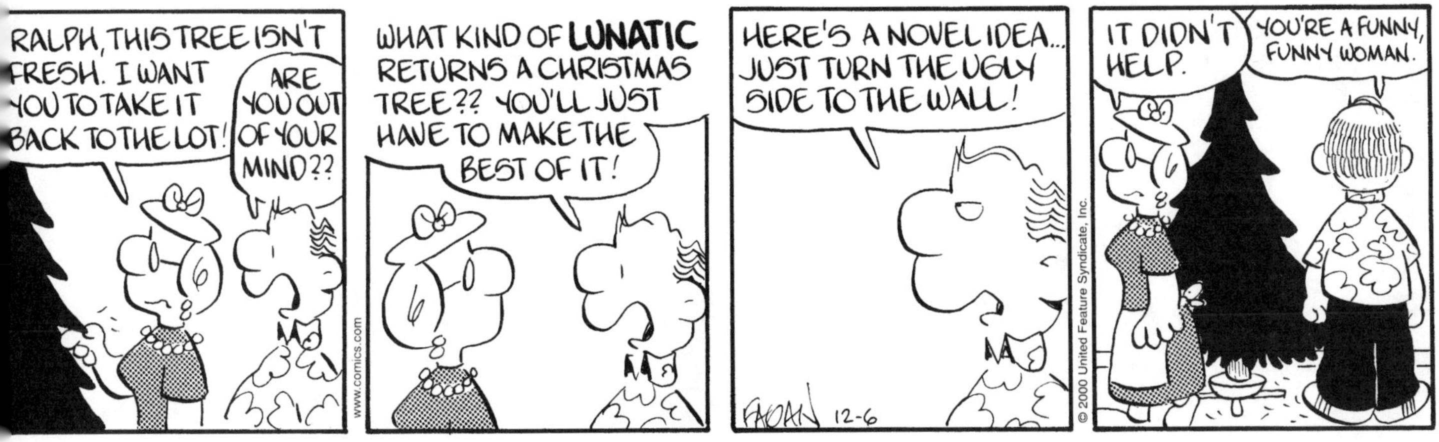
RALPH, THIS TREE ISN'T FRESH. I WANT YOU TO TAKE IT BACK TO THE LOT!
ARE YOU OUT OF YOUR MIND??
www.comics.com
WHAT KIND OF LUNATIC RETURNS A CHRISTMAS TREE?? YOU'LL JUST HAVE TO MAKE THE BEST OF IT!
HERE'S A NOVEL IDEA... JUST TURN THE UGLY SIDE TO THE WALL!
FAGAN 12-6
© 2000 United Feature Syndicate, Inc.
IT DIDN'T HELP.
YOU'RE A FUNNY, FUNNY WOMAN.

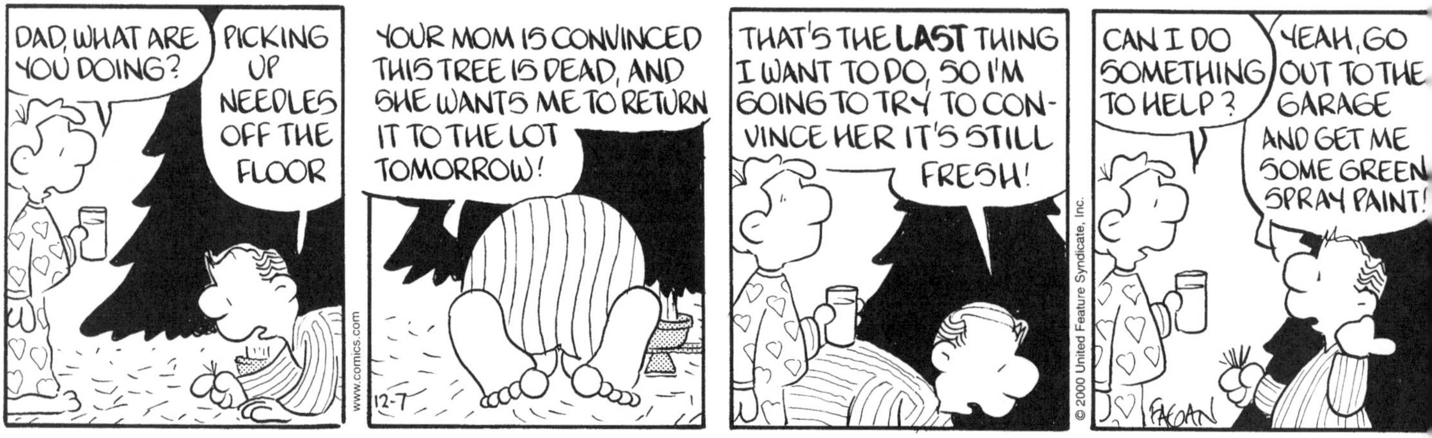
DAD, WHAT ARE YOU DOING?
PICKING UP NEEDLES OFF THE FLOOR
www.comics.com
12-7
YOUR MOM IS CONVINCED THIS TREE IS DEAD, AND SHE WANTS ME TO RETURN IT TO THE LOT TOMORROW!
THAT'S THE **LAST** THING I WANT TO DO, SO I'M GOING TO TRY TO CONVINCE HER IT'S STILL FRESH!
© 2000 United Feature Syndicate, Inc.
CAN I DO SOMETHING TO HELP?
YEAH, GO OUT TO THE GARAGE AND GET ME SOME GREEN SPRAY PAINT!
FAGAN

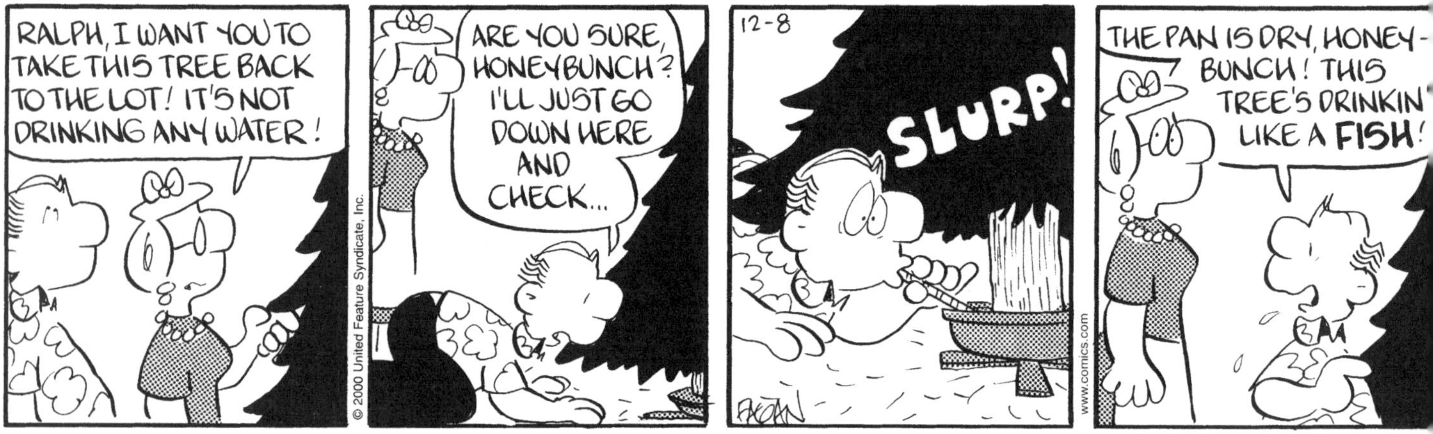
RALPH, I WANT YOU TO TAKE THIS TREE BACK TO THE LOT! IT'S NOT DRINKING ANY WATER!
© 2000 United Feature Syndicate, Inc.
ARE YOU SURE, HONEYBUNCH? I'LL JUST GO DOWN HERE AND CHECK...
12-8
SLURP!
FAGAN
www.comics.com
THE PAN IS DRY, HONEYBUNCH! THIS TREE'S DRINKIN' LIKE A **FISH**!

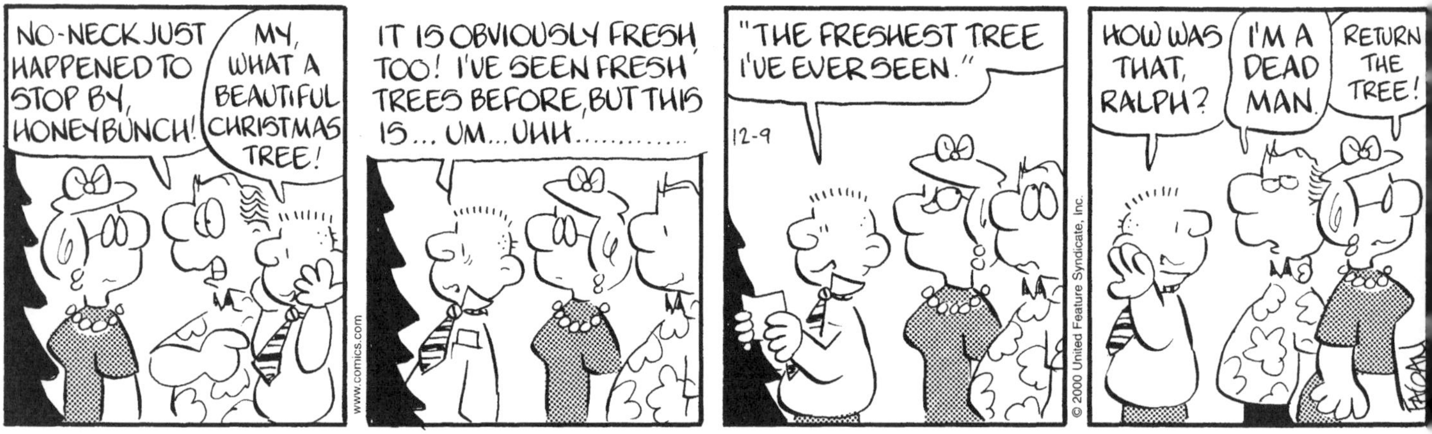
NO-NECK JUST HAPPENED TO STOP BY, HONEYBUNCH!
MY, WHAT A BEAUTIFUL CHRISTMAS TREE!
www.comics.com
IT IS OBVIOUSLY FRESH TOO! I'VE SEEN FRESH TREES BEFORE, BUT THIS IS... UM... UHH............
"THE FRESHEST TREE I'VE EVER SEEN."
12-9
© 2000 United Feature Syndicate, Inc.
HOW WAS THAT, RALPH?
I'M A DEAD MAN.
RETURN THE TREE!
FAGAN

DRABBLE® By KEVIN FAGAN

SCREEECH!
© 2000 United Feature Syndicate, Inc.
12-17
www.comics.com
WHAT A COINCIDENCE! WE JUST HAPPEN TO HAVE A FRUITCAKE FOR YOU, TOO!
FAGAN

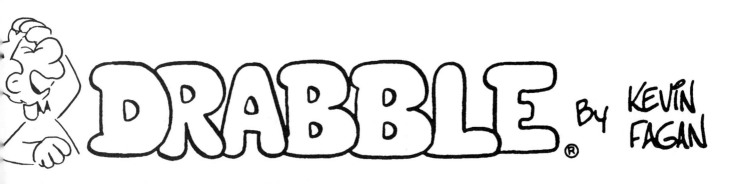

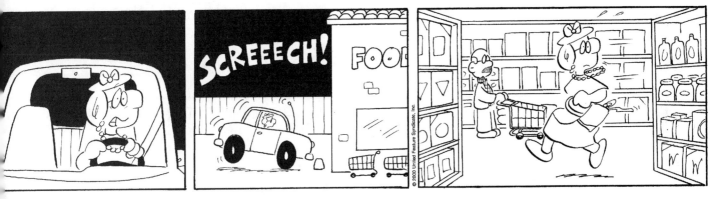

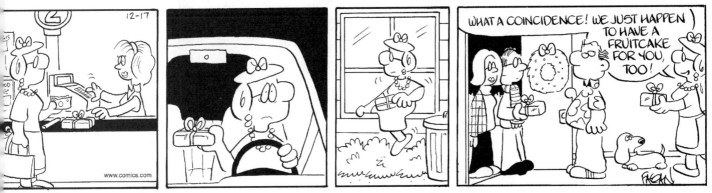

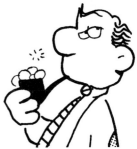

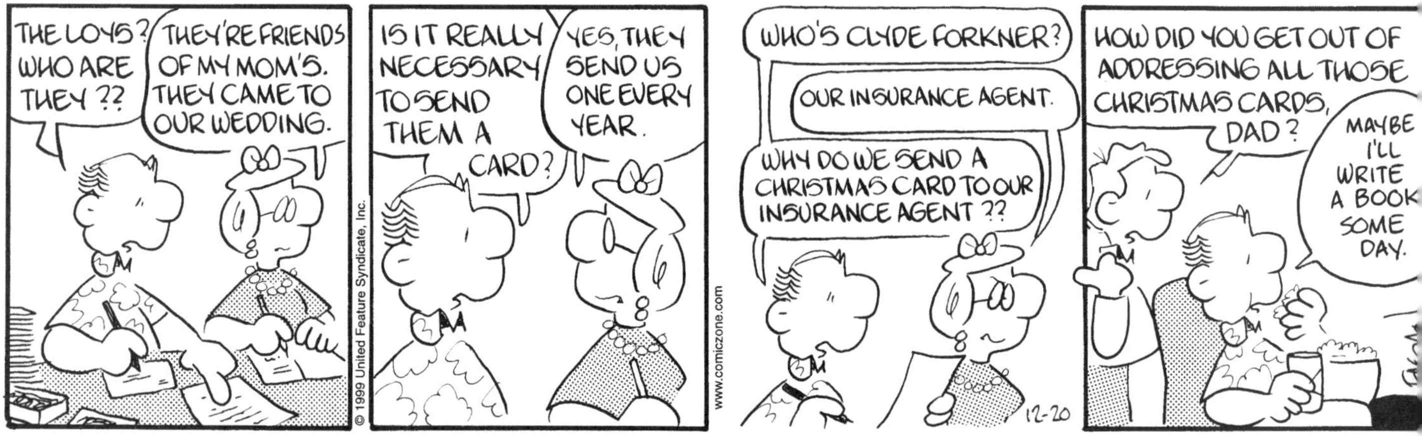
THE LOYS? WHO ARE THEY ??
THEY'RE FRIENDS OF MY MOM'S. THEY CAME TO OUR WEDDING.
© 1999 United Feature Syndicate, Inc.
IS IT REALLY NECESSARY TO SEND THEM A CARD?
YES, THEY SEND US ONE EVERY YEAR.
www.comiczone.com
WHO'S CLYDE FORKNER?
OUR INSURANCE AGENT.
WHY DO WE SEND A CHRISTMAS CARD TO OUR INSURANCE AGENT ??
12-20
HOW DID YOU GET OUT OF ADDRESSING ALL THOSE CHRISTMAS CARDS, DAD?
MAYBE I'LL WRITE A BOOK SOME DAY.

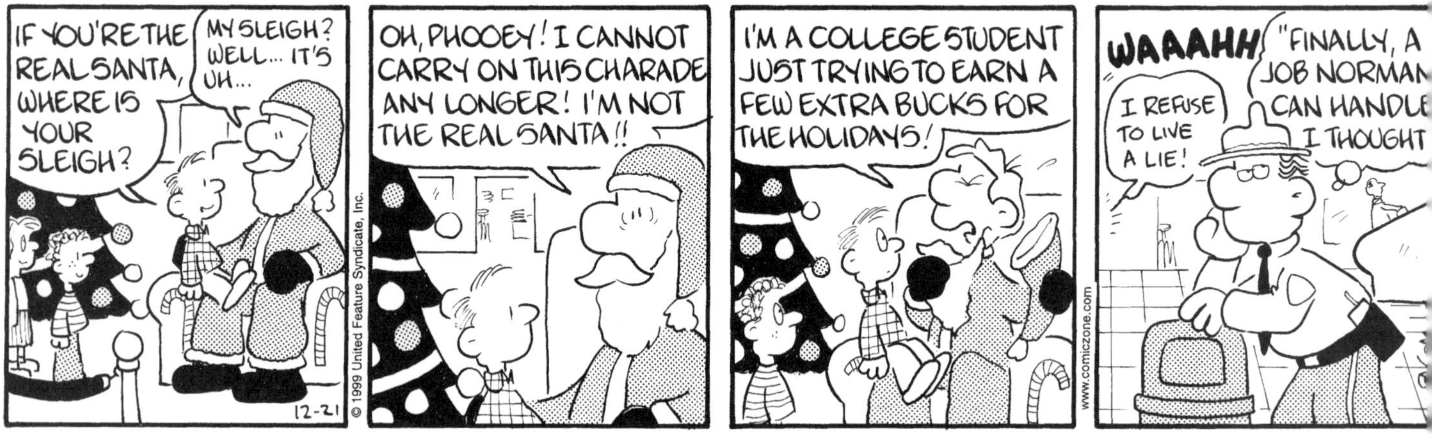
IF YOU'RE THE REAL SANTA, WHERE IS YOUR SLEIGH?
MY SLEIGH? WELL... IT'S UH...
12-21
© 1999 United Feature Syndicate, Inc.
OH, PHOOEY! I CANNOT CARRY ON THIS CHARADE ANY LONGER! I'M NOT THE REAL SANTA!!
I'M A COLLEGE STUDENT JUST TRYING TO EARN A FEW EXTRA BUCKS FOR THE HOLIDAYS!
www.comiczone.com
WAAAHH
I REFUSE TO LIVE A LIE!
"FINALLY, A JOB NORMAN CAN HANDL
I THOUGHT

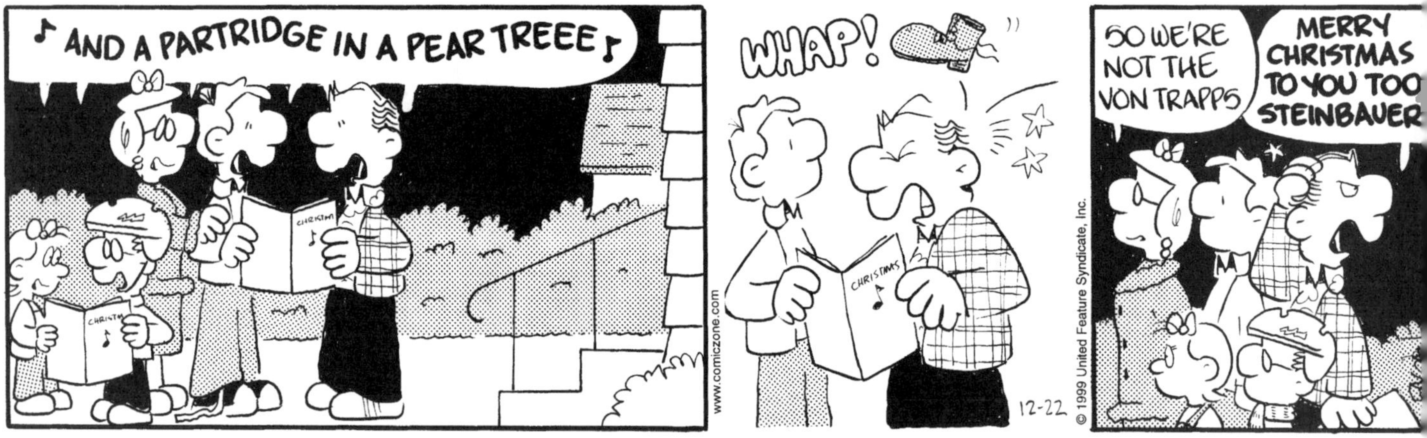
♪ AND A PARTRIDGE IN A PEAR TREEE ♪
CHRISTMAS
www.comiczone.com
WHAP!
CHRISTMAS
12-22
© 1999 United Feature Syndicate, Inc.
SO WE'RE NOT THE VON TRAPPS
MERRY CHRISTMAS TO YOU TOO STEINBAUER

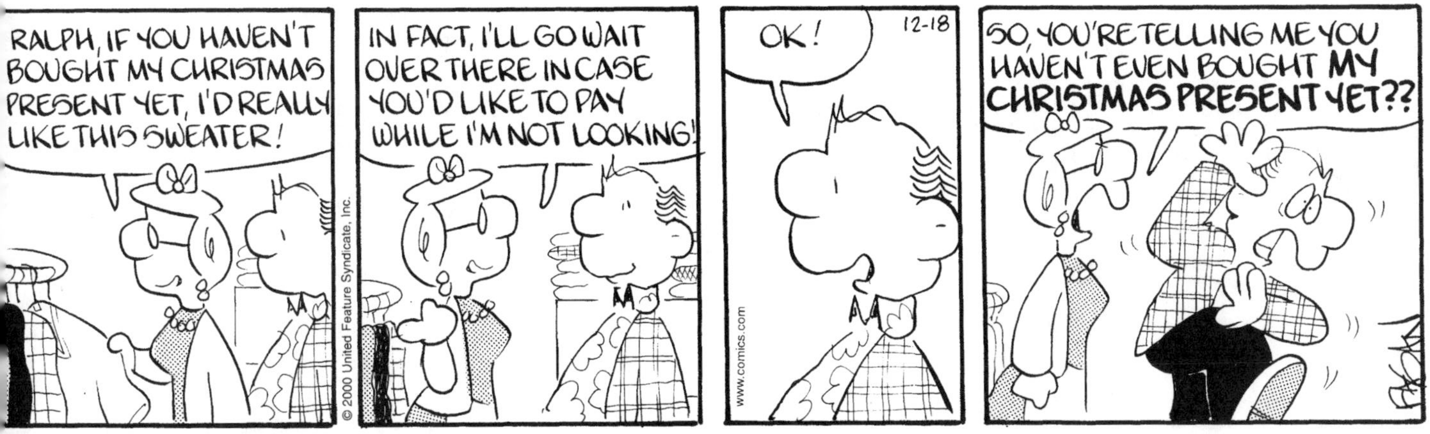
RALPH, IF YOU HAVEN'T BOUGHT MY CHRISTMAS PRESENT YET, I'D REALLY LIKE THIS SWEATER!
© 2000 United Feature Syndicate, Inc.
IN FACT, I'LL GO WAIT OVER THERE IN CASE YOU'D LIKE TO PAY WHILE I'M NOT LOOKING!
www.comics.com
OK!
12-18
SO, YOU'RE TELLING ME YOU HAVEN'T EVEN BOUGHT **MY CHRISTMAS PRESENT** YET??
FAGAN

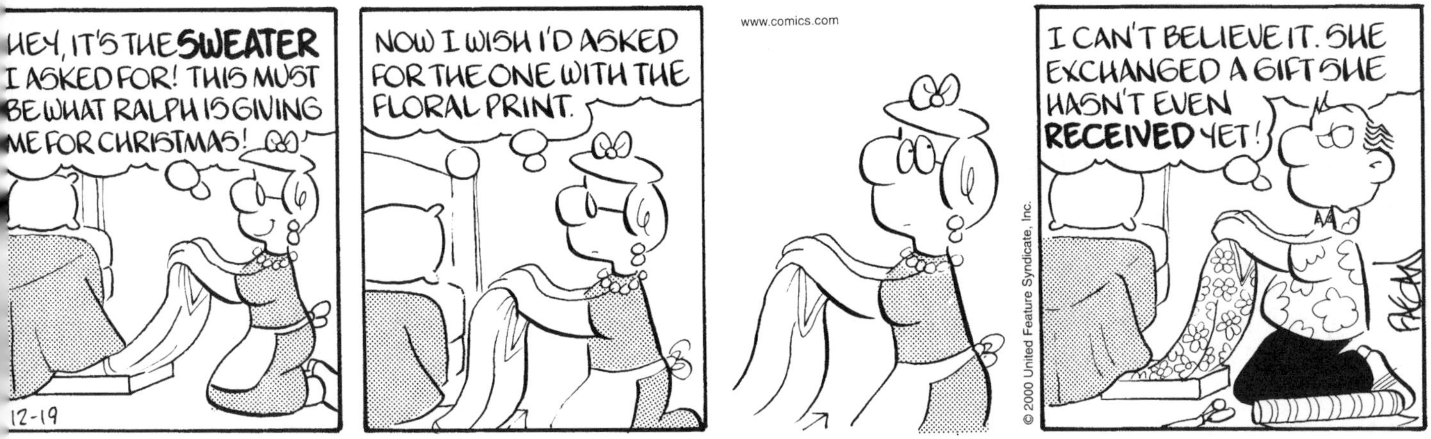
HEY, IT'S THE **SWEATER** I ASKED FOR! THIS MUST BE WHAT RALPH IS GIVING ME FOR CHRISTMAS!
12-19
NOW I WISH I'D ASKED FOR THE ONE WITH THE FLORAL PRINT.
www.comics.com
© 2000 United Feature Syndicate, Inc.
I CAN'T BELIEVE IT. SHE EXCHANGED A GIFT SHE HASN'T EVEN **RECEIVED** YET!
FAGAN

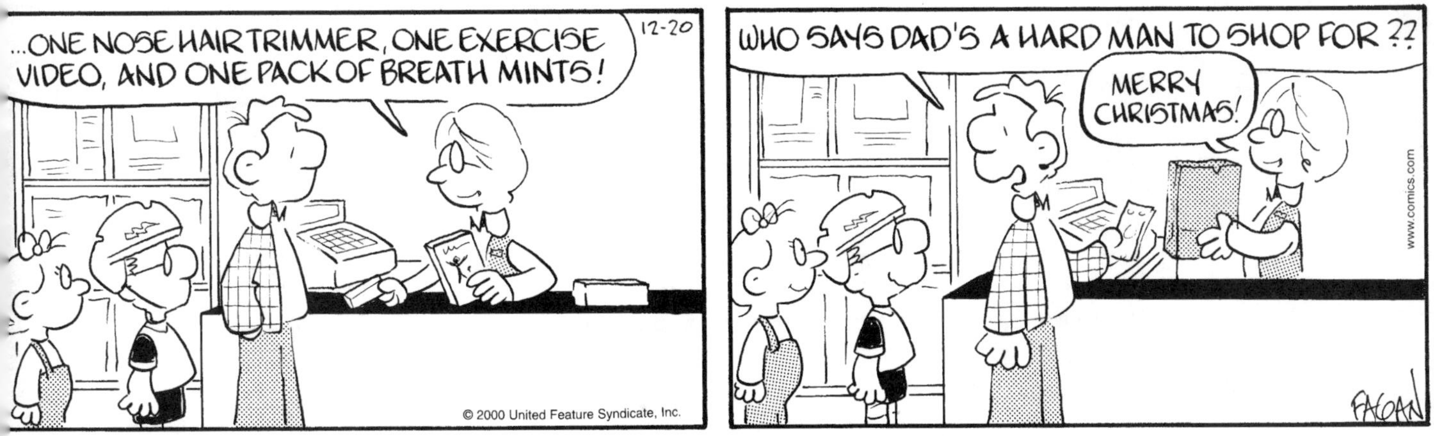
...ONE NOSE HAIR TRIMMER, ONE EXERCISE VIDEO, AND ONE PACK OF BREATH MINTS!
12-20
© 2000 United Feature Syndicate, Inc.
WHO SAYS DAD'S A HARD MAN TO SHOP FOR??
MERRY CHRISTMAS!
www.comics.com
FAGAN

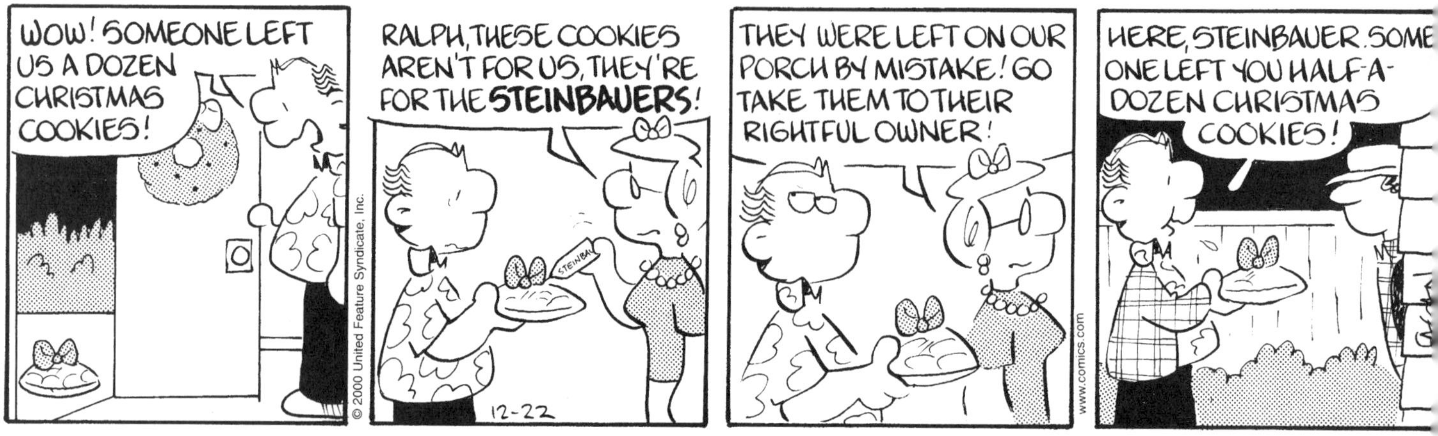

WOW! SOMEONE LEFT US A DOZEN CHRISTMAS COOKIES!
RALPH, THESE COOKIES AREN'T FOR US, THEY'RE FOR THE STEINBAUERS!
STEINBA
THEY WERE LEFT ON OUR PORCH BY MISTAKE! GO TAKE THEM TO THEIR RIGHTFUL OWNER!
HERE, STEINBAUER. SOME ONE LEFT YOU HALF-A-DOZEN CHRISTMAS COOKIES!
© 2000 United Feature Syndicate, Inc.
www.comics.com
12-22

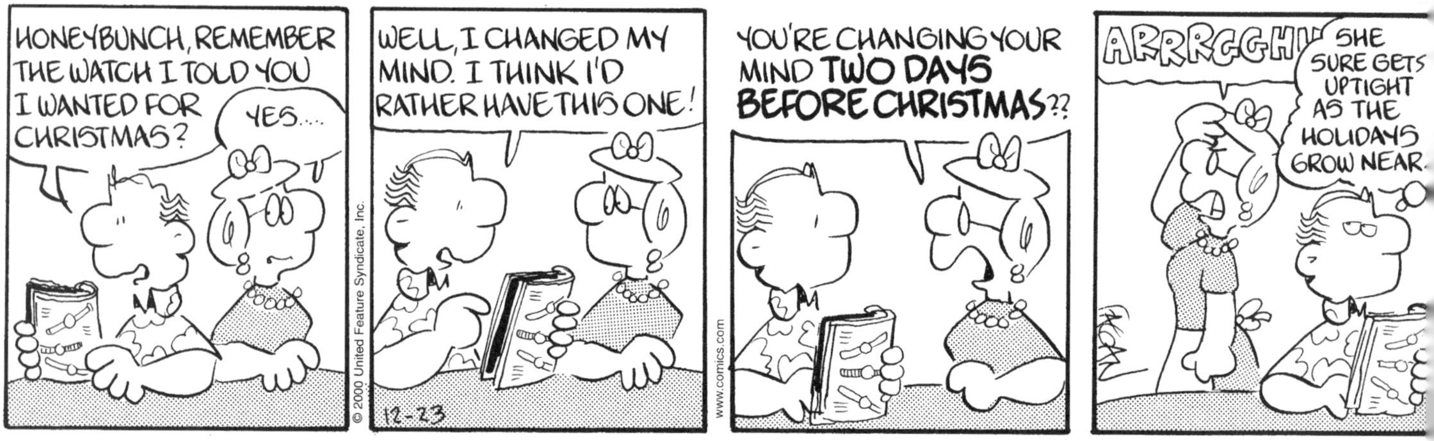

HONEYBUNCH, REMEMBER THE WATCH I TOLD YOU I WANTED FOR CHRISTMAS?
YES....
WELL, I CHANGED MY MIND. I THINK I'D RATHER HAVE THIS ONE!
YOU'RE CHANGING YOUR MIND TWO DAYS BEFORE CHRISTMAS??
ARRRGGH!!
SHE SURE GETS UPTIGHT AS THE HOLIDAYS GROW NEAR.
© 2000 United Feature Syndicate, Inc.
www.comics.com
12-23

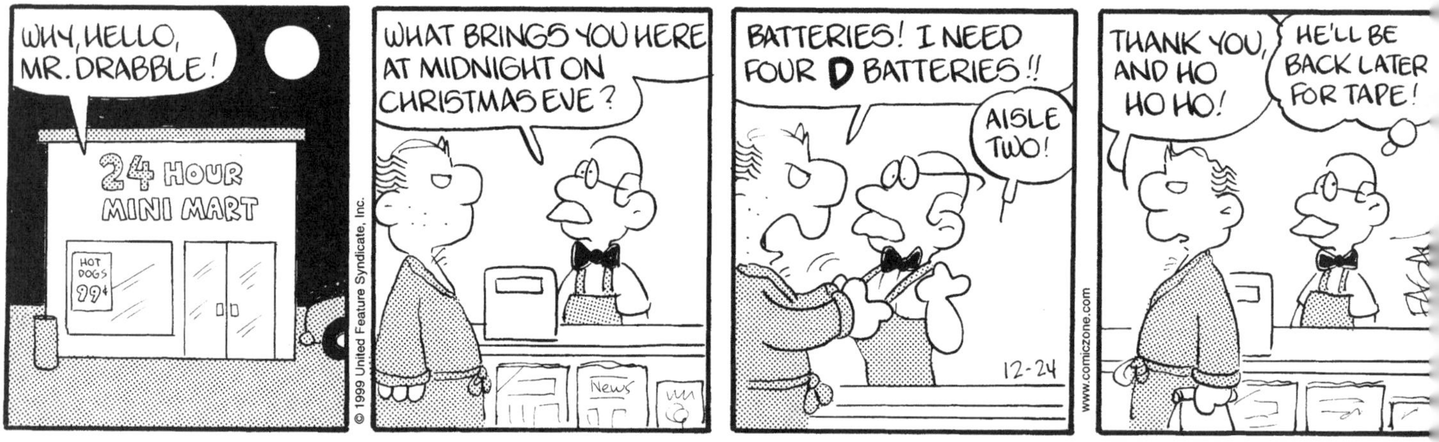

WHY, HELLO, MR. DRABBLE!
24 HOUR MINI MART
HOT DOGS 99¢
WHAT BRINGS YOU HERE AT MIDNIGHT ON CHRISTMAS EVE?
News
BATTERIES! I NEED FOUR D BATTERIES!!
AISLE TWO!
THANK YOU, AND HO HO HO!
HE'LL BE BACK LATER FOR TAPE!
© 1999 United Feature Syndicate, Inc.
www.comiczone.com
12-24

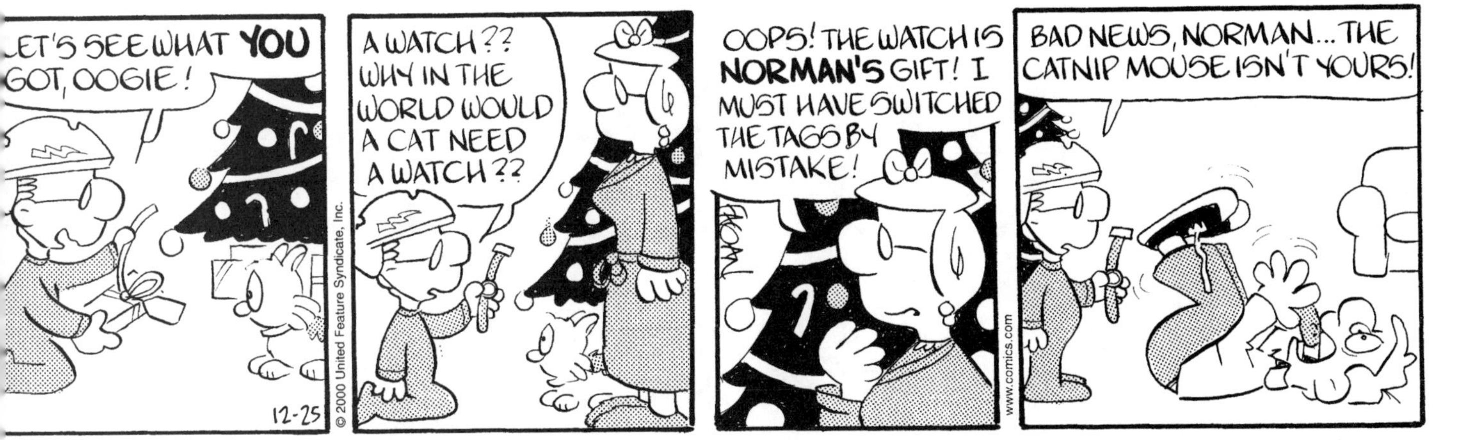
LET'S SEE WHAT **YOU** GOT, OOGIE!
A WATCH?? WHY IN THE WORLD WOULD A CAT NEED A WATCH??
OOPS! THE WATCH IS **NORMAN'S** GIFT! I MUST HAVE SWITCHED THE TAGS BY MISTAKE!
BAD NEWS, NORMAN... THE CATNIP MOUSE ISN'T YOURS!
© 2000 United Feature Syndicate, Inc.
www.comics.com
12-25

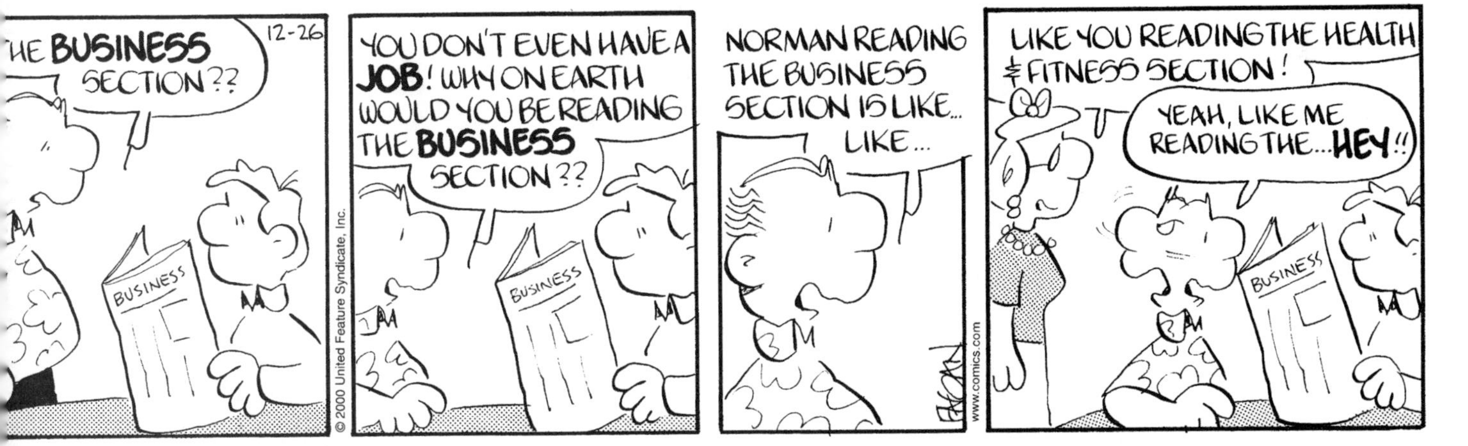
THE **BUSINESS** SECTION??
BUSINESS
YOU DON'T EVEN HAVE A **JOB**! WHY ON EARTH WOULD YOU BE READING THE **BUSINESS** SECTION??
NORMAN READING THE BUSINESS SECTION IS LIKE... LIKE...
LIKE YOU READING THE HEALTH & FITNESS SECTION!
YEAH, LIKE ME READING THE... **HEY**!!
© 2000 United Feature Syndicate, Inc.
www.comics.com
12-26

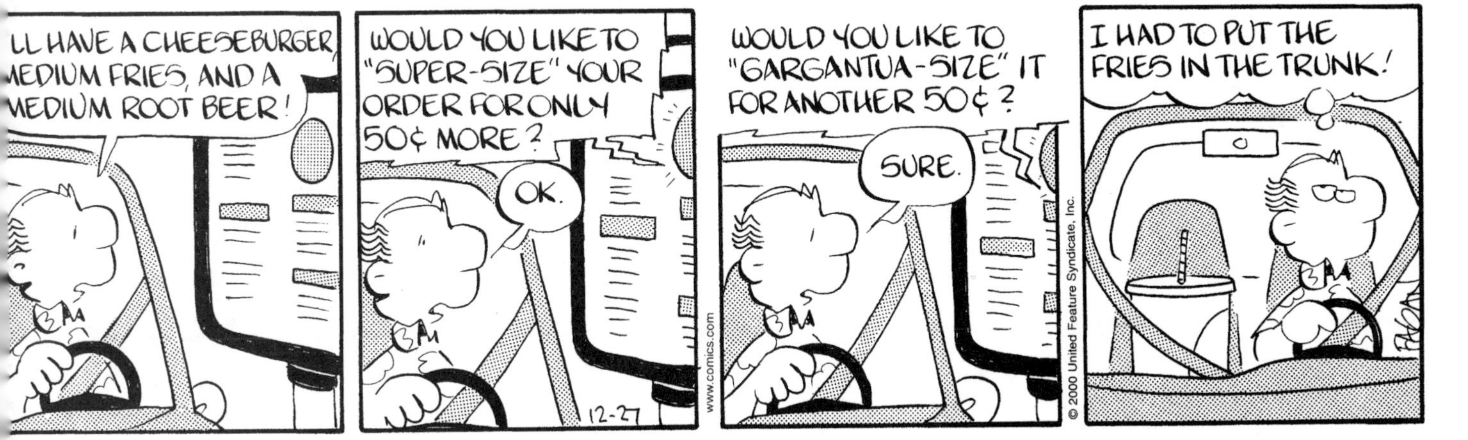
I'LL HAVE A CHEESEBURGER, MEDIUM FRIES, AND A MEDIUM ROOT BEER!
WOULD YOU LIKE TO "SUPER-SIZE" YOUR ORDER FOR ONLY 50¢ MORE?
OK.
WOULD YOU LIKE TO "GARGANTUA-SIZE" IT FOR ANOTHER 50¢?
SURE.
I HAD TO PUT THE FRIES IN THE TRUNK!
© 2000 United Feature Syndicate, Inc.
www.comics.com
12-27

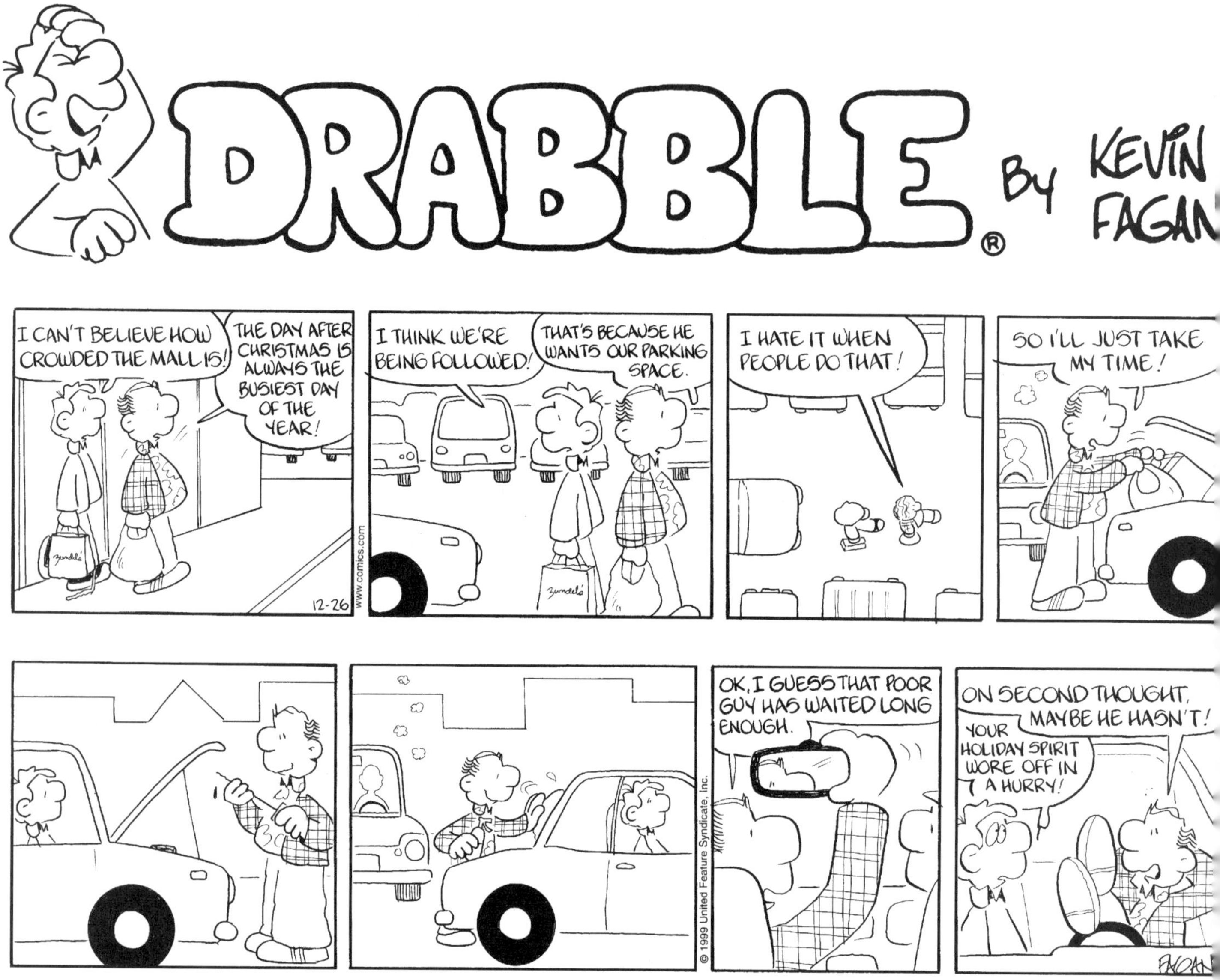
DRABBLE
By KEVIN FAGAN
I CAN'T BELIEVE HOW CROWDED THE MALL IS!
THE DAY AFTER CHRISTMAS IS ALWAYS THE BUSIEST DAY OF THE YEAR!
12-26
www.comics.com
I THINK WE'RE BEING FOLLOWED!
THAT'S BECAUSE HE WANTS OUR PARKING SPACE.
I HATE IT WHEN PEOPLE DO THAT!
SO I'LL JUST TAKE MY TIME!
© 1999 United Feature Syndicate, Inc.
OK, I GUESS THAT POOR GUY HAS WAITED LONG ENOUGH.
ON SECOND THOUGHT, MAYBE HE HASN'T!
YOUR HOLIDAY SPIRIT WORE OFF IN A HURRY!
FAGAN

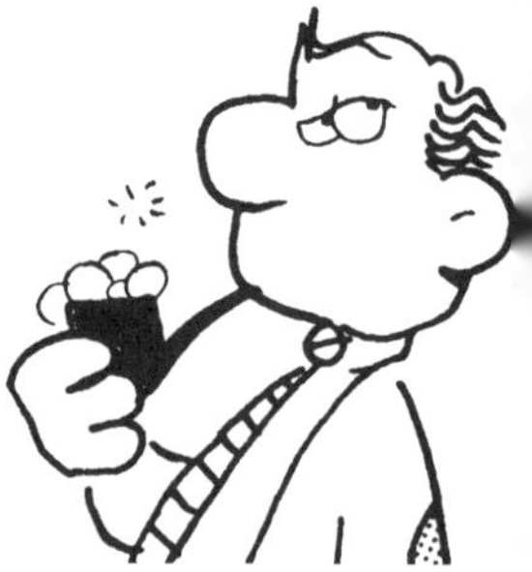

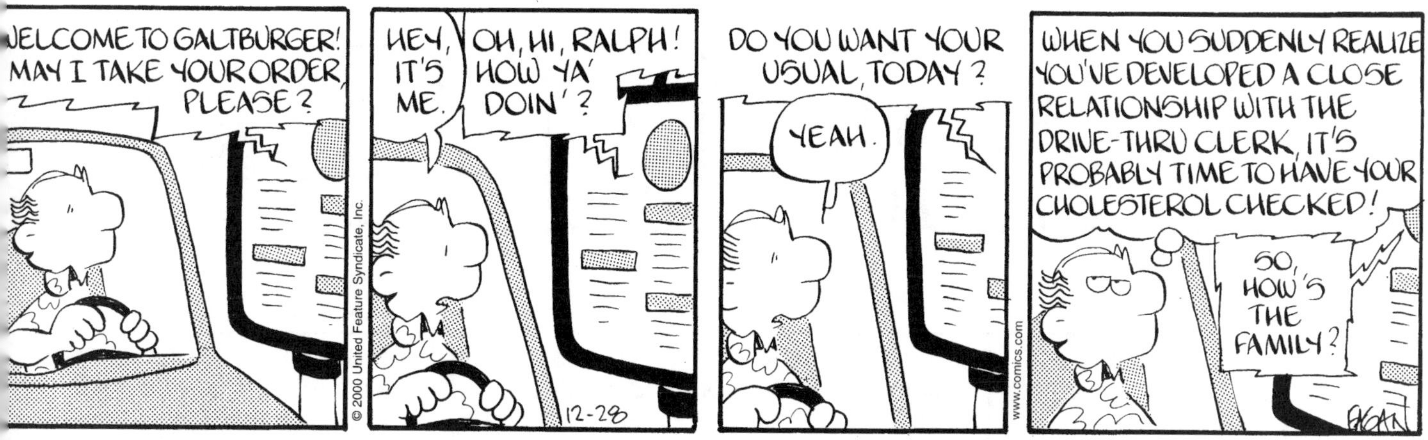
WELCOME TO GALTBURGER! MAY I TAKE YOUR ORDER, PLEASE?
© 2000 United Feature Syndicate, Inc.
HEY, IT'S ME.
OH, HI, RALPH! HOW 'YA' DOIN'?
12-28
DO YOU WANT YOUR USUAL, TODAY?
YEAH.
www.comics.com
WHEN YOU SUDDENLY REALIZE YOU'VE DEVELOPED A CLOSE RELATIONSHIP WITH THE DRIVE-THRU CLERK, IT'S PROBABLY TIME TO HAVE YOUR CHOLESTEROL CHECKED!
SO, HOW'S THE FAMILY?
FAGAN

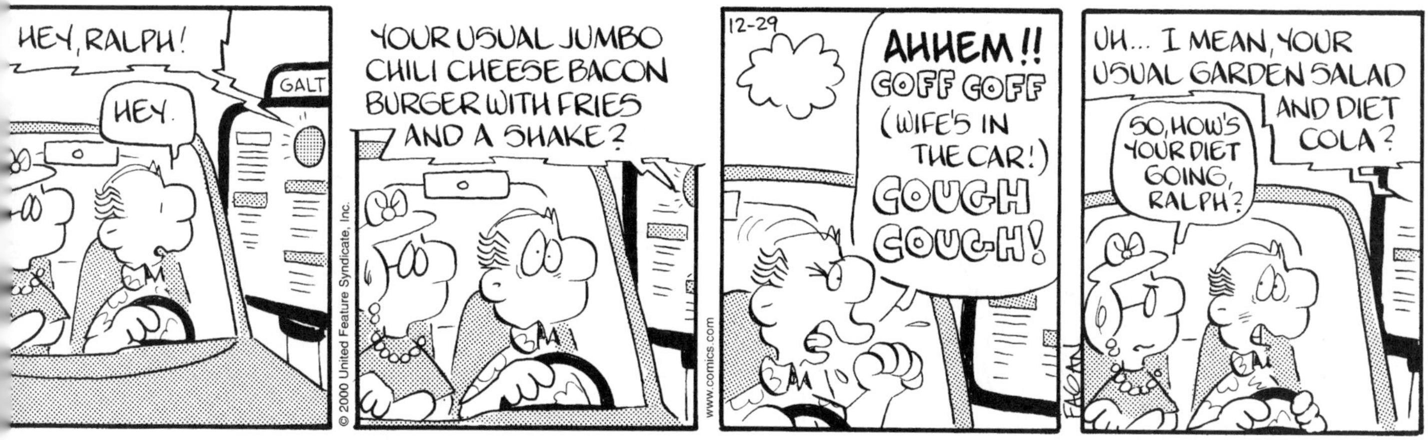
HEY, RALPH!
HEY.
GALT
© 2000 United Feature Syndicate, Inc.
YOUR USUAL JUMBO CHILI CHEESE BACON BURGER WITH FRIES AND A SHAKE?
www.comics.com
12-29
AHHEM!! GOFF GOFF (WIFE'S IN THE CAR!) GOUGH GOUGH!
FAGAN
UH... I MEAN, YOUR USUAL GARDEN SALAD AND DIET COLA?
SO, HOW'S YOUR DIET GOING, RALPH?

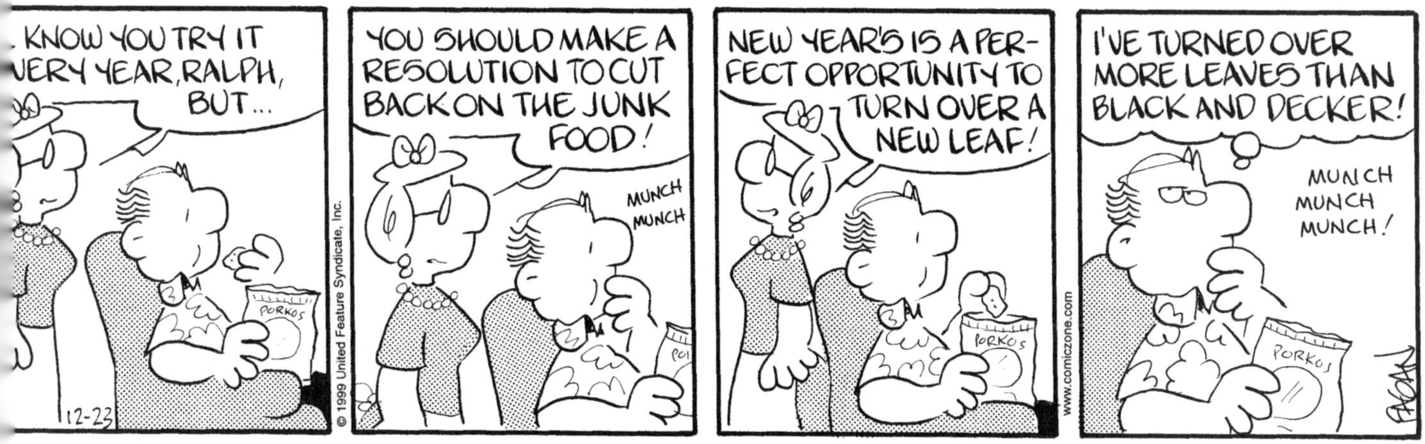
I KNOW YOU TRY IT EVERY YEAR, RALPH, BUT...
12-23
© 1999 United Feature Syndicate, Inc.
YOU SHOULD MAKE A RESOLUTION TO CUT BACK ON THE JUNK FOOD!
MUNCH MUNCH
NEW YEAR'S IS A PERFECT OPPORTUNITY TO TURN OVER A NEW LEAF!
PORKOS
www.comiczone.com
I'VE TURNED OVER MORE LEAVES THAN BLACK AND DECKER!
MUNCH MUNCH MUNCH!
PORKOS
FAGAN

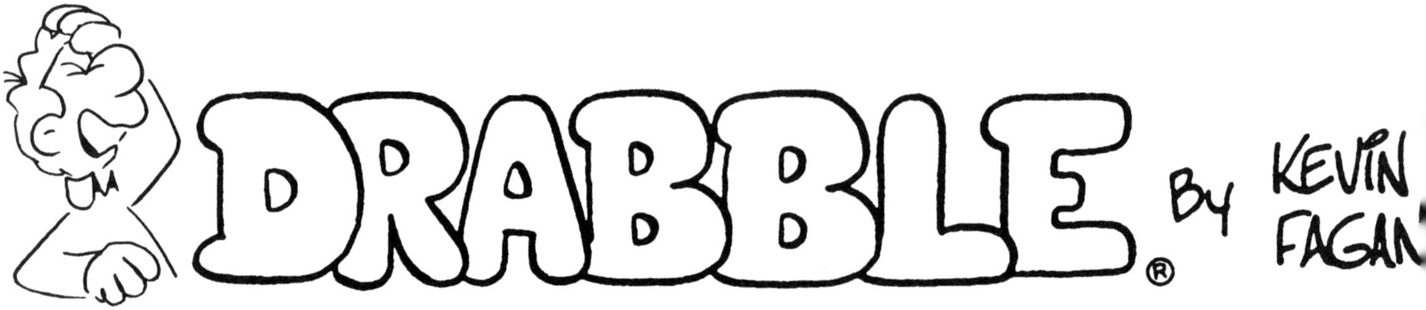
DRABBLE®
By KEVIN FAGAN

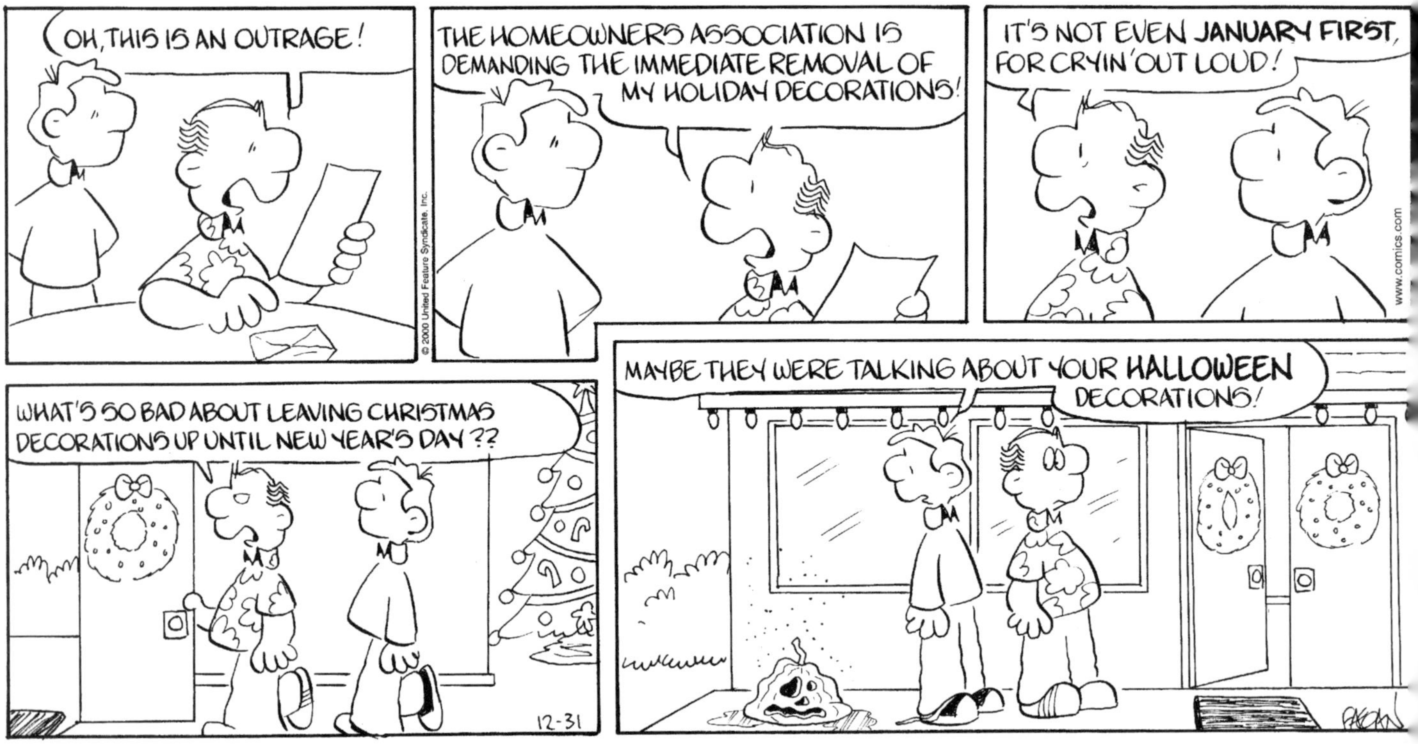
OH, THIS IS AN OUTRAGE!
THE HOMEOWNERS ASSOCIATION IS DEMANDING THE IMMEDIATE REMOVAL OF MY HOLIDAY DECORATIONS!
IT'S NOT EVEN JANUARY FIRST, FOR CRYIN' OUT LOUD!
WHAT'S SO BAD ABOUT LEAVING CHRISTMAS DECORATIONS UP UNTIL NEW YEAR'S DAY??
MAYBE THEY WERE TALKING ABOUT YOUR HALLOWEEN DECORATIONS!
© 2000 United Feature Syndicate, Inc.
www.comics.com
12-31
FAGAN

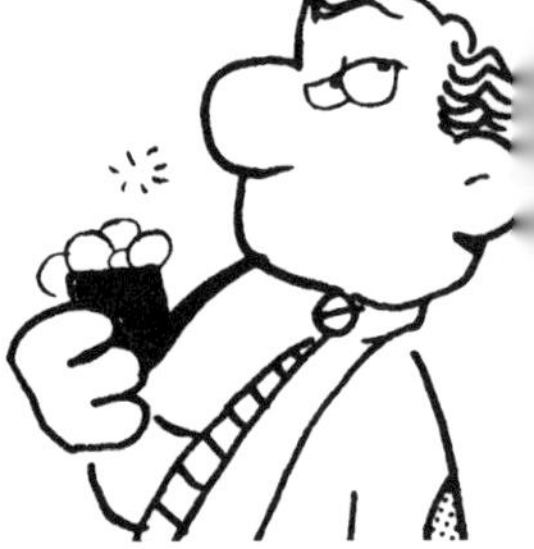

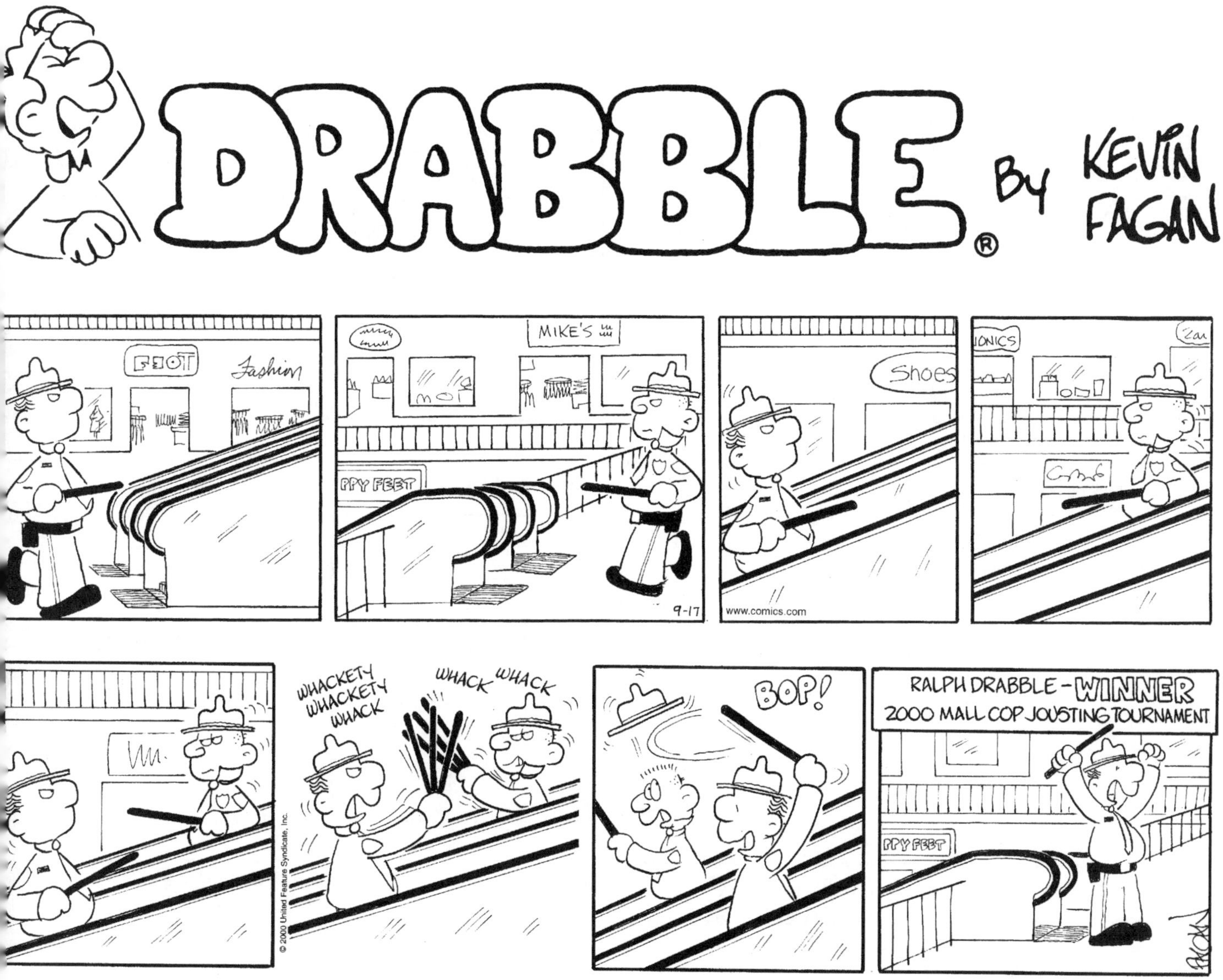
DRABBLE®
By KEVIN FAGAN
Fashion
MIKE'S
PPY FEET
9-17
Shoes
www.comics.com
IONICS
© 2000 United Feature Syndicate, Inc.
WHACKETY WHACKETY WHACK
WHACK WHACK
BOP!
RALPH DRABBLE - WINNER
2000 MALL COP JOUSTING TOURNAMENT
PPY FEET

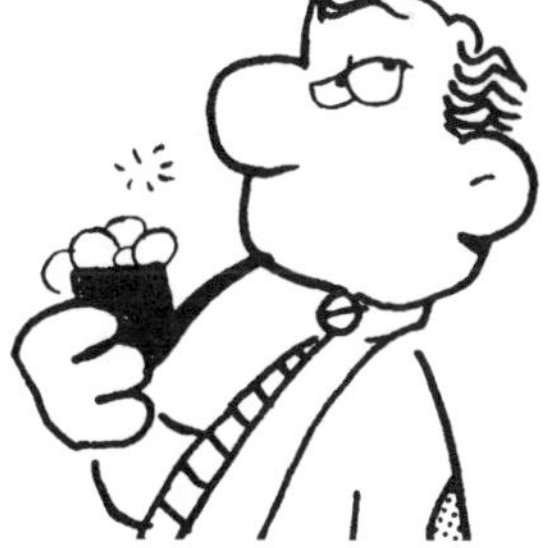

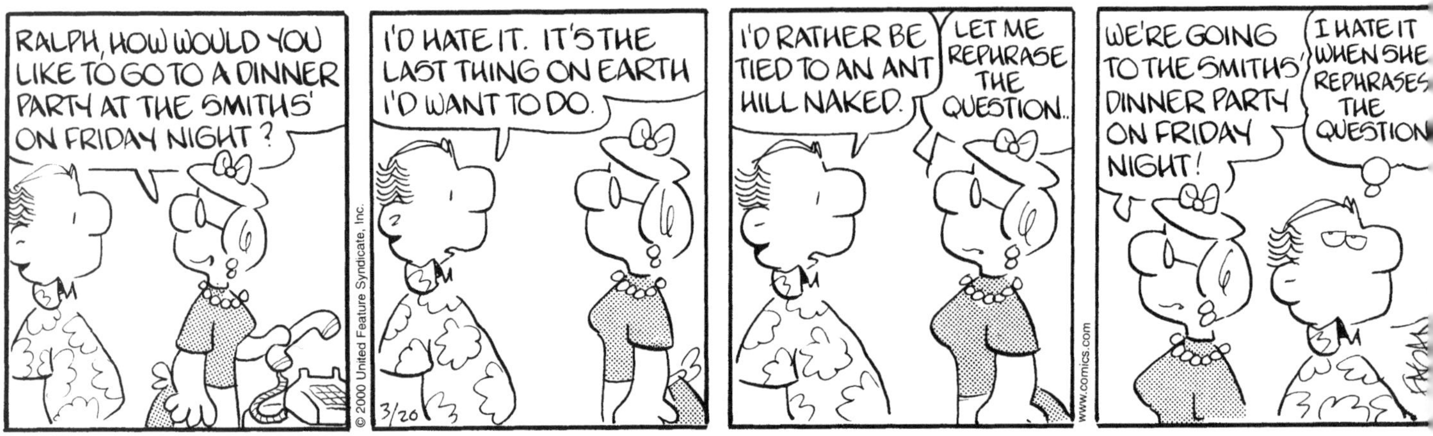
RALPH, HOW WOULD YOU LIKE TO GO TO A DINNER PARTY AT THE SMITHS' ON FRIDAY NIGHT ?
I'D HATE IT. IT'S THE LAST THING ON EARTH I'D WANT TO DO.
I'D RATHER BE TIED TO AN ANT HILL NAKED.
LET ME REPHRASE THE QUESTION..
WE'RE GOING TO THE SMITHS' DINNER PARTY ON FRIDAY NIGHT!
I HATE IT WHEN SHE REPHRASES THE QUESTION
© 2000 United Feature Syndicate, Inc.
3/20
www.comics.com

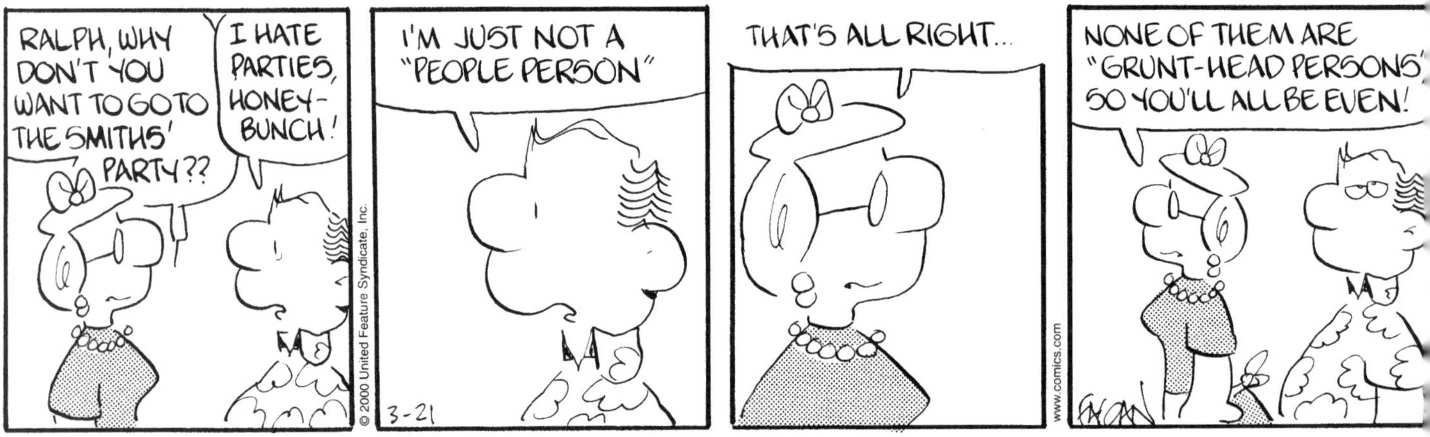
RALPH, WHY DON'T YOU WANT TO GO TO THE SMITHS' PARTY??
I HATE PARTIES, HONEY-BUNCH!
I'M JUST NOT A "PEOPLE PERSON"
THAT'S ALL RIGHT...
NONE OF THEM ARE "GRUNT-HEAD PERSONS" SO YOU'LL ALL BE EVEN!
© 2000 United Feature Syndicate, Inc.
3-21
www.comics.com

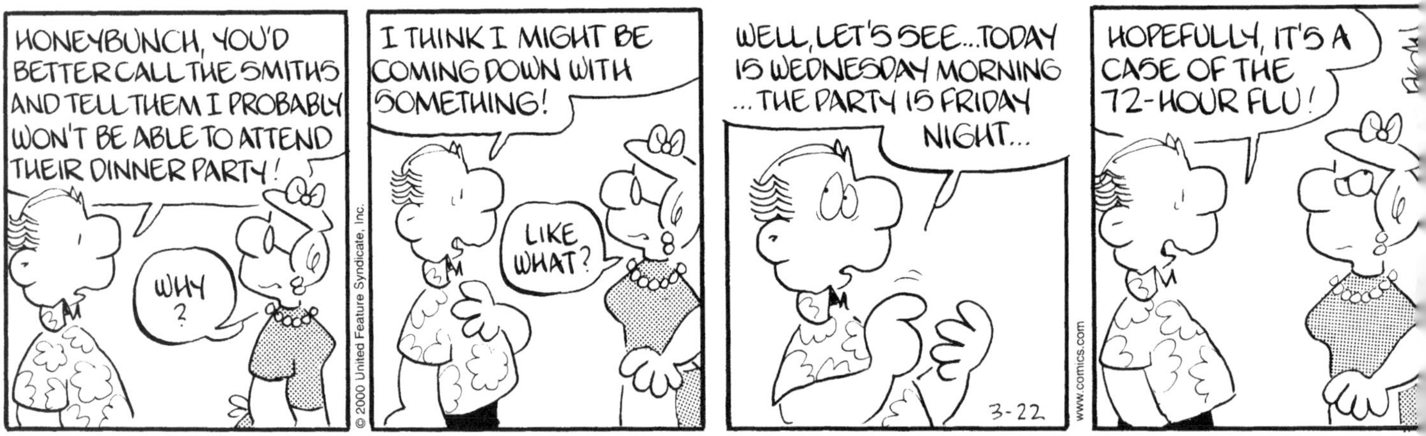
HONEYBUNCH, YOU'D BETTER CALL THE SMITHS AND TELL THEM I PROBABLY WON'T BE ABLE TO ATTEND THEIR DINNER PARTY!
WHY ?
I THINK I MIGHT BE COMING DOWN WITH SOMETHING!
LIKE WHAT?
WELL, LET'S SEE...TODAY IS WEDNESDAY MORNING ...THE PARTY IS FRIDAY NIGHT...
HOPEFULLY, IT'S A CASE OF THE 72-HOUR FLU!
© 2000 United Feature Syndicate, Inc.
3-22
www.comics.com

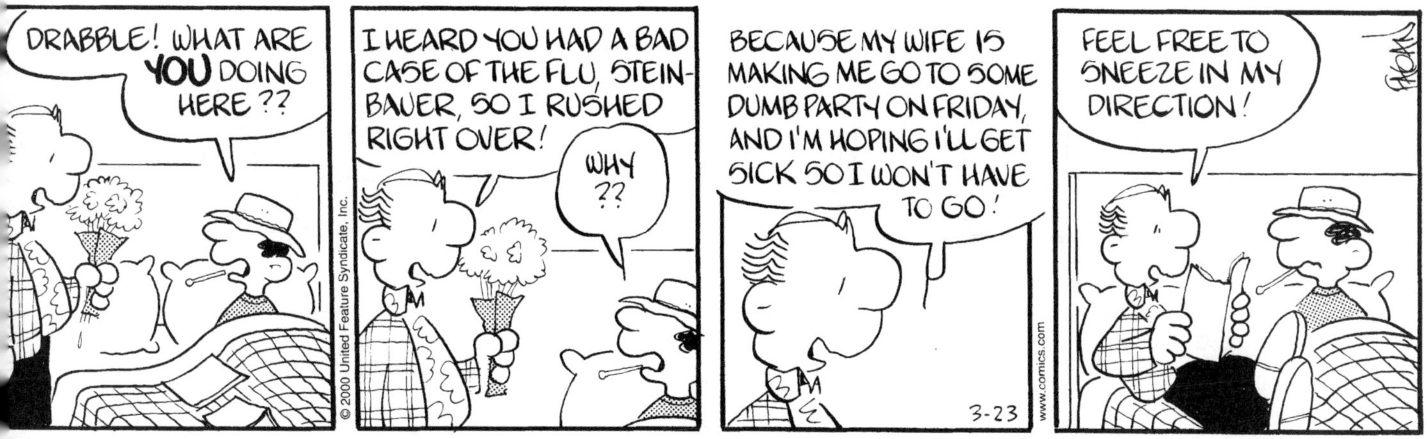
DRABBLE! WHAT ARE YOU DOING HERE??
I HEARD YOU HAD A BAD CASE OF THE FLU, STEINBAUER, SO I RUSHED RIGHT OVER!
WHY ??
BECAUSE MY WIFE IS MAKING ME GO TO SOME DUMB PARTY ON FRIDAY, AND I'M HOPING I'LL GET SICK SO I WON'T HAVE TO GO!
3-23
FEEL FREE TO SNEEZE IN MY DIRECTION!
© 2000 United Feature Syndicate, Inc.
www.comics.com

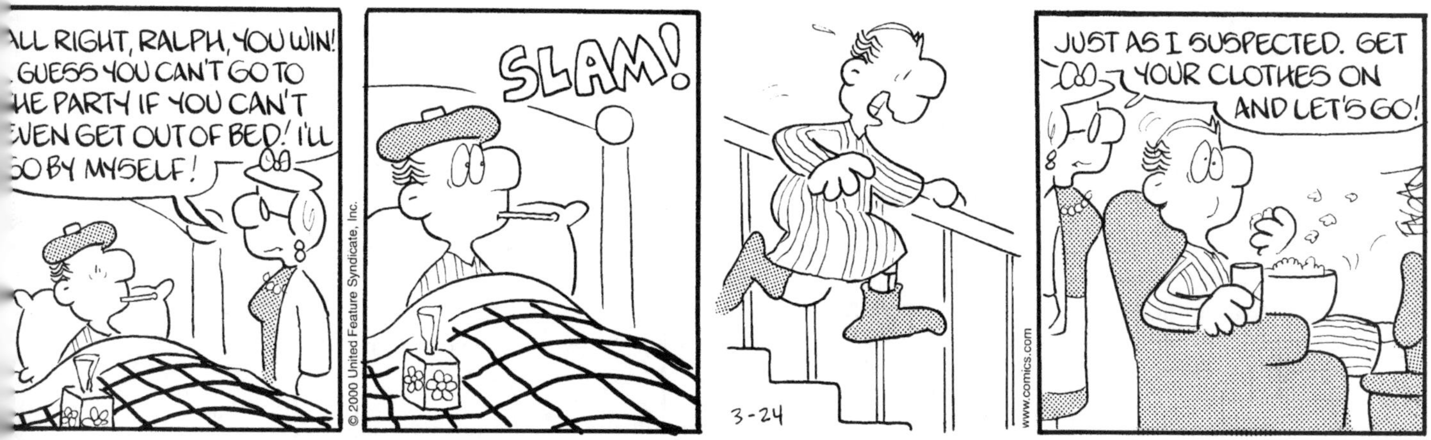
LL RIGHT, RALPH, YOU WIN! GUESS YOU CAN'T GO TO HE PARTY IF YOU CAN'T VEN GET OUT OF BED! I'LL O BY MYSELF!
SLAM!
3-24
JUST AS I SUSPECTED. GET YOUR CLOTHES ON AND LET'S GO!
© 2000 United Feature Syndicate, Inc.
www.comics.com

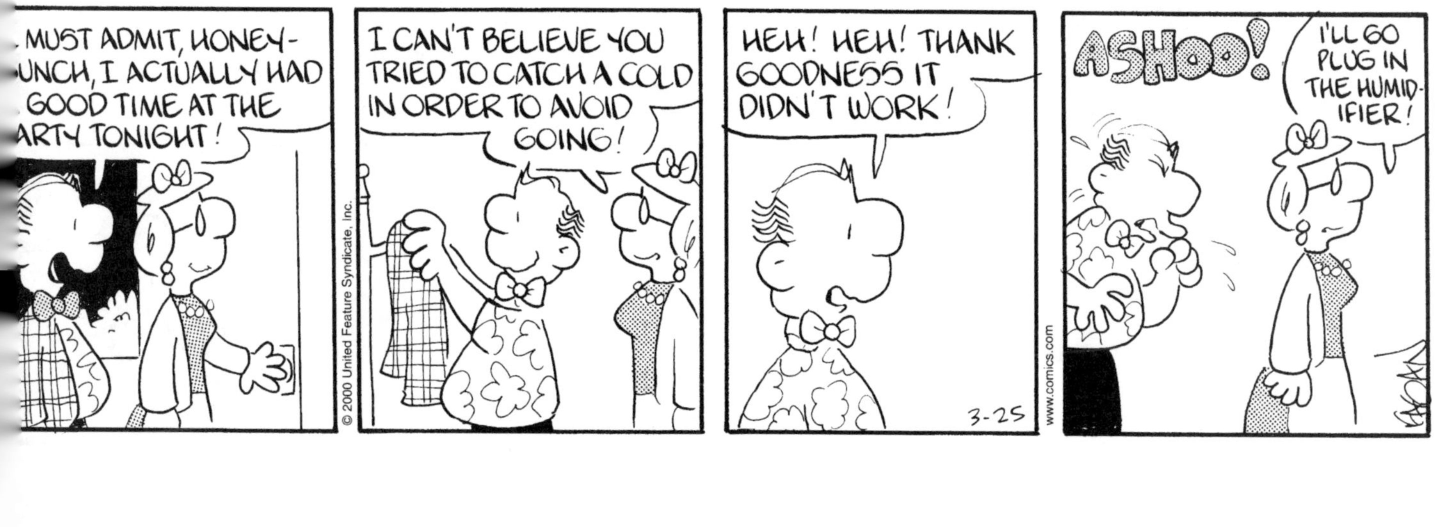
MUST ADMIT, HONEY-UNCH, I ACTUALLY HAD GOOD TIME AT THE ARTY TONIGHT!
I CAN'T BELIEVE YOU TRIED TO CATCH A COLD IN ORDER TO AVOID GOING!
HEH! HEH! THANK GOODNESS IT DIDN'T WORK!
3-25
ASHOO!
I'LL GO PLUG IN THE HUMIDIFIER!
© 2000 United Feature Syndicate, Inc.
www.comics.com

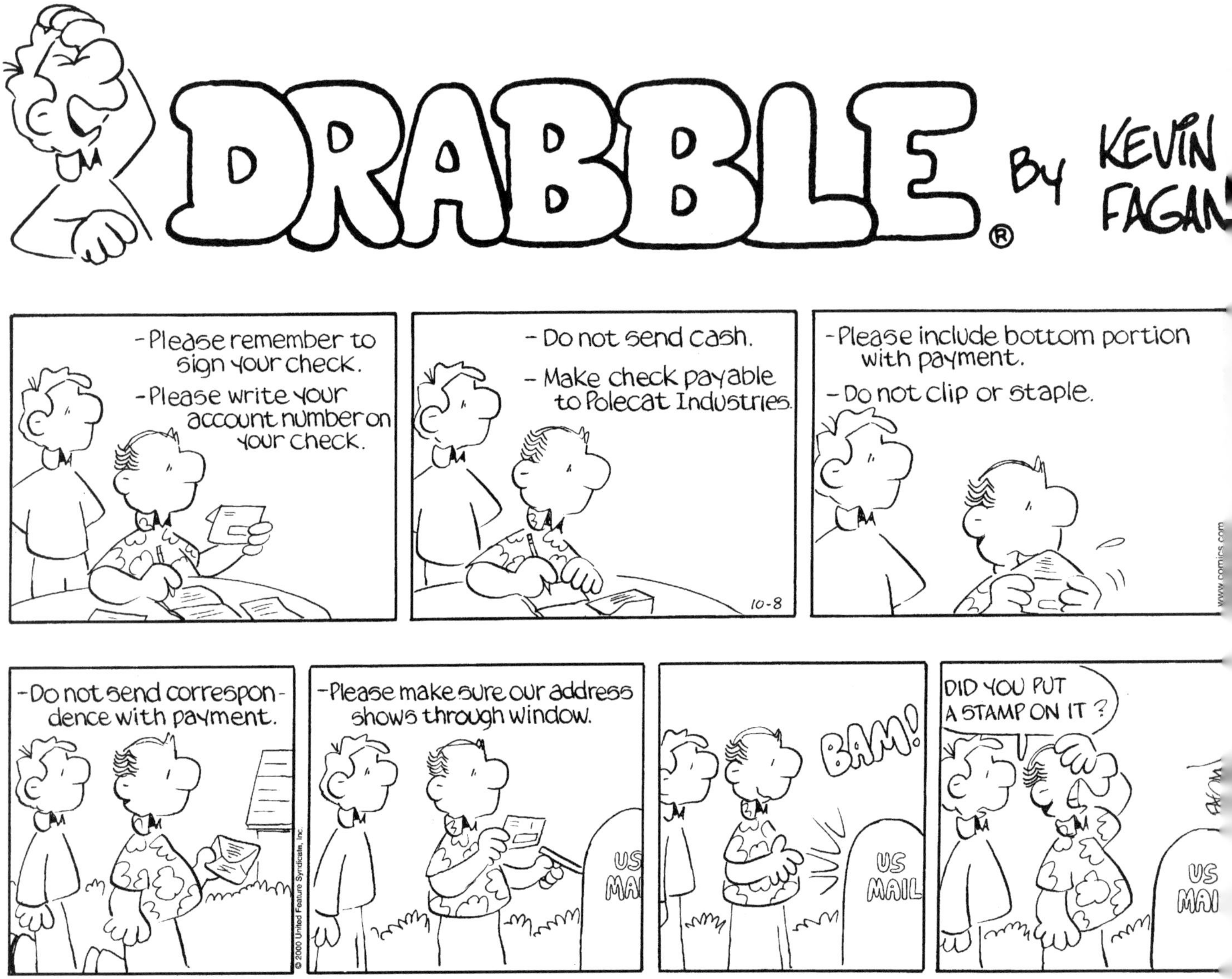
DRABBLE® By KEVIN FAGAN
-Please remember to sign your check.
-Please write your account number on your check.
- Do not send cash.
- Make check payable to Polecat Industries.
10-8
-Please include bottom portion with payment.
- Do not clip or staple.
www.comics.com
-Do not send correspondence with payment.
© 2000 United Feature Syndicate, Inc.
-Please make sure our address shows through window.
US MAIL
BAM!
US MAIL
DID YOU PUT A STAMP ON IT ?
US MAI

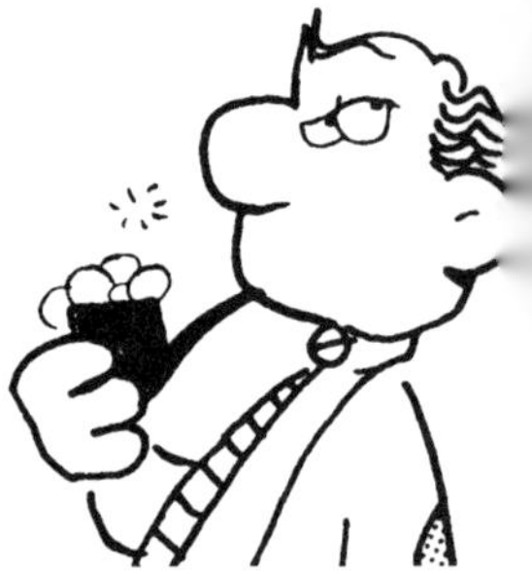

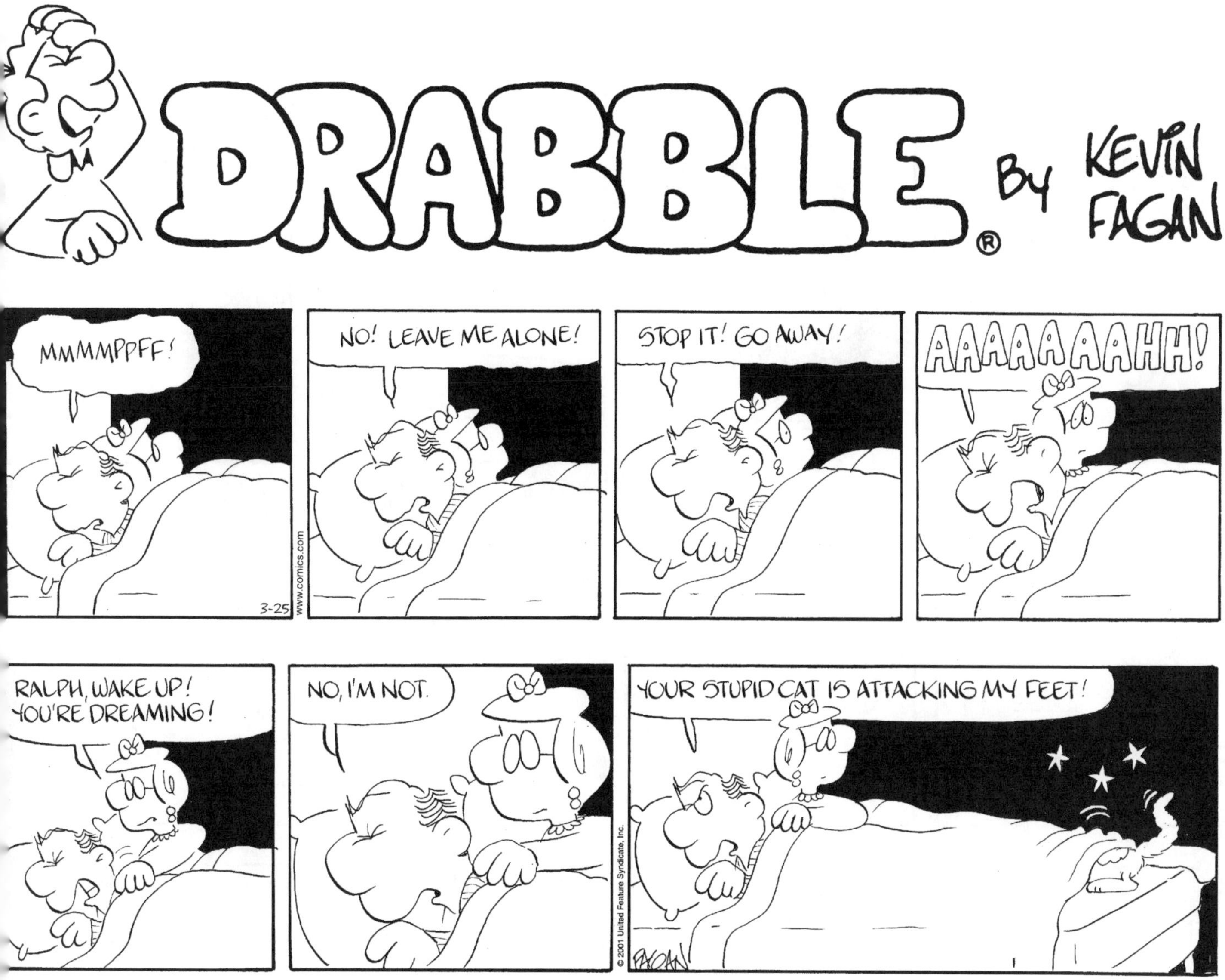
DRABBLE®
By KEVIN FAGAN
MMMMPPFF!
NO! LEAVE ME ALONE!
STOP IT! GO AWAY!
AAAAAAAHH!
3-25
www.comics.com
RALPH, WAKE UP! YOU'RE DREAMING!
NO, I'M NOT.
© 2001 United Feature Syndicate, Inc.
YOUR STUPID CAT IS ATTACKING MY FEET!
FAGAN

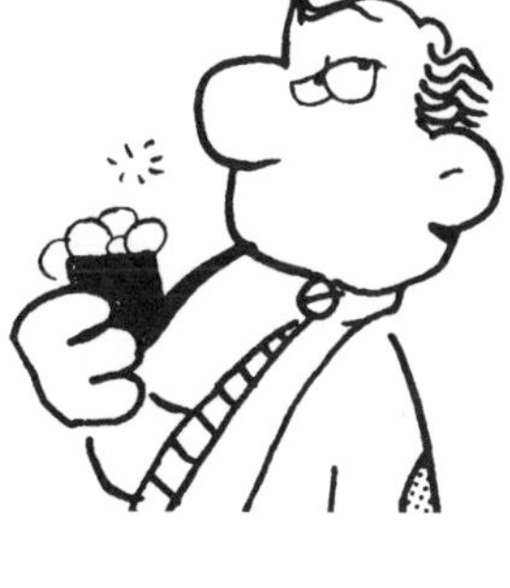

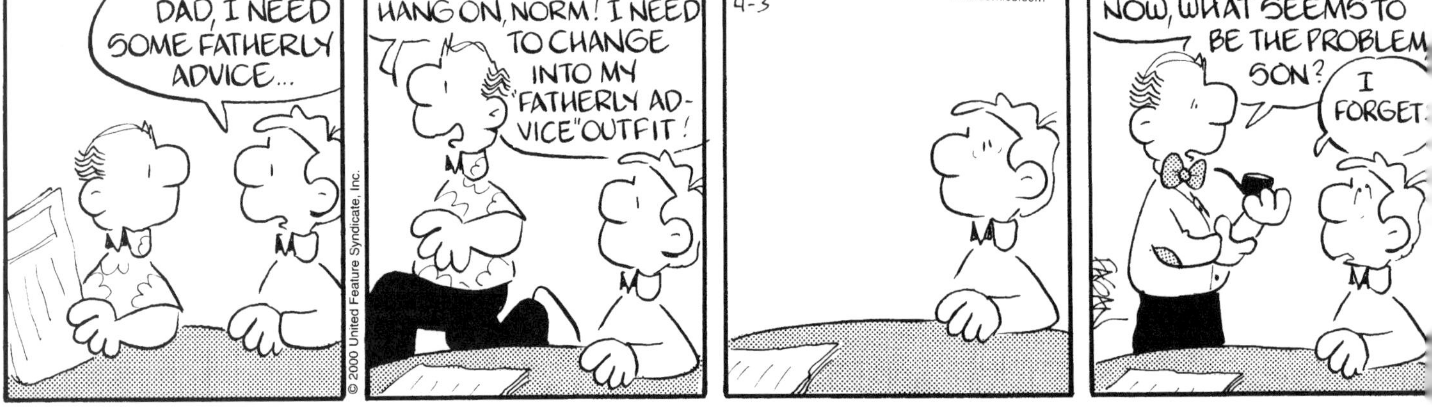
DAD, I NEED SOME FATHERLY ADVICE...
HANG ON, NORM! I NEED TO CHANGE INTO MY "FATHERLY ADVICE" OUTFIT!
4-3
www.comics.com
NOW, WHAT SEEMS TO BE THE PROBLEM SON?
I FORGET.
© 2000 United Feature Syndicate, Inc.

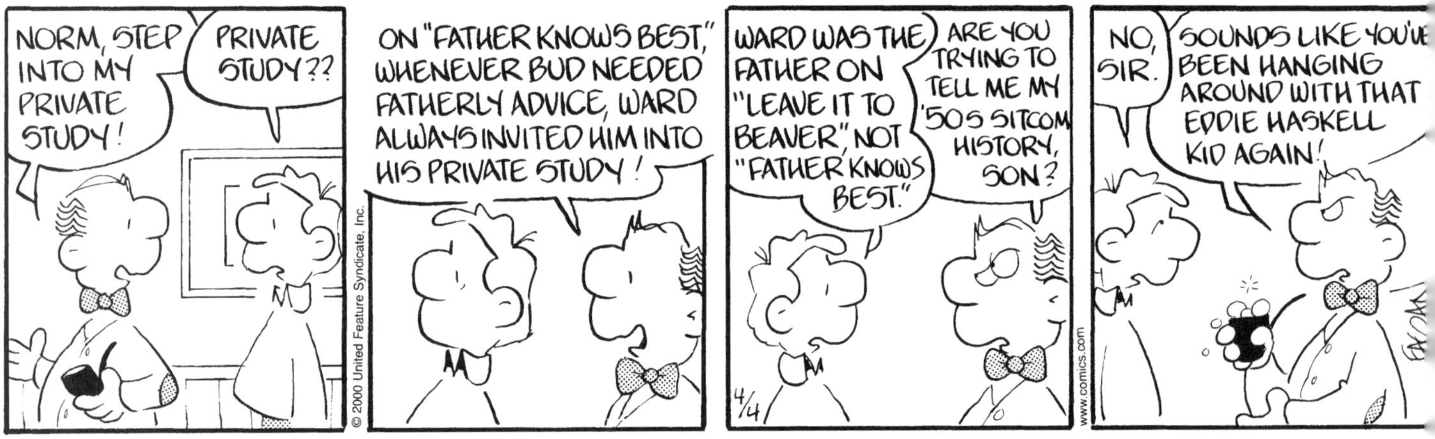
NORM, STEP INTO MY PRIVATE STUDY!
PRIVATE STUDY??
ON "FATHER KNOWS BEST," WHENEVER BUD NEEDED FATHERLY ADVICE, WARD ALWAYS INVITED HIM INTO HIS PRIVATE STUDY!
WARD WAS THE FATHER ON "LEAVE IT TO BEAVER", NOT "FATHER KNOWS BEST."
ARE YOU TRYING TO TELL ME MY '50S SITCOM HISTORY, SON?
4/4
NO, SIR.
SOUNDS LIKE YOU'VE BEEN HANGING AROUND WITH THAT EDDIE HASKELL KID AGAIN!
www.comics.com
© 2000 United Feature Syndicate, Inc.

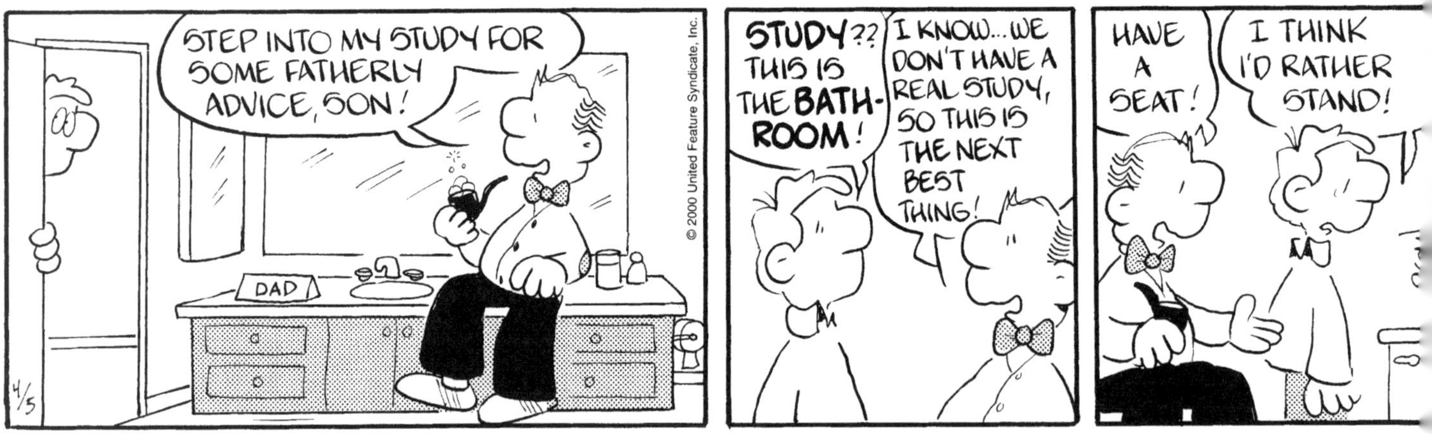
STEP INTO MY STUDY FOR SOME FATHERLY ADVICE, SON!
DAD
4/5
STUDY?? THIS IS THE BATHROOM!
I KNOW... WE DON'T HAVE A REAL STUDY, SO THIS IS THE NEXT BEST THING!
HAVE A SEAT!
I THINK I'D RATHER STAND!
© 2000 United Feature Syndicate, Inc.

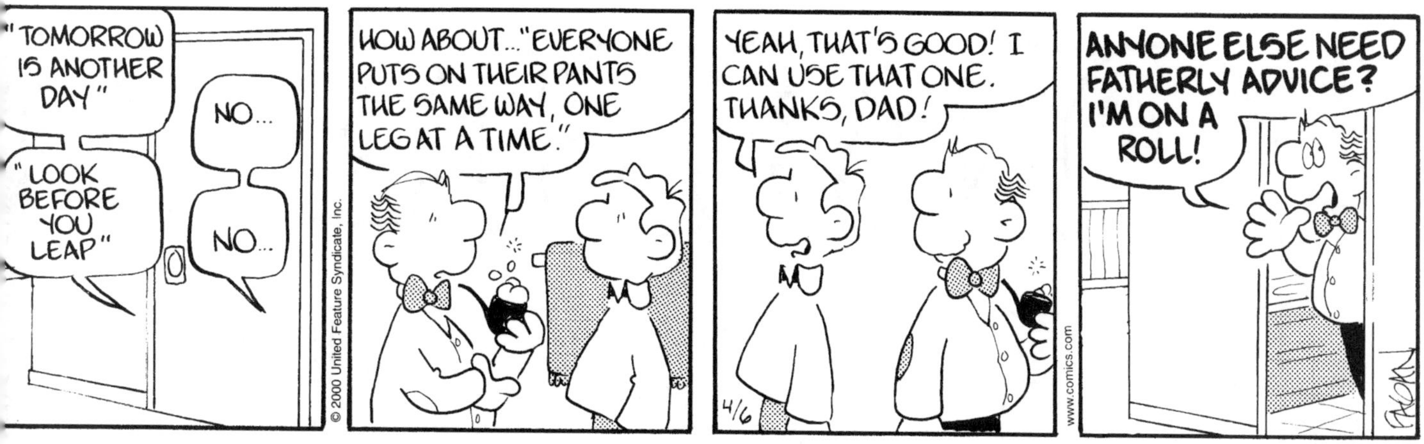
"TOMORROW IS ANOTHER DAY"
NO...
"LOOK BEFORE YOU LEAP"
NO...
© 2000 United Feature Syndicate, Inc.
HOW ABOUT..."EVERYONE PUTS ON THEIR PANTS THE SAME WAY, ONE LEG AT A TIME."
YEAH, THAT'S GOOD! I CAN USE THAT ONE. THANKS, DAD!
4/6
www.comics.com
ANYONE ELSE NEED FATHERLY ADVICE? I'M ON A ROLL!

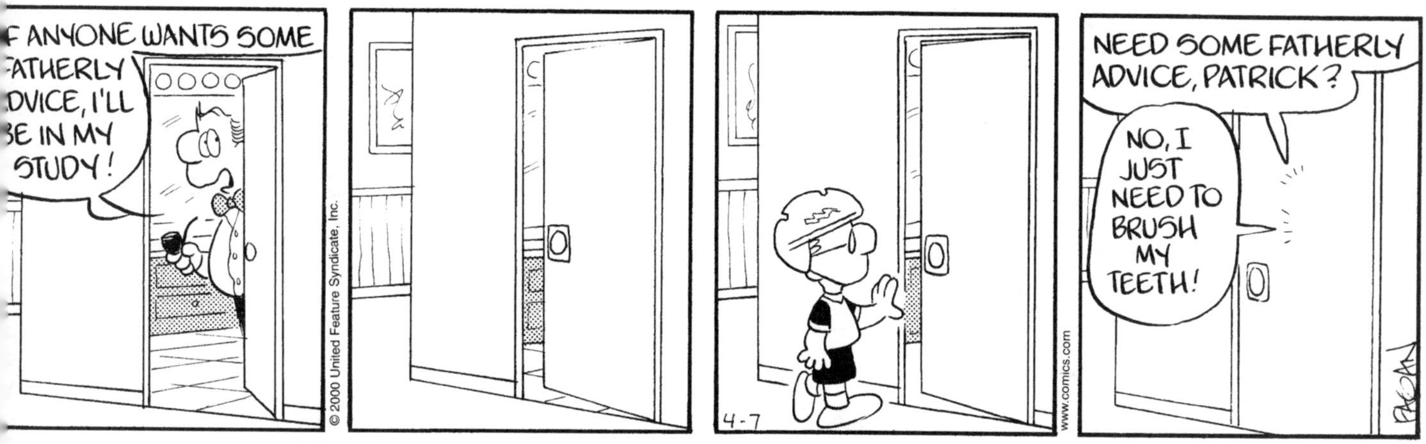
F ANYONE WANTS SOME ATHERLY DVICE, I'LL BE IN MY STUDY!
© 2000 United Feature Syndicate, Inc.
4-7
www.comics.com
NEED SOME FATHERLY ADVICE, PATRICK?
NO, I JUST NEED TO BRUSH MY TEETH!

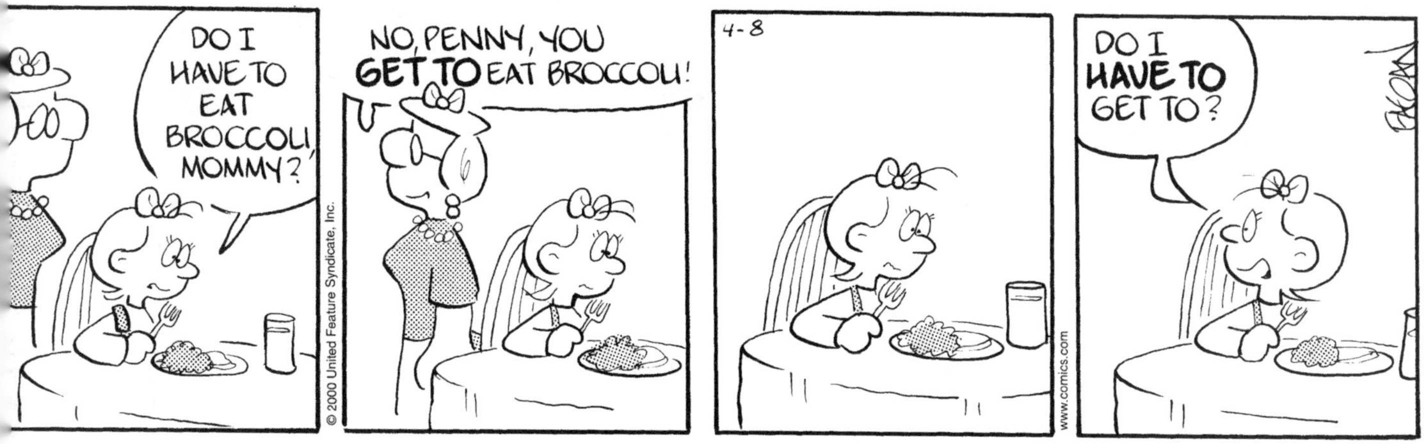
DO I HAVE TO EAT BROCCOLI, MOMMY?
© 2000 United Feature Syndicate, Inc.
NO, PENNY, YOU GET TO EAT BROCCOLI!
4-8
www.comics.com
DO I HAVE TO GET TO?

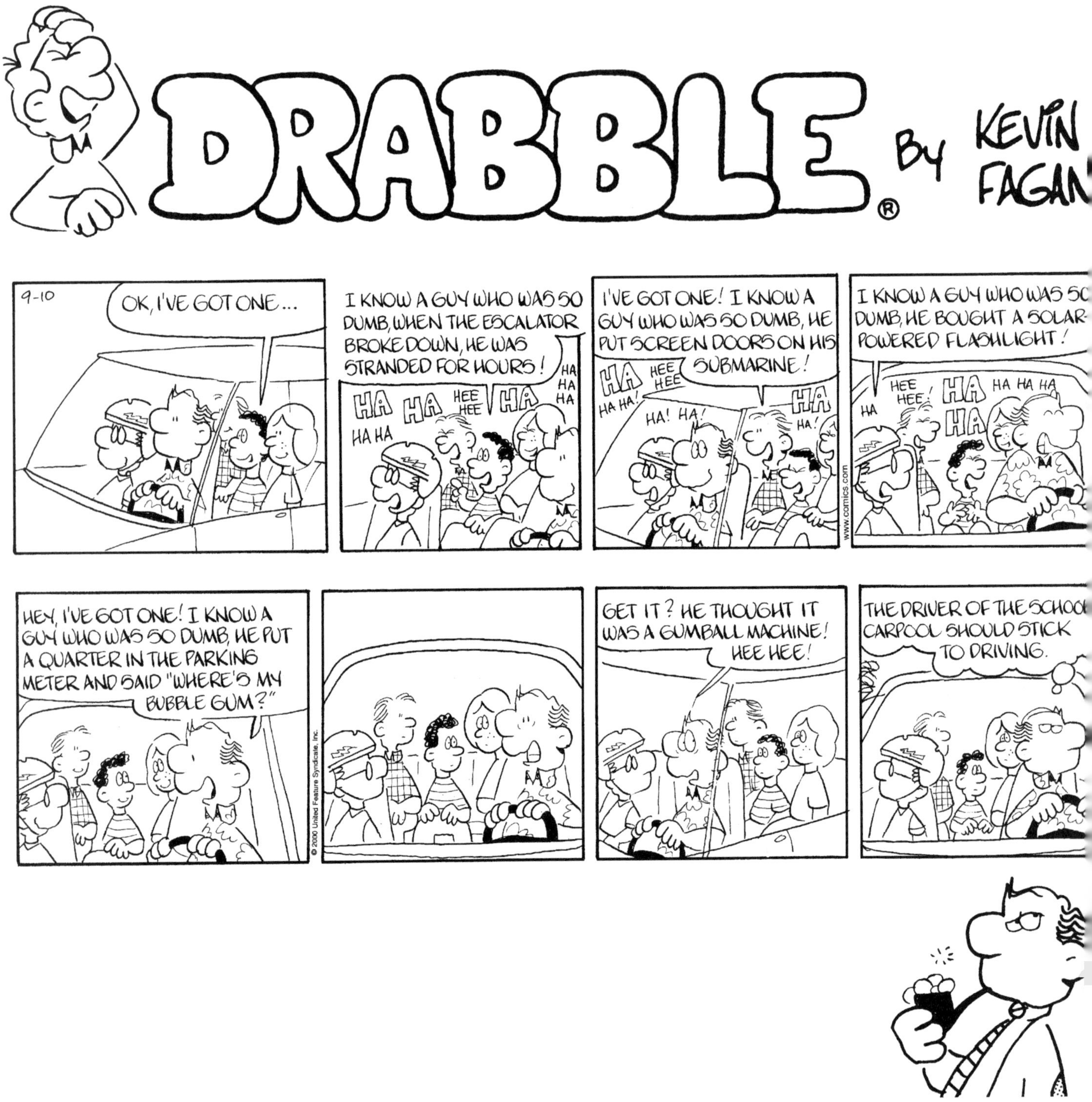
DRABBLE®
By KEVIN FAGAN
9-10
OK, I'VE GOT ONE...
I KNOW A GUY WHO WAS SO DUMB, WHEN THE ESCALATOR BROKE DOWN, HE WAS STRANDED FOR HOURS!
HA HA HA HA HEE HEE HA HA HA HA
I'VE GOT ONE! I KNOW A GUY WHO WAS SO DUMB, HE PUT SCREEN DOORS ON HIS SUBMARINE!
HA HEE HEE HA HA! HA! HA! HA HA!
www.comics.com
I KNOW A GUY WHO WAS SO DUMB, HE BOUGHT A SOLAR-POWERED FLASHLIGHT!
HA HEE HEE! HA HA HA HA HA
HEY, I'VE GOT ONE! I KNOW A GUY WHO WAS SO DUMB, HE PUT A QUARTER IN THE PARKING METER AND SAID "WHERE'S MY BUBBLE GUM?"
© 2000 United Feature Syndicate, Inc.
GET IT? HE THOUGHT IT WAS A GUMBALL MACHINE! HEE HEE!
THE DRIVER OF THE SCHOOL CARPOOL SHOULD STICK TO DRIVING.

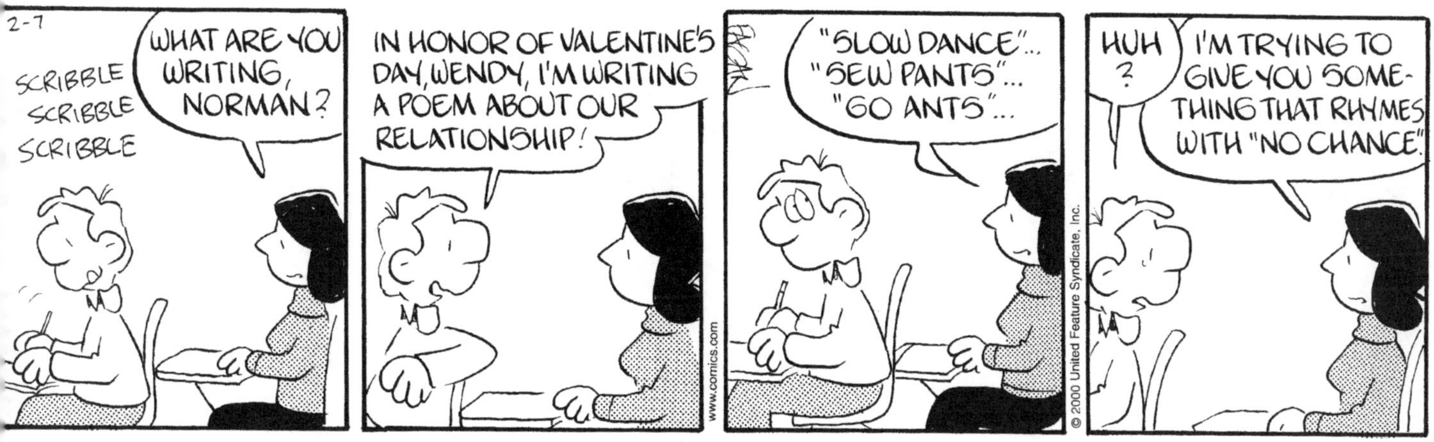
2-7
SCRIBBLE SCRIBBLE SCRIBBLE
WHAT ARE YOU WRITING, NORMAN?
IN HONOR OF VALENTINE'S DAY, WENDY, I'M WRITING A POEM ABOUT OUR RELATIONSHIP!
"SLOW DANCE"... "SEW PANTS"... "GO ANTS"...
HUH ?
I'M TRYING TO GIVE YOU SOMETHING THAT RHYMES WITH "NO CHANCE"
www.comics.com
© 2000 United Feature Syndicate, Inc.

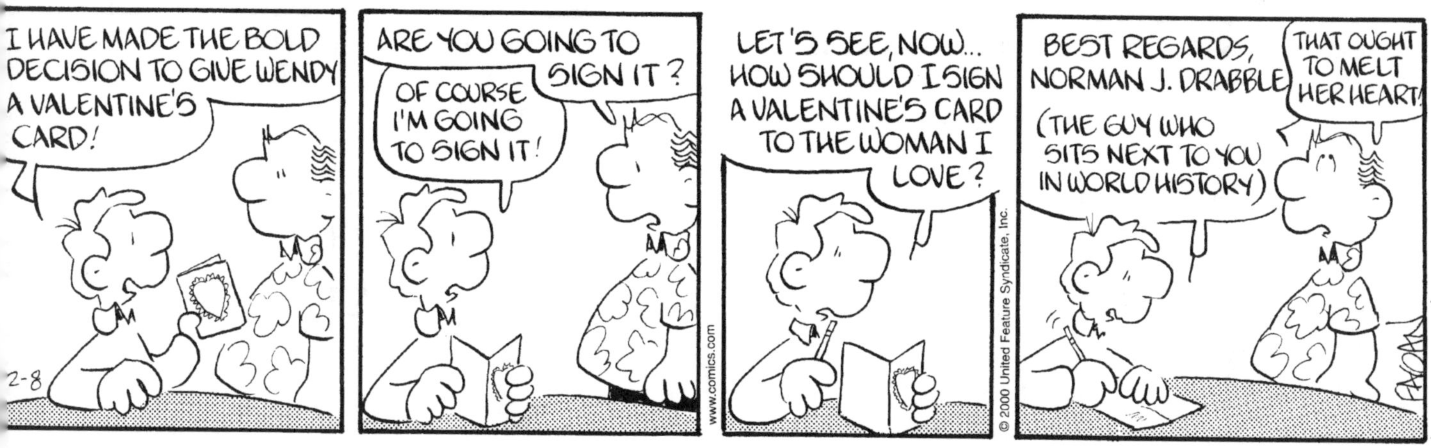
I HAVE MADE THE BOLD DECISION TO GIVE WENDY A VALENTINE'S CARD!
2-8
ARE YOU GOING TO SIGN IT?
OF COURSE I'M GOING TO SIGN IT!
LET'S SEE, NOW... HOW SHOULD I SIGN A VALENTINE'S CARD TO THE WOMAN I LOVE?
BEST REGARDS, NORMAN J. DRABBLE (THE GUY WHO SITS NEXT TO YOU IN WORLD HISTORY)
THAT OUGHT TO MELT HER HEART!
www.comics.com
© 2000 United Feature Syndicate, Inc.

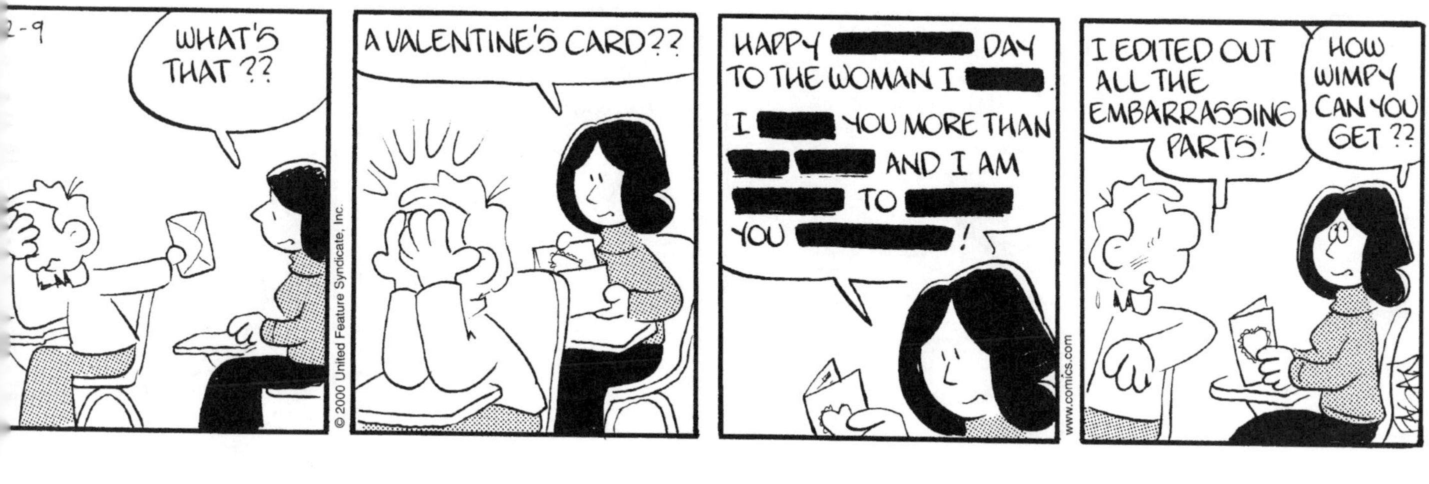
2-9
WHAT'S THAT ??
A VALENTINE'S CARD??
HAPPY [redacted] DAY TO THE WOMAN I [redacted]. I [redacted] YOU MORE THAN [redacted] AND I AM [redacted] TO [redacted] YOU [redacted]!
I EDITED OUT ALL THE EMBARRASSING PARTS!
HOW WIMPY CAN YOU GET ??
© 2000 United Feature Syndicate, Inc.
www.comics.com

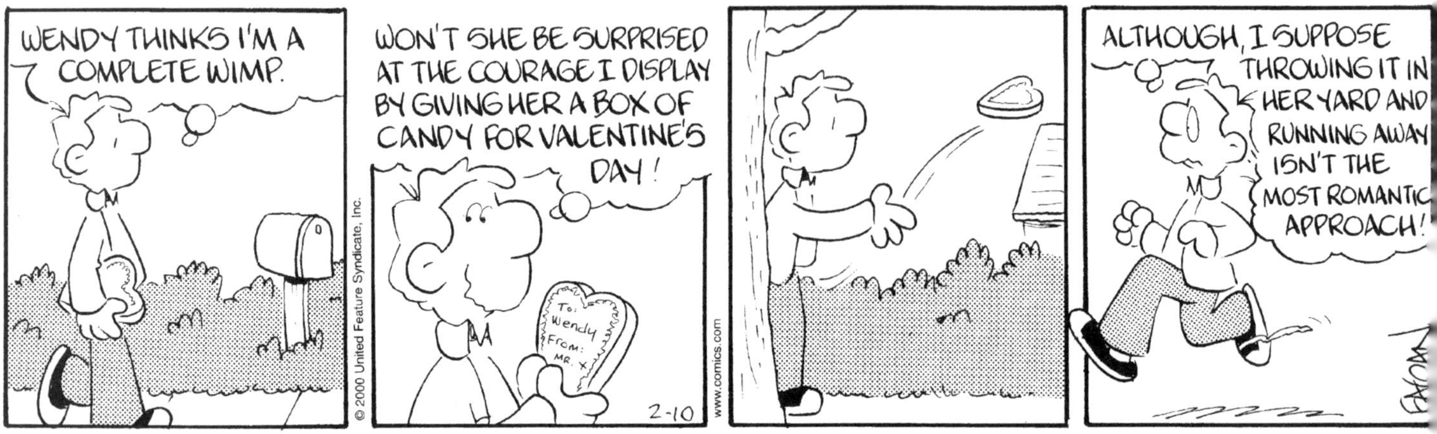
WENDY THINKS I'M A COMPLETE WIMP.
WON'T SHE BE SURPRISED AT THE COURAGE I DISPLAY BY GIVING HER A BOX OF CANDY FOR VALENTINE'S DAY!
To: Wendy From: MR. X
© 2000 United Feature Syndicate, Inc.
2-10
www.comics.com
ALTHOUGH, I SUPPOSE THROWING IT IN HER YARD AND RUNNING AWAY ISN'T THE MOST ROMANTIC APPROACH!

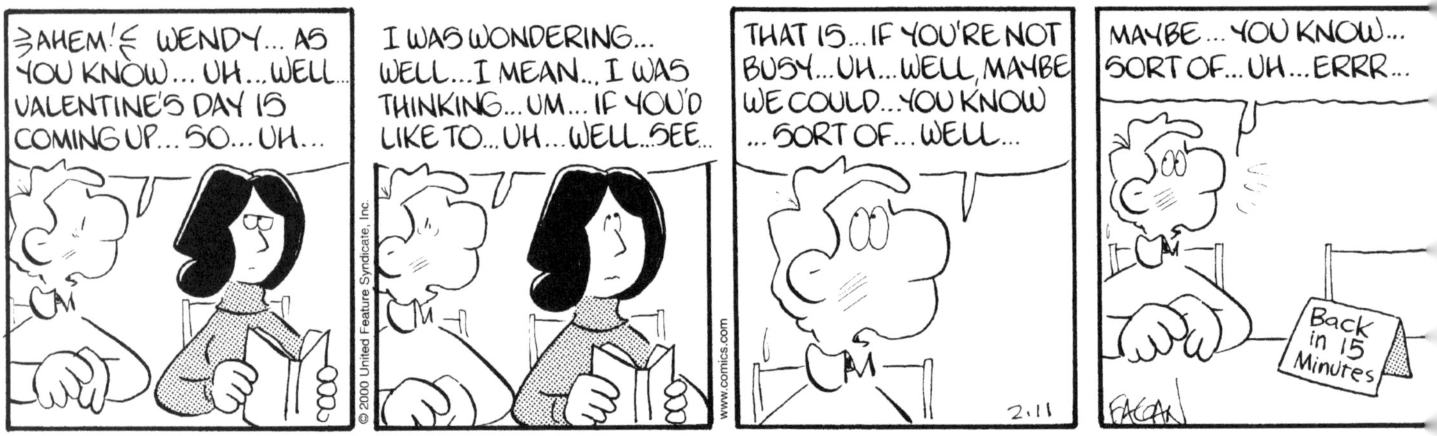
AHEM! WENDY... AS YOU KNOW... UH... WELL... VALENTINE'S DAY IS COMING UP... SO... UH...
I WAS WONDERING... WELL... I MEAN... I WAS THINKING... UM... IF YOU'D LIKE TO... UH... WELL... SEE...
© 2000 United Feature Syndicate, Inc.
THAT IS... IF YOU'RE NOT BUSY... UH... WELL, MAYBE WE COULD... YOU KNOW ... SORT OF... WELL...
www.comics.com
2-11
MAYBE... YOU KNOW... SORT OF... UH... ERRR...
Back in 15 Minutes

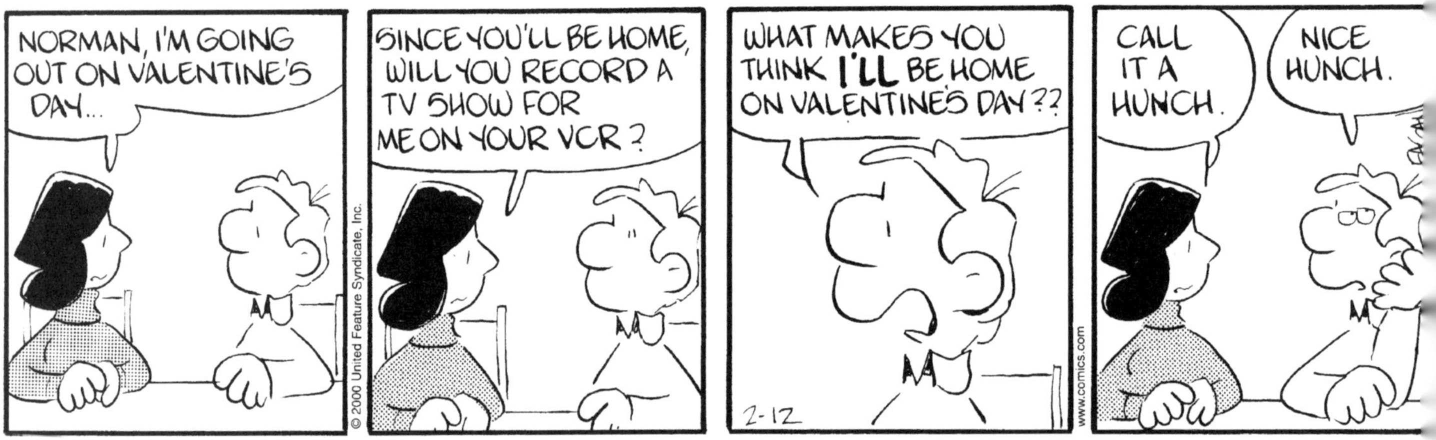
NORMAN, I'M GOING OUT ON VALENTINE'S DAY...
© 2000 United Feature Syndicate, Inc.
SINCE YOU'LL BE HOME, WILL YOU RECORD A TV SHOW FOR ME ON YOUR VCR?
WHAT MAKES YOU THINK I'LL BE HOME ON VALENTINE'S DAY??
2-12
www.comics.com
CALL IT A HUNCH.
NICE HUNCH.

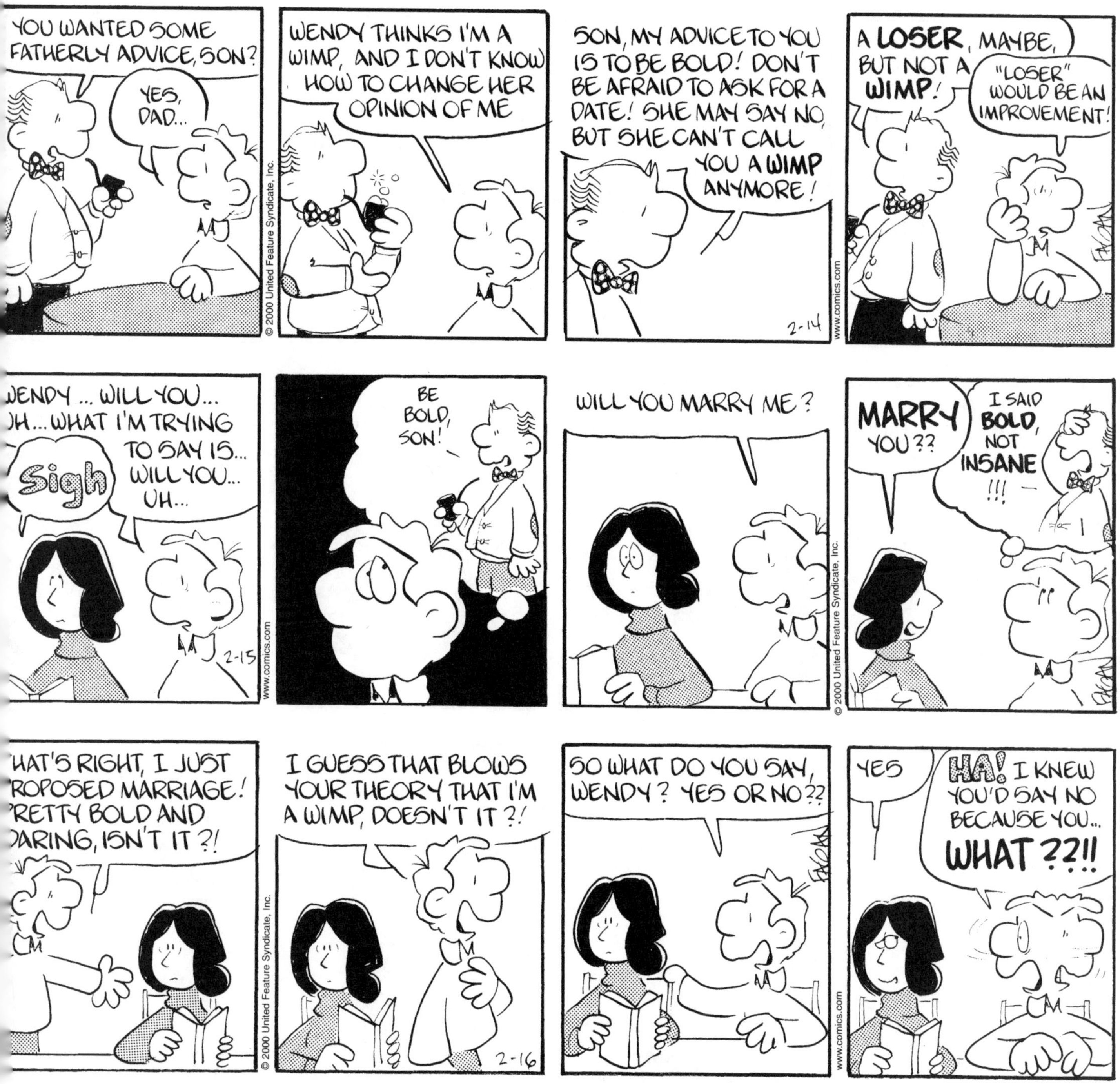
YOU WANTED SOME FATHERLY ADVICE, SON?
YES, DAD...
WENDY THINKS I'M A WIMP, AND I DON'T KNOW HOW TO CHANGE HER OPINION OF ME
© 2000 United Feature Syndicate, Inc.
SON, MY ADVICE TO YOU IS TO BE BOLD! DON'T BE AFRAID TO ASK FOR A DATE! SHE MAY SAY NO, BUT SHE CAN'T CALL YOU A WIMP ANYMORE!
2-14
www.comics.com
A LOSER, MAYBE, BUT NOT A WIMP!
"LOSER" WOULD BE AN IMPROVEMENT!
ENDY ... WILL YOU... H... WHAT I'M TRYING TO SAY IS... WILL YOU... UH...
Sigh
2-15
www.comics.com
BE BOLD, SON!
WILL YOU MARRY ME?
© 2000 United Feature Syndicate, Inc.
MARRY YOU??
I SAID BOLD, NOT INSANE!!!
HAT'S RIGHT, I JUST ROPOSED MARRIAGE! RETTY BOLD AND ARING, ISN'T IT?!
© 2000 United Feature Syndicate, Inc.
I GUESS THAT BLOWS YOUR THEORY THAT I'M A WIMP, DOESN'T IT?!
2-16
SO WHAT DO YOU SAY, WENDY? YES OR NO??
www.comics.com
YES
HA! I KNEW YOU'D SAY NO BECAUSE YOU... WHAT??!!

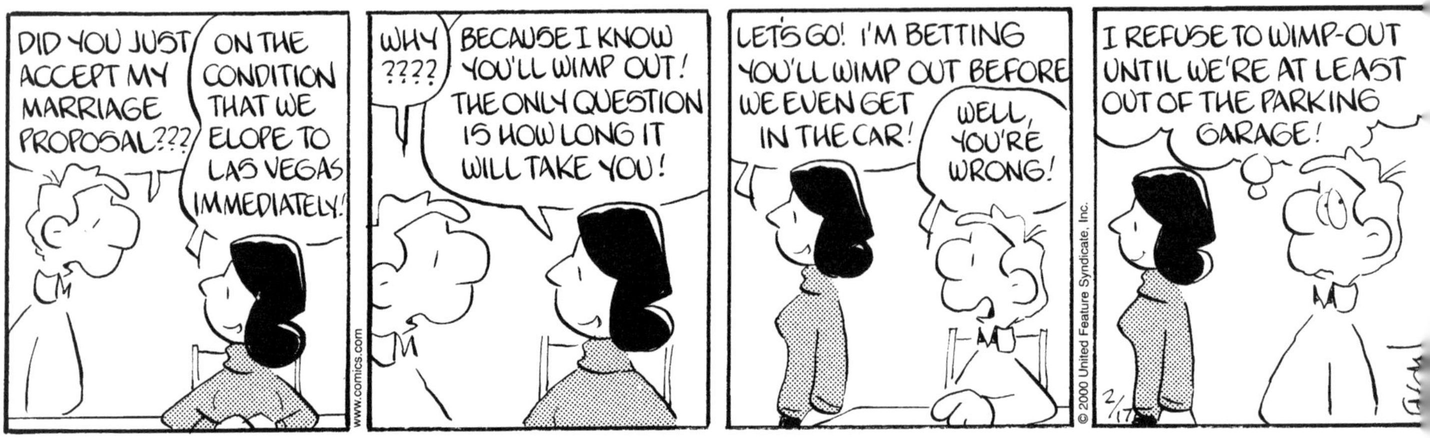
DID YOU JUST ACCEPT MY MARRIAGE PROPOSAL???
ON THE CONDITION THAT WE ELOPE TO LAS VEGAS IMMEDIATELY!
www.comics.com
WHY ????
BECAUSE I KNOW YOU'LL WIMP OUT! THE ONLY QUESTION IS HOW LONG IT WILL TAKE YOU!
LET'S GO! I'M BETTING YOU'LL WIMP OUT BEFORE WE EVEN GET IN THE CAR!
WELL, YOU'RE WRONG!
© 2000 United Feature Syndicate, Inc.
I REFUSE TO WIMP-OUT UNTIL WE'RE AT LEAST OUT OF THE PARKING GARAGE!
2/17

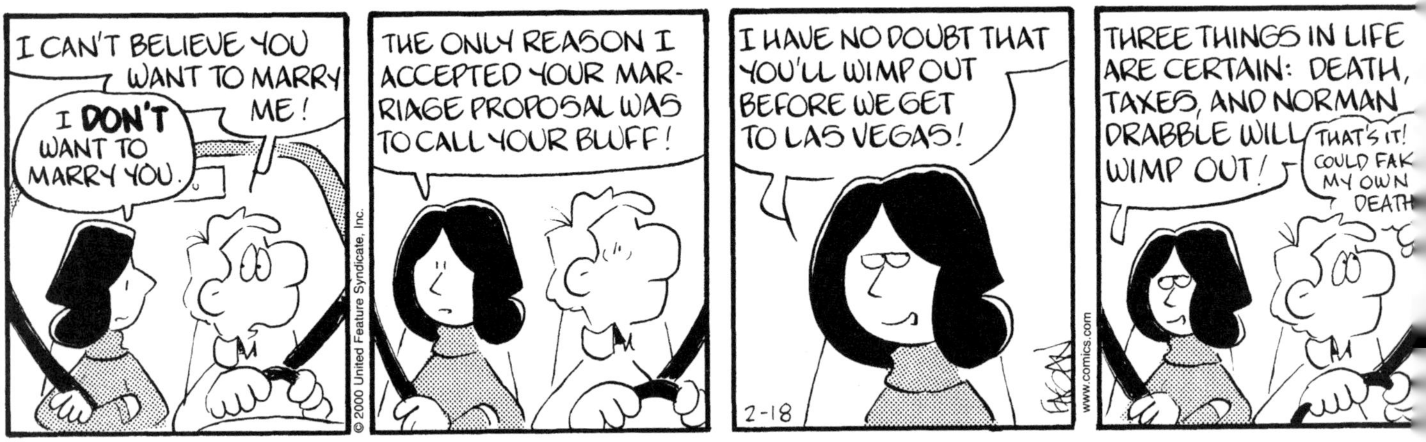
I CAN'T BELIEVE YOU WANT TO MARRY ME!
I DON'T WANT TO MARRY YOU.
© 2000 United Feature Syndicate, Inc.
THE ONLY REASON I ACCEPTED YOUR MARRIAGE PROPOSAL WAS TO CALL YOUR BLUFF!
I HAVE NO DOUBT THAT YOU'LL WIMP OUT BEFORE WE GET TO LAS VEGAS!
2-18
www.comics.com
THREE THINGS IN LIFE ARE CERTAIN: DEATH, TAXES, AND NORMAN DRABBLE WILL WIMP OUT!
THAT'S IT! COULD FAK MY OWN DEATH

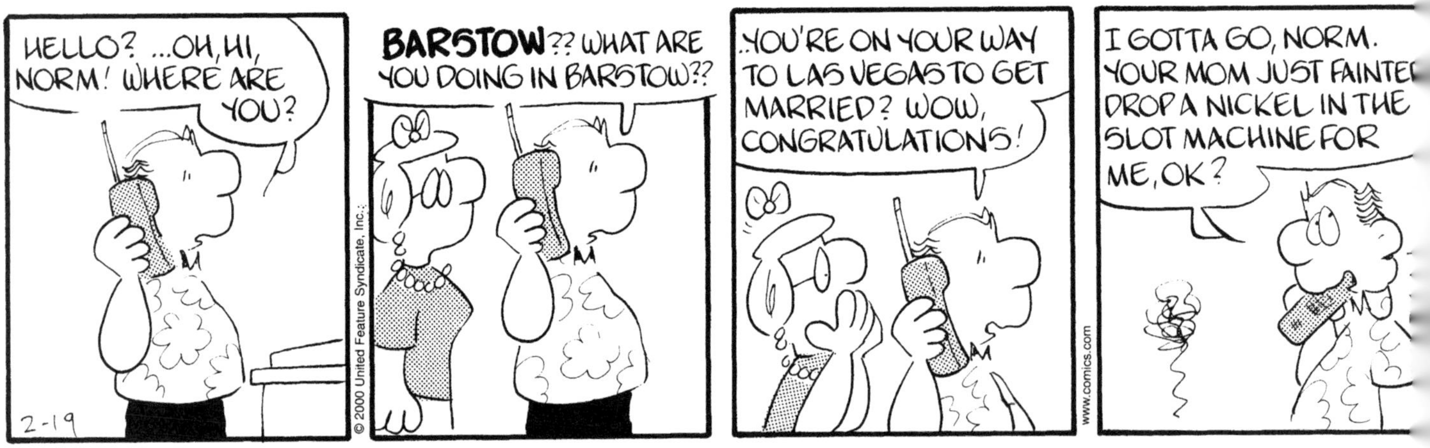
HELLO? ...OH, HI, NORM! WHERE ARE YOU?
2-19
© 2000 United Feature Syndicate, Inc.
BARSTOW?? WHAT ARE YOU DOING IN BARSTOW??
...YOU'RE ON YOUR WAY TO LAS VEGAS TO GET MARRIED? WOW, CONGRATULATIONS!
www.comics.com
I GOTTA GO, NORM. YOUR MOM JUST FAINTE DROP A NICKEL IN THE SLOT MACHINE FOR ME, OK?

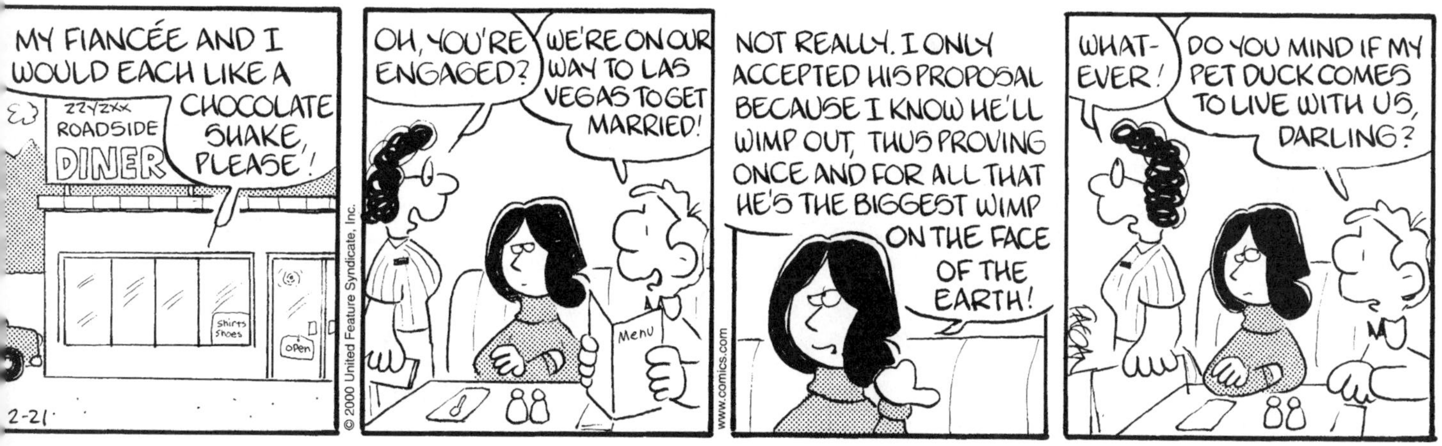
MY FIANCÉE AND I WOULD EACH LIKE A CHOCOLATE SHAKE, PLEASE!
ZZYZXX ROADSIDE DINER
Shirts Shoes
Open
2-21
© 2000 United Feature Syndicate, Inc.
OH, YOU'RE ENGAGED?
WE'RE ON OUR WAY TO LAS VEGAS TO GET MARRIED!
Menu
www.comics.com
NOT REALLY. I ONLY ACCEPTED HIS PROPOSAL BECAUSE I KNOW HE'LL WIMP OUT, THUS PROVING ONCE AND FOR ALL THAT HE'S THE BIGGEST WIMP ON THE FACE OF THE EARTH!
WHAT-EVER!
DO YOU MIND IF MY PET DUCK COMES TO LIVE WITH US, DARLING?

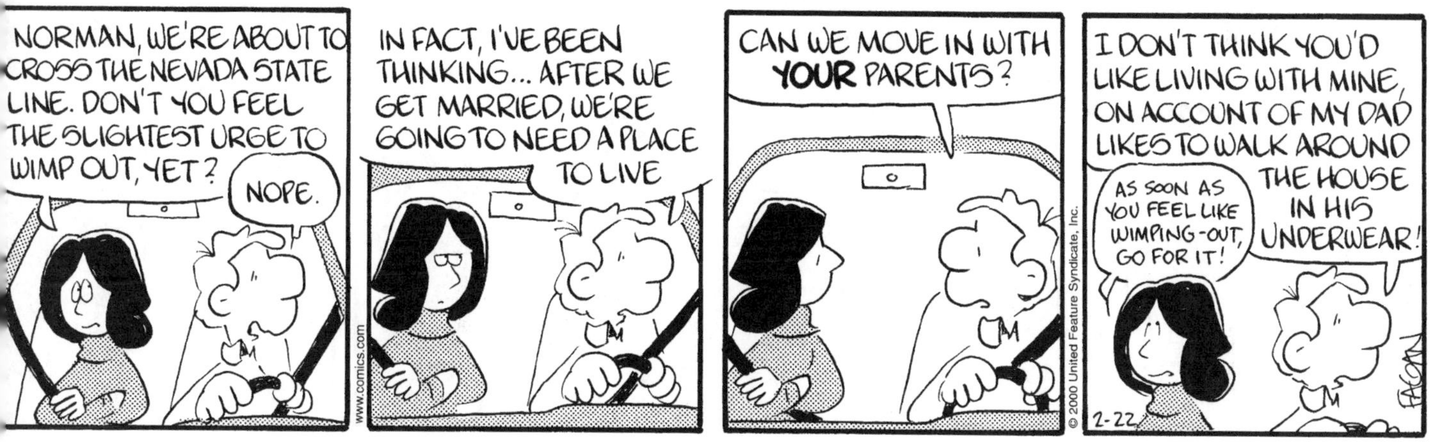
NORMAN, WE'RE ABOUT TO CROSS THE NEVADA STATE LINE. DON'T YOU FEEL THE SLIGHTEST URGE TO WIMP OUT, YET?
NOPE.
www.comics.com
IN FACT, I'VE BEEN THINKING... AFTER WE GET MARRIED, WE'RE GOING TO NEED A PLACE TO LIVE
CAN WE MOVE IN WITH **YOUR** PARENTS?
© 2000 United Feature Syndicate, Inc.
I DON'T THINK YOU'D LIKE LIVING WITH MINE, ON ACCOUNT OF MY DAD LIKES TO WALK AROUND THE HOUSE IN HIS UNDERWEAR!
AS SOON AS YOU FEEL LIKE WIMPING-OUT, GO FOR IT!
2-22

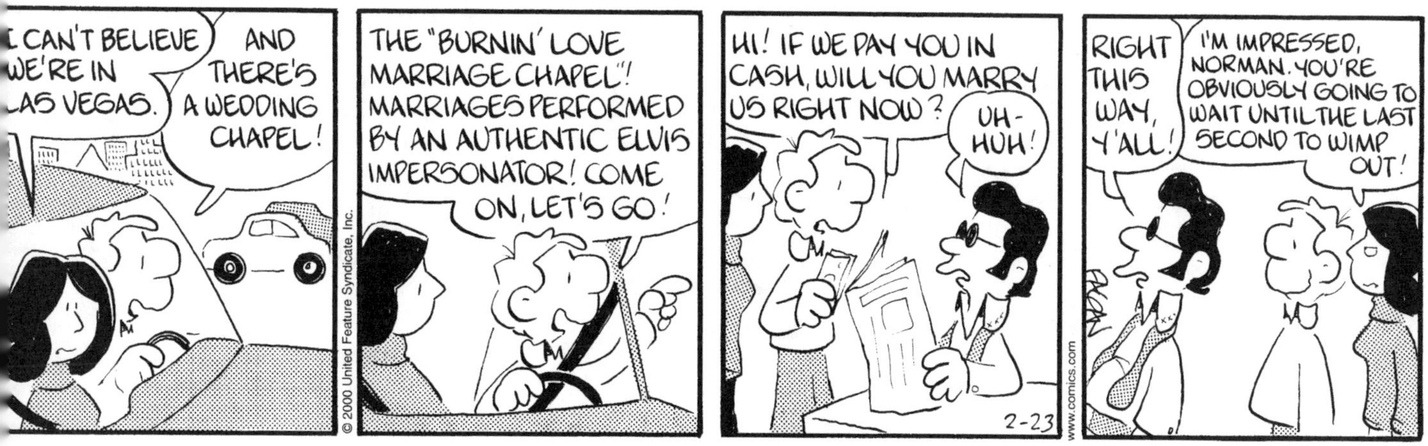
I CAN'T BELIEVE WE'RE IN LAS VEGAS.
AND THERE'S A WEDDING CHAPEL!
© 2000 United Feature Syndicate, Inc.
THE "BURNIN' LOVE MARRIAGE CHAPEL"! MARRIAGES PERFORMED BY AN AUTHENTIC ELVIS IMPERSONATOR! COME ON, LET'S GO!
HI! IF WE PAY YOU IN CASH, WILL YOU MARRY US RIGHT NOW?
UH-HUH!
2-23
www.comics.com
RIGHT THIS WAY, Y'ALL!
I'M IMPRESSED, NORMAN. YOU'RE OBVIOUSLY GOING TO WAIT UNTIL THE LAST SECOND TO WIMP OUT!

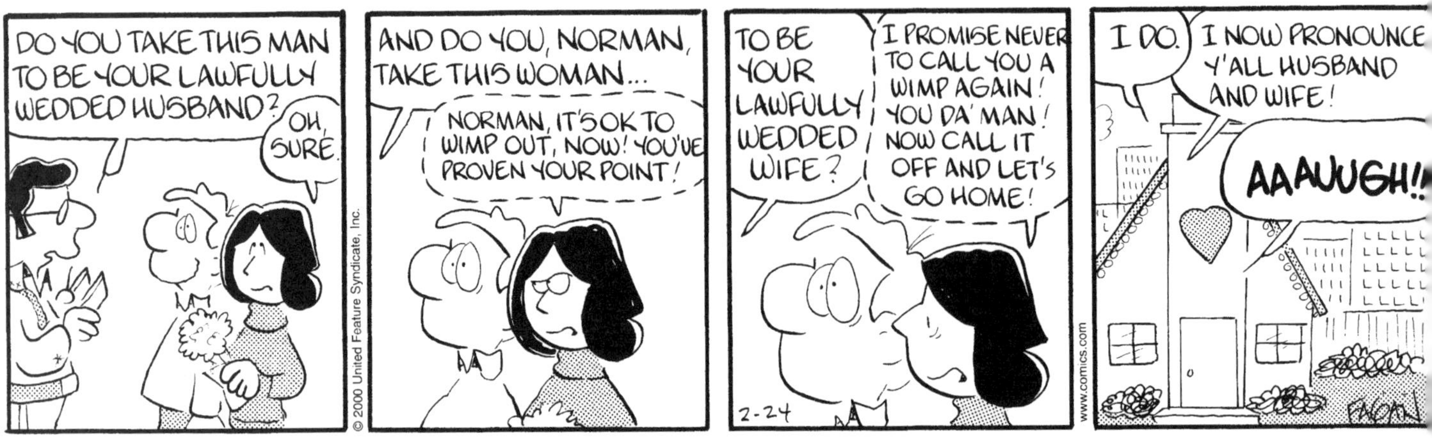
DO YOU TAKE THIS MAN TO BE YOUR LAWFULLY WEDDED HUSBAND?
OH, SURE.
© 2000 United Feature Syndicate, Inc.
AND DO YOU, NORMAN, TAKE THIS WOMAN...
NORMAN, IT'S OK TO WIMP OUT, NOW! YOU'VE PROVEN YOUR POINT!
TO BE YOUR LAWFULLY WEDDED WIFE?
I PROMISE NEVER TO CALL YOU A WIMP AGAIN! YOU DA' MAN! NOW CALL IT OFF AND LET'S GO HOME!
2-24
www.comics.com
I DO.
I NOW PRONOUNCE Y'ALL HUSBAND AND WIFE!
AAAUUGH!!
FAGAN

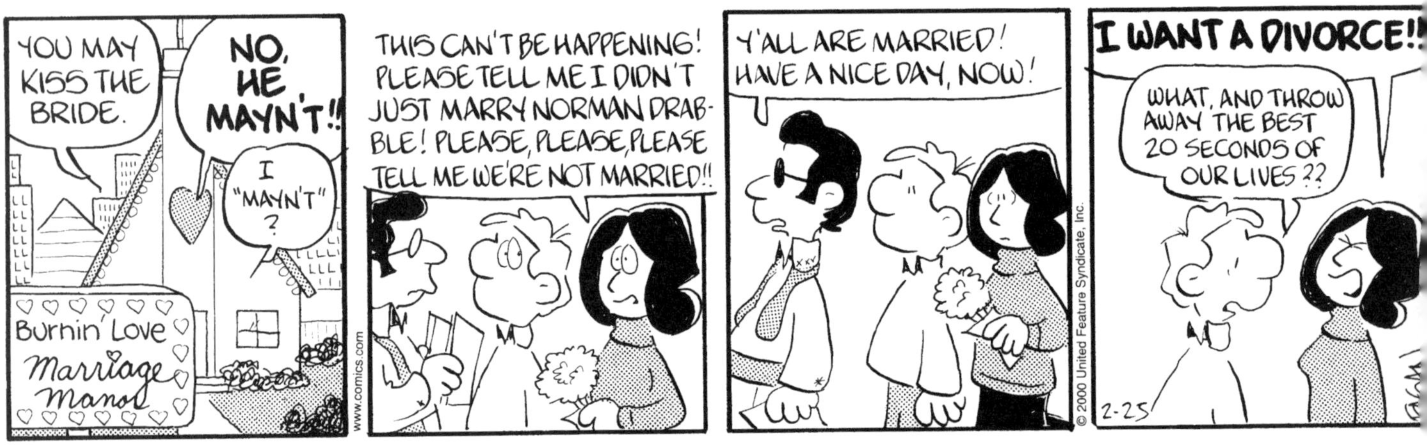
YOU MAY KISS THE BRIDE.
NO, HE MAYN'T!!
I "MAYN'T"?
Burnin' Love
Marriage Manor
www.comics.com
THIS CAN'T BE HAPPENING! PLEASE TELL ME I DIDN'T JUST MARRY NORMAN DRABBLE! PLEASE, PLEASE, PLEASE TELL ME WE'RE NOT MARRIED!!
Y'ALL ARE MARRIED! HAVE A NICE DAY, NOW!
© 2000 United Feature Syndicate, Inc.
I WANT A DIVORCE!!
WHAT, AND THROW AWAY THE BEST 20 SECONDS OF OUR LIVES??
2-25

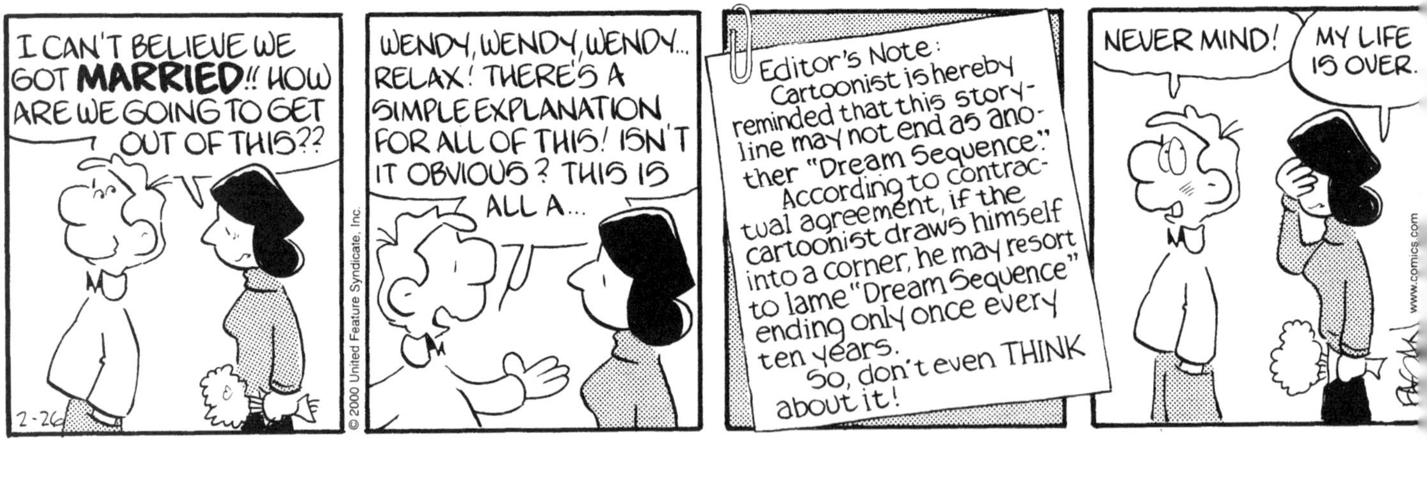
I CAN'T BELIEVE WE GOT MARRIED!! HOW ARE WE GOING TO GET OUT OF THIS??
2-26
© 2000 United Feature Syndicate, Inc.
WENDY, WENDY, WENDY... RELAX! THERE'S A SIMPLE EXPLANATION FOR ALL OF THIS! ISN'T IT OBVIOUS? THIS IS ALL A...
Editor's Note:
Cartoonist is hereby reminded that this storyline may not end as another "Dream Sequence."
According to contractual agreement, if the cartoonist draws himself into a corner, he may resort to lame "Dream Sequence" ending only once every ten years.
So, don't even THINK about it!
NEVER MIND!
MY LIFE IS OVER.
www.comics.com

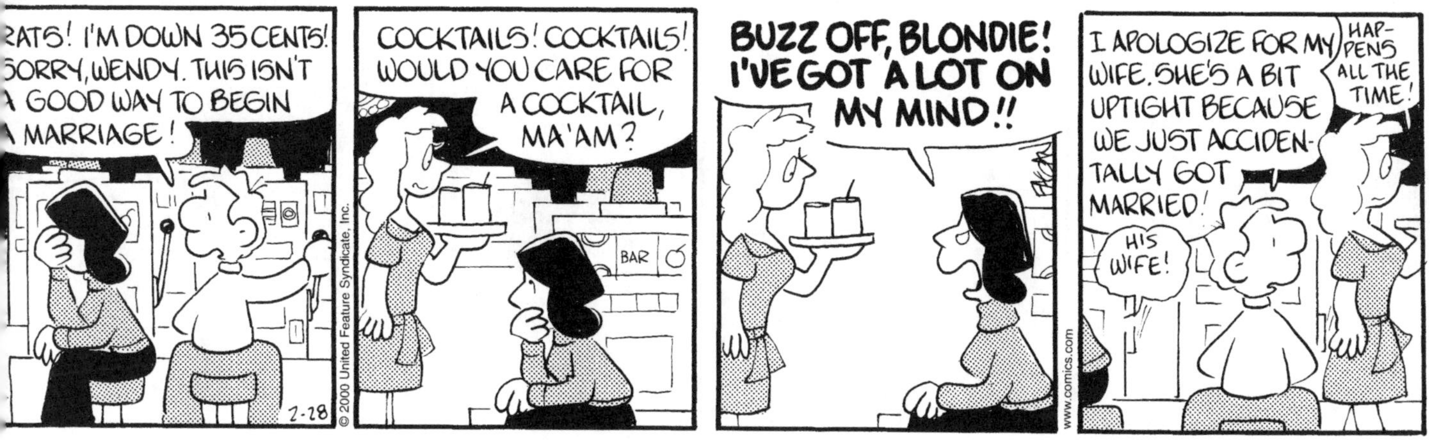
RATS! I'M DOWN 35 CENTS! SORRY, WENDY. THIS ISN'T A GOOD WAY TO BEGIN A MARRIAGE!
2-28
© 2000 United Feature Syndicate, Inc.
COCKTAILS! COCKTAILS! WOULD YOU CARE FOR A COCKTAIL, MA'AM?
BAR
BUZZ OFF, BLONDIE! I'VE GOT A LOT ON MY MIND!!
www.comics.com
I APOLOGIZE FOR MY WIFE. SHE'S A BIT UPTIGHT BECAUSE WE JUST ACCIDENTALLY GOT MARRIED!
HAPPENS ALL THE TIME!
HIS WIFE!

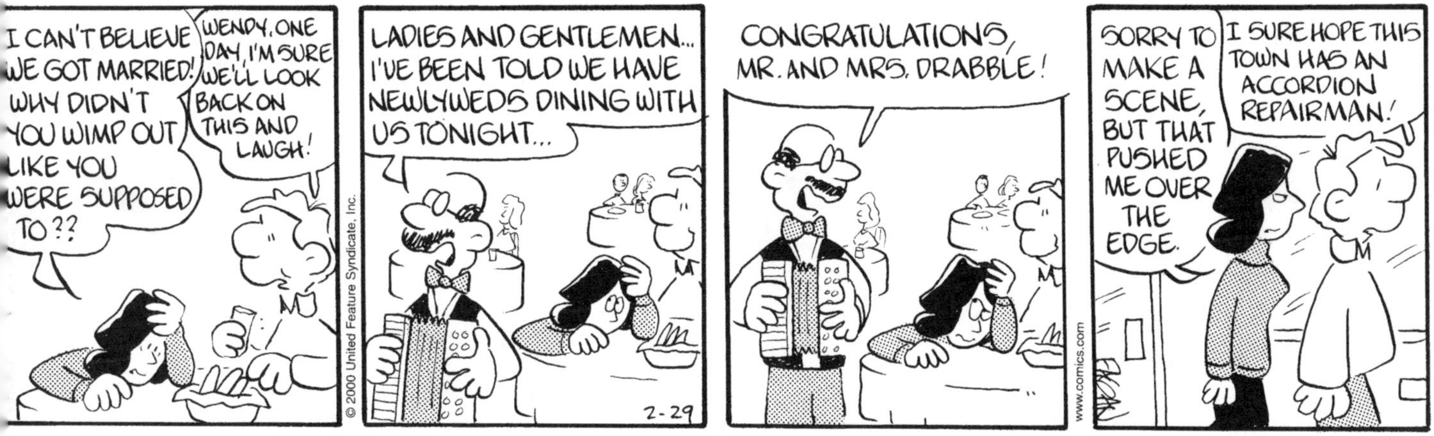
I CAN'T BELIEVE WE GOT MARRIED! WHY DIDN'T YOU WIMP OUT LIKE YOU WERE SUPPOSED TO??
WENDY, ONE DAY, I'M SURE WE'LL LOOK BACK ON THIS AND LAUGH!
© 2000 United Feature Syndicate, Inc.
LADIES AND GENTLEMEN... I'VE BEEN TOLD WE HAVE NEWLYWEDS DINING WITH US TONIGHT...
2-29
CONGRATULATIONS, MR. AND MRS. DRABBLE!
www.comics.com
SORRY TO MAKE A SCENE, BUT THAT PUSHED ME OVER THE EDGE.
I SURE HOPE THIS TOWN HAS AN ACCORDION REPAIRMAN!

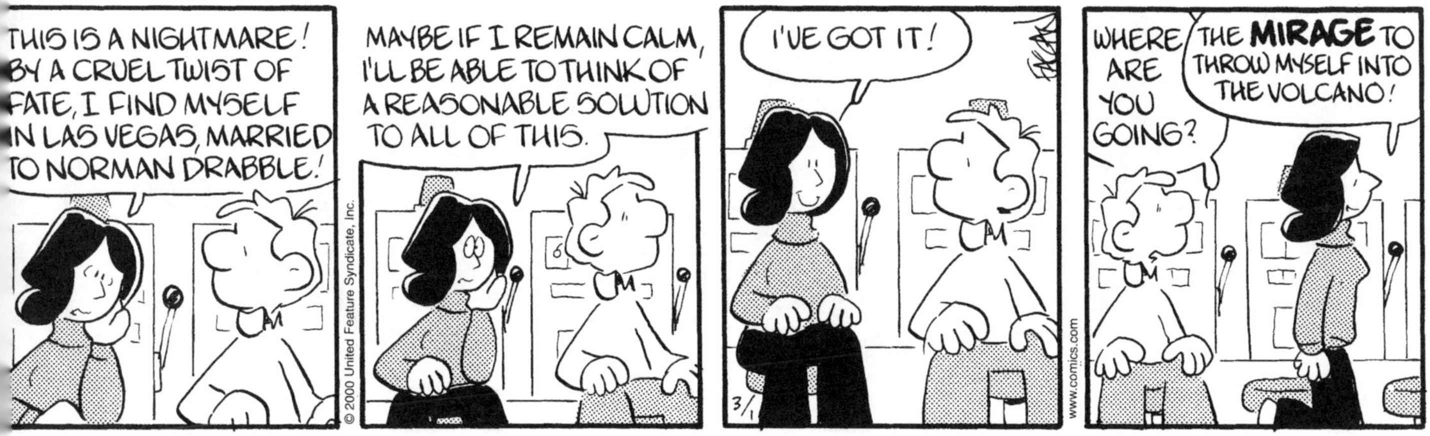
THIS IS A NIGHTMARE! BY A CRUEL TWIST OF FATE, I FIND MYSELF IN LAS VEGAS, MARRIED TO NORMAN DRABBLE!
© 2000 United Feature Syndicate, Inc.
MAYBE IF I REMAIN CALM, I'LL BE ABLE TO THINK OF A REASONABLE SOLUTION TO ALL OF THIS.
I'VE GOT IT!
3/1
www.comics.com
WHERE ARE YOU GOING?
THE MIRAGE TO THROW MYSELF INTO THE VOLCANO!

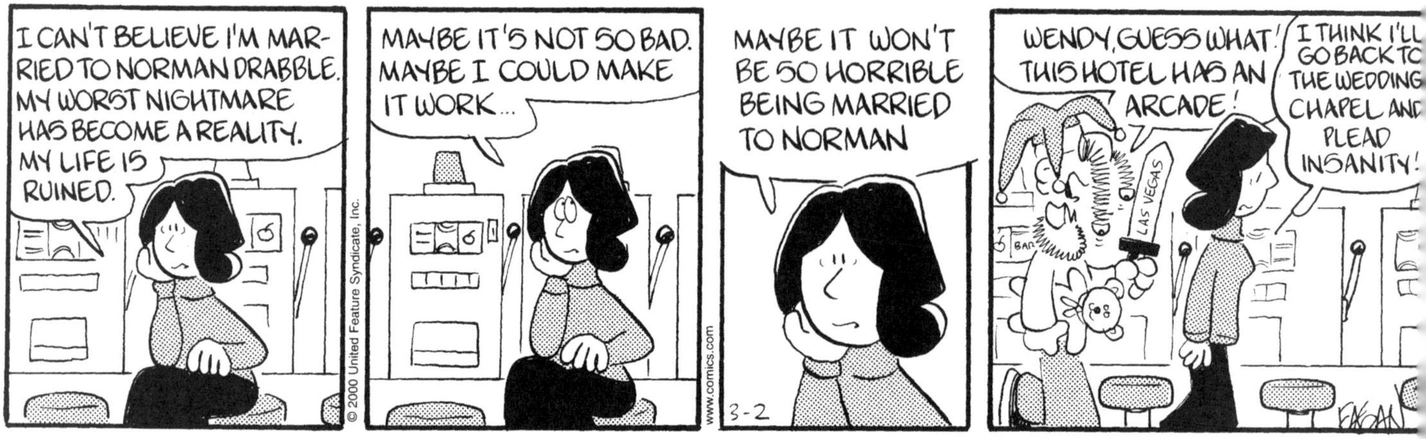
I CAN'T BELIEVE I'M MARRIED TO NORMAN DRABBLE. MY WORST NIGHTMARE HAS BECOME A REALITY. MY LIFE IS RUINED.
© 2000 United Feature Syndicate, Inc.
MAYBE IT'S NOT SO BAD. MAYBE I COULD MAKE IT WORK...
www.comics.com
MAYBE IT WON'T BE SO HORRIBLE BEING MARRIED TO NORMAN
3-2
WENDY, GUESS WHAT! THIS HOTEL HAS AN ARCADE!
I THINK I'LL GO BACK TO THE WEDDING CHAPEL AND PLEAD INSANITY!
LAS VEGAS
FAGAN

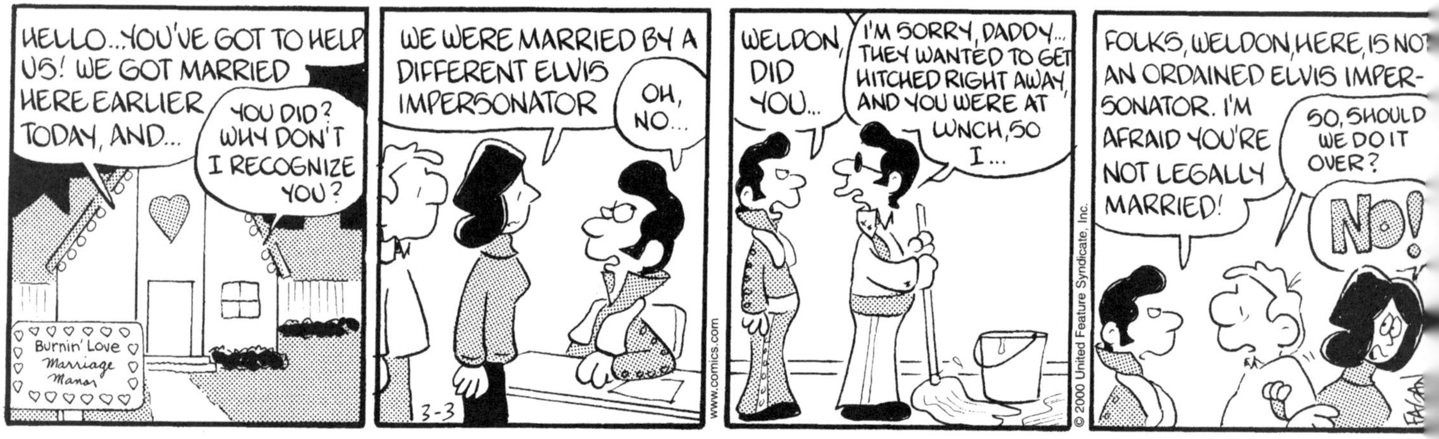
HELLO...YOU'VE GOT TO HELP US! WE GOT MARRIED HERE EARLIER TODAY, AND...
YOU DID? WHY DON'T I RECOGNIZE YOU?
Burnin' Love Marriage Manor
WE WERE MARRIED BY A DIFFERENT ELVIS IMPERSONATOR
OH, NO...
3-3
www.comics.com
WELDON, DID YOU...
I'M SORRY, DADDY... THEY WANTED TO GET HITCHED RIGHT AWAY, AND YOU WERE AT LUNCH, SO I...
© 2000 United Feature Syndicate, Inc.
FOLKS, WELDON, HERE, IS NOT AN ORDAINED ELVIS IMPERSONATOR. I'M AFRAID YOU'RE NOT LEGALLY MARRIED!
SO, SHOULD WE DO IT OVER?
NO!

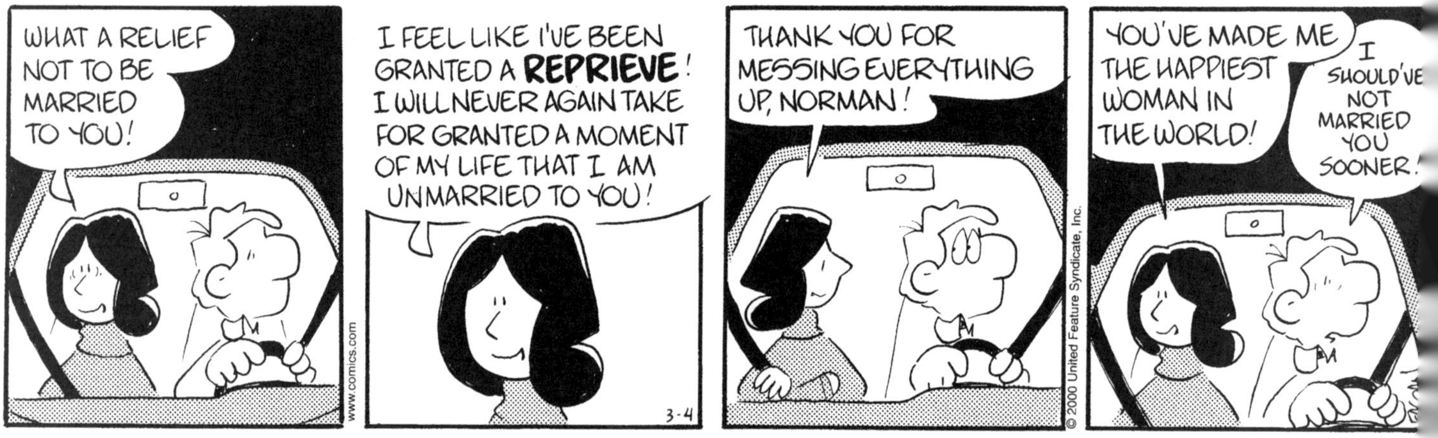
WHAT A RELIEF NOT TO BE MARRIED TO YOU!
www.comics.com
I FEEL LIKE I'VE BEEN GRANTED A REPRIEVE! I WILL NEVER AGAIN TAKE FOR GRANTED A MOMENT OF MY LIFE THAT I AM UNMARRIED TO YOU!
3-4
THANK YOU FOR MESSING EVERYTHING UP, NORMAN!
© 2000 United Feature Syndicate, Inc.
YOU'VE MADE ME THE HAPPIEST WOMAN IN THE WORLD!
I SHOULD'VE NOT MARRIED YOU SOONER!

DRABBLE®

By Kevin Fagan

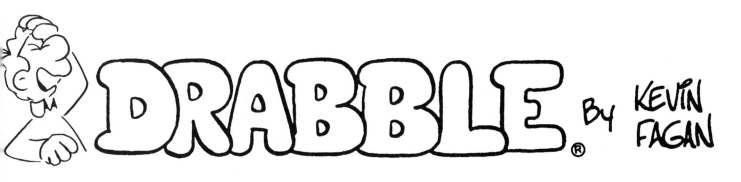

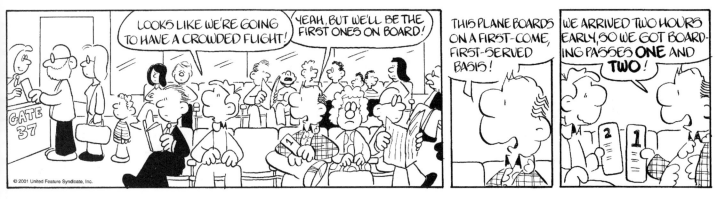

LOOKS LIKE WE'RE GOING TO HAVE A CROWDED FLIGHT!
YEAH, BUT WE'LL BE THE FIRST ONES ON BOARD!
GATE 37
© 2001 United Feature Syndicate, Inc.
THIS PLANE BOARDS ON A FIRST-COME, FIRST-SERVED BASIS!
WE ARRIVED TWO HOURS EARLY, SO WE GOT BOARDING PASSES **ONE** AND **TWO**!
POLECAT AIRLINES ANNOUNCES PRE-BOARDING OF FLIGHT 807! ALL PASSENGERS WHO ARE ELDERLY, REQUIRE PHYSICAL ASSISTANCE, TRAVELING WITH SMALL CHILDREN, OR HAVE SPECIAL NEEDS, MAY NOW BOARD AT GATE 37!
POLECAT AIRLINES NOW ANNOUNCES BOARDING FOR PASSENGERS **1** THROUGH **20**.
THAT'S US!
GATE 37
www.comics.com 2-11
FAGAN

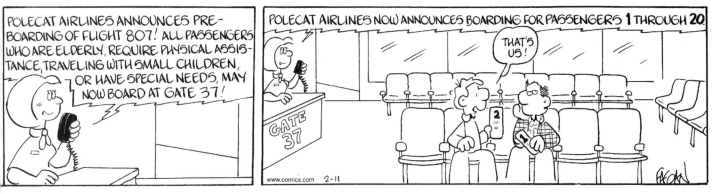

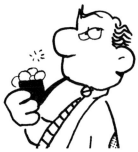

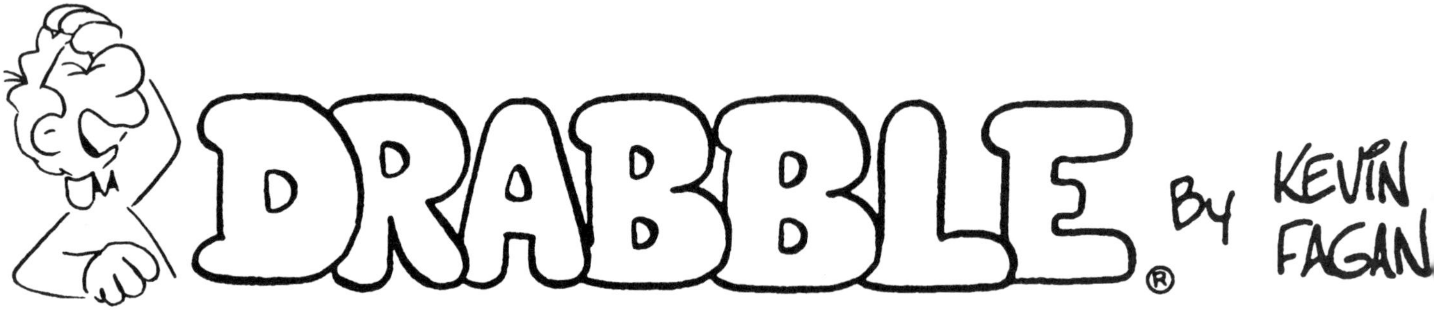
DRABBLE®
By KEVIN FAGAN

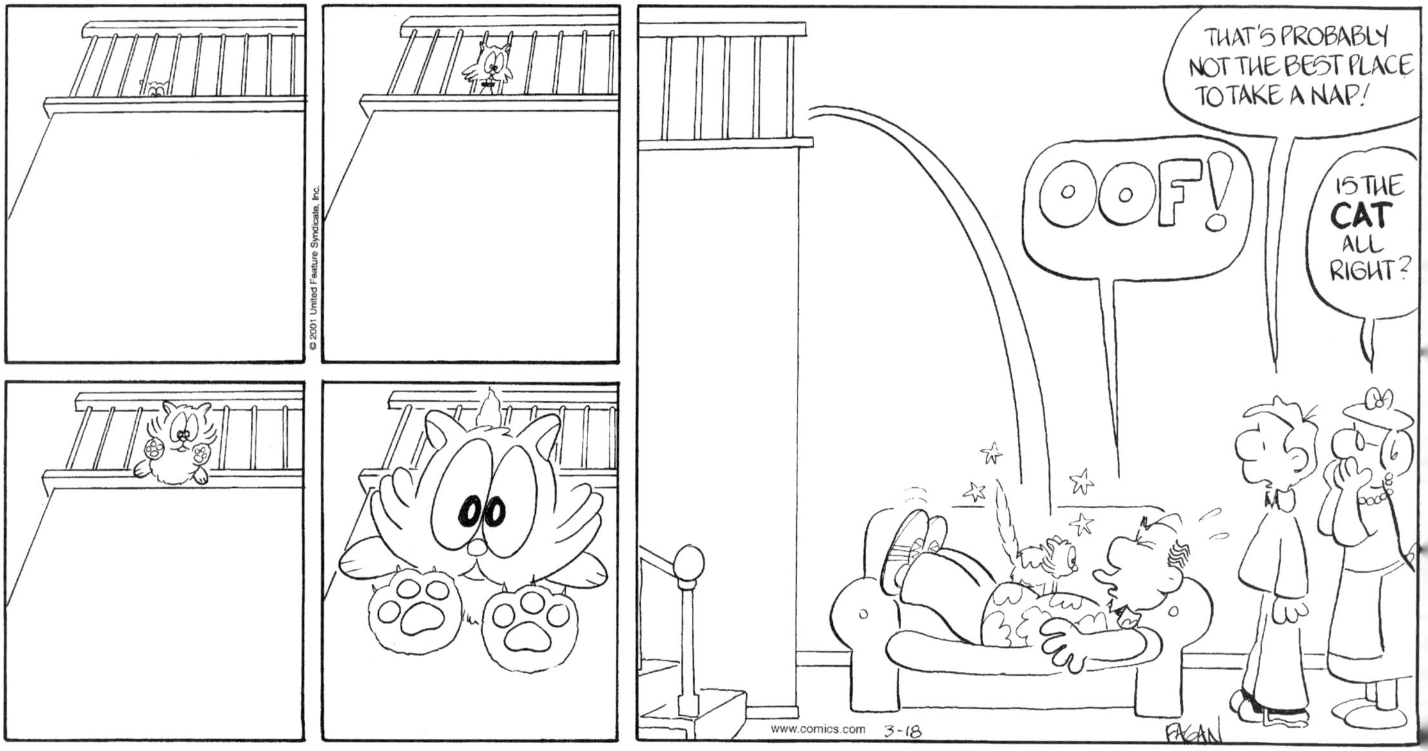
© 2001 United Feature Syndicate, Inc.
OOF!
THAT'S PROBABLY NOT THE BEST PLACE TO TAKE A NAP!
IS THE CAT ALL RIGHT?
www.comics.com
3-18
FAGAN

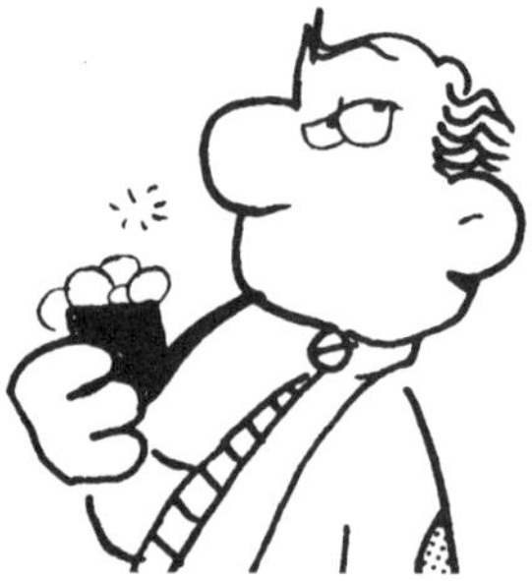

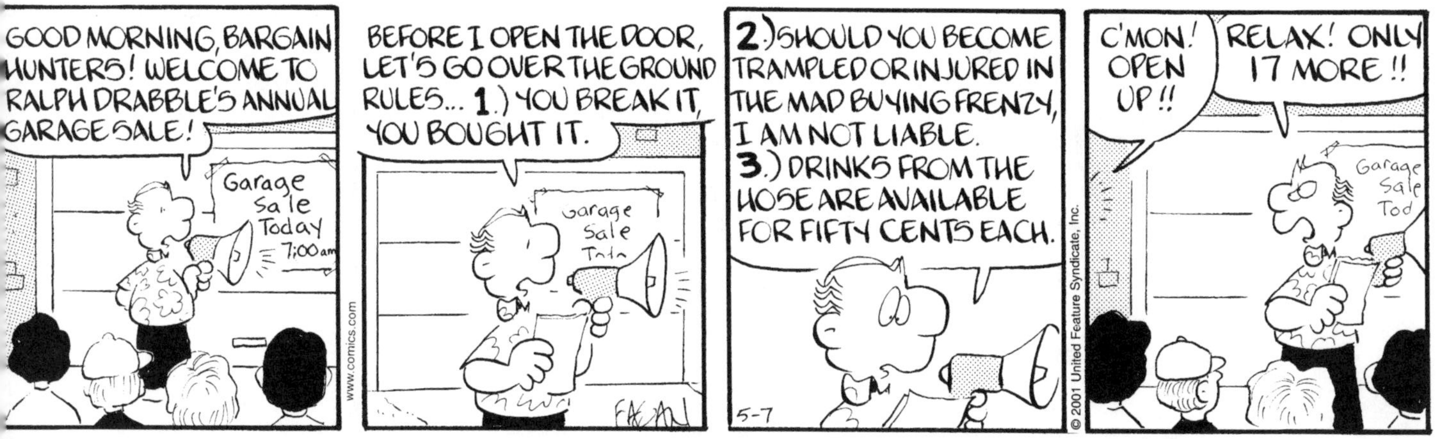
GOOD MORNING, BARGAIN HUNTERS! WELCOME TO RALPH DRABBLE'S ANNUAL GARAGE SALE!
Garage Sale Today 7:00 am
www.comics.com
BEFORE I OPEN THE DOOR, LET'S GO OVER THE GROUND RULES... 1.) YOU BREAK IT, YOU BOUGHT IT.
2.) SHOULD YOU BECOME TRAMPLED OR INJURED IN THE MAD BUYING FRENZY, I AM NOT LIABLE. 3.) DRINKS FROM THE HOSE ARE AVAILABLE FOR FIFTY CENTS EACH.
5-7
© 2001 United Feature Syndicate, Inc.
C'MON! OPEN UP!!
RELAX! ONLY 17 MORE!!

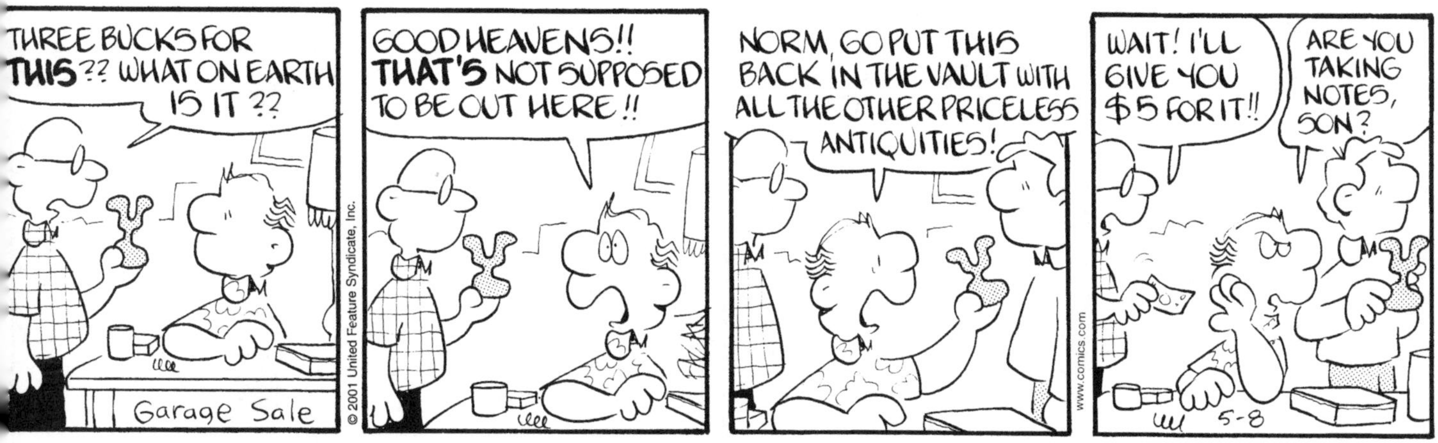
THREE BUCKS FOR THIS?? WHAT ON EARTH IS IT??
Garage Sale
© 2001 United Feature Syndicate, Inc.
GOOD HEAVENS!! THAT'S NOT SUPPOSED TO BE OUT HERE!!
NORM, GO PUT THIS BACK IN THE VAULT WITH ALL THE OTHER PRICELESS ANTIQUITIES!
www.comics.com
WAIT! I'LL GIVE YOU $5 FOR IT!!
ARE YOU TAKING NOTES, SON?
5-8

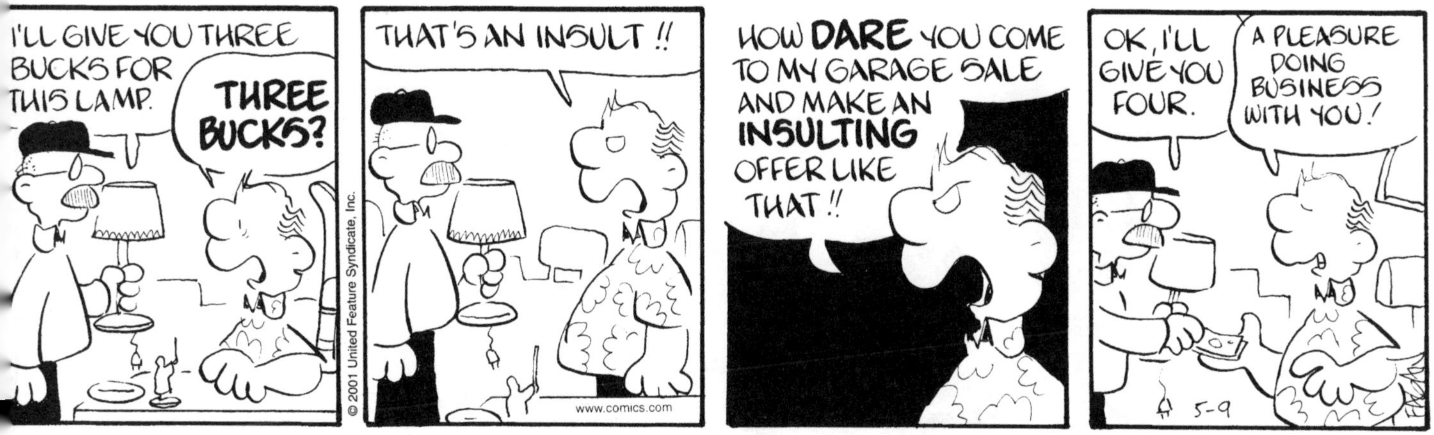
I'LL GIVE YOU THREE BUCKS FOR THIS LAMP.
THREE BUCKS?
© 2001 United Feature Syndicate, Inc.
THAT'S AN INSULT!!
www.comics.com
HOW DARE YOU COME TO MY GARAGE SALE AND MAKE AN INSULTING OFFER LIKE THAT!!
OK, I'LL GIVE YOU FOUR.
A PLEASURE DOING BUSINESS WITH YOU!
5-9

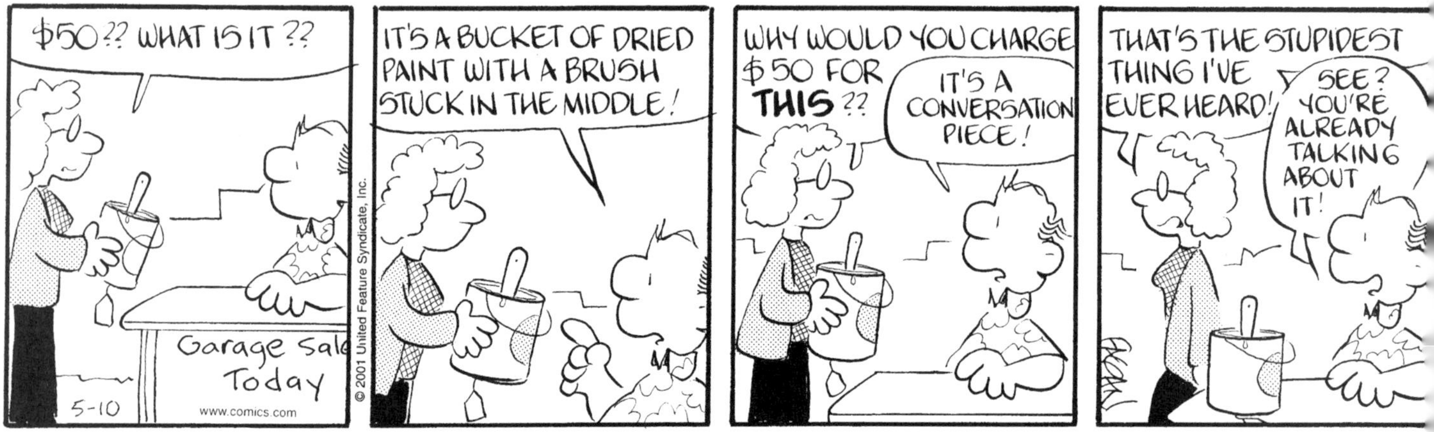

$50?? WHAT IS IT??
Garage Sale Today
5-10
www.comics.com
© 2001 United Feature Syndicate, Inc.
IT'S A BUCKET OF DRIED PAINT WITH A BRUSH STUCK IN THE MIDDLE!
WHY WOULD YOU CHARGE $50 FOR THIS??
IT'S A CONVERSATION PIECE!
THAT'S THE STUPIDEST THING I'VE EVER HEARD!
SEE? YOU'RE ALREADY TALKING ABOUT IT!
FAGAN

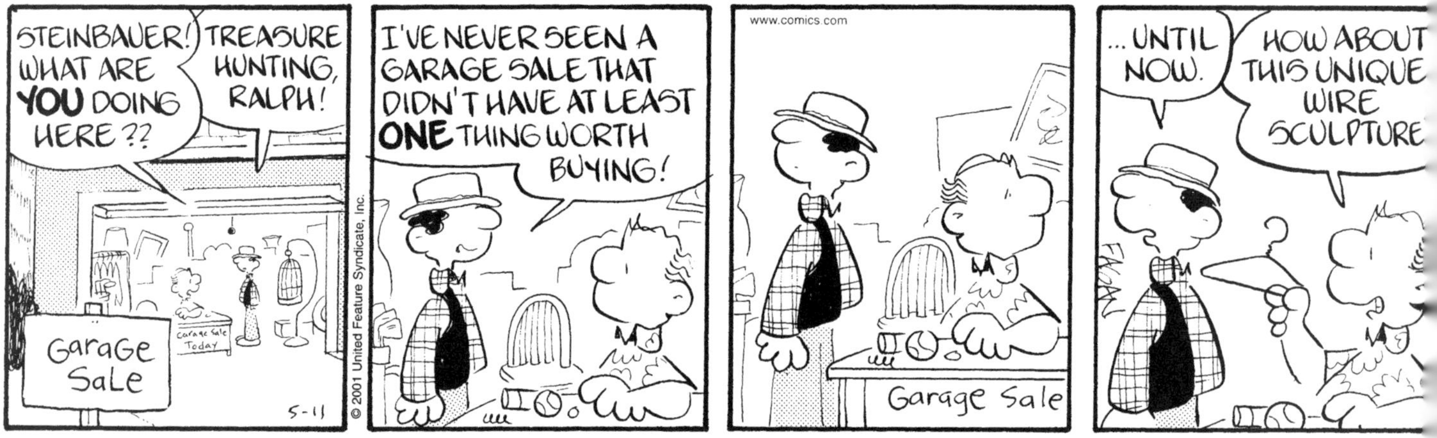

STEINBAUER! WHAT ARE YOU DOING HERE??
TREASURE HUNTING, RALPH!
Garage Sale
Garage Sale Today
5-11
© 2001 United Feature Syndicate, Inc.
I'VE NEVER SEEN A GARAGE SALE THAT DIDN'T HAVE AT LEAST ONE THING WORTH BUYING!
www.comics.com
Garage Sale
...UNTIL NOW.
HOW ABOUT THIS UNIQUE WIRE SCULPTURE
FAGAN

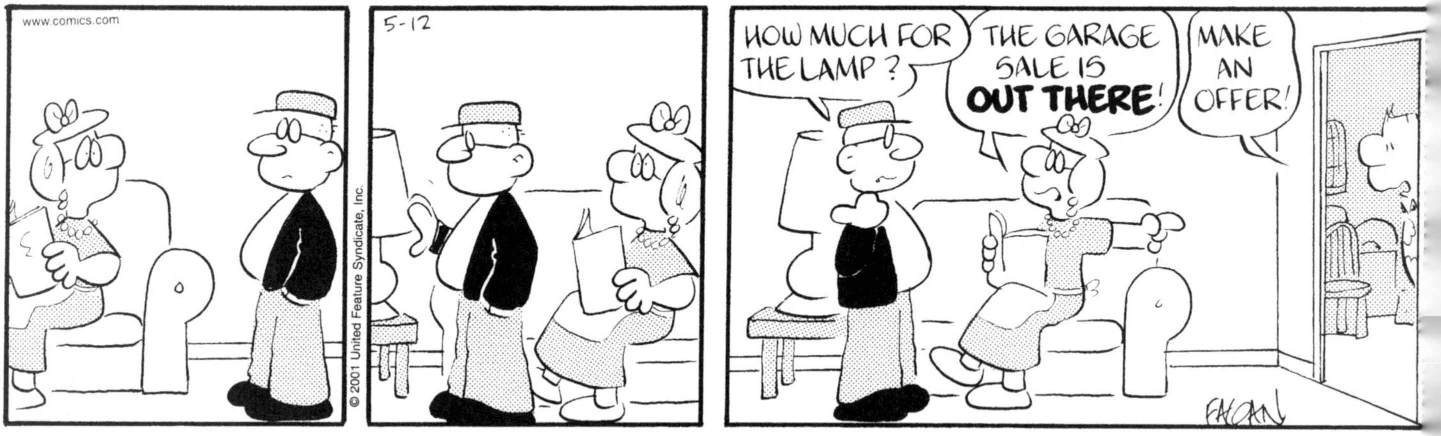

www.comics.com
© 2001 United Feature Syndicate, Inc.
5-12
HOW MUCH FOR THE LAMP?
THE GARAGE SALE IS OUT THERE!
MAKE AN OFFER!
FAGAN

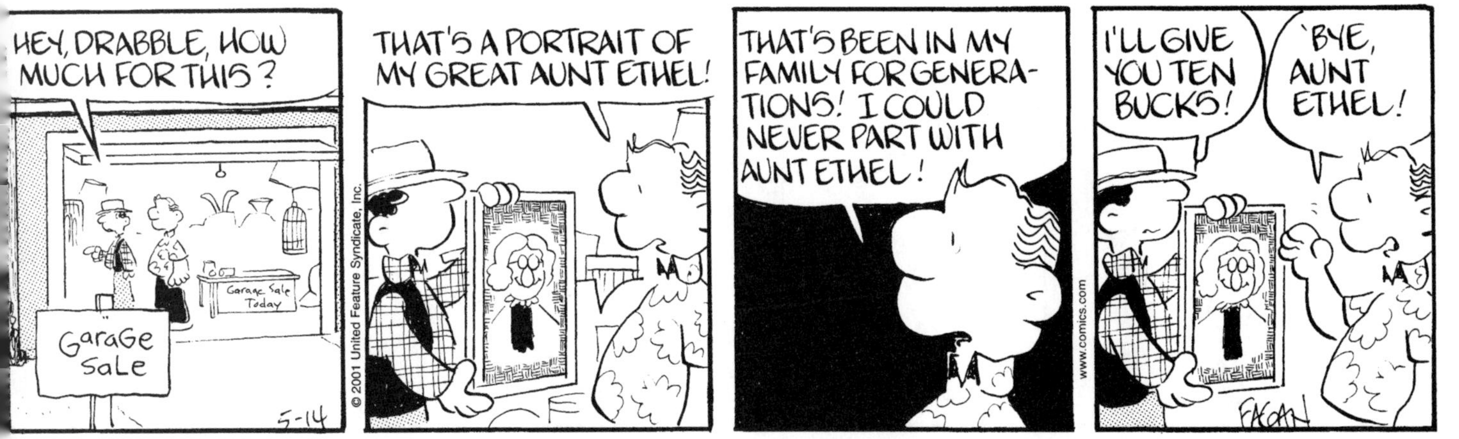
HEY, DRABBLE, HOW MUCH FOR THIS?
Garage Sale Today
GaraGe SaLe
5-14
THAT'S A PORTRAIT OF MY GREAT AUNT ETHEL!
© 2001 United Feature Syndicate, Inc.
THAT'S BEEN IN MY FAMILY FOR GENERA-TIONS! I COULD NEVER PART WITH AUNT ETHEL!
www.comics.com
I'LL GIVE YOU TEN BUCKS!
`BYE, AUNT ETHEL!
FAGAN

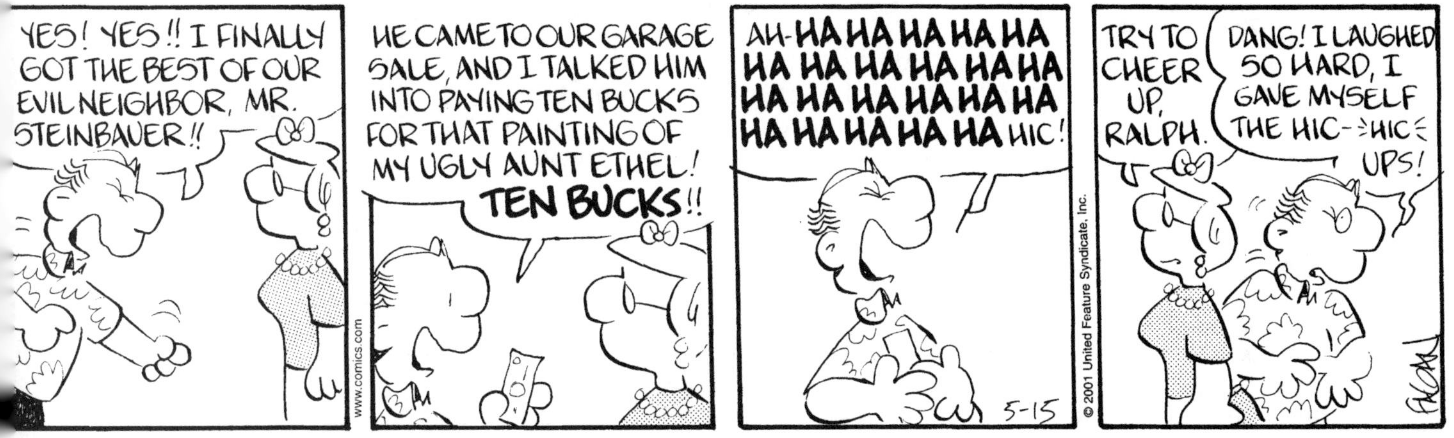
YES! YES!! I FINALLY GOT THE BEST OF OUR EVIL NEIGHBOR, MR. STEINBAUER!!
www.comics.com
HE CAME TO OUR GARAGE SALE, AND I TALKED HIM INTO PAYING TEN BUCKS FOR THAT PAINTING OF MY UGLY AUNT ETHEL! TEN BUCKS!!
AH-HA HA HA HA HA HA HA HA HA HA HA HA HA HA HA HA HA HA HA HA HA HA HA HA HA HA HIC!
5-15
© 2001 United Feature Syndicate, Inc.
TRY TO CHEER UP, RALPH.
DANG! I LAUGHED SO HARD, I GAVE MYSELF THE HIC-HIC-UPS!
FAGAN

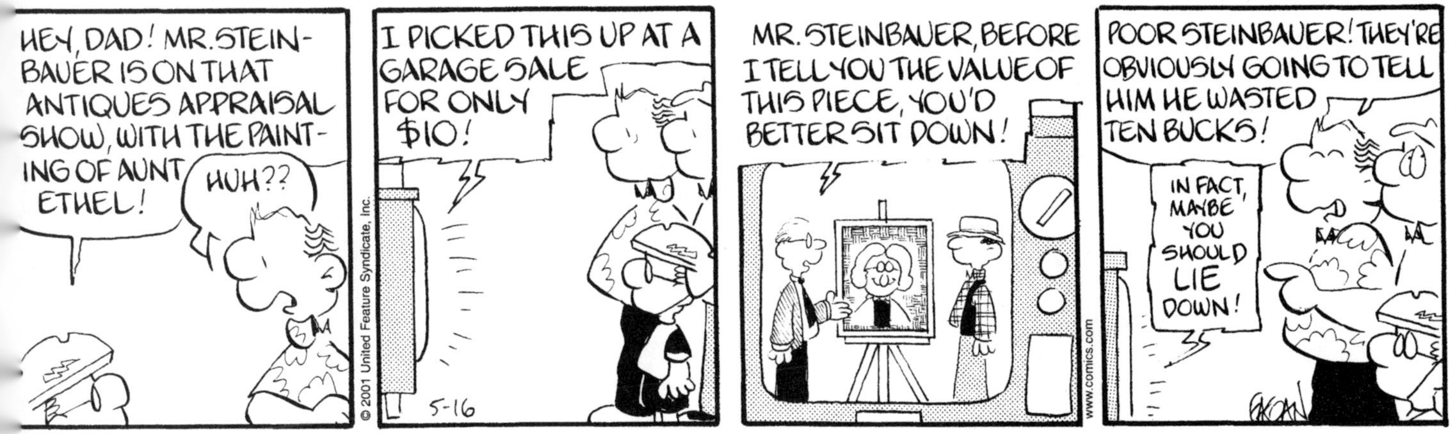
HEY, DAD! MR. STEIN-BAUER IS ON THAT ANTIQUES APPRAISAL SHOW, WITH THE PAINT-ING OF AUNT ETHEL!
HUH??
© 2001 United Feature Syndicate, Inc.
I PICKED THIS UP AT A GARAGE SALE FOR ONLY $10!
5-16
MR. STEINBAUER, BEFORE I TELL YOU THE VALUE OF THIS PIECE, YOU'D BETTER SIT DOWN!
www.comics.com
POOR STEINBAUER! THEY'RE OBVIOUSLY GOING TO TELL HIM HE WASTED TEN BUCKS!
IN FACT, MAYBE YOU SHOULD LIE DOWN!
FAGAN

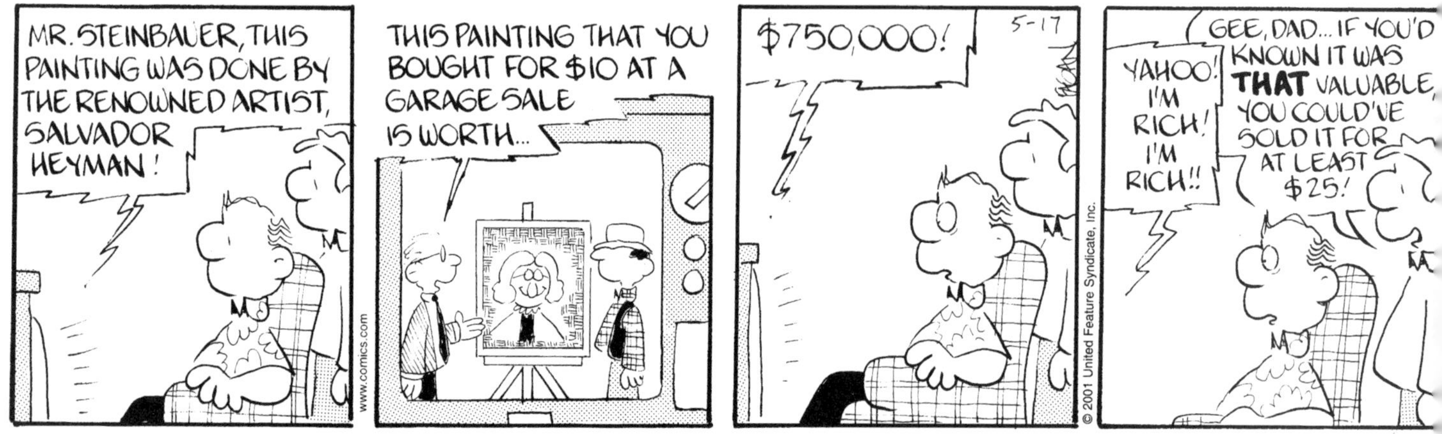
MR. STEINBAUER, THIS PAINTING WAS DONE BY THE RENOWNED ARTIST, SALVADOR HEYMAN!
www.comics.com
THIS PAINTING THAT YOU BOUGHT FOR $10 AT A GARAGE SALE IS WORTH...
$750,000!
5-17
YAHOO! I'M RICH! I'M RICH!!
GEE, DAD... IF YOU'D KNOWN IT WAS **THAT** VALUABLE, YOU COULD'VE SOLD IT FOR AT LEAST $25!
© 2001 United Feature Syndicate, Inc.

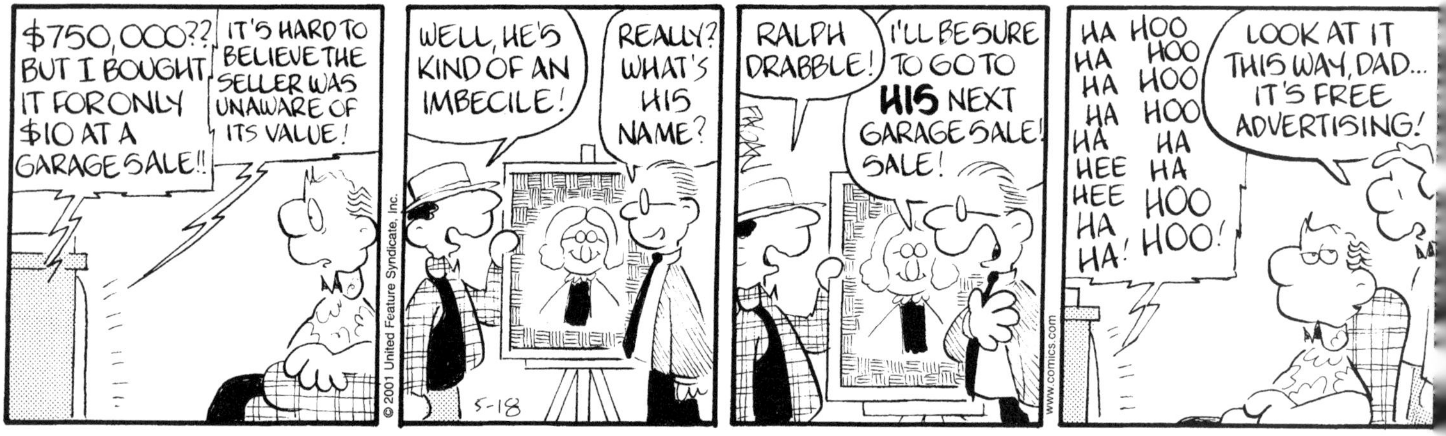
$750,000?? BUT I BOUGHT IT FOR ONLY $10 AT A GARAGE SALE!!
IT'S HARD TO BELIEVE THE SELLER WAS UNAWARE OF ITS VALUE!
© 2001 United Feature Syndicate, Inc.
WELL, HE'S KIND OF AN IMBECILE!
REALLY? WHAT'S HIS NAME?
5-18
RALPH DRABBLE!
I'LL BE SURE TO GO TO **HIS** NEXT GARAGE SALE! SALE!
www.comics.com
HA HA HA HA HA HEE HEE HA HA! HOO HOO HOO HOO HA HA HOO HOO!
LOOK AT IT THIS WAY, DAD... IT'S FREE ADVERTISING!

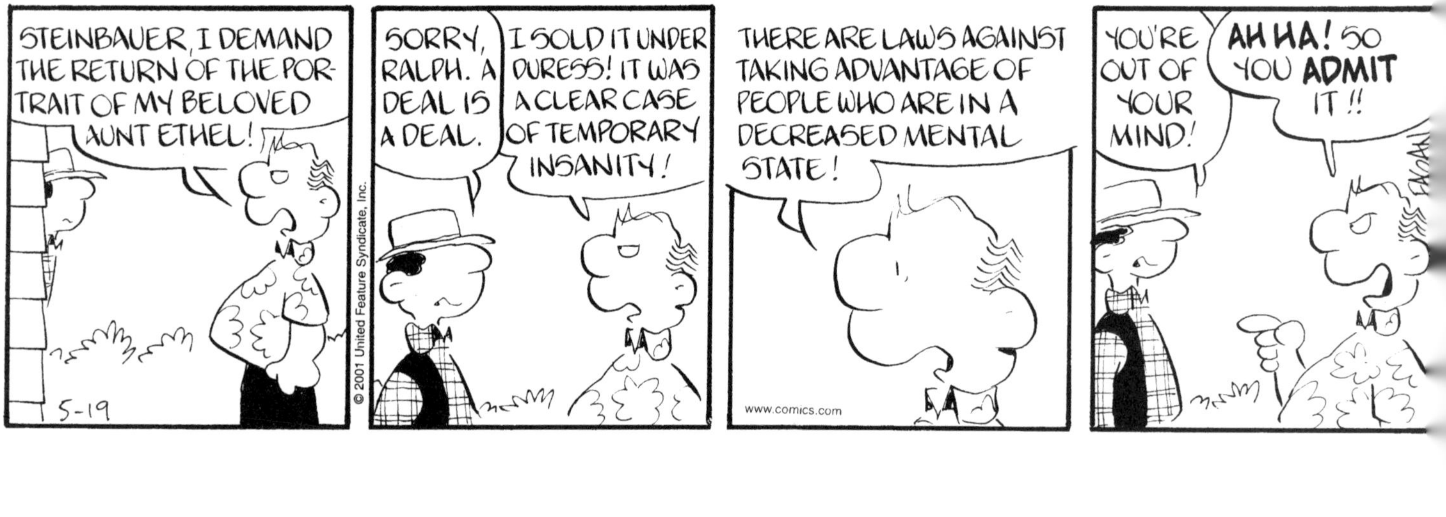
STEINBAUER, I DEMAND THE RETURN OF THE PORTRAIT OF MY BELOVED AUNT ETHEL!
5-19
© 2001 United Feature Syndicate, Inc.
SORRY, RALPH. A DEAL IS A DEAL.
I SOLD IT UNDER DURESS! IT WAS A CLEAR CASE OF TEMPORARY INSANITY!
THERE ARE LAWS AGAINST TAKING ADVANTAGE OF PEOPLE WHO ARE IN A DECREASED MENTAL STATE!
www.comics.com
YOU'RE OUT OF YOUR MIND!
AH HA! SO YOU **ADMIT** IT!!

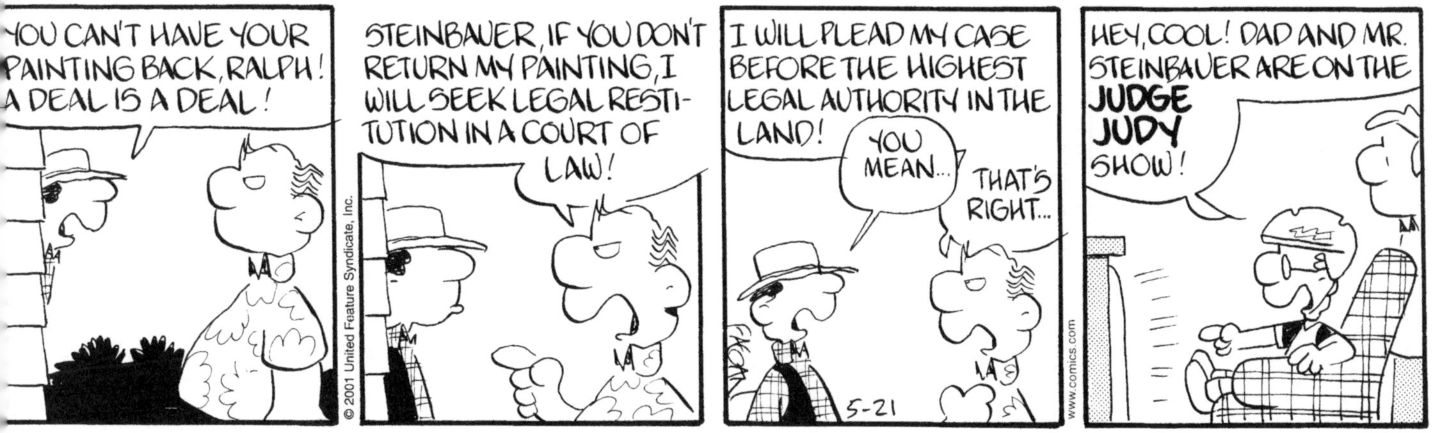
YOU CAN'T HAVE YOUR PAINTING BACK, RALPH! A DEAL IS A DEAL!
© 2001 United Feature Syndicate, Inc.
STEINBAUER, IF YOU DON'T RETURN MY PAINTING, I WILL SEEK LEGAL RESTITUTION IN A COURT OF LAW!
I WILL PLEAD MY CASE BEFORE THE HIGHEST LEGAL AUTHORITY IN THE LAND!
YOU MEAN...
THAT'S RIGHT...
5-21
www.comics.com
HEY, COOL! DAD AND MR. STEINBAUER ARE ON THE JUDGE JUDY SHOW!

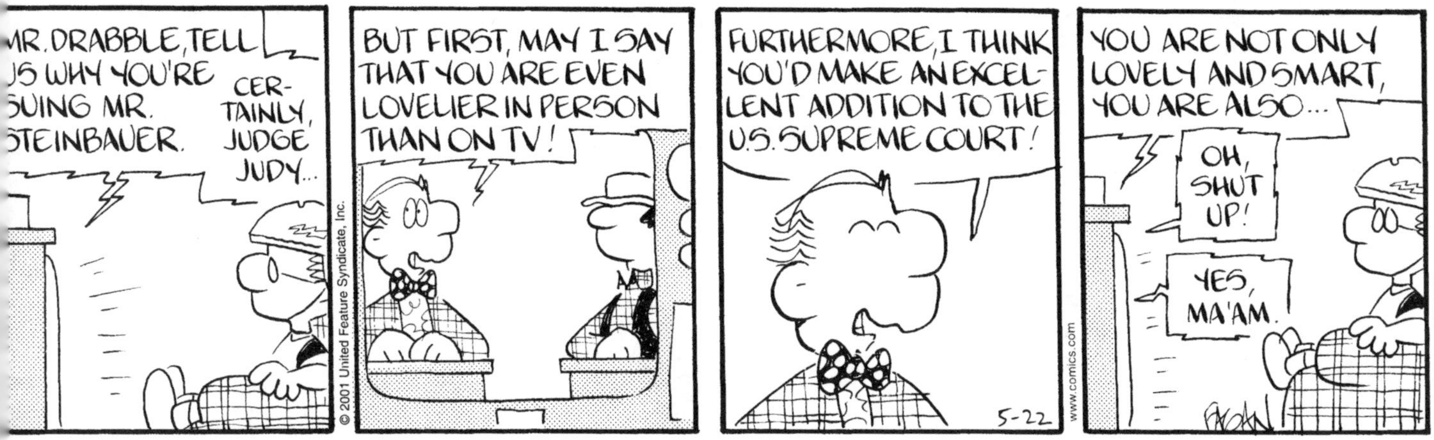
MR. DRABBLE, TELL US WHY YOU'RE SUING MR. STEINBAUER.
CERTAINLY, JUDGE JUDY...
© 2001 United Feature Syndicate, Inc.
BUT FIRST, MAY I SAY THAT YOU ARE EVEN LOVELIER IN PERSON THAN ON TV!
FURTHERMORE, I THINK YOU'D MAKE AN EXCELLENT ADDITION TO THE U.S. SUPREME COURT!
5-22
www.comics.com
YOU ARE NOT ONLY LOVELY AND SMART, YOU ARE ALSO...
OH, SHUT UP!
YES, MA'AM.

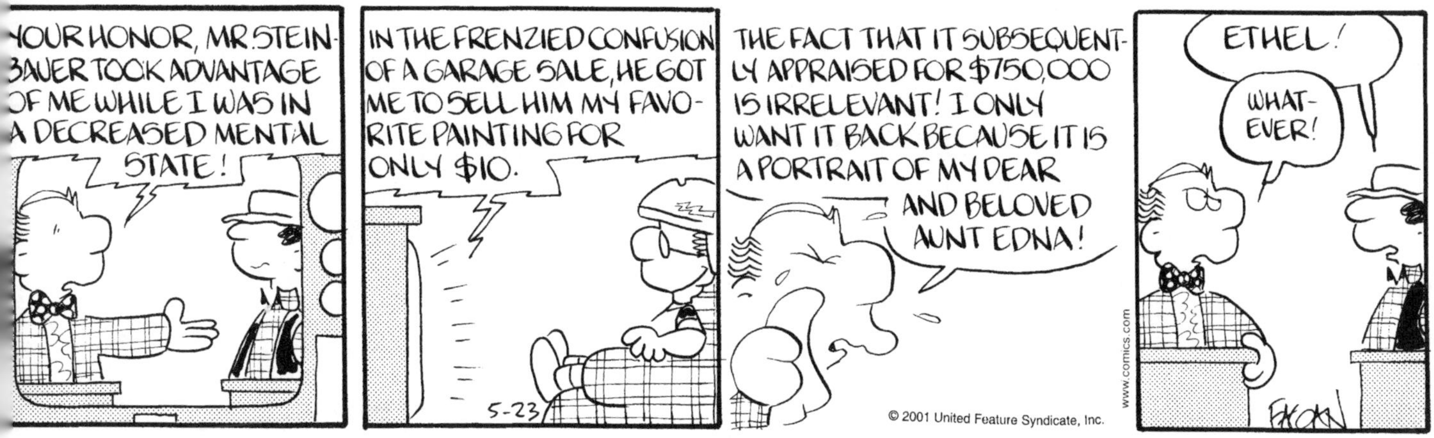
YOUR HONOR, MR. STEINBAUER TOOK ADVANTAGE OF ME WHILE I WAS IN A DECREASED MENTAL STATE!
IN THE FRENZIED CONFUSION OF A GARAGE SALE, HE GOT ME TO SELL HIM MY FAVORITE PAINTING FOR ONLY $10.
5-23
THE FACT THAT IT SUBSEQUENTLY APPRAISED FOR $750,000 IS IRRELEVANT! I ONLY WANT IT BACK BECAUSE IT IS A PORTRAIT OF MY DEAR
AND BELOVED AUNT EDNA!
© 2001 United Feature Syndicate, Inc.
www.comics.com
ETHEL!
WHATEVER!

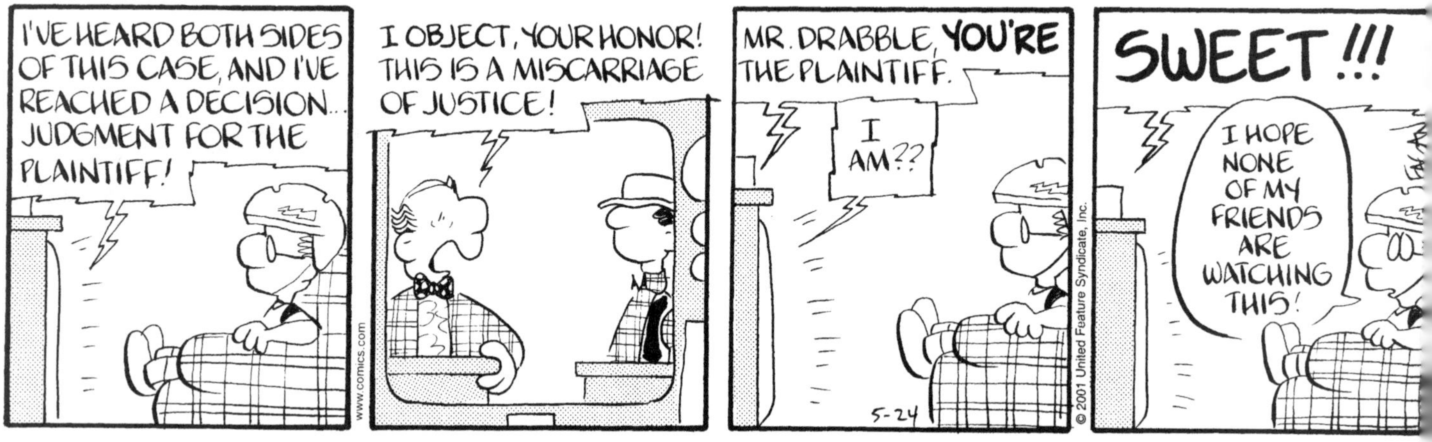
I'VE HEARD BOTH SIDES OF THIS CASE, AND I'VE REACHED A DECISION... JUDGMENT FOR THE PLAINTIFF!
www.comics.com
I OBJECT, YOUR HONOR! THIS IS A MISCARRIAGE OF JUSTICE!
MR. DRABBLE, YOU'RE THE PLAINTIFF.
I AM??
5-24
© 2001 United Feature Syndicate, Inc.
SWEET!!!
I HOPE NONE OF MY FRIENDS ARE WATCHING THIS!

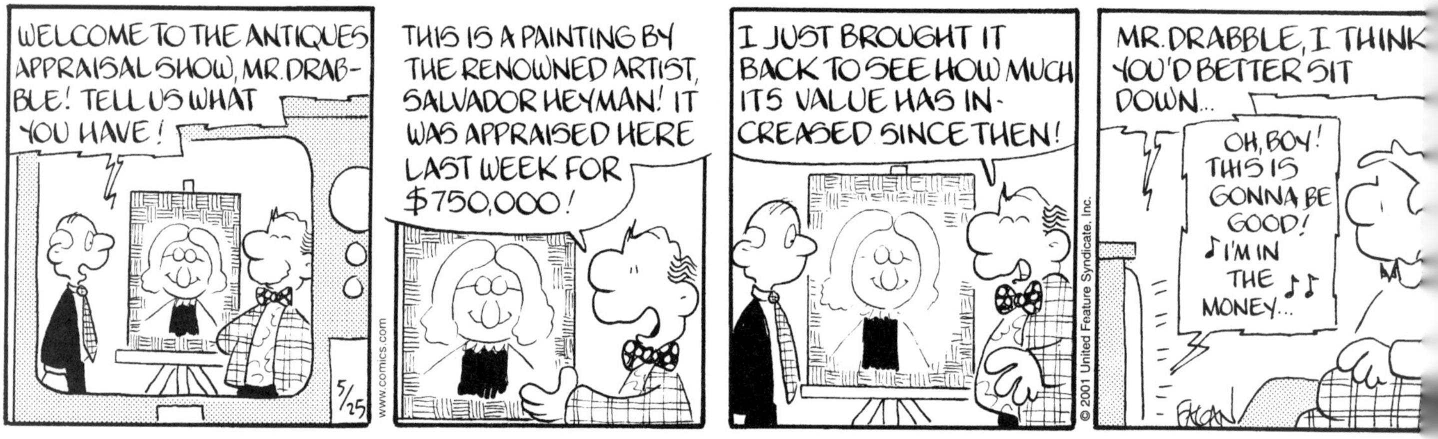
WELCOME TO THE ANTIQUES APPRAISAL SHOW, MR. DRABBLE! TELL US WHAT YOU HAVE!
5/25
www.comics.com
THIS IS A PAINTING BY THE RENOWNED ARTIST, SALVADOR HEYMAN! IT WAS APPRAISED HERE LAST WEEK FOR $750,000!
I JUST BROUGHT IT BACK TO SEE HOW MUCH ITS VALUE HAS INCREASED SINCE THEN!
© 2001 United Feature Syndicate, Inc.
MR. DRABBLE, I THINK YOU'D BETTER SIT DOWN...
OH, BOY! THIS IS GONNA BE GOOD! ♪ I'M IN THE MONEY... ♪♪
FAGAN

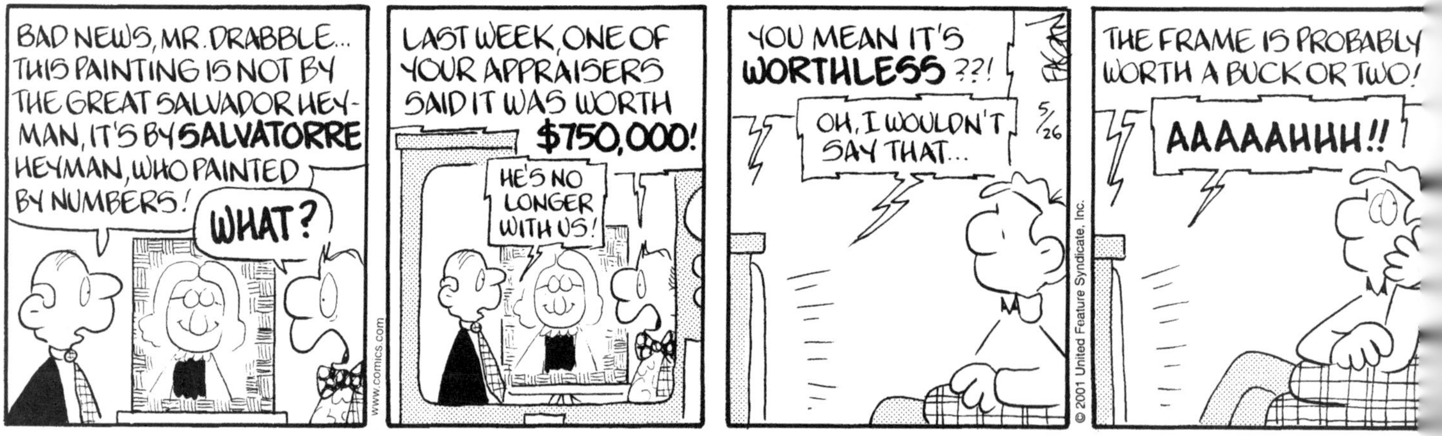
BAD NEWS, MR. DRABBLE... THIS PAINTING IS NOT BY THE GREAT SALVADOR HEYMAN, IT'S BY SALVATORRE HEYMAN, WHO PAINTED BY NUMBERS!
WHAT?
www.comics.com
LAST WEEK, ONE OF YOUR APPRAISERS SAID IT WAS WORTH $750,000!
HE'S NO LONGER WITH US!
YOU MEAN IT'S WORTHLESS??!
OH, I WOULDN'T SAY THAT...
5/26
© 2001 United Feature Syndicate, Inc.
THE FRAME IS PROBABLY WORTH A BUCK OR TWO!
AAAAAHHH!!

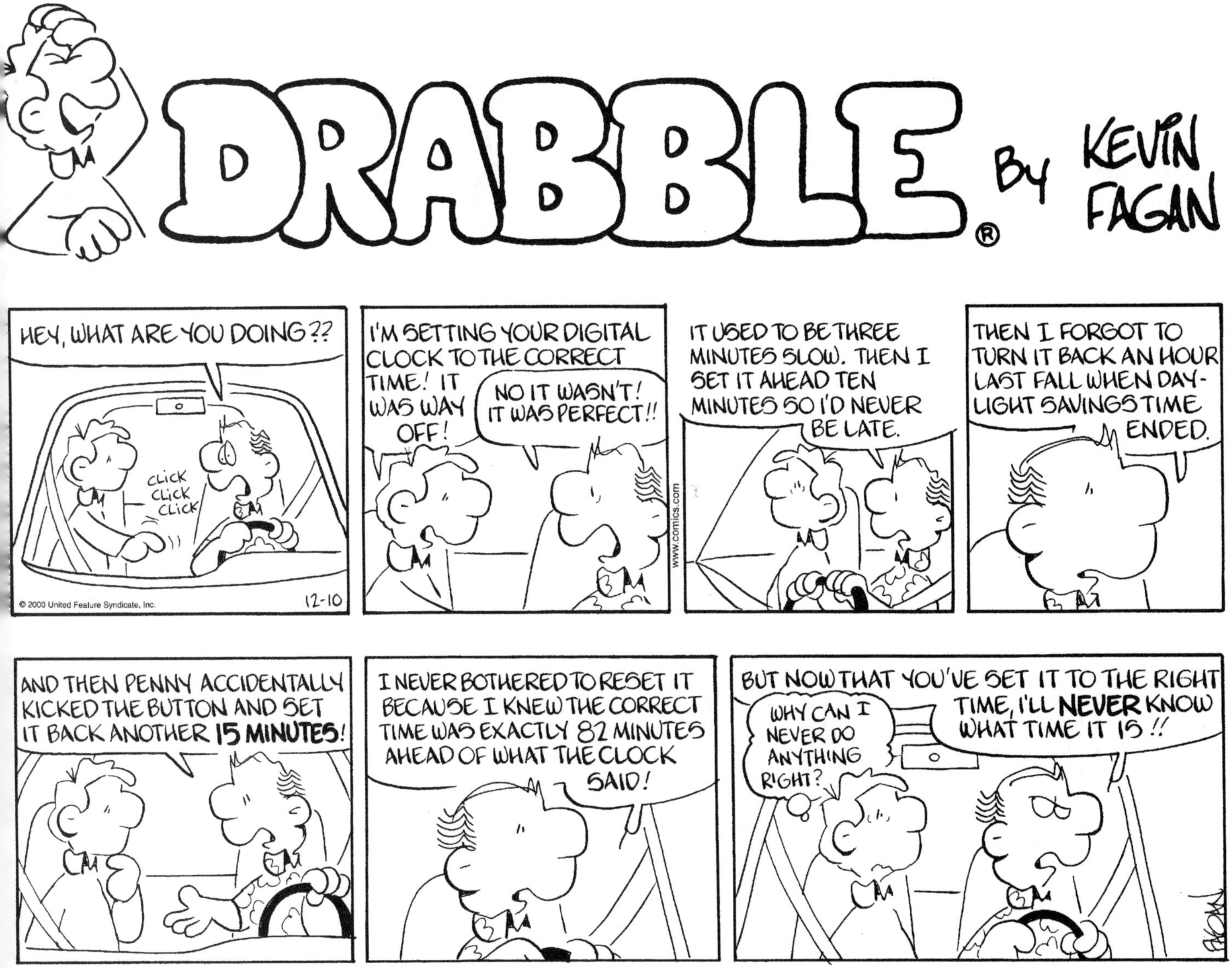
DRABBLE® By KEVIN FAGAN
HEY, WHAT ARE YOU DOING??
CLICK CLICK CLICK
© 2000 United Feature Syndicate, Inc.
12-10
I'M SETTING YOUR DIGITAL CLOCK TO THE CORRECT TIME! IT WAS WAY OFF!
NO IT WASN'T! IT WAS PERFECT!!
www.comics.com
IT USED TO BE THREE MINUTES SLOW. THEN I SET IT AHEAD TEN MINUTES SO I'D NEVER BE LATE.
THEN I FORGOT TO TURN IT BACK AN HOUR LAST FALL WHEN DAY-LIGHT SAVINGS TIME ENDED.
AND THEN PENNY ACCIDENTALLY KICKED THE BUTTON AND SET IT BACK ANOTHER **15 MINUTES**!
I NEVER BOTHERED TO RESET IT BECAUSE I KNEW THE CORRECT TIME WAS EXACTLY 82 MINUTES AHEAD OF WHAT THE CLOCK SAID!
BUT NOW THAT YOU'VE SET IT TO THE RIGHT TIME, I'LL **NEVER** KNOW WHAT TIME IT IS!!
WHY CAN I NEVER DO ANYTHING RIGHT?

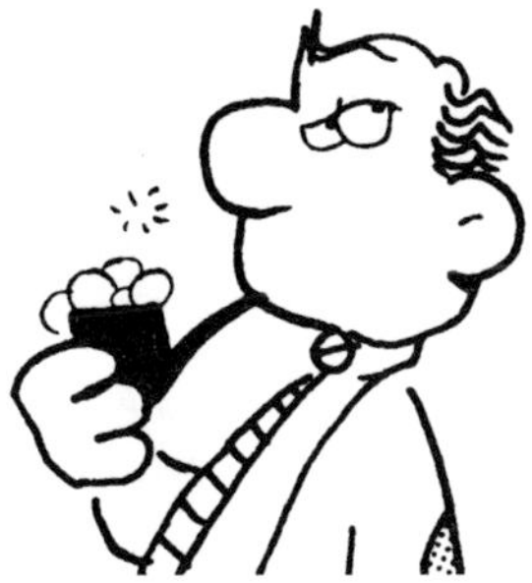

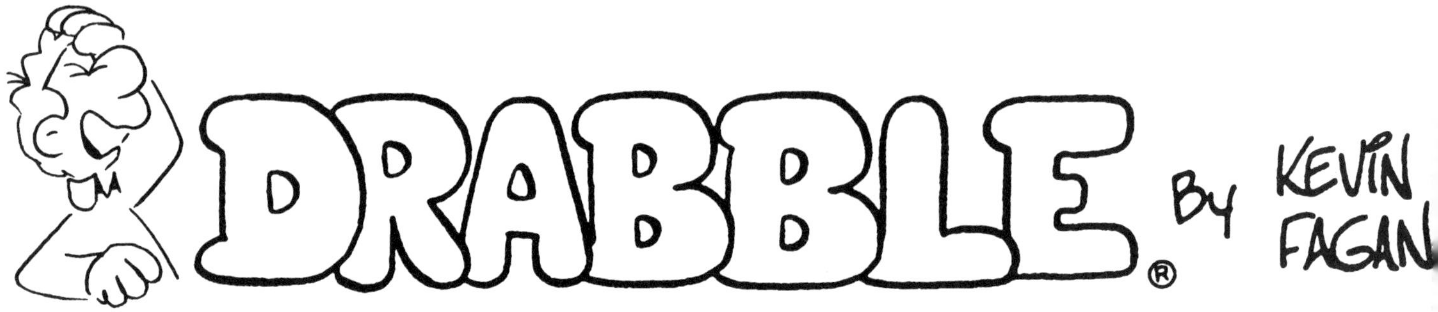
DRABBLE®
By KEVIN FAGAN

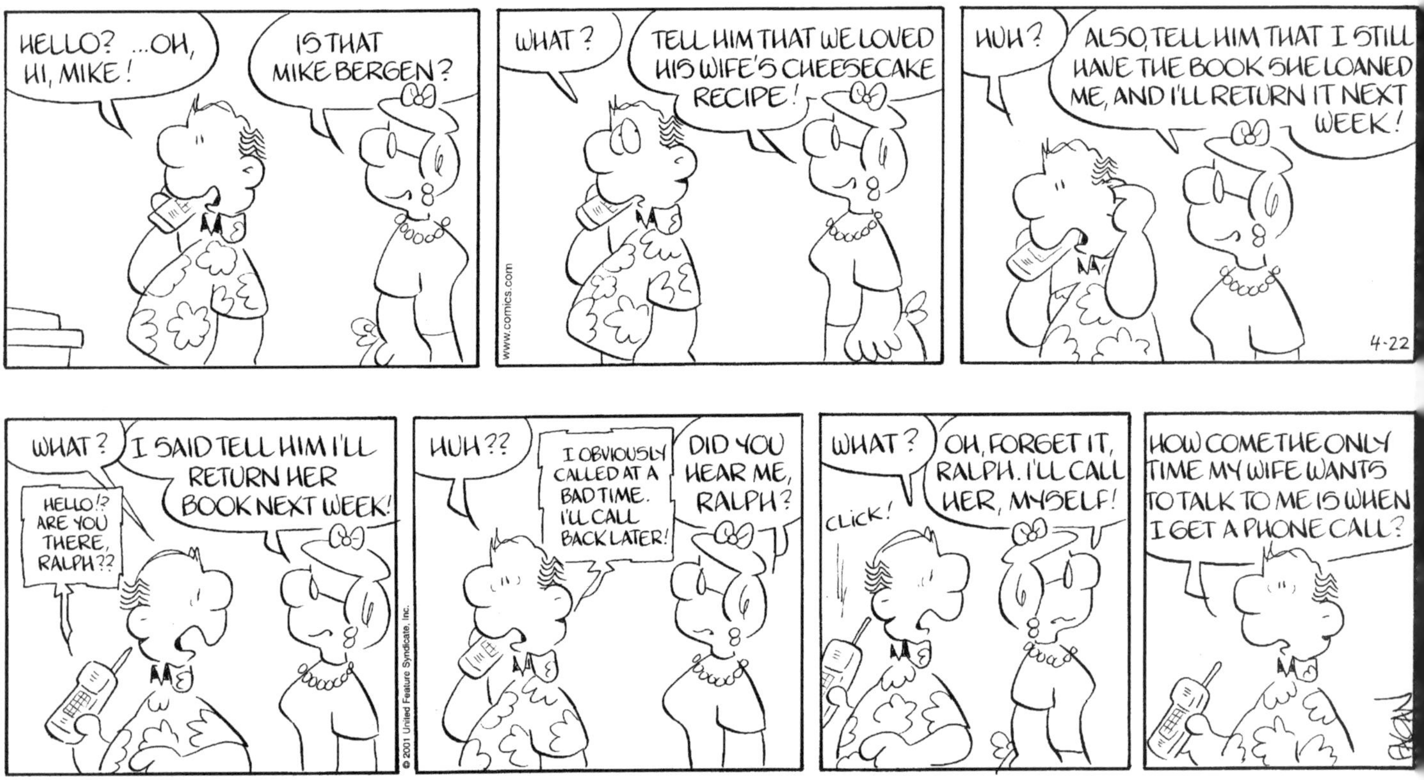
HELLO? ...OH, HI, MIKE!
IS THAT MIKE BERGEN?
WHAT?
TELL HIM THAT WE LOVED HIS WIFE'S CHEESECAKE RECIPE!
www.comics.com
HUH?
ALSO, TELL HIM THAT I STILL HAVE THE BOOK SHE LOANED ME, AND I'LL RETURN IT NEXT WEEK!
4-22
WHAT?
I SAID TELL HIM I'LL RETURN HER BOOK NEXT WEEK!
HELLO!? ARE YOU THERE, RALPH??
© 2001 United Feature Syndicate, Inc.
HUH??
I OBVIOUSLY CALLED AT A BAD TIME. I'LL CALL BACK LATER!
DID YOU HEAR ME, RALPH?
WHAT?
OH, FORGET IT, RALPH. I'LL CALL HER, MYSELF!
CLICK!
HOW COME THE ONLY TIME MY WIFE WANTS TO TALK TO ME IS WHEN I GET A PHONE CALL?

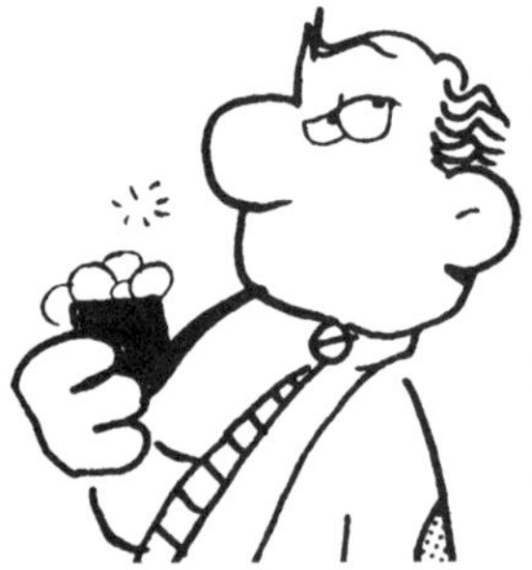

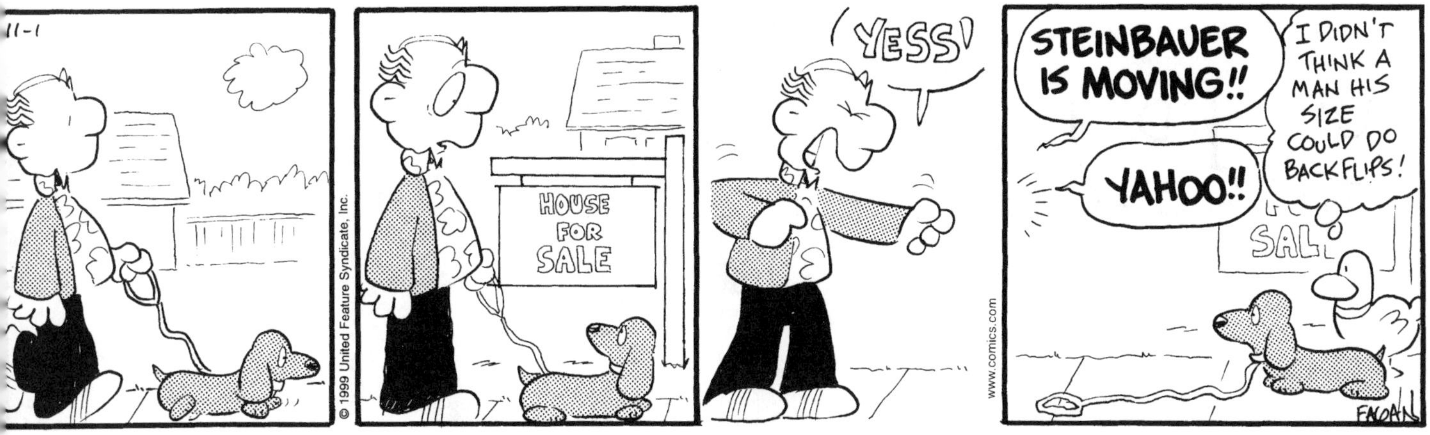
11-1
HOUSE FOR SALE
© 1999 United Feature Syndicate, Inc.
YESS!
www.comics.com
STEINBAUER IS MOVING!!
YAHOO!!
I DIDN'T THINK A MAN HIS SIZE COULD DO BACKFLIPS!
FAGAN

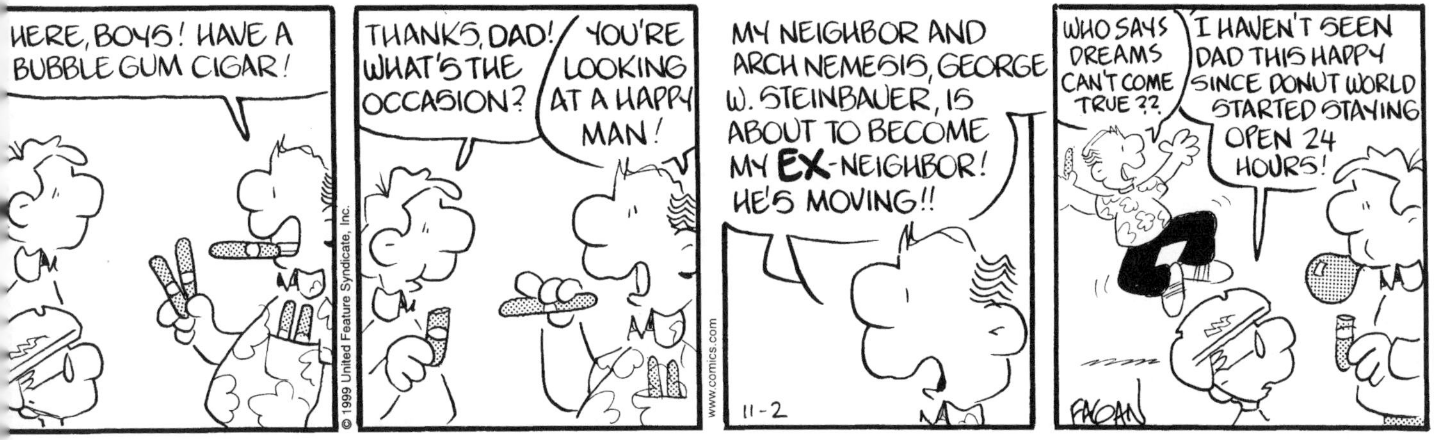
HERE, BOYS! HAVE A BUBBLE GUM CIGAR!
© 1999 United Feature Syndicate, Inc.
THANKS, DAD! WHAT'S THE OCCASION?
YOU'RE LOOKING AT A HAPPY MAN!
www.comics.com
MY NEIGHBOR AND ARCH NEMESIS, GEORGE W. STEINBAUER, IS ABOUT TO BECOME MY EX-NEIGHBOR! HE'S MOVING!!
11-2
WHO SAYS DREAMS CAN'T COME TRUE??
I HAVEN'T SEEN DAD THIS HAPPY SINCE DONUT WORLD STARTED STAYING OPEN 24 HOURS!
FAGAN

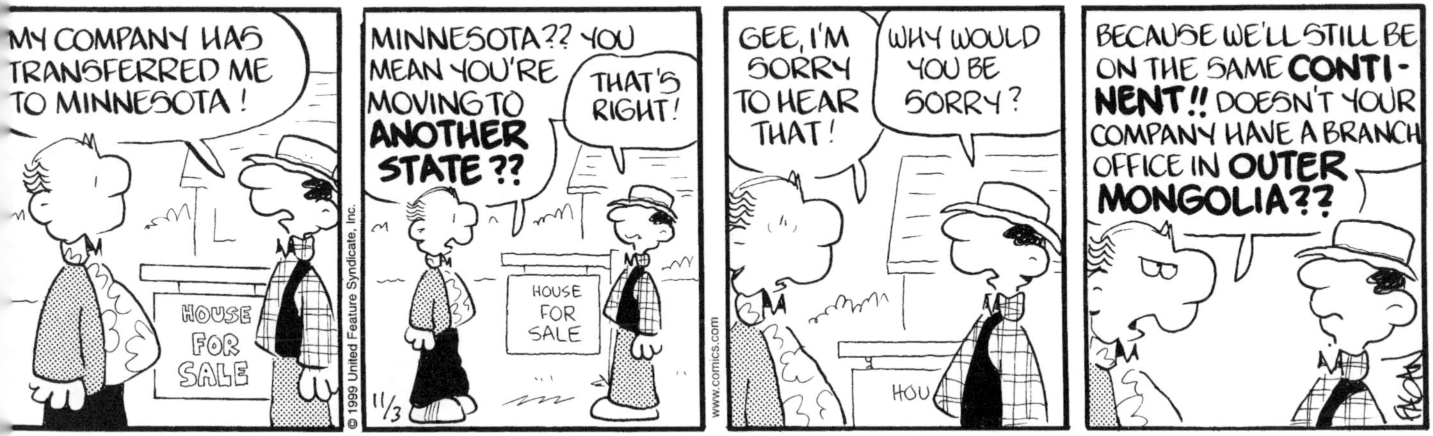
MY COMPANY HAS TRANSFERRED ME TO MINNESOTA!
HOUSE FOR SALE
© 1999 United Feature Syndicate, Inc.
MINNESOTA?? YOU MEAN YOU'RE MOVING TO ANOTHER STATE??
THAT'S RIGHT!
HOUSE FOR SALE
11/3
www.comics.com
GEE, I'M SORRY TO HEAR THAT!
WHY WOULD YOU BE SORRY?
HOU
BECAUSE WE'LL STILL BE ON THE SAME CONTI-NENT!! DOESN'T YOUR COMPANY HAVE A BRANCH OFFICE IN OUTER MONGOLIA??
FAGAN

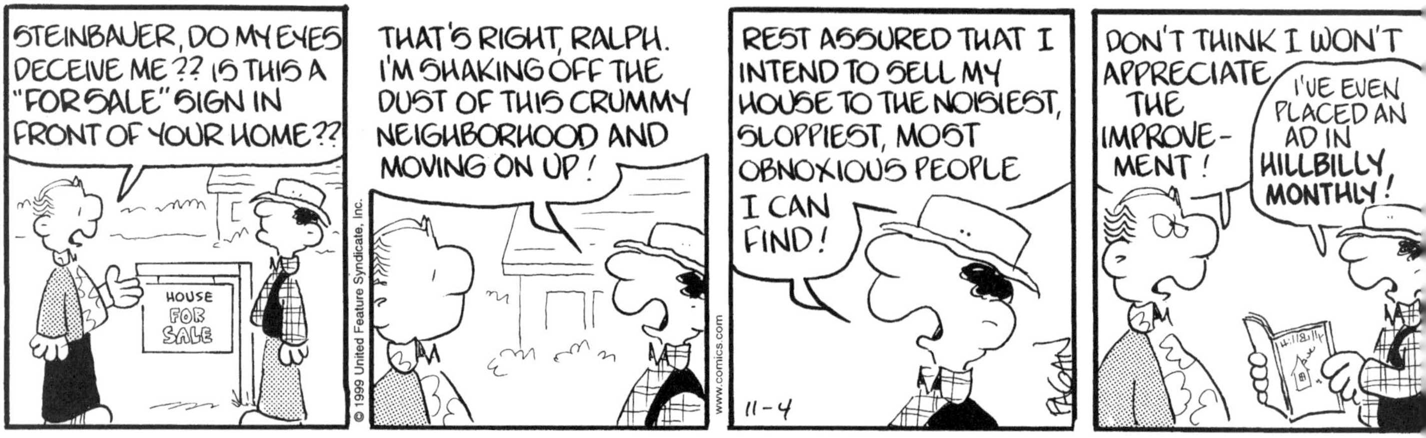
STEINBAUER, DO MY EYES DECEIVE ME?? IS THIS A "FOR SALE" SIGN IN FRONT OF YOUR HOME??
HOUSE FOR SALE
THAT'S RIGHT, RALPH. I'M SHAKING OFF THE DUST OF THIS CRUMMY NEIGHBORHOOD AND MOVING ON UP!
© 1999 United Feature Syndicate, Inc.
www.comics.com
REST ASSURED THAT I INTEND TO SELL MY HOUSE TO THE NOISIEST, SLOPPIEST, MOST OBNOXIOUS PEOPLE
I CAN FIND!
11-4
DON'T THINK I WON'T APPRECIATE THE IMPROVEMENT!
I'VE EVEN PLACED AN AD IN HILLBILLY MONTHLY!

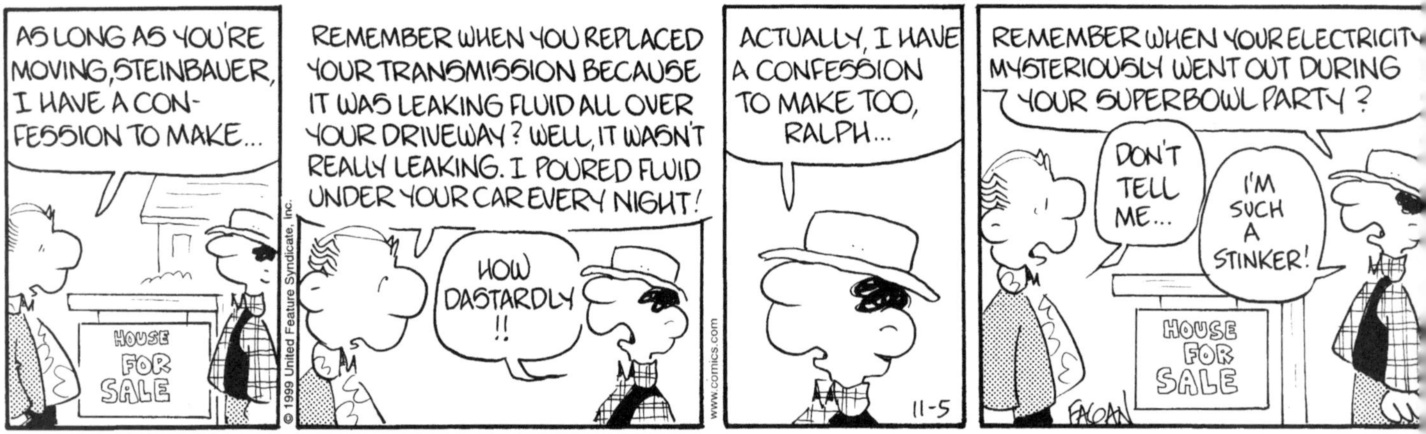
AS LONG AS YOU'RE MOVING, STEINBAUER, I HAVE A CONFESSION TO MAKE...
HOUSE FOR SALE
REMEMBER WHEN YOU REPLACED YOUR TRANSMISSION BECAUSE IT WAS LEAKING FLUID ALL OVER YOUR DRIVEWAY? WELL, IT WASN'T REALLY LEAKING. I POURED FLUID UNDER YOUR CAR EVERY NIGHT!
HOW DASTARDLY!!
© 1999 United Feature Syndicate, Inc.
www.comics.com
ACTUALLY, I HAVE A CONFESSION TO MAKE TOO, RALPH...
11-5
REMEMBER WHEN YOUR ELECTRICITY MYSTERIOUSLY WENT OUT DURING YOUR SUPERBOWL PARTY?
DON'T TELL ME...
I'M SUCH A STINKER!
HOUSE FOR SALE
FAGAN

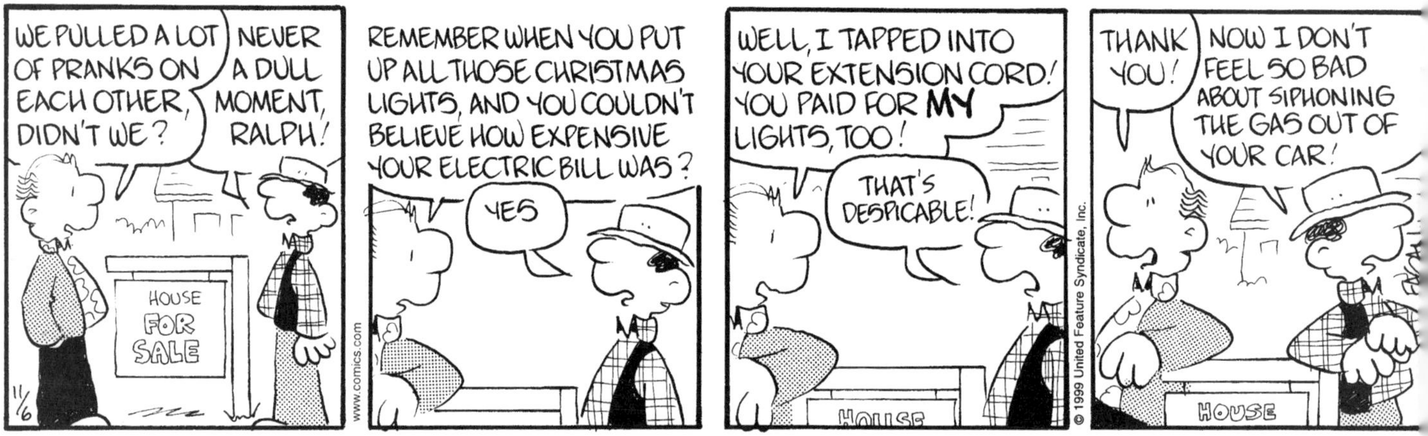
WE PULLED A LOT OF PRANKS ON EACH OTHER, DIDN'T WE?
NEVER A DULL MOMENT, RALPH!
HOUSE FOR SALE
11/6
REMEMBER WHEN YOU PUT UP ALL THOSE CHRISTMAS LIGHTS, AND YOU COULDN'T BELIEVE HOW EXPENSIVE YOUR ELECTRIC BILL WAS?
YES
www.comics.com
WELL, I TAPPED INTO YOUR EXTENSION CORD! YOU PAID FOR MY LIGHTS, TOO!
THAT'S DESPICABLE!
© 1999 United Feature Syndicate, Inc.
THANK YOU!
NOW I DON'T FEEL SO BAD ABOUT SIPHONING THE GAS OUT OF YOUR CAR!
HOUSE

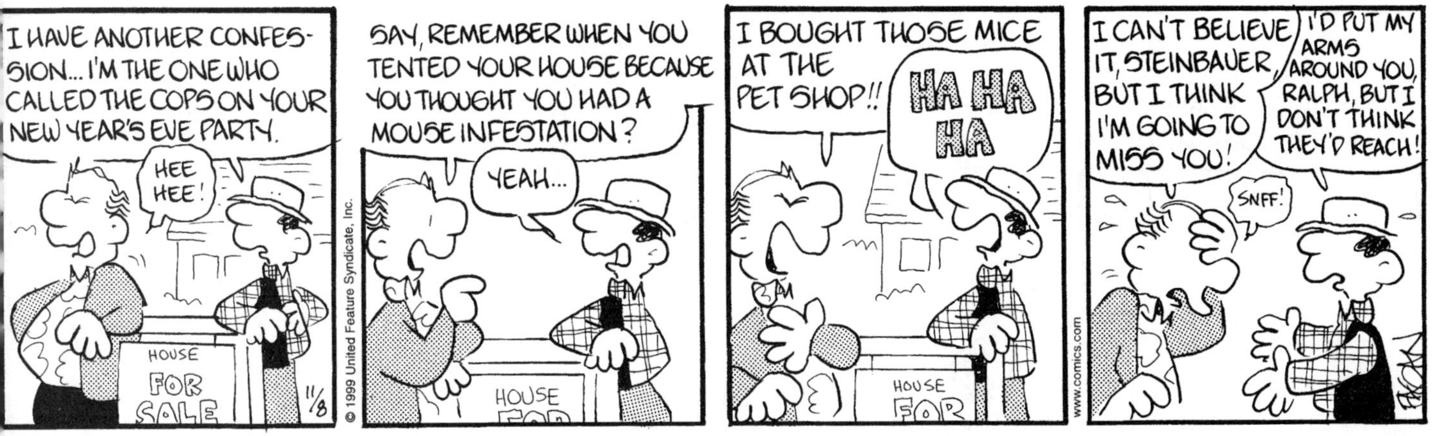
I HAVE ANOTHER CONFESSION... I'M THE ONE WHO CALLED THE COPS ON YOUR NEW YEAR'S EVE PARTY.
HEE HEE!
HOUSE FOR SALE
11/8
© 1999 United Feature Syndicate, Inc.
SAY, REMEMBER WHEN YOU TENTED YOUR HOUSE BECAUSE YOU THOUGHT YOU HAD A MOUSE INFESTATION?
YEAH...
HOUSE
I BOUGHT THOSE MICE AT THE PET SHOP!!
HA HA HA
HOUSE
www.comics.com
I CAN'T BELIEVE IT, STEINBAUER, BUT I THINK I'M GOING TO MISS YOU!
SNFF!
I'D PUT MY ARMS AROUND YOU, RALPH, BUT I DON'T THINK THEY'D REACH!

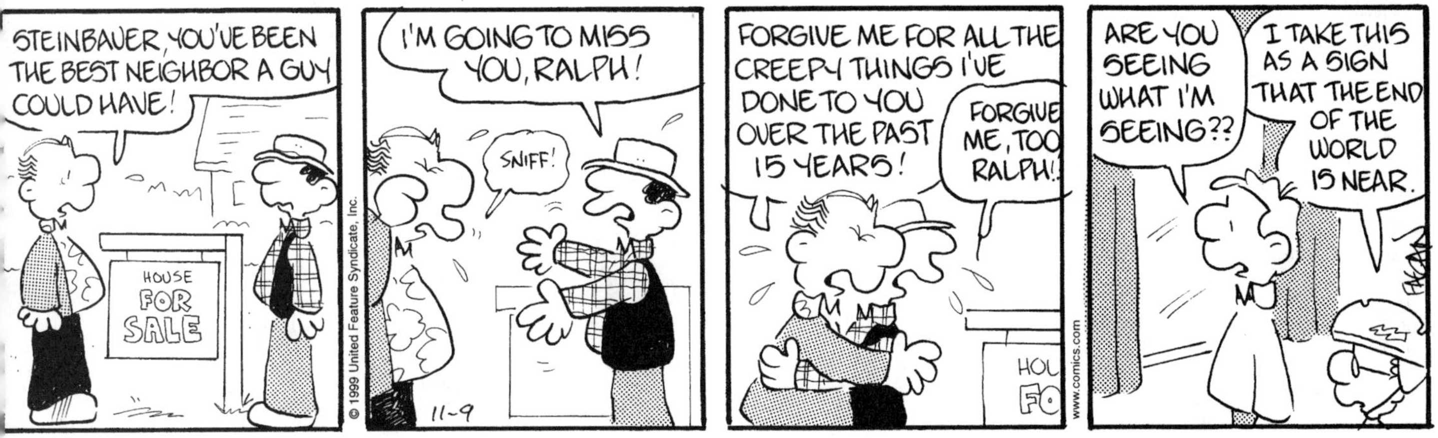
STEINBAUER, YOU'VE BEEN THE BEST NEIGHBOR A GUY COULD HAVE!
HOUSE FOR SALE
© 1999 United Feature Syndicate, Inc.
I'M GOING TO MISS YOU, RALPH!
SNIFF!
11-9
FORGIVE ME FOR ALL THE CREEPY THINGS I'VE DONE TO YOU OVER THE PAST 15 YEARS!
FORGIVE ME, TOO RALPH!
www.comics.com
ARE YOU SEEING WHAT I'M SEEING??
I TAKE THIS AS A SIGN THAT THE END OF THE WORLD IS NEAR.

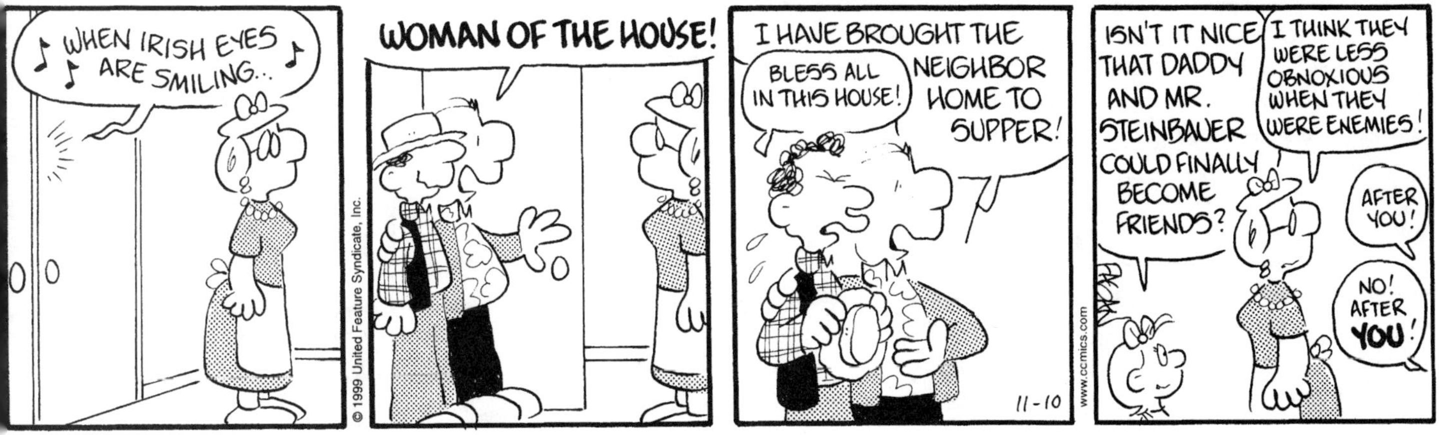
♪ WHEN IRISH EYES ♪ ARE SMILING... ♪
© 1999 United Feature Syndicate, Inc.
WOMAN OF THE HOUSE!
I HAVE BROUGHT THE NEIGHBOR HOME TO SUPPER!
BLESS ALL IN THIS HOUSE!
11-10
www.comics.com
ISN'T IT NICE THAT DADDY AND MR. STEINBAUER COULD FINALLY BECOME FRIENDS?
I THINK THEY WERE LESS OBNOXIOUS WHEN THEY WERE ENEMIES!
AFTER YOU!
NO! AFTER YOU!

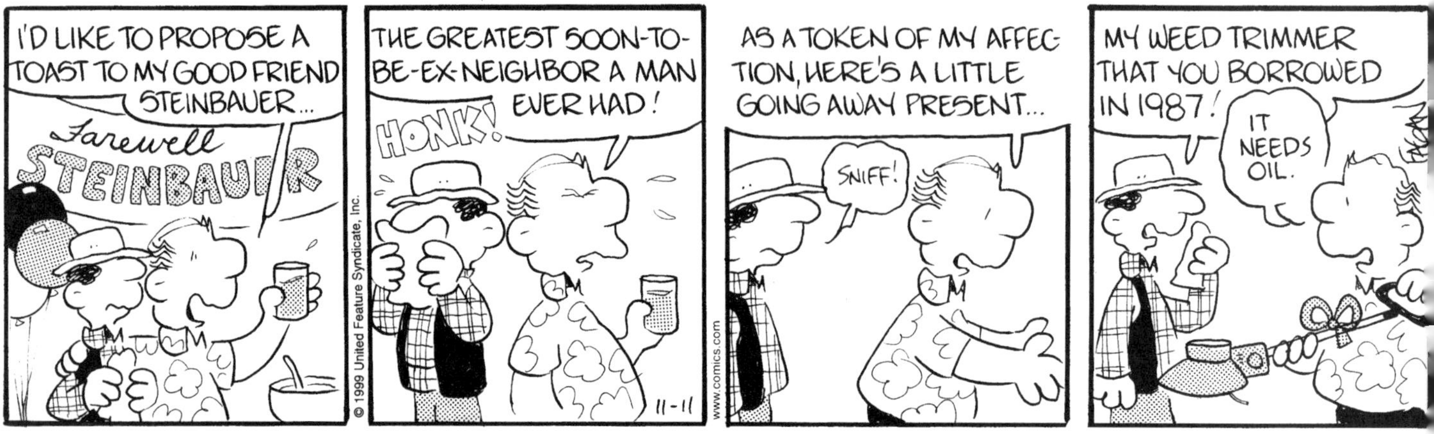
I'D LIKE TO PROPOSE A TOAST TO MY GOOD FRIEND STEINBAUER...
Farewell
THE GREATEST SOON-TO-BE-EX-NEIGHBOR A MAN EVER HAD!
HONK!
© 1999 United Feature Syndicate, Inc.
11-11
AS A TOKEN OF MY AFFECTION, HERE'S A LITTLE GOING AWAY PRESENT...
SNIFF!
www.comics.com
MY WEED TRIMMER THAT YOU BORROWED IN 1987!
IT NEEDS OIL.

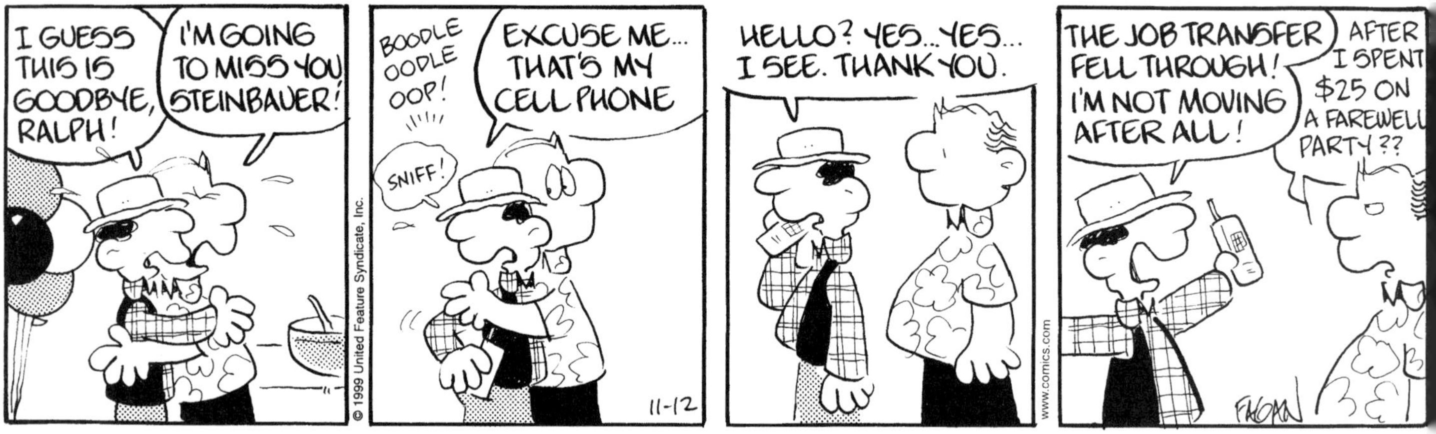
I GUESS THIS IS GOODBYE, RALPH!
I'M GOING TO MISS YOU STEINBAUER!
BOODLE OODLE OOP!
EXCUSE ME... THAT'S MY CELL PHONE
SNIFF!
© 1999 United Feature Syndicate, Inc.
11-12
HELLO? YES... YES... I SEE. THANK YOU.
www.comics.com
THE JOB TRANSFER FELL THROUGH! I'M NOT MOVING AFTER ALL!
AFTER I SPENT $25 ON A FAREWELL PARTY??
FAGAN

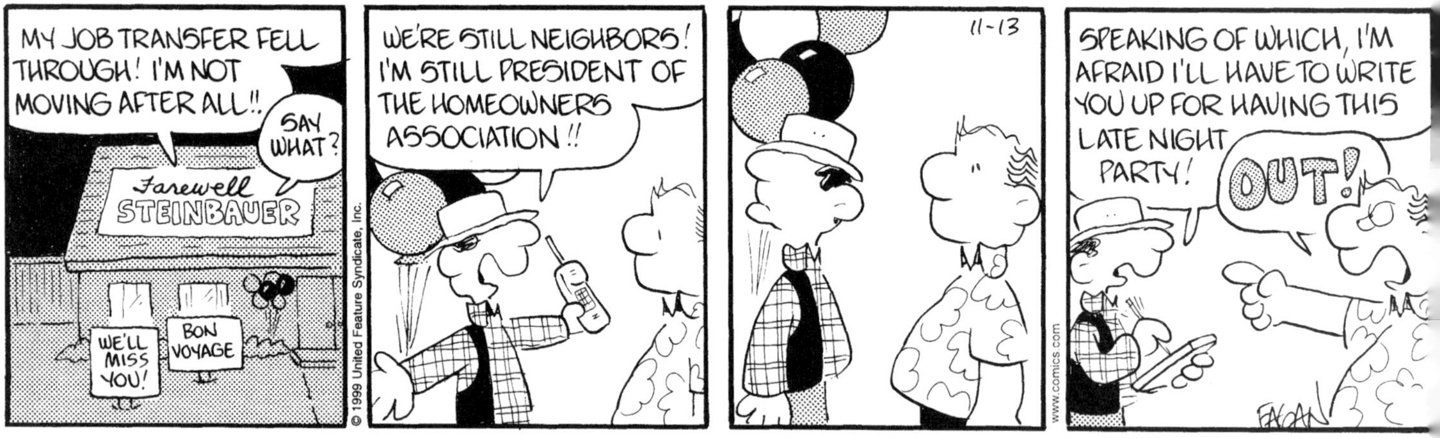
MY JOB TRANSFER FELL THROUGH! I'M NOT MOVING AFTER ALL!!
SAY WHAT?
Farewell STEINBAUER
WE'LL MISS YOU!
BON VOYAGE
© 1999 United Feature Syndicate, Inc.
WE'RE STILL NEIGHBORS! I'M STILL PRESIDENT OF THE HOMEOWNERS ASSOCIATION!!
11-13
www.comics.com
SPEAKING OF WHICH, I'M AFRAID I'LL HAVE TO WRITE YOU UP FOR HAVING THIS LATE NIGHT PARTY!
OUT!
FAGAN